Berlioz the Critic

Eastman Studies in Music

Ralph P. Locke, Senior Editor
Eastman School of Music

Additional Titles of Interest

Beethoven's Century: Essays on Composers and Themes
Hugh Macdonald

Berlioz in Time: From Early Recognition to Lasting Renown
Peter Bloom

Berlioz: Past, Present, Future: Bicentenary Essays
Edited by Peter Bloom

Berlioz: Scenes from the Life and Work
Edited by Peter Bloom

Berlioz's Semi-Operas: "Roméo et Juliette" and "La Damnation de Faust"
Daniel Albright

Beyond Fingal's Cave: Ossian in the Musical Imagination
James Porter

Canonic Repertories and the French Musical Press: Lully to Wagner
William Weber, Beverly Wilcox

*The Musical Madhouse: An English Translation
of Berlioz's "Les Grotesques de la musique"*
Hector Berlioz
Translated and Edited by Alastair Bruce
Introduction by Hugh Macdonald

Nadia Boulanger: Thoughts on Music
Edited by Jeanice Brooks, Kimberly Francis

Rossini and Post-Napoleonic Europe
Warren Roberts

A complete list of titles in the Eastman Studies in Music Series
may be found on our website, www.urpress.com

Berlioz the Critic

Selected Writings from 1837 to 1850

Translated with commentary by Roger Nichols
Edited by Julian Rushton
Introduction by Peter Bloom

UNIVERSITY OF ROCHESTER PRESS

The University of Rochester Press gratefully acknowledges support from the Trustees of the New Berlioz Edition for the publication of this book.

Copyright © 2025 Roger Nichols

All rights reserved. Except as permitted under current legislation, no part of this work may be photocopied, stored in a retrieval system, published, performed in public, adapted, broadcast, transmitted, recorded, or reproduced in any form or by any means, without the prior permission of the copyright owner.

First published 2025

University of Rochester Press
668 Mt. Hope Avenue, Rochester, NY 14620, USA
www.urpress.com
and Boydell & Brewer Limited
PO Box 9, Woodbridge, Suffolk IP12 3DF, UK
www.boydellandbrewer.com

Our Authorised Representative for product safety in the EU is Easy Access System Europe - Mustamäe tee 50, 10621 Tallinn, Estonia, gpsr.requests@easproject.com

ISBN-13: 978-1-64825-073-6
ISSN: 1071-9989

Library of Congress Cataloging-in-Publication Data
Names: Berlioz, Hector, 1803–1869, author. | Nichols, Roger, translator. | Rushton, Julian, editor. | Bloom, Peter, writer of introduction.
Title: Berlioz the critic : selected writings from 1837 to 1850 / translated with commentary by Roger Nichols ; edited by Julian Rushton ; introduction by Peter Bloom.
Other titles: Eastman studies in music ; 201.
Description: Rochester : University of Rochester Press, 2025. | Series: Eastman studies in music, 1071-9989 ; 201 | Includes bibliographical references and index.
Identifiers: LCCN 2024055809 (print) | LCCN 2024055810 (ebook) | ISBN 9781648250736 (hardback) | ISBN 9781805433750 (epub) | ISBN 9781805433743 (pdf)
Subjects: LCSH: Berlioz, Hector, 1803–1869. | Musical criticism—France—19th century. | Music—19th century—History and criticism. | LCGFT: Music criticism and reviews.
Classification: LCC ML410.B5 A25 2025 (print) | LCC ML410.B5 (ebook) | DDC 780.9/034—dc23/eng/20241206
LC record available at https://lccn.loc.gov/2024055809
LC ebook record available at https://lccn.loc.gov/2024055810

A catalogue record for this title is available from the British Library.

Contents

	Translator's Preface and Acknowledgments	ix
	Sources and Abbreviations Used in the Text and Notes	xi
	Editor's Note	xiii
	Introduction	1
	Peter Bloom	
1	On Imitation in Music (I)	20
2	On Imitation in Music (II)	27
3	Conservatoire de Musique, Ninth Concert: On Beethoven's *Eroica* and Taste in General	32
4	*Esmeralda*: On Fair Artistic Judgement	35
5	Paris Opéra: Revival of *Le Siège de Corinthe*	38
6	Third Conservatoire Concert (The Critic's Life)	41
7	Théâtre-Italien, *Le nozze di Figaro*: Benefit Performanc for Lablache	45
8	Second Concert of the *Gazette musicale*: Mlle Pauline Garcia – Gluck's *Orphée*	49
9	Adolphe Nourrit	58
10	Musical Instruments: Exhibition of Industrial Products	63
11	Théâtre de la Renaissance, First Staging of *Lucie de Lammermoor*: Music by Donizetti, Libretto by Alphonse Royer and Gustave Vaez	67
12	Letter to Liszt: Music in Paris and London	74
13	Review of Kastner's *Treatise on Instrumentation*	83
14	Théâtre de la Renaissance	90
15	First Conservatoire Concert: A Few Words on Early Music (I)	94
16	First Conservatoire Concert: A Few Words on Early Music (II)	101

17	Paris Opéra: Revival of *Fernand Cortez*; Liszt and Batta in London	108
18	Third Conservatoire Concert	112
19	Paris Opéra: Revival of *Don Giovanni* (I)	116
20	Liszt's Concerts	118
21	Paris Opéra: Revival of *Don Giovanni* (II)	120
22	Liszt's Concert at the Conservatoire	123
23	Paris Opéra: Poultier's Debut in *Guillaume Tell*	126
24	The Saint-Denis Organ	130
25	Fourth Conservatoire Concert	131
26	Cherubini	134
27	Sixth Conservatoire Concert	143
28	Thalberg's Concerts	145
29	German Theatre: First Performance of *Jessonda*	147
30	*Castor et Pollux*; the Score	151
31	Théâtre de l'Opéra-Comique: Revival of *Le Déserteur*	156
32	M. Berlioz's Concert at the Théâtre-Italien	162
33	Théâtre de l'Odéon: Premiere of *Antigone*	166
34	Large-Scale Concert at the Opéra: 'Le Droit des pauvres'	169
35	Michel de Glinka	172
36	Conservatoire Concert: Spontini, *La Vestale*	178
37	Cherubini's *Messe du Sacre* in Saint-Eustache	190
38	Music Festival in Bonn: The Beethoven Statue	192
39	New Method of Instrumental Practice	203
40	Inauguration of Rossini's Statue	205
41	Théâtre de l'Opéra-Comique: Revival of *Zémire et Azor*	208
42	On the Harmonium	214
43	Paris Opéra: Premiere of *Robert Bruce*, a Pastiche in Three Acts, Music by Rossini	218
44	Adolphe Sax's New Concert Hall	228

45	To M. Friedland in Prague	231
46	Opening of the Théâtre de la Nation: The Théâtre-National, or Opéra (Old Style)	233
47	The Opéra: Mme de Lagrange's Debut; Duprez, *Otello*	238
48	Distribution of Prizes at the Paris Conservatoire	244
49	Théâtre de l'Opéra-Comique: Premiere of *Le Caïd*	247
50	Second Séance of the Société des Concerts: Beethoven, Haydn, and Others	255
51	Third Séance of the Société des Concerts	259
52	Sixth Séance of the Société des Concerts	264
53	Industrial Exhibition, Musical Instruments: The 'Droit des Pauvres' Applied to Instrument-Makers; MM. Érard, Boisselot, Weulfel, Sax, and Vuillaume	266
54	The Death of Johann Strauss	274
55	The Death of Chopin	276
56	A Method of Telephony by M. Sudre	279
57	M. Niedermayer's *Messe solennelle*	282
58	Gluck's *Alceste*	287
	Index of Names	293

Translator's Preface and Acknowledgments

Berlioz's first article, the first of three entitled *Polémique musicale*, was published in *Le Corsaire* on 12 August 1823 when he was nineteen. He asked of Spontini's opera *La Vestale*, among other things, 'Why does the orchestra make so much noise?' Berlioz's propensity for causing trouble lasted throughout his career as critic; but at the same time, he was happy distributing praise when he felt it to be deserved. Other outlets in these early years included *Le Correspondant* (1829), the *Berliner allgemeine musikalische Zeitung* (1829), which published eight articles translated into German, the *Revue européenne* (1832), *L'Europe littéraire* (1833), *Le Rénovateur* (1833–5), *L'Italie pittoresque* (1834), *Le Monde dramatique* (1835), and *La Chronique de Paris* (1837–8).

There were two journals to which he remained loyal to the end of his critical career, if one counts as one the weekly *Gazette musicale de Paris* (1834–5), which became the *Revue et Gazette musicale de Paris* (*RGM*) in 1835 (so before the period covered in this selection of articles). This was a specialist publication, as its name implies, edited by Maurice-Adolphe Schlesinger (1798–1871), also a music publisher of works by Berlioz and his teacher Jean-François Le Sueur among others; contributors to Schlesinger's periodical included Robert Schumann, Liszt, Wagner, and George Sand. The other was the *Journal des débats* (*JD*), a political daily for which Berlioz first wrote in 1835. A fuller account of these journals, their editors and owners, and Berlioz's connections to them, personal and professional, may be found in Peter Bloom's introduction.

Extracts of varying lengths are presented in this collection; only a few are included complete. The choice of extracts has been made to exclude a good deal that seems of ephemeral interest and, more broadly, to translate only articles that have not previously been published in English. Only a few articles are exceptions, or partial exceptions, to the latter condition. They are included because their intrinsic interest outweighs the existence of previous translations and also outweighs the possibility that Berlioz reused them in his books, even though all of these have been translated. Details are given in the introductions to each article.

Berlioz's articles have been published in ten volumes as *Hector Berlioz, Critique musicale* (*CM*). These contain all Berlioz's journalism from 1823 to 1863.[1] A translation of selected articles edited by Katherine Kolb was published in 2015.[2] After her untimely death in 2018, this was not followed up; the present volume, covering thirteen more years, is conceived as a sequel, in the hope that a third, covering 1850–63, may follow.

Acknowledgments

I am grateful to Hugh Macdonald for lending me his copies of the *Critique musicale* and for following the process of writing with invaluable acumen and devotion; and to the Trustees of the New Berlioz Edition for generously funding the project.

Roger Nichols

---

1. Peter Bloom has identified as by Berlioz an article from 1865 (*RGM*, 20 August) that is highly critical of Wagner. It is signed 'X'. Peter Bloom, 'Wagner', in Julian Rushton (ed.), *The Cambridge Berlioz Encyclopedia* (Cambridge: Cambridge University Press, 2018), p. 356.
2. *Berlioz on Music. Selected Criticism 1824–1837* (ed. Katherine Kolb, translated by Samuel Rosenberg). New York: Oxford University Press, 2015. Selections in this and the present volume are representative and necessarily comprise only a small proportion of Berlioz's vast output of articles.

Sources and Abbreviations Used in the Text and Notes

CG	Hector Berlioz, *Correspondance générale* (ed. Pierre Citron et al.), 8 vols. Paris: Flammarion, 1972–2003, abbreviated *CG* vol. 1, 2, etc.
CG IX	*Nouvelles Lettres de Berlioz, de sa famille, de ses contemporains* (ed. Peter Bloom, Joël-Marie Fauquet, Hugh J. Macdonald, Cécile Reynaud). Paris: Actes Sud/Palazzetto Bru Zane, 2016; abbreviated *Nouvelles Lettres*.
CM	Hector Berlioz, *Critique musicale*. 10 vols. (1996–2020). Vols. 1–6, Paris: Buchet/Castel; vols. 7–10, Paris: Société française de musicologie. Vols. 4–7 were used to prepare these translations. See also the introduction.
Memoirs	*Mémoires d'Hector Berlioz*. Paris: private issue, 1865; Paris: Michel Lévy frères, 1870. Annotated edition, ed. Peter Bloom. Paris: Vrin, 2019. Translation by David Cairns: *The Memoirs of Hector Berlioz*. Second revised edition: London: Everyman's Library, 2002.
Traité	*Grande Traité d'instrumentation et d'orchestration modernes*. Paris: Schonenberger, 1843; modern edition ed. and annotated Peter Bloom (New Berlioz Edition vol. 24), Kassel: Bärenreiter, 2003; translated and annotated by Hugh Macdonald as *Berlioz's Orchestration Treatise*, Cambridge: Cambridge University Press, 2002.
Holoman, *Berlioz*	D. Kern Holoman, *Berlioz*. Cambridge, Mass.: Harvard University Press, and London: Faber & Faber, 1989, with list of concerts: pp. 612–27.
JD	*Journal des débats*.
M	Monsieur (Mr)
Mlle	Mademoiselle (Miss or Ms)

Mme	Madame (Mrs or Ms)
MM	Messieurs (plural of M.)
Opéra	The Paris Opéra, variously known as Académie royale / nationale / impériale de musique
RGM	*Revue et Gazette musicale*

See also: D. Kern Holoman, *Catalogue of the Works of Hector Berlioz.* New Berlioz Edition vol. 25. Kassel: Bärenreiter, 1987. Catalogue of Berlioz's articles, pp. 435–88.

Editor's Note

With the compiler and translator of these essays unfortunately in poor health, I was asked to help with final editorial revisions necessary for publication. My interventions are mainly concerned with checking and supplementing the notes and organizing the preliminaries and index. Clarifications added to the text itself are in brackets. The commentary on the translations provided by the introductions to each article and the footnotes are the combined work of Roger Nichols and myself, with assistance from Peter Bloom and Ralph P. Locke.

Some aspects of the policy in translating should be mentioned here. Berlioz would sometimes use a French form of a foreign name; for instance, in the first article, he wrote 'Jules Romain' for 'Giulio Romano'. These usages seem part of the flavour, as it were, of Berlioz's writing and are retained with the original name appearing in footnotes. Berlioz refers courteously to living persons by including a French form of title; here abbreviations are used for 'Monsieur', 'Madame', and 'Mademoiselle': for instance, 'M. Meyerbeer', 'Mme Viardot', and 'Mlle Nathan'. Notes are provided for people Berlioz mentions, many of them singers and some of whose details have proved impossible to trace. Later allusions to them are referred back to the first citation.

With titles of works, mindful of the fact that readers may like to dip in and out, composers' names have been inserted in brackets. An exception is made of works by Berlioz, which are included under his name in the index. Also in the index, in the interests of space, where an entry consists of a surname and one forename, the first of the often-multiple forenames mentioned in the notes is used, even when it is not the forename usually employed. An example would be the author and composer Louis-Hector Berlioz. He was always addressed as Hector and signed himself HB.

I am most grateful to Ralph P. Locke, senior editor of the Eastman Studies in Music series, for his enthusiastic support and many helpful comments and suggested improvements; to Peter Bloom for the same, and also for his richly informative introduction and constant vigilance with reference to sources; and to the editors of the *Critique musicale* whose annotations have proved indispensable in preparing the information in the notes. My thanks also to the Trustees of the New Berlioz Edition for offering me this editorial task; and to Roger Nichols for his splendid work on translating, in which he so often catches the subtleties of tone, serious, ironic, mock serious as it often is, in Berlioz's writings.

Julian Rushton

Introduction

There was a time when 'Berlioz the critic' would have been the title of a lesser chapter in the larger biography of the composer. Now that his complete literary works have become available in modern critical editions, however, it has been possible to wonder, with more than a modicum of seriousness, whether Berlioz displayed his greatest talents as a musician or as a writer. For Berlioz himself, this was not a question. Setting down words, he often said, as in chapter 21 of his *Memoirs*, was 'work', while setting down notes was a 'delight'. Many are the passages in his letters where he tells of the thrill of musical ideas coming to him so fast as to be unmanageable: 'To tell you the truth, for several days I have been unable to sleep, I've lost touch with reality, so absorbed have I been by my work [*Roméo et Juliette*]'; 'the music settled readily upon the words like a bird on a ripe fruit [the love scene from act 4 of *Les Troyens*]'; 'the music is crowding my brain; I cannot even tell which number I prefer [in *Béatrice et Bénédict*]'.[1] Years earlier, at the very moment he veered away from the medical study prescribed by his father in order to embrace harmony and counterpoint, he expressed extraordinary confidence in his musical future: 'I am involuntarily drawn to a magnificent career', he wrote in 1824; 'I am certain that I shall distinguish myself in music [...]; I should like to make a name for myself; I should like to leave upon this earth a trace of my existence'.[2]

In a nation where literature has always been revered as occupying the apex of the arts, Berlioz's obsessive commitment to music led some of his later contemporaries to take seriously his perfectly ironic remark about being 'three-quarters German'. In fact, despite various disclaimers, Berlioz was deeply possessed by literature, classic and modern, French and foreign. From the astonishing number of citations found in his writings, from Virgil, from Shakespeare, from La Fontaine, from the neo-classical French dramatists and the modernists around Victor Hugo, we know that he read a great deal and that he remembered a great deal of what he read. This made him very much a man of his time and a man of his country, a man as French as French could be. It must never be forgotten that what sparked Berlioz's musical passion was not playing, not listening, but *reading* – the lives of Gluck and

---

1 *CG* vol. 2, p. 539; *CG* vol. 8, p. 425; *CG* vol. 8, p. 494.
2 *CG* vol. 1, p. 64.

Haydn, in Louis-Gabriel Michaud's far-reaching *Biographie universelle ancienne et moderne*, to which his father was a faithful subscriber, and to which he himself remained devoted until the very end, perusing various articles in the library at the Institut de France before attending the weekly *séances* of the Académie des Beaux-Arts. In his *Memoirs*, choosing the word with care, Berlioz referred to his own *embarquement* upon a journalistic career as a *fatalité* – by which he intended to suggest both *reluctance*, because he wished of course to be remembered as a composer, and *inevitability*, because he early on sensed that his gifts as a polemicist might serve his cause and enhance his renown. In 1856, when after five previous attempts Berlioz was elected to the Institut de France, a detractor quipped of the institution that 'what it needed was a musician, what it chose was a journalist' ('il fallait un musicien, c'est un journaliste qu'on a choisi'). That detractor – Paul Scudo, one of Berlioz's most implacable enemies, here cleverly paraphrasing Figaro in Beaumarchais' play *Le Mariage de Figaro* ('il fallait un calculateur, ce fut un danseur qui l'obtint'; 'what was needed was a mathematician; a dancer got the job') – was unwittingly uttering a compliment.[3] Berlioz's work as musician and writer spanned essentially the same four decades of his life, from the mid-1820s to the mid-1860s, and he carried it out with equal attention to tone, rhythm, and detail. That his colleagues at the Académie des Beaux-Arts urged him to seek the post of perpetual secretary of the organization when it became vacant in 1862 is testimony to their high regard for his literary talents, for the post was one that required a *writer* – of requests, reviews, and reports.

The larger context of Berlioz's literary career is summarized with remarkable insight in Katherine Kolb's *Berlioz on Music*, a judiciously selective compendium of articles covering the early thirteen-year period, from January 1824 to October 1837, to which the present volume, which extends for a 'middle' thirteen-year period (January 1837 to March 1850) may be seen as a generous complement.[4] (A subsequent volume could encompass a 'final' thirteen-year period, 1850 to 1863, in which year Berlioz submitted his resignation to the *Journal des débats*.) These publications owe their existence to the *Critique musicale*, the modern edition of Berlioz's critical writings of which the first six volumes were published in Paris by Buchet/Chastel between 1996 and 2007, and the final four by the Société française de musicologie between 2013 and 2020. This magnificent project was founded in the 1990s by H. Robert Cohen and Yves Gérard, who themselves edited the first volume; Professor Gérard edited the second (1998) with Marie-Hélène

---

3   *Revue des deux mondes* (15 July 1856), p. 444.
4   *Berlioz on Music. Selected Criticism 1824–1837* (ed. Katherine Kolb, translated by Samuel Rosenberg). New York: Oxford University Press, 2015.

Coudroy-Saghaï, and the third with Madame Coudroy-Saghaï and Anne Bongrain. Mesdames Bongrain and Coudroy-Saghaï then edited the following seven volumes, with the assistance of an editorial committee comprising Pierre Citron, Joël-Marie Fauquet, Yves Gérard, Catherine Massip, Jean Mongrédien, and the author of this introduction.[5] Let it be hoped that this fundamental tool for research – with its accurate texts and copious annotations that identify the thousands of persons and works considered by Berlioz in his critiques – will soon be digitized and uploaded to a website open to all. All who have worked on the current volume acknowledge with gratitude their reliance on information found in the *Critique musicale*.

At the beginning of her essay, Katherine Kolb takes note of the fact that Berlioz 'earned his living by his pen'.[6] This was of course the case for most men of letters of the time, and in fact Berlioz's sources of income were many and varied, and included in the early years allowances from his well-to-do father and the liberal government stipend that supported him for the five years after his victory in the 1830 Prix de Rome competition. From February 1839 he received a salary as librarian at the Paris Conservatoire, and from 1856 honoraria as a Membre de l'Institut; there were profits over the years from some of his concerts and from contracts with publishers. There was a family inheritance and, last but by no means least, his journalism. Berlioz began writing for journals and newspapers at a time when such publications were becoming more central to the political, intellectual, and artistic life of the French nation. For historians of the nineteenth century these periodic mirrors of the daily life of the people of all classes of society are of conspicuous importance, especially after Émile de Girardin's foundation in 1836 of *La Presse*, the first of the inexpensive newspapers whose operating costs were newly offset not only by subscriptions but also by advertising and whose circulations were thus exponentially enlarged. The mirrors are *tinted*, of course; the subtitle of the biography of the owner of the *Journal des débats*, 'the birth of opinion', says it all; the moguls of the press, then as now, were never simply disinterested observers desirous of offering to the public some sort of 'objective' view of the news.[7] They rather harboured points of view that they wished overtly and covertly to convey to their readers. The extent to which literary critics, art critics, and music critics were obliged to toe these lines, however, has never been easy to appraise: these 'impotent writers', as Balzac

---

[5] While it is possible to access most of Berlioz's articles online, thanks to such resources as RIPM (*Répertoire international de la presse musicale*, founded by Professor Cohen), and Retronews.com, developed by the Bibliothèque nationale de France, this was not the case when the *Critique musicale* came into existence.

[6] *Berlioz on Music*, p. 1.

[7] Jean-Paul Clément, *Bertin, ou La Naissance de l'opinion*. Paris: Fallois, 2018.

sardonically called them, were in fact men of letters of conviction and with talents that could arguably rival those of the artists whose works they were remunerated to review.[8]

Berlioz's first three articles were letters to the editor of *Le Corsaire*, a daily newspaper concerned with performance, literature, art, lifestyle, and fashion that first appeared on 11 July 1823 and which lasted for some thirty-five years. It is noteworthy that Berlioz nowhere mentions *Le Corsaire* in his *Memoirs*, perhaps because of its reputation at the time as a journal of the liberal opposition to the monarchy. The newspaper he *does* mention, when seeking to voice the anti-Italianism that characterizes much of his early criticism and in particular his disapproval of the 'Rossinistes' who denigrated the school of Gluck and Spontini, is *La Quotidienne*, the well-known *légitimiste* (pro-Bourbon) newspaper owned by the same Michaud brothers who published the *Biographie universelle*.

> I was in need of a reputable tribune. I wrote to Monsieur Michaud, editor-in-chief and owner of *La Quotidienne*, at the time a rather popular newspaper. I explained to him my hopes and my opinions, promising that I would enter this critical battle in a manner that would be as fair as it would be forceful. My letter, serious but not without wit, apparently pleased him. He wrote back immediately with a positive reaction. My proposition was accepted! My first article was awaited with impatience! Jumping for joy, I cried out, 'Ah, I've got you, you miserable louts!' But I was mistaken, I had no one, I had nothing. My inexperience as a writer was all too obvious, my ignorance of the world and of the conventions of the press was all but absolute, and my musical passions were so strong that I was inevitably bound, at this early stage, to make a terrible faux pas. The article I took to Monsieur Michaud, ill-conceived and ill-organized, went far beyond the limits of even the most ardent polemics. On hearing me read it, Monsieur Michaud, astounded by my cheekiness, said to me: 'What you say may be true, but your way of saying it is entirely beyond the pale. I cannot possibly publish such a thing in *La Quotidienne*'. I went out, promising to revise the article. But my sloth and my distaste for all the changes that would be required to make the article palatable soon took over, and I did nothing more about it.[9]

This may explain, in a way, why Berlioz, who had not yet proclaimed the atheism that estranged him from the Catholic Church, soon turned to the less 'conservative' outlet that was *Le Corsaire*.

---

8   'Il existe dans tout critique un auteur impuissant'. *Monographie de la presse parisienne*, in Balzac, *Oeuvres complètes* (ed. Marcel Bouteron and Henri Longnon). Paris: Conard, 1912–40, vol. 40, p. 577.
9   *Mémoires d'Hector Berlioz* (ed. Peter Bloom). Paris: Vrin, 2019, p. 243.

In 1829 and 1830, Berlioz wrote four important articles for *Le Correspondant*, a journal that gave voice to young Catholic intellectuals and artists who wished to have their voices heard during the political tensions that marked the later years of the reign of King Charles X, and especially to counteract the 'rationalism' for which *Le Globe*, soon to be the voice of the proto-socialist Saint-Simonian movement, 'was the dangerous advocate'.[10] One of the co-founders of *Le Correspondant*, which became the *Revue européenne* in 1831, was the historian and politician Louis de Carné, whom Berlioz regarded as a fair and impartial fellow. When the vehemence of Berlioz's anti-Italianism struck him as 'overly harsh', Carné, whose associates were the ultra-royalist deputy Augustin de Meaux and the politician turned priest Edmond de Cazalès, asked Berlioz to write something ... on another subject. Berlioz quipped to his friend Humbert Ferrand, 'so you see that the prostitute finds lovers even among the religious faithful!'[11] When, after winning the Prix de Rome in the summer of 1830, the composer attempted to convince the authorities to make an exception to the rules and allow him to remain in Paris while enjoying his five-year stipend, one of those who wrote to the administration in support of this highly unusual request was none other than Louis de Carné.

For a brief period in 1829, Berlioz acted as the Paris correspondent for the *Berliner allgemeine musikalische Zeitung*, a progressive periodical founded in 1824 by the music theorist Adolf Bernhard Marx in conjunction with the Berlin music publisher Adolph Martin Schlesinger. Marx became an admirer of Berlioz on reading the score of *Huit Scènes de Faust*, published in 1829. Schlesinger (whom, when he met him briefly, Berlioz found 'annoying') was the father of Maurice Schlesinger, who, as we shall see, would publish what became the most significant music periodical of the French nineteenth century, the *Revue et Gazette musicale*.[12]

Two other magazines employed Berlioz as their music critic before he became permanently associated with the periodicals represented in the present volume. *L'Europe littéraire*, founded in 1833 by Victor Bohain and Alphonse Royer, aspired to be a kind of 'universal library' that would feature articles from around the world, that would bring together the artists and the public, that would eschew politics, and that would 'allow all parties

---

10   Alban Ramaut, 'Berlioz critique, entre lecture et création: l'article du 22 octobre 1830', in Sylvie Triaire and François Brunet (eds.), *Aspects de la critique musicale au XIXe siècle*. Montpellier: Presses universitaires de la Méditerranée, 2002, note 1.
11   *CG* vol. 1, p. 257.
12   *CG* vol. 1, p. 257.

and all opinions peacefully to coexist'.[13] Berlioz may have met Bohain in 1827, when he was director of the Théâtre des Nouveautés where Berlioz, for several months, was a member of the chorus. In 1828 the two men were to collaborate on a *Faust* ballet for the Opéra, but the project came to nothing. For *L'Europe littéraire*, among whose writers were such luminaries as Alexandre Dumas, Charles Nodier, Alfred de Musset, Honoré de Balzac, Victor Hugo, Heinrich Heine, and Jules Michelet, Berlioz organized several concerts for the subscribers to the journal, something that would enhance the readership's sense of community. But despite the prestige of that assembly, the magazine met financial difficulties in the summer of 1833 and dissolved in February the following year.

Le Rénovateur, founded as a weekly in 1832 by the *légitimiste* and Catholic Pierre-Sébastien Laurentie (earlier an editor at *La Quotidienne*) in conjunction with other leaders of the pro-Bourbon party, became a daily newspaper in 1833 and soon thereafter merged with *Le Courrier de l'Europe* to become *Le Rénovateur—Courrier de L'Europe*, whose political stance was firmly in opposition to the July Monarchy of Louis-Philippe and firmly in support of the 'legitimate monarchy' of Charles X that had been deposed by the Revolution of 1830.[14] Berlioz wrote some *eighty-nine* articles for *Le Rénovateur* in 1834 and 1835 and clearly came to know the editors well. Not long after Laurentie had resumed his responsibilities at *La Quotidienne*, he asked Berlioz to serve as a correspondent for that journal. But by that time Berlioz was working both for Maurice Schlesinger's new *Gazette musicale de Paris*, to which over a two-year period (1834–5) he contributed some *thirty-eight* articles, and, more importantly (because of its daily appearance and its much larger circulation), for the *Journal des débats*, which paid him handsomely for his contributions, and which no doubt allowed him a freer hand, when sensitive matters came into play, than he would have had at *La Quotidienne*.[15] Berlioz nonetheless remained in contact with Laurentie, welcomed him in January 1850 as a patron of his new Société philharmonique de Paris, and years later thanked him for his generous review of the concert of 1 March 1866, when Berlioz conducted Léon Kreutzer's *Concerto-symphonique* in E-flat major, with Louise-Aglaé Massart as the piano

---

13 See Peter Bloom and D. Kern Holoman, 'Berlioz's Music for *L'Europe littéraire*', *Music Review*, 39 (1978), pp. 98–109.
14 See Estelle Berthereau, 'The Impossible Modernization of Legitimate Monarchy after 1830: The Journalists Pierre-Sébastien Laurentie and Eugène de Genoude', *History of European Ideas* (Taylor & Francis online, 2021), pp. 1–11.
15 *CG* vol. 2, p. 284.

soloist.[16] (This turned out to be the last time Berlioz appeared in Paris as a conductor.)

Berlioz flirted with other newspapers with keen points of view – he intended first to publish his 1834 biography of Gluck in *Le Publiciste*, for example, a 'journal de législation et d'administration publique', no doubt because he was invited to do so by his friend Jean-Gabriel Cappot, known as Capo de Feuillide, the editor of a number of journals at the time.[17]

But let us now turn our attention to the *Revue et Gazette musicale* and the *Journal des débats*, from which the fifty-eight articles translated in the present volume have been selected: eighteen from the weekly musical magazine, forty from the daily newspaper. The *Revue et Gazette musicale* (*RGM*) began its existence with two fathers, as it were: it was born of the *Revue musicale* and the *Gazette musicale de Paris*. The *Revue musicale*, founded in 1827 by François-Joseph Fétis, the organist, composer, theorist, and historian who also devoted a good deal of his time to criticism for the daily and weekly press, was the first serious French journal uniquely devoted to music. As professor of composition and librarian at the Conservatoire, Fétis came to know the young Berlioz and to review his early compositions with both sympathy and encouragement, until an unfortunate falling out led to a feud in the early 1830s that lasted for over twenty years.[18] On 20 May 1828, Berlioz wrote a letter to the editor and sent it to at least three publications, including *Le Corsaire* and *Le Figaro*. Fétis immediately printed the letter in the issue of the *Revue musicale* that appeared on the very next day, thus implicitly seconding Berlioz's message: that his desire to produce a concert of his own music, scheduled for 26 May 1828, was the product not of pretentiousness or arrogance but rather of the desire simply to make his music, and his presence, known.[19]

In 1834, when the *Revue musicale* was in its seventh year of operation, Maurice Schlesinger, who had begun his now highly successful music publishing business in Paris in 1821, sensed that there was room in the capital for another serious music journal, with an editorial environment different

---

16   *CG* vol. 3, p. 681, and *CG* vol. 7, p. 395–6.
17   See *CG* vol. 2, p. 165. The director of *Le Publiciste* is listed as 'V. Rondy', one of the pseudonyms used by Capo de Feuillide.
18   The falling out was provoked by Berlioz's mockery of Fétis in the libretto of *Le Retour à la vie*. This led to Fétis's negative review of Franz Liszt's transcription of the *Symphonie fantastique* in the *Revue musicale* (1 February 1835) and to Robert Schumann's remarkable analysis of the work in the *Neue Zeitschrift für Musik* of later that year. Both essays are translated in Edward T. Cone (ed.), *Berlioz: Fantastic Symphony*. New York, W. W. Norton and London: Chappell, 1971, pp. 215–48.
19   *CG* vol. 1, p. 185.

from Fétis's stuffy erudition, and began bringing out his *Gazette musicale de Paris*: here he turned his attention to the younger artists of the romantic generation as well, of course, to the composers – among them the fashionable Meyerbeer and the fledgling Berlioz – whose music he was publishing at the time. In November 1835, when Fétis – now living in Belgium as chapel master to King Leopold I and director of the new Conservatoire de Bruxelles – found it impossible to continue editing the *Revue musicale*, he published a valedictory essay, claiming credit for developing readers for the history, theory, and aesthetics of music as well as for developing music schools, musical institutions, and a taste for philosophizing about the art: 'If well-rounded and deeply knowledgeable musicians are still rarely to be found, it is at least certain that there exist today writers on music who firmly grasp the questions they treat and who express themselves appropriately'.[20]

On the same day, Maurice Schlesinger officially absorbed Fétis's pioneering enterprise, renamed his house organ the *Revue et Gazette musicale de Paris* and announced a sort of military victory: 'The *Revue musicale*, with its arms and ammunition, with its battle-hardened colours flying high, has now come over to the *Gazette musicale*'.[21] Fétis, often at odds with Schlesinger, now signed on as one of his regular contributors and published hundreds of articles over the next three decades.

Maurice Schlesinger was a feisty character whose personality was well-captured by the writer Maxime du Camp: 'He was an avid businessman who was involved in twenty different things at the same time: directing an important publishing house, inhaling from afar the scent of a woman and abandoning his wife in order to chase the first petticoat that appeared at the corner of the street; he was a past master at advertising, he threw gold coins out the window, yet stooped to pick up pennies in the street'.[22] Heinrich Heine also knew him well: 'When I was still in the good graces of the director of the *Gazette musicale* (alas, due to a childish indiscretion, I fell out of favour), I had many opportunities to observe with my own eyes how so many illustrious artists simply prostrated themselves before him, shamelessly grovelling at his feet in order to receive a word of praise in his journal'. On the laurel wreaths of even the most celebrated virtuosos, Heine went on, 'one still finds the dust from the boots of Maurice Schlesinger'.[23]

---

20   *Revue musicale* (1 November 1835).
21   *Revue et Gazette musicale* (1 November 1835).
22   Maxime Du Camp, *Souvenirs littéraires*. Paris: Hachette, 1892, vol. 2, pp. 337–8.
23   Heinrich Heine, *Lutezia I* [and] *II* (ed. Volkmar Hansen). Hamburg: Hoffmann und Campe, 1988/1990, vols. 14/2, p. 181; 13/2, p. 1507. Heine's 'indiscretion' was castigating the French public at Schlesinger's *Revue et Gazette musicale* concert of 4 February 1841 (in the Augsburg *Allgemeine*

Schlesinger's relationships with Franz Liszt (extensive) and Richard Wagner (brief) were advantageous for both musicians but fraught with aggravation. His relationship with the popular pianist Henri Herz led to legal proceedings, pistols, and protracted propaganda.[24] For Berlioz, however, Schlesinger, the most important publisher of the early part of his career (he brought out many works from Berlioz's 'Opus 1', *Huit Scènes de Faust*, to the *Symphonie fantastique*, and on to the *Symphonie funèbre et triomphale*), seems always to have been a much-trusted partner. Indeed, when Schlesinger was away from his desk or from Paris, he apparently delegated his editorial duties to none other than Berlioz. 'I have indeed been charged with replacing Schlesinger while he is taking the waters I know not where', wrote the composer, with a smile, in August 1836.[25] Among Berlioz's letters there are dozens such as this, which lies unpublished in the Berlin Staatsbibliothek: 'My dear Maurice, I would be very grateful to you if you could find space in the *Gazette* for the several lines I include here about my concert of yesterday. A thousand thanks! I have time only to shake your hand and to thank you in advance'.[26] Berlioz and Schlesinger surely had in common a lively sense of humour. As a German, Schlesinger would have been delighted, for example, to hear how Berlioz, in conversation with the king of Prussia, the deeply religious Frederick William IV, the dedicatee of Berlioz's *Grand Traité d'instrumentation*, caused the king to laugh out loud, a rare feat for anyone.[27]

It must nonetheless be understood, when reading Berlioz in the *RGM*, that the eyes of Schlesinger were upon him, indulgent though they may well have been. In 1837, for example, when he had successfully recruited Balzac to contribute to the *RGM*, Schlesinger accepted with pleasure his short story *Gambara*, which has been read as a tribute to the art and science of Meyerbeer (although the matter is more complex than that), but then rejected Balzac's *Massimila Doni*, which has been read as an *hommage à*

Zeitung, 29 April 1841) for failing to appreciate the beautiful 'German soul' of Sophie Loewe's singing of Beethoven's *Adelaide*.

24 See Shaena Weitz, 'Propaganda and Reception in Nineteenth-Century Music Criticism', *19th-Century Music* 43/1 (Summer 2019), pp. 38–60.

25 *CG* vol. 2, p. 306. Schlesinger was on holiday at Trouville with Élise Foucault, the woman who passed for but who was not yet his wife, the woman with whom the teenage Flaubert fell hopelessly in love and whose person he later eternalized as Madame Arnoux in *L'Éducation sentimentale*.

26 'Mon cher Maurice, / Voulez-vous donner place dans la *Gazette* aux quelques lignes ci-jointes sur mon concert d'hier? Vous m'obligerez beaucoup. / Mille amitiés. Je n'ai que le temps de vous serrer la main et de vous remercier d'avancer. H. Berlioz' (Staatsbibliothek zu Berlin, N. Mus. Ep. 2339).

27 *CG* vol. 3, p. 438.

Rossini, and thus antithetical to the artistic politics of the journal.[28] Berlioz would have done likewise. But on *political* politics, it is likely that Berlioz and Schlesinger did not see eye-to-eye. Berlioz was appalled by the Revolution of 1848 and ever more openly, in letters, expressed his anti-republicanism. Schlesinger, on the other hand, having sold his business in January 1846 to his young German associate Louis Brandus, became a member of the Club de la Société républicaine centrale and thus a man who, after the coup d'état of Napoléon III, would have been seen as a suspicious character.[29] Brandus, whose younger brother Gemmy became his partner in 1850, immediately brought out Berlioz's *Roméo et Juliette* (1847) and *Harold en Italie* (1848), and would follow up with editions of the *Te Deum* (1855) and the vocal score of *Béatrice et Bénédict* (1863). For Berlioz, the Brandus brothers figured among the small number of courageous publishers who were willing to risk investing in work whose nature was not guaranteed immediate success.[30] Unlike Schlesinger, one would imagine, those brothers seem to have worked unproblematically during the authoritarian regime of Napoleon III. At a time when, as I have suggested, friendships between artists and publishers were crucial to successful business operations, they certainly remained close to Berlioz. Which is why, if the family anecdote is to be believed, Berlioz permitted himself to lean over to Gemmy Brandus at the premiere of Gounod's *Faust* and say to him, 'J'espère bien que vous n'allez pas publier cette cochonnerie!' ('I certainly hope you aren't going to publish this rubbish!')[31]

The *RGM* and other journals of that kind were officially nonpolitical, a status that allowed them to avoid the large security deposit required of the main daily newspapers whose raison d'être was political, and whose choice of words was carefully overseen by the censors. The circulation of Schlesinger's weekly was small; it could be measured in the hundreds. On the other hand, during the July Monarchy, the *Journal des débats*, the organ that far more than any other projected Berlioz's voice to the larger reading public, enjoyed a daily circulation, national and international, of between twelve and thirteen thousand copies.[32] The *Débats* was of course overtly political, and its stance for most of its history was calculatedly moderate and supportive of the

---

28 See Jacques Blamont, 'Les Deux éditeurs de la musique romantique: Schlesinger et Brandus', *Bulletin de la Société Alkan*, 76–7 (2014), pp. 9–45, here 14–16.
29 Blamont, 'Les Deux éditeurs', p. 20.
30 Berlioz, *Journal des débats* (23 July 1861).
31 Blamont, p. 36. (The writer is the great-grandson of Louis Brandus's daughter, Blanche.)
32 Clément, *Bertin*, p. 235.

régime in power: first, the Napoleonic Empire, then, the Bourbon restoration, then, after the July Revolution, the monarchy of Louis-Philippe—whose administration 'secretly supported' the newspaper.[33] In later years the *Débats* veered left and right, distancing itself from the Prince-President after the coup d'état of 2 December 1851, when criticism of the new régime could lead to imprisonment (the *Débats* remained discreetly loyal to the Orléanist pretender to the throne, Philippe, comte de Paris), yet many years later embracing the collaborationist government of Philippe Pétain.

We know from many sources, including, for example, the correspondence between Victor Hugo and his principal critic, Charles-Augustin Sainte-Beuve, that Louis-François Bertin—the 'Monsieur Bertin' of the great portrait by Jean-Auguste-Dominique Ingres that came to define the era—was a close reader of the texts he published, including the *feuilletons* at the bottom of page 1 (these were dubbed 'foolitons' by a satirist), and wished to publish nothing, Hugo told Sainte-Beuve, that was 'contrary to the political colour of the journal'.[34] Indeed, two of the leading writers for the *Débats*, Alfred-Auguste Cuvillier-Fleury and Jules Janin, were openly enthusiastic supporters of the July Monarchy, the former acting as a kind of publicist for the Orléans family from the interior of the palace, the latter archiving for posterity the grand achievements of the reign of Louis-Philippe.[35] Of these, one was the promotion and development of the French railway network, something Janin celebrated in his 'Chant des chemins de fer', a poetic encomium to the railroads set to music by Berlioz and premiered in June 1846 at the opening of the new line that stretched from Paris to Lille. Earlier, in the mid-1830s, it was in part thanks to the connections between the Bertin family and the director of the Opéra (which institution from time immemorial has been a symbol of the regime in power) that Berlioz was offered a commission for what became the thrillingly original yet ill-fated opera *Benvenuto Cellini*.

Louise Bertin, the daughter of Bertin aîné, as he was called, studied musical composition with Fétis and Antoine Reicha and became in the 1830s a thoroughly professional composer whose operas *Fausto* and *La Esmeralda* in particular revealed her lively compositional imagination. Berlioz was an admirer of her skills and honoured her, in his way, by dedicating to her the

---

33 Marie-Ève Thérenty, 'The "Fooliton": A French Media Invention', *Victorian Review*, 38/2 (Autumn 2021), pp. 35–8, here p. 36.

34 See note 30. Éric Bertin and Michel Brix, 'Vingt-trois lettres inédites de Sainte-Beuve à Victor Hugo (1830–1845)', *Revue d'histoire littéraire de la France*, 119/2 (April–June 2019), p. 420.

35 See Grégoire Franconie, 'Une écriture militante: La critique littéraire et la royauté dans le *Journal des débats* (1830–48)', *Nineteenth-Century French Studies*, 74/3–4 (Spring–Summer 2019), pp. 278–89.

first version of *Les Nuits d'été*, for voice and piano, and by addressing to her the seventh letter of his *Voyage musical en Allemagne*, which appeared serially in the *Journal des débats*, in his first book, and in his *Memoirs*.

When Louis-François Bertin died, on 13 September 1841 (Berlioz attended the funeral), his younger son Armand immediately took over the direction of the journal: his name first appears as editor-in-chief on 14 September. On Armand's death in 1854, his older brother, the already famous painter Édouard, assumed the editorship. Armand possessed the same imposing girth as his father, as we read in the caption provided for his portrait in pencil by Ingres, at the Metropolitan Museum of Art, 'but a much gentler demeanour'.[36] This no doubt contributed to Berlioz's establishment of an enduring friendship with the new editor, consecrated some years earlier with the dedication to him of the overture *Le Roi Lear*, composed in Nice in the spring of 1831. The dedication on the title page of that score is a later addition; it suggests that Berlioz made the younger Bertin's acquaintance only after his return from Italy in 1832 and made the dedication shortly before the publication in 1840. In May 1834, aware that the composer needed an opera commission to take the first major steps of his career, Armand wrote on Berlioz's behalf to the then-director of the Opéra, Louis-Désiré Véron, and urged him to offer Berlioz a libretto for a forthcoming production.[37] That Berlioz and the younger Bertin worked well together is indicated by various mentions in Berlioz's correspondence, including one in a letter to his friend Albert Du Boys regarding a review of Du Boys's novel, *Rodolphe de Francon*, that was delayed; Berlioz notes that that reviewer had little influence at the *Débats*, 'while I, on the other hand, have an influence equal to that of two'; and another, in a letter to 'Monsieur Armand' himself regarding the outstanding success of his concert in Vienna on 16 November 1845, where Berlioz joyously adds 'a thousand compliments to you and to all of my colleagues and friends at the *Journal des débats*'.[38] Nonetheless, when, after his lengthy travels in Russia in 1847, Berlioz wished to publish the account of his trip as a series of open letters, Armand Bertin was reluctant to publish *Voyage en Russie* because he wished not to air the schism between Berlioz's appreciation of the Russian society that received him and the imperialistic aspirations of Russian rulers who stood in opposition to current French foreign policy (which supported the

---

36 https://artsandculture.google.com/asset/armand-bertin.
37 *CG* vol. 9, p. 128.
38 'Berlioz notes': *CG* vol. 2, p. 250 (21 September 1835). Berlioz's own short note on the novel appears in the *Débats* of 20 September 1835. 'And another': *CG* vol. 9, p. 265.

endangered Ottoman empire) – this in the wake of the virulent censorship established by the newly authoritarian post-coup republic.

In January 1852, Berlioz told his sister Adèle that Armand Bertin was newly anxious to have his articles, and newly anxious that they be the first to report on new developments, because the *Débats* 'was no longer concerned itself with politics'.[39] For Victor Hugo and like-minded republicans, the dictatorial manoeuvrings of Louis Napoleon were famously disastrous. But for Berlioz, the dawn of the new day was bright:

> The President is getting better and better. His government is the realization of all of my dreams. He is sublimely intelligent, logical, firm and decisive. Last night, he came to the Comédie-Française where, as he entered and as he departed, he was met with acclamations and interminable applause. My admiration for him is without self-interest, because I am certain that for all official ceremonies, such as the one that has just taken place at Notre Dame, he will always engage the usual suspects – the tired old men and the tired old works.[40]

The selections of the present volume do not extend to that later period of Berlioz's journalistic career, but the point of view that Berlioz articulates here with especial clarity is one that undergirds much of the thinking that lies beneath the surface of most of his mature writing as a journalist: he was a member of the party of order; the disarray of republicanism was not his cup of tea; he supported the emergent empire, authoritarian though it was; and he long sought imperial assistance for his work.

The first of the articles newly translated in this volume was published in January 1837. In December that year, after a long series of disappointments, Berlioz was finally able to bring to performance his *Grande Messe des morts* (*Requiem*), one of the monumental works that would ensure his lasting renown. Initially commissioned by the administration of Louis-Philippe to honour those who were killed in an assassination attempt against the king on the fifth anniversary of the July Revolution, the *Requiem* was finally performed at the funeral service for Général Damrémont and the officers and soldiers killed during the siege of Constantine in October of that year. The article is a philosophical disquisition on the nature and meaning of 'imitation' in music, a subject dear to Berlioz's principal composition teacher's heart: one of Le Sueur's earliest essays is an *Exposé détaillé d'une musique une, imitative, et particulière à chaque solennité*, whose fourth part, we read, 'treats the means of composing music that is at once unified and *imitative*,

---

39   *CG* vol. 4, p. 101 (16 January 1852).
40   *CG* vol. 4, p. 102 (16 January 1852). The *Te Deum* at Notre Dame on 1 January 1852 included music by Le Sueur and Adolphe Adam.

inventiveness, organization, design on the large and small scale, proportions, contrasts, effects, formal liberties, continuity, the drama appropriate to solemn occasions and vocal and instrumental expression as well as the elegance, truth, and beauty of that expression'.[41] Many of the terms here refer to matters with which Berlioz – as the composer of a *Symphonie fantastique* with a programme that long caused sceptics to accuse him of asking of music to express more than it was capable of expressing – would concern himself for a lifetime. It is not impossible that Le Sueur himself might have been pleased by Berlioz's ruminations (he died later in the same year, on 6 October).

Berlioz's concern with *imitation* was forced on him already in November 1830 when Fétis, reacting to the programme of *Symphonie fantastique*, was among the first to suggest that the composer was perhaps mistaken about the goals of the art by requiring of music that it paint material facts and express abstract ideas.[42] He may have been more immediately prompted by reading *Le Haydine, ou Lettres sur la vie et les ouvrages du célèbre compositeur Haydn* by Giuseppe Carpani, who holds a place, with Georg August Griesinger and Albert Christoph Dies, as one of Haydn's earliest biographers. A selection from Carpani's work, published originally in Italian in 1812, was printed in Niort in June 1836 by Robin, in a translation by the novelist Dominique Mondo, who dedicated his work to Désiré Beaulieu, Prix de Rome winner in 1811, now living in Niort. The brochure no doubt piqued Berlioz's interest (he quotes from it) as he had been interested in Haydn from the beginning. It is not inconceivable that he encountered the new French translation of Carpani through his publisher Adolphe Catelin, with whom he began to work in the mid-1830s.[43] It is also possible that Mondo himself alerted Berlioz to his new publication; to his later translation of Peter Lichtenthal's *Dictionnaire de musique*, for example, Mondo added a number of bits of his own, including a word about Berlioz, who was 'to be noticed as a composer of instrumental music'.[44]

Berlioz's essay 'De l'imitation musicale' sparked a significant part of the book by Jacques Barzun that itself sparked the modern Berlioz renaissance. In the first 'interchapter' of *Berlioz and the Romantic Century*, entitled 'Program Music and the Unicorn', Barzun interrogates at length, as we continue to do even today, the nature and elusive existence of such a category

---

41 Lesueur, *Exposé*. Paris: Veuve Hérissant, 1787, p. vii.
42 *Revue musicale* (27 November 1830).
43 Mondo's complete translation of Carpani appeared, in Niort from Robin and in Paris from Schwartz and Gagnot, as *Haydn, sa vie, ses ouvrages, ses voyages et ses aventures*, in December 1837. It was reissued by Adolphe Catelin in Paris in 1838.
44 Peter Lichtenthal, *Dictionnaire de musique*. Paris: Troupenas, 1839, p. 432.

as 'program(me) music'; after much exposition and development, he comes essentially to the conclusion that Berlioz reached some 150 years earlier: music 'is an art *sui generis*, self-sufficing, and able to exert its spell without recourse to any kind of imitation whatsoever'.[45]

The last of the articles included here was published in 1850, in which year Berlioz set forth upon his adventure, all too short-lived, as founder, impresario, and conductor of the new Société philharmonique de Paris. On the programme of the second of five concerts given during that first season we find seven excerpts from act 1 of Gluck's *Alceste*: the choruses 'O ciel! Qu'allons-nous devenir' and 'Dieu puissant'; the *Marche religieuse*; the oracle scene 'Apollon est sensible à nos gémissements'; the soprano aria 'Non, ce n'est point un sacrifice!'; the bass aria 'Déjà la mort s'apprête'; and the soprano aria 'Divinités du Styx'. Gluck, for Berlioz 'the first of the romantics', was for him always larger than music itself: his various writings on the opera span almost thirty years, from two articles in the *Gazette musicale* of June 1834 to a series of six articles in the *JD* of October, November, and December 1861. It is altogether fitting, then, that this anthology conclude with Berlioz's midcentury remarks on *Alceste*, in which, with an exhortation characteristic of much of his writing, he employs the imperative mode: 'Écoutez ce morceau instrumental!' 'Entendez cette mélodie douce!' ('*Listen* to this instrumental movement'; '*Listen* to this gentle melody'), urgings of a sort designed by Berlioz from the beginning to have his readers hear and admire at least *something* of what he knew, in his heart and mind, was the essence of high art.

The year 1850 was one that for Berlioz was filled with drama. The forty-seven-year-old composer witnessed the successful first season of his Société philharmonique in the spring; he opened the second in the autumn; he directed a monumental performance of the *Requiem* at Saint-Eustache in May. In the same month he learned of the death of his sister, Nanci Pal, and in August, in the company of such notables as Victor Hugo, Gérard de Nerval, Alexandre Dumas *père* and *fils*, he attended the funeral of Honoré de Balzac. (In the first column he published after the death of Louis-Philippe, on 26 August 1850, Berlioz said nothing of the lately overthrown king.) In September he accompanied his sixteen-year-old son to Le Havre and bid adieu to the boy (who would eventually become a master mariner) as he entered upon his first adventure as an apprentice sailor on the high seas. Berlioz had little time for composition but by the end of the year had made some sketches for what would later become the oratorio *L'Enfance du Christ*. He furthermore completed thirteen major articles for the *JD* (not

---

45   Jacques Barzun, *Berlioz and the Romantic Century*, third edition. New York: Columbia University Press, 1969, vol. 1, p. 172.

included here) and one for the *RGM* (which brings this selection to a close). If the year 1850 was not a watershed in his career, much as we might like to use it as a point of demarcation, it was nonetheless filled with numerous trials and tribulations that a less practised and precautious individual would not easily have been able to meet and surmount, including Harriet Smithson's several strokes (Berlioz was separated from his wife but always saw to her financial well-being).[46]

It would be possible to elaborate upon the larger context, biographical and artistic, of each and every one of the fifty-eight articles in this anthology, as I have done here upon the first and last. But our aim in this publication is rather more simply to convey to the English-speaking world a generous selection of the writings that made of Berlioz the most significant music critic of his generation. A reading of the complete criticism is tantamount to a reading of the history of music in the middle third of the nineteenth century. A reading of this selection will serve that purpose ... selectively, while demonstrating something of the magic of his pen and the magnitude of his learning, as well as many of the themes that preoccupied him during those three decades and more that he worked as a word-weaver: the trials and tribulations of the critic, who must *feuilletoniser* (one of a number of neologisms invented by Berlioz, who loved them), and who no matter what stance he takes is criticised for taking it.[47] In this regard he echoes one of his heroes, Lord Byron, who wrote to his friend Thomas Moore on 2 January 1821 that he felt writing 'as a torture': something to 'get rid of but never a pleasure. On the contrary', he said, it was 'a great pain'.[48] It is conceivable that Berlioz read those very words in the French translation of Byron's letters by Louise Swanton-Belloc, published in Paris in the very same year.[49] Madame Belloc was the translator of Moore's *Irish Melodies*, some of which, rendered into verse by Thomas Gounet, were set to music in Berlioz's own *Mélodies irlandaises*, first published in Paris in 1830 as *Neuf Mélodies*.

One of the principal themes of Berlioz's criticism is the exaltation of the glory of his gods, Gluck and Beethoven, Virgil and Shakespeare; another is the excoriation of his nemeses, the makers of *arrangements*, sometimes accompanied by the painful admission (because he, too, penned them) of

---

46 I have elsewhere suggested that the main caesuras of Berlioz's artistic career, separating periods playfully labelled 'initiation', 'innovation', and 'introspection', occurred around the revolutions of 1830 and 1848. Peter Bloom, *The Life of Berlioz*. Cambridge: Cambridge University Press, 1998.

47 In *Le Rénovateur* (5 October 1835).

48 *Letters and Journals of Lord Byron*. London: John Murray, 1830, p. 436.

49 *Mémoires de Lord Byron* published by Thomas Moore [*Letters and Journals of Lord Byron*], translated into English by Mme Louise Sw.-Belloc. Paris: A. Mesnier, 1830.

their occasional legitimacy. He is inspired to defend the virtues of instrumental music, and to demonstrate the centrality of the Beethoven symphonies in the realm of romantic music; he is happy to cheer on the new and talented singers; he is sad to see the shenanigans of the untalented opera directors and the underwhelming success of their enterprise. He sings of the emptiness of *la routine* and, as he summarises the plots of so many operas-comiques, the nefariousness of so many *idées reçues*. In the strictly musical arena, he pontificates about the size of the orchestra and chorus and the spatial layout of the places in which they play and sing; he appreciates the grandeur of Les Invalides, for example, for whose resonance he designed the *Requiem*, and finds it conversely absurd to attempt to make any music whatsoever in the open air. He is preoccupied by matters of intonation of both singers and players (that Berlioz had absolute pitch seems certain); and he is much taken by the capacity of the modern timpani, for example, to tune to notes both high and low. He is enthusiastic about new instruments – saxophones, for example, capable of sounding like 'echoes of echoes' – and enjoys playing upon other instruments' names: the 'cacophonium' (a fictional cousin of the *mélodium*); the 'grandmother' of the E-flat clarinet! In his reviews as in his treatise on orchestration, he is obsessed with enharmonic equivalents: fascinated with the differing implications of the notes D-sharp and E-flat, for example, and fearful that when played simultaneously they will create dissonance in the extreme.

Berlioz's political preferences, which we have mentioned, do not often come to the fore in his criticism, but they bubble up now and again in unexpected places. During the short-lived Second Republic, proclaimed by the revolutionaries on 28 February 1848 and repudiated by the rising emperor in 1852, he admits that by stirring the passions, music is likely to contribute to the 'progress' of revolutions, but adds with veiled bitterness that revolutions are unlikely to contribute to the 'progress' of music.[50] Berlioz no doubt had to restrain his more radical opinions in order to remain employed, but he could not resist some roguish remarks on the reopening of the Opéra, recently renamed 'Théâtre de la Nation'. In 1847 Adolphe Adam had formed a new company called 'Théâtre National' and Berlioz in July 1848 mulled over the difference between the two: 'Happily, the question is no more serious than knowing whether one should say "the shape" or "the form" of a hat; the great thing, at the moment, is to have both a hat and a head …'.[51]

Like music marked for the intelligent listener, intelligent behaviour, too, at that postrevolutionary hour, seemed to Berlioz to be in short supply.

---

50   *JD*, 5 December 1848.
51   *JD*, 26 July 1848 (see article 46).

Here, as elsewhere, in his diatribes and dialogues (so clever and convincing as to have caused later critics to take them as having occurred!), we see and savour Berlioz's inevitable, indeed incorrigible irony, cynicism, and mirth. Of these one further example must stand for many. Describing the great conductor François-Antoine Habeneck's desire to have the audience pay attention to his programme, Berlioz puts into his mouth this urgent command: 'Now listen, you pitiless gossipers, frivolous cavatina fans, be finally, totally, completely, absolutely quiet! No moving about, no breathing (no point asking you to stop thinking!)'. Because *thinking*, obviously, *never even crossed your mind*. The principal weapon in Berlioz's polemical arsenal, first, last, and always, is humour.[52]

Berlioz did not hanker for *systems* of thought; he did not fancy the word 'aesthetics' and went so far as to suggest that the pedant who invented it should be brought before a firing squad: 'Esthétique!! Je voudrais bien voir fusiller le cuistre qui a inventé ce mot-là!'[53] If, in his critical writings, certain themes emerge and recur rather like *Leitmotifs* or, to use the more Berliozian term, *idées fixes*, Berlioz remains nonetheless something of an improviser, ready to surprise readers with opinions different from and on occasion contradictory to those they might have expected from him. It is rather in his *music*, popular notions of his hallucinatory abandon to the contrary notwithstanding, that he acts with great rationality and premeditation. *Forget* the opium-induced nightmare of the *programme* of the *Fantastique*; *look* at the composer's chiselled musical hand; *listen* to the Pilgrims' March from *Harold en Italie*, the Offertory from the *Requiem*, the Funeral March from *Roméo et Juliette*, and the love duet from *Les Troyens*; and *dare to say* that these exquisite moments are anything other than sober and controlled in their elaboration and execution.

Traduttore, traditore; traduction, trahison. It is ironic that in English, for this ancient formula about the futility of translation, we have no such paronyms; *translator, traitor* is an unduly harsh metaphor for something unavoidable and, why not say so, urgent. Even Berlioz – who read Shakespeare in English and, while grousing, in French – admitted the necessity of translations, attempting as he did to separate those that were faithful from those that were flawed. 'I have corrected in my edition [of Shakespeare's *Othello*] I don't know how many absurdities by Monsieur Benjamin Laroche', Berlioz told his friend Ferrand, speaking of the translator upon whose version of *Much Ado about Nothing* he had relied for his own *Béatrice et Bénédict*, 'and

---

52   See Eric Bordas, 'Polémique, style', in Jean-Pierre Bartoli, Peter Bloom, Pierre Citron, and Cécile Reynaud (eds.), *Dictionnaire Berlioz* (Paris: Fayard, 2003), pp. 431–2.
53   *JD*, 16 February 1840.

yet he is the most faithful and least ignorant of the lot'.[54] (Sixty years later an American who closely examined the text remarked that 'Laroche's mistakes are remarkably few'.)[55] Readers of these fifty-eight articles in translation will miss something of the sound and fury of Berlioz's French. They will nonetheless hear the wealth of his wit and wisdom in Roger Nichols's terse and elegant English. They will be pulled 'irresistibly into his world', as Katherine Kolb wrote in her introduction to the present book's predecessor and made 'to want to read on'.[56]

Peter Bloom

---

54   *CG* vol. 7, p. 139.
55   Margaret Gilman, *Othello in French*. Paris: Champion, 1925, p. 114.
56   *Berlioz on Music*, p. 26.

1

On Imitation in Music (I)

RGM, 1 January 1837

Berlioz's article 'De l'Imitation musicale', published in the RGM *(1 and 8 January 1837), has twice been published in English translation: by Jacques Barzun, but with cuts, and the same translation with cuts restored and translated by Edward T. Cone.*[1] *But given that Cone's version dates from over forty-five years ago, and Barzun's from over seventy, I feel it is worth bringing out a new version of this important essay. Why Berlioz should have chosen this subject in 1837 is uncertain: it would seem unlikely that anyone had complained, some six years after the first performance of* Symphonie fantastique, *about the noise of the guillotine.*[2] *But the idea of imitation in music continued to exercise composers and critics for years, with many declaring the innate superiority of 'pure' music. Satie's quip on the first movement ('From dawn to midday at sea') in Debussy's* La Mer, *that 'there was especially a little moment between half-past ten and a quarter to eleven that I found amazing', took aim at the composer's chronological exactitude. Likewise, Ravel in 1922 refused to accept a widespread reaction that* La Valse *tapped into the violence of World War I, saying, 'You should see in it only what comes from the music'.*

I'm not talking here about imitation in the sense generally accepted in connection with the writing of fugues but about the *reproduction* of certain sounds, and also about the *description* or musical *painting* of things whose existence is revealed to us only *by our eyes*. There are no great composers of any school who have not, with greater or lesser success, tried their hand at this interesting side of music, which has, one must admit straight away, tempted several of them into errors and deplorable absurdities. One must

---

1   Jacques Barzun, *Pleasures of Music.* New York: Viking Press, 1951; Edward T. Cone (ed.), Berlioz: *Fantastic Symphony.* New York, W. W. Norton, 1971.
2   As Peter Bloom mentions in his introduction, the stimulus was possibly the recently published French translation of Carpani (see note 3).

admit that this branch of music has rarely been treated at any length or examined with meticulous attention. But it's a matter of the greatest importance, which eccentric spirits among musical columnists raise from time to time without ever receiving an answer. I'm going to try and shed some light on the dark corners of this question and discover at the same time the point where its practice ceases to be worthy of the art or accepted by good taste and sinks into the absurd by way of the inane and the grotesque.

M. Joseph Carpani, an excellent Italian critic to whom we owe, among other remarkable writings, a collection of letters on Haydn's life and works, will be helpful to us in this task.[3] His opinions on the matter seem to us in general to be those of a man with a true feeling for music and for what in particular constitutes good musical manners. Even so, it seems to me that his words have not highlighted several crucial aspects of the question; and it is to supply these missing elements as they occur that I am going to proceed, point by point.

In one of his letters, about the well-known oratorio *The Creation*, in which the composer makes great use of the 'descriptive style', M. Carpani remarks that composers before Haydn had already often turned to the means of imitation that music offers; and he identifies two types, the 'physical' and the 'emotional'.

'By physical imitation', says M. Carpani, 'I mean that of sounds generated in animals' throats, or of those produced by vibrations in the air in various ways around the bodies these vibrations encounter. This element turns all bodies into musical instruments, provided they offer resistance. Air rustles through the leaves, roars in caves, murmurs along uneven ground, rumbles, resounds and thunders when it escapes with a rush from a narrow space into a wider one, etc. The physical imitation of these sounds, these noises, belongs by right to music. But that is not the finest of its capabilities, even if imitation nonetheless has its difficulties as well as its merits. A Greek was asked one day to go and listen to a man who could whistle a perfect imitation of a nightingale; to which he replied, 'I'm staying here. I've heard a real nightingale'. I don't see why that reply has been praised. My retort to him would have been, 'My dear philosopher, precisely because it's not a nightingale singing, that's why it should be heard and admired'. If someone was invited to see a battle painting by Jules Romain and replied 'I've seen real battles', what sense would that make? He'd be told, 'It's precisely because

---

3   Giuseppe Antonio Carpani (1752–1825) made Italian translations of librettos for Dalayrac, Grétry, and Kreutzer as well as for Haydn's *Creation*. His *Le Haydine ovvero Lettere su la vita e le opere del celebre maestro Giuseppe Haydn* was published in Italian in 1812 and in French in 1837.

you've seen real battles that you ought to find pleasure in seeing how art has been able to copy them using just a touch of coloured earth'.[4]

Here M. Carpani seems to have strayed outside his subject in borrowing a means of comparison from painting. This art in fact cannot and should not have any other object than reproduction or imitation that is more or less beautiful and true to nature, while music, in the great majority of cases, is an art sui generis, sufficient to itself, which knows how to delight without having recourse to any kind of imitation. Painting could never encroach on the domain of music; music, on the other hand, can obviously act on the imagination with its own resources, so as to create impressions similar to those produced by art. But this pertains to the second of the two types we identified initially, to the imitation M. Carpani calls *indirect* or *emotional*. As for the first of these, the *physical*, direct imitation of sounds and noises in nature, here is what I think, and what our writer does not say.

The first requirement for this kind of imitation to be included among the resources of musical art, without diminishing that art's nobility and power, is that that imitation should never be an *end*, but only a *means*; that it should never be considered (except with rare exceptions) as the musical idea itself, but as the complement to that idea, to which it is linked logically and naturally.

The second requirement for an imitation to be acceptable is that it should be used only on subjects worthy of retaining the hearer's attention and should not be used (at least in any serious work) to emphasise sounds, movements, or objects that are set too far below the level at which art could never operate without cheapening itself.

The third requirement would be that the imitation, without becoming a reality by substituting nature exactly for art, should nonetheless be faithful enough to ensure that the composer's intention could not be misunderstood by an attentive and experienced audience. Finally, the fourth requirement would be that this material imitation should never take the place of *emotional* imitation (expression) and should not make an exaggerated display of its descriptive trifles when the drama is proceeding by leaps and bounds and passion alone demands to be heard.

Therefore, to support the distinctions we have just made, I shall choose examples taken from the great composers and also from the great poets (since poetry and music, in this respect, are at one with each other). The storm from Beethoven's *Pastoral Symphony* seems to be a magnificent exception

---

4   From 'By physical imitation' to 'coloured earth' Berlioz cites Carpani almost word for word. Jules Romain is Giulio Romano (born Giulio Pippi, 1499–1546), a pupil of Raphael. His masterpiece of architecture and painting is the set of illusionist frescos in the Palazzo del Te in Mantua.

to our first rule, of allowing imitation only as a means and not an end, since this movement is entirely devoted to reproducing various noises caused by a violent storm suddenly breaking over a village celebration; the rain falls drop by drop, the wind gets up, the thunder growls dully in the distance, the squawking birds seek shelter, then the squall comes closer, the trees lose branches, men and animals disperse howling with terror, the lightning cracks furiously, the sky becomes a torrent, the elements are in disarray, it's chaos ... However, this sublime painting, which leaves far behind everything that had ever been attempted of the same kind, still belongs in the category of *contrasts* and *dramatic effects* imposed by the work's subject, given that it's preceded and followed by scenes of gentleness and good humour, to which it acts as a foil; and that is so true that this storm in the *Pastoral Symphony*, if transplanted to some other composition where its presence was not motivated, would certainly lose a great deal of its effectiveness. So, this imitation is really just a means of contrast, carried off with the immeasurable power of genius.

In *Fidelio*, on the other hand, another work by the same composer, we find a musical imitation very different from the one we've been discussing. It comes in the famous tomb duet: the gaoler and Fidelio are digging the grave in which Florestan is to be buried; in the middle of their labours the two diggers unearth a huge rock and with great effort roll it to the edge of the grave; at this moment the contrabasses play a bizarre, very brief phrase (not to be confused with their ostinato phrase that runs through the whole piece), by which, so we're told, Beethoven intended to imitate *the muted sound of the rolling rock*.[5]

This imitation, which was in no way necessary either for the drama or for its musical effect, is therefore truly an *end* for the composer: he imitates for imitation's sake and also loses out, for there is neither poetry, nor music, nor drama, nor truth in such an imitation: it's a lamentable piece of puerility over which one is as sad as surprised to have to reproach a great man. We can say the same about Handel if it's true, as is claimed, that in his oratorio *Israel in Egypt* he wanted to copy the 'movements of the locusts' in the very rhythmic passages of the vocal parts.[6] Certainly it's a very unfortunate imitation of an even more unfortunate activity, unworthy of music in general and a hundred times more so of the oratorio's noble and elevated style.

---

5 The duet in act 2, no. 12, bars 45–6. The passage is on cellos, double-basses, and contrabassoon, marked *forte*. The stage direction is that the rock, earlier and with difficulty lifted by the jailer Rocco and Leonora, *falls* rather than rolls.

6 The chorus in part 1 on the words 'and the locusts came without number'.

In *The Creation* and *The Seasons*, essentially descriptive works, Haydn does not, on the contrary, seem to me to have lowered his style greatly when, obeying the dictates of the libretto, he applied musical imitation to the graceful sounds of the cooing of doves, an imitation which is in any case very convincing. This leads us back directly to Beethoven and the *Pastoral Symphony*. People have often criticised the song of the three birds we hear at the end of the 'Scene by the Brook'. As to the appropriateness of this imitation, it seems to me self-evident: the majority of the calm voices of sky, earth, and water find a quite natural place here and contribute effortlessly to the serene mood of the countryside. But they don't all appear in a faithful reproduction. The quail, the cuckoo, and the nightingale are the birds Beethoven has chosen to copy in his orchestra. Now we cannot possibly fail to instantly recognize the first two named, but for the other there's no escaping the fact that an uninstructed listener, hearing the flute, would never guess that it's the nightingale that it's claiming to imitate. The reason is that the *fixed sounds* of the cuckoo and quail belong naturally to our musical scale, while those of the nightingale – sometimes plaintive, sometimes brilliant, but never steady – does not.

It's strange that this observation has escaped numerous composers who have tried, all of them unsuccessfully, to copy the inimitable *vocalises* of this nocturnal singer. On the other hand, several of them have courted ridicule by substituting, for the imitation of certain sounds, these sounds themselves in all their anti-musical reality. For example, an Italian composer, whose name escapes me, having written a symphony on the death of Werther, decided the best way to imitate the suicidal pistol shot was to include an actual pistol shot in his orchestration – the height of absurdity.[7] When Méhul and Weber wanted to include the noise of a firearm, the former in his overture to *Le jeune Henri*, the latter in the 'Infernal Hunt' of *Der Freischütz*, they succeeded absolutely without overstepping the boundaries of art, by means of a simple, carefully judged drum beat. If M. Meyerbeer in *Les Huguenots* used real bells instead of imitating them imperfectly with the orchestra, that's because the dramatic situation demanded it forcefully, as is proved by the terrifying effect of these sinister vibrations booming out in the Paris Opéra; and even if such success were not the ultimate justification, we may reasonably say that since bells are, when it comes to it, *musical instruments*, there has never been a happier occasion for using them.

There's also the case of imitations which are not absolutely condemned by reason but which, when appearing in the public domain, become trivialised and so demand of the composer who includes them the utmost skill, or a flash of inspiration, to give them a new and more noble appearance. In

---

[7] The orchestral suite *Werther* by Gaetano Pugnani (1731–98).

a duet in *Guillaume Tell*, for example, there's a passage for Arnold, 'I tread on the fields of glory', beneath which there's a long rhythmic pedal for the trumpet, which I hear as being deliberately vulgar. In any case it's open to severe criticism, as an error a man of M. Rossini's calibre should be the last to commit. On the other hand, in Gluck's *Armide*, the warlike noise with which he accompanies Ubalde's exclamation, 'Our general summons you back' ['Notre général vous rappelle!'] electrifies the most phlegmatic listener and, whatever revolutions may happen in the world of music, will always shine out as a brilliant flash of genius.

There is finally, in the use of actual *imitation* as a *means*, a trap which the greatest poets have not always avoided and which I shall point out to musicians. It's the difficulty of using it only in the right place, and especially being careful never to substitute it for that most powerful of all imitations, the one that reproduces feelings and passions, namely *expression*. When Talma, in the role of Orestes, cried out, with hissing 'esses' 'For whom are these snakes that hiss above your heads?', far from leaving me moved, it always made me want to laugh; because it seemed obvious to me, then as now, that this attempt by Orestes to imitate the hissing of snakes when his soul is full of terror, his heart with despair and his head with foul visions, was in direct opposition to all ideas we have of truth and dramatic verisimilitude.[8] Orestes is really not in the business of *describing* the Furies: far from it, he imagines he is seeing them, he summons them, he entreats them, he defies them, and unquestionably one has to exercise considerable charity not to find risible an imitation of this sort put into the mouth of such a desperate man, at such a moment.

On the other hand, any number of passages in Virgil strike me as quite unusually telling, because he has taken the trouble to place them only in speeches made by the characters or in descriptions made by the poet himself:

> Ruit alto a culmine Troja.
> Nox atra cava circumvolat umbra.
> Quadrupedante putrem sonitu quatit ungula campum.
> Procumbit humi bos.[9]

---

8 Berlioz saw the tragedian François-Joseph Talma (1763–1826) on stage almost as soon as he arrived in Paris. The line quoted is from the final scene of Racine's *Andromaque*: 'Pour qui sont ces serpents qui sifflent sur vos têtes?'

9 From different parts of the *Aeneid*: II.90 ('Troy falls in ruins from its great height'); II.360 ('Black night envelops us with its hollow shadows'); VIII. 596 ('Galloping hooves shake the soft earth with their noise'; V.481 ('The ox is felled to the ground'). In this last line, Virgil substitutes the single syllable 'bos' for the word of two or three syllables that normally ends a hexameter.

These are wonderful imitations. But if, instead of placing the penultimate one of these quotations in an epic narration, the poet had set it as a kind of dramatic intervention in the mouth of a wounded, straggling soldier with his feet in the stirrups, riding his horse in the middle of the battlefield, we may concur that the coolness of this man, busy describing the galloping horses that are overwhelming him, would have struck us as utterly ridiculous. Is Orestes far less so?

In my next article I shall examine the second kind of imitation, which M. Carpani labels *indirect or emotional*, and which I shall call, depending on the situation, *musical image* or *expression*.

2

On Imitation in Music (II)

RGM, 8 January 1837

Before turning to the second kind of imitation, which consists, as I have already said, in reproducing the tone of passions and feelings, and even in reproducing in music the image of objects that are only visible, I shall say a few more words about physical imitation.

This kind of imitation, according to M. Carpani, was taken to such an excess in seventeenth-century Italy that the composer Melani, in his opera *Le Bailli de Coloniola*, set to music the following words and asked his orchestra to take on the roles of the animals mentioned below:[1]

> Sometimes the frog in the mud
> Sings cheerfully: kouà kouà rà;
> The cricket goes: tri tri tri,
> And the little lamb: bè bè;
> The nightingale goes: kiou kiou kiou,
> And the cock: couri ki ki.

But long before Melani, in antiquity this kind of imitation was employed by the Greeks in their plays, as in Aristophanes's *The Frogs* and *The Birds*. Although Haydn was careful and discerning about using it in his famous oratorios, one can't help regretting that the subjects he chose often led him to embrace such childishness. No doubt he judged them at their true worth, and perhaps he found place for them in his scores merely to please certain amateurs of the kind one finds in society, who are more taken by such instrumental tours de force than by feats of sublime inspiration. Baron van Swieten, among others, bullied the great composer to include frogs.[2] At least

---

1 Jacopo Melani (1623–76), *Il potestà di Colognole*, premiered in Florence in 1656.

2 Gottfried Bernhard, baron van Swieten (1733–1803) was a diplomat and music-lover of Dutch origin. He composed a few opéras-comiques but is best

in *The Seasons* Haydn stuck to his guns and refused, unlike the Greek playwright, to wallow in the mud just to appeal to the taste of the ultra-classical van Swieten.

The best kind of physical imitation is one which, without committing the excesses noted in my first article, would be truthful enough for its message not to be misunderstood, would not fashion the sound to be exactly what it is in nature but would content itself with a reference that was lightly coloured. There I leave physical imitation.

What M. Carpani calls *emotional* imitation has the intention of using sound to stir different feelings in our hearts and to inspire, using our hearing alone, sensations which we humans only feel in nature through the mediation of our other senses. This is the aim of *expression*, of *painting*, and of *musical images*. As for power of expression, I doubt that the arts of drawing and even of poetry possess it to the same degree as music. It required all the enthusiasm of the defenders of a celebrated master, together with a total lack of education and an utterly barbaric intelligence, for them to claim (in the single task of defending their idol from the criticism) that all tones of music were entirely interchangeable, and that the composer of *Otello* [Rossini] was not guilty of the senselessness he was accused of since music has no sense; nor was he guilty of writing a number of *absurd* pieces because there is no such thing as *true* music. He took it upon himself to send them immortal proof to the contrary in *Guillaume Tell*. But I should be doing my readers a disservice if I laboured the point any further.

Musical *painting*, which as we shall see shortly is not at all the same thing as an *image*, is in my opinion far from possessing such an incontestable reality. The famous naturalist Lacépède, who according to his fellow scientists also had claim to being an excellent composer, says somewhere, 'Music has nothing but sounds at its disposal; it can act only through sounds. So for it to be able to interpret the signs of our emotions, it is necessary that these should themselves be sounds'.[3] But how to express in music something that has neither sound nor echo? For example, the density of a wood, the coolness of a meadow, the path of the moon, etc. 'By interpreting' says Lacépède, 'the emotions they inspire'. Our Italian critic, M. Carpani, finds such imitation noble, beautiful, enchanting; he finds in it the highest point of music.

---

known for commissioning C.P.E. Bach's symphonies and Mozart's reorchestrations of Handel, and for preparing the texts for Haydn's *The Creation* and *The Seasons*.

3   Bernard Germain Étienne Médard de la Ville-sur-Illon, Comte de Lacépède (1756–1825), studied cello and piano, and on Gluck's advice took lessons from Gossec. He composed a few operas but none received professional performance and they appear to be lost. His scientific and philosophical works had more success.

I am far from totally sharing his opinion. On the contrary, I am strongly inclined to think him misled, like many others, by a play on words, or, if you like, by the evident imprecision with which the terms of the argument have been formulated. Do we really have a constant, identical response on seeing a wood, a meadow, or the serene path of the moon across the sky? Of course not. The wood, whose coolness and darkness draw tender sighs from the lover remembering the delights he enjoyed there, will provoke gnashing of teeth from the ignored or deceived lover and fill his heart with rage as it reminds him of a rival's success. The hunter will enter it filled with burning, vigorous happiness, the young girl with a secret terror; the heavily armed robber will one day establish himself with grim ferocity in his ambush on the fringe of the wood and next day will be dragging his wounded body back there, terrified that his most secret hideout will not protect him from the furious policemen on his track.

Music is good at expressing success in love, jealousy, positive and carefree joy, anxious modesty, violent threat, suffering, and fear. But for these various emotions to be aroused by the sight of a wood or anything else is something it can never achieve, and the claim to extend the power of musical expression beyond these already generous limits seems to me utterly untenable. As a result, there have been few composers of merit who have wasted time and effort pursuing such a chimera, since they have had better things to do than to engage with these so-called imitations. If there have been some who have been led to abandon music for what is, ultimately, neither music nor painting, they are abandoning their prey for its reflection.[4] I'm strongly inclined to believe that art has not lost a great deal, and that reflection and prey were on the same level. Handel, however, decided in one of his works to paint a natural phenomenon which has neither sound nor echo nor even a *silent rhythm*, the result of which does not, I think, leave anybody with a very specific impression, namely that of falling snow. I am at a total loss to understand how he hoped to succeed in such a project by choosing snow as the subject for musical imitation.[5]

I shall probably be told that these are excellent examples of painting in music which deserve recognition, at least as exceptions. We shall see, when we examine them, that these poetic beauties do not, even so, break out of the vast circle in which the nature of music has enclosed them. The fact is

---

4   One of Berlioz's many references to the fables of Lafontaine. The seventeenth fable of book 6 is copied from Aesop, and ends, 'This dog, seeing his prey mirrored in the water / Abandoned it for its reflection, and thought he would drown. / The river suddenly became rough; / With great difficulty he made it to the bank, / But lost both reflection and prey'.

5   This is apparently a misattribution of the depiction of falling snow in Haydn's *The Creation*.

that these imitations are not presented as pictures of visible objects, but only as *images* or comparisons, restoring sensations to which music undoubtedly possesses analogies. Furthermore, for the original source of these *images* to be clearly understood, it is vital that the listener be informed by some other means about the composer's intention, and that the point of comparison should be plainly set out. Rossini, for example, is regarded as having described the action of rowing in *Guillaume Tell* by means of regular accents in the orchestra, an *image* of the in/out movements of the oarsmen whose arrival has already been announced by other characters.

Weber portrayed moonlight in the accompaniment to Agathe's aria in act 2 of *Der Freischütz* ['Leise, leise, fromme Weise'] because the veiled colouring, the calm and melancholy of his harmonies and the *chiaroscuro* of his orchestration are a faithful *image* of pale moonlight; he also express wonderfully the dreamy mood to which the lovers so willingly lend themselves, gazing at the moon whose aid Agathe is imploring at this very moment.

One may say of certain works that they represent a vast horizon, an immensity, because the composer, by the expansiveness of his melodies, the majesty and clarity of his harmonies, all set in opposition to each other to obtain a variety of effects, has been able to conjure up *to the ear* similar impressions to those felt by a traveller who has reached the summit of a mountain, looking out on a vast space, a superb panorama suddenly unfolding *before his eyes*. Again, the truth of the *image* will only be appreciated thanks to explanation beforehand of the subject treated by the composer.

We can see that this faculty of affecting emotions through images which only the written word, whether spoken or sung, has the capacity to bring about, is a very long way from the pretention, as pointless as it is ambitious, of accurately identifying objects that are soundless or unrhythmical with the help of just those rhythmical, sonorous means possessed by music.

Then there is the kind of *image* which, being attached to words in vocal music, merely hinders the expression of overall feeling by drawing attention to details that often have nothing to do with the meaning of the phrase or of the overall idea; the result is often puerile and shabby. Spontini, it's true, has written a superb example in these lines from *La Vestale*:

The gods, to send a sign of their almighty wrath,
Will they in chaos plunge the universe once more?[6]

But in order to relish the magnificent descent from the first syllable of 'chaos' to the second [a minor ninth, from D-flat down to C], how much rubbish we have to endure in countless works by more or less familiar composers! One such can't mention 'sky' without giving it a high note, another would

---

6   'Les dieux, pour signaler leur colère éclatante, / Vont-ils dans le chaos replonger l'univers?'

consider himself disgraced if he didn't place 'hell' in the voice's lowest register, this one makes dawn 'break', that one makes night 'fall' etc., etc. There's nothing more unbearable than this craze for endlessly playing with words. A craze from which, in fact, we are starting to emerge, and which, to judge by the harsh words with which Jean-Jacques Rousseau attacked French composers of his own time, has never been as widespread nor as intense as it was in the last century.

3

Conservatoire de Musique, Ninth Concert: On Beethoven's *Eroica* and Taste in General

RGM, 29 April 1838

The concert at the Conservatoire on 22 April 1838 was the ninth and last of the season. It also included, among other items, excerpts from Méhul's operas Joseph *and* Le jeune Henri, *movements from Beethoven's Septet, and a scene from Mozart's* Idomeneo. *The short final passage dealing with these is omitted here.*

The performance was of Beethoven's *Eroica* Symphony [no. 3]. The first movement filled me with inexpressible admiration. A feeling of deep, one might say 'antique', sadness was dominant throughout, and I have never better understood or admired the grandeur and power of music. On the other hand, when the last chord had sounded and this audience, which passes for the best educated and most responsive of all Paris audiences, seemed to have been so little affected by such an outpouring of nobility, of melancholy, of sublime fury, of grace and pride, I could not help but weep for the unhappiness of the composer who, afire with such enthusiasm, could not make himself understood, even by an elite audience, to the point of elevating them to the heights of his inspiration. It was all the sadder because this same audience, on other occasions, comes alight, their hearts beating and weeping with him. They exhibit true, lively passion for some of his other compositions which, it's true, are equally admirable but not more beautiful than this one: they appreciate the true value of the A minor Adagio of the Seventh Symphony [*sic*: it is an Allegretto], the Allegretto scherzando of the Eighth, the finale of the Fifth and the scherzo of the Ninth; they even seemed deeply moved by the funeral march of the one mentioned here [the *Eroica*]; but as for the first movement, it's impossible to be mistaken. I first noticed their response over six years ago: the public listens to it with equanimity, and beyond that ... nothing.

There's no way to make sense of it. One may well say it was always the same everywhere and for every work of high quality, that the causes of poetic emotion are secret and unanalysable, that the feeling for certain sorts of beauty with which some individuals are blessed is absolutely absent among the masses and that it's impossible it should be otherwise ... There's no consolation in that, nor does it calm the instinctive, involuntary, and even pointless indignation the heart feels, faced with a miracle misunderstood, a superhuman creation that the mob looks at without seeing, hears without understanding, and allows to go past without turning their heads, as though it were a question of something mediocre and everyday. What I find beautiful is 'beauty' for me, but it may not be for my best friend. Someone whose feelings are normally the same as mine will be affected differently from me. It's possible that a work which transports me, affects me like a fever, and drives me to floods of tears, will leave him cold or even offend and infuriate him ...

Most of the great poets either have no feeling for music or else only like trivial, puerile tunes. Many important people have no idea of the emotions it can excite; for Napoleon, certainly, it [music] didn't exist. These are sad truths, palpable, obvious ones that only the pig-headedness of some intellects can deny. I've seen a bitch who used to howl with delight when she heard a major third played by double-stopping on a violin. But she had puppies on whom neither that third, nor the fifth, nor the sixth, nor the octave, nor any chord, consonant or dissonant, ever produced the slightest effect. In the matter of higher musical responses, the public, however it's made up, is like that dog and her puppies. There are certain nerves that vibrate to certain frequencies, but because susceptibility, very incomplete as it may be, is unequally provided and infinitely varied, it follows that it's almost crazy to rely on some aspects of music rather than others to make an impact. So, the composer can only obey his own feelings blindly and resign himself beforehand to the workings of chance.

I'm coming out of the Conservatoire with three or four *dilettanti* one day after a performance of the Ninth Symphony.[1] One of them asks me, 'What

---

1   Berlioz explained the term 'dilettanti' in his second review in *Le Corsaire* (11 January 1824): 'They are people of taste ... who only patronise the Théâtre-Italien, never read scores, for one good reason that we can guess at, and decide without appeal on the merits of pieces, singers and orchestras. Their sensibility is such that they can no longer breathe when they hear a certain *pathetic* item from [Rossini's] *La gazza ladra*, at the moment when the servant girl is led to her death, and yet that they retain the greatest composure at performances of

do you think of that work?' – 'Immense! Magnificent! Overwhelming!'– 'And you?' he asks, turning to an Italian ... 'Oh! As for me, I find it unintelligible, or rather unbearable, there are no tunes. Look, here are several newspapers that mention it. They say: "Beethoven's Choral Symphony represents the culminating point of modern music. The art has produced nothing that can compare with it for nobility of style, grandeur of conception and accuracy of detail". (Another paper): "Beethoven's Choral Symphony is a monstrosity". (Another paper): "This work is not totally deprived of ideas, but they're clumsily put together and form merely an incoherent mass divested of charm". (Another): "Beethoven's last symphony, the one with chorus, contains admirable passages, but one can see that he lacked ideas and that, since his exhausted imagination could no longer come to his aid, he had to work especially hard, often successfully, in order to replace inspiration with technique. Various passages in the work are treated with supreme skill and organised in a perfectly clear and logical order. All in all, it's a highly interesting work from a *worn-out genius*"'.

Where is the truth? Or the untruth? Everywhere and nowhere. Each of them is right: what is beautiful for one is not for the other, as we see from the simple fact that one has been moved and the other has remained impassive, that the first has experienced great enjoyment and the second gross fatigue. What's to be done? Nothing. But it's awful. I prefer to be insane and believe in absolute beauty ... [2]

---

the [Gluck's] *Iphigénies*, [Salieri's] *Les Danaides*, etc.' Although Berlioz claims this definition came from another musician, its concurrence with his own known views makes his own authorship likely.

[2] This audience reaction is reminiscent of what Berlioz had experienced many years before at a performance of Beethoven's String Quartet in C-sharp minor, op. 131. *Le Correspondant*, 1829, translated in the *Berlioz Society Bulletin* 220 (December 2023), pp. 61–2.

4

Esmeralda: On Fair Artistic Judgement

JD, 15 July 1838

Berlioz had already reviewed this opera by Louise-Angélique Bertin (1805–77), on a libretto by Victor Hugo, adapted from his novel Notre-Dame de Paris *(*RGM, *20 November 1836). While recognizing aspects that spoke of her inexperience, he could at least find it in him to praise beauties 'that overall give evidence of a feeling for style and a power of invention that are extremely rare'.*[1] *This extract translates four paragraphs from the middle of the feuilleton.*

Before turning to a study of this work [*Esmeralda*], which is remarkable from many points of view, it may perhaps not be irrelevant to mention the cause of a number of inaccurate criticisms about which composers, more than other artists, have undoubted reason to complain. This cause is *prejudice*.

There is in fact no art more vulnerable to suffering from such unfair judgments than music. Painters, sculptors, engravers, architects, poets, and prose writers all have a real advantage in the fixity of their work: once out of hands of its maker, it can be immediately seen by the critic without its message being undermined, changed or weakened in any way. A painting or a statue is always the same; nothing can prevent the critic from seeing it as it is and understanding it perfectly. If an initial inspection is not enough to judge it overall and in detail, then the critic is free to come back next day, the day after, and several days in a row: the work is there waiting for him, immobile and unalterable.

The score of a musical composition can, of course up to a point, enjoy the same privileges, but members of the public, who are its most important critics,

---

[1] Berlioz had assisted the composer, who was physically handicapped, at rehearsals; he was, of course, indebted to her family who owned the *Journal des débats*. It was falsely rumoured that he had even composed the most popular item, Quasimodo's 'Bell Song'.

don't read scores, and understandably so. They listen to works as best they may and appreciate them in a performance that is more or less faithful, during which the composer's ideas pass rapidly without the possibility of stopping for a moment to allow them to enjoy a leisurely examination. What's more (and here I must offer my personal view of the matter), although many people boast of being able to read a score as they do a book and claim to appreciate it perfectly at first sight without needing to hear a single note, my many observations of extremely competent musicians have proved to me – beyond the possibility of chance – that this claim is, to say the least, considerably exaggerated. From the page one can distinguish a vulgar style from one that isn't, one can see if the harmony is correct and lively, if the instrumentation is carefully applied, if the themes are interesting, or if the work fails through faults in the opposite direction. But as to enjoying a complete understanding, as to being *moved deeply* by it, as one could be by a fine performance, this I categorically deny.

Music is the art of sounds, it has no powers but theirs, and to say the eyes can in all honesty replace the ear in transmitting impressions is on the same level as confusing an account of something with the thing itself, or the idea with the sensation. More crucially, reading a score (especially in the present state of the art) does not even give a true notion of what it contains. One often finds there something the performance lacks, and even more often the reader fails to see the cause of certain truly new and beautiful effects which can arouse an enthusiastic response in the listener. This is so much the case that when the relevant composers aren't present, conductors have found themselves forced to conduct works which they have read meticulously, have thought about at length, and come to believe that they have thoroughly understood. Yet they have still made so many serious errors and entirely misinterpreted any number of passages, changing their colour and ultimately destroying the work's basic character. It has even happened that, being preoccupied with details clearly marked in the score, the conductors didn't realize at rehearsals that the overall effect was lacking; this has led to horrendous gaps in the orchestral sound which by bad luck they only perceived rather too late, and which would undoubtedly not have occurred had the artist charged with conducting the work previously heard it.

It's clear that, even for highly competent musicians, arriving at a true judgment of an important piece of music by reading the score is almost impossible. But if an accurate, spirited, colourful performance is absolutely necessary for the composer, it's also vital, if justice is to be done to him, that no anti-musical element come to work on his listeners and remove them from his influence. It's important that his judges be entirely free of prejudice. Sadly, this is very rarely the case. A few examples will show to what heights of ridicule this malign disposition can bring the judges of art, even when it doesn't lead to the most unhappy consequences for artists.

Everyone knows about Méhul's delightful prank when, borrowing the name Fioraventi as the composer's name for his opera *L'irato, ou L'Emporté*, he gained applause for it from Napoleon, who didn't think any French composer worthy of such favour.[2] Informed of his mistake, the First Consul was happy to forgive the composer for his joke and did not revise his opinion of the work. But such honesty, however natural it may seem, is not generally found any more often than Napoleon's other fine qualities. Another composer had proof of this fact shortly afterwards ...

In those days provincial choir schools were flourishing, and several were headed by men of real talent. One of these was anxious to make an appearance in one of the Paris theatres and, after spending a lot of time in fruitless attempts to find an opera libretto and have the result played, was on the brink of returning, sad and discouraged, to his little home town. At this point Lesueur, whose character was always as exemplary as his talent and whose works were extremely popular at the time, came to the young man's aid. He found him a libretto and, with the agreement of its author, put about the news that he, Lesueur, was setting it to music. Some months went by, the score was finished and published under the name of Lesueur.[3] It was then accepted and almost immediately put into rehearsal. The first night was a success, confirmed over the next three. On the fifth night, M. Lesueur owned up to his generous trick, at which the theatre's directors exploded with rage. This music, which had been excellent the night before, now in a flash became execrable. Performances were instantly abandoned and the administrators were almost on the point of asking M. Lesueur for damages with interest. The opera, entitled *Arabelle et Vascos*, was never performed again. The composer, called Marc, if I am not mistaken, died in poverty and almost entirely forgotten.[4]

---

2   This opera was premiered at the Salle Favart, Paris, in 1801.

3   Jean-François Le Sueur (1760–1837); Berlioz habitually spelled his name 'Lesueur'. In 1804 Napoleon had ordered the Opéra to perform Le Sueur's opera *Ossian, ou Les Bardes*. Le Sueur also composed much religious music, including thirty-three masses. He was chapel-master at the Tuileries and one of the original teachers at the Paris Conservatoire; Berlioz studied with him in the 1820s, at first privately. One historian remarks that by his demand for sumptuous productions and the impact he made with massed choruses and large orchestral forces, he was one of the creators of romantic opera. For Edward J. Dent, with *Ossian* 'we are in the full flood of Romanticism': *The Rise of Romantic Opera*. Cambridge: Cambridge University Press, 1976, p. 87. For Jean Mongrédien, in *Ossian* we find 'many dramatic situations and writing processes that are already those of romantic opera' ('quantité de situations dramatiques ou de procédés d'écriture qui sont déjà ceux de l'opéra romantique'): *La Musique en France des Lumières au Romantisme 1789–1830*. Paris: Flammarion, 1986, p. 76.

4   François Marc (1745–1819) became maître de chapelle of the cathedral of Le Mans. His opera was premiered at the Salle Favart, Paris, in 1801.

5

Paris Opéra: Revival of *Le Siège de Corinthe*

JD, 5 November 1838

Rossini's Le Siège de Corinthe, *a revision of* Maometto II, *was first given at the Paris Opéra on 9 October 1826. The revival took place on 22 October 1838. Although, as noted above, Berlioz was no lover of 'dilettanti', his initially low opinion of Rossini had been revised upwards, especially after getting to know* Guillaume Tell; *Rossini could not be held responsible for the works of his many imitators. This extract translates the first six paragraphs of Berlioz's review.*

This was the first Rossini opera to have been staged at our Académie royale de musique. At its first appearance it unleashed a storm against the Opéra's director: he was bitterly reproached for putting on the stage of the French Opéra, a stage essentially devoted to the dramatic and the serious, the work of an Italian who had made an opera of *Le Barbier de Séville*.

There were only two things the defenders of the national, dramatic genre forgot. The first is that the main works that had for thirty years underpinned the repertoire of our great theatre, and that created its character of grandeur and lyricism, were composed by Italians and one German: Piccinni, Sacchini, Spontini, and Gluck are not Frenchmen. The second point which should not be forgotten is that *Il barbiere di Siviglia*, given the supreme skill with which each of its characters is drawn and developed, was the best guarantee any composer could have given of his understanding of staging and the finesse of his feeling for drama. What's more, this same *Barbier* had been furiously whistled at by the Romans, which must be considered a fairly good recommendation of its composer.[1]

---

1   Rossini's *Il barbiere di Siviglia* had annoyed audiences by seeming to challenge Paisiello's well-liked opera (1782), also based on Beaumarchais's *Le Barbier de Séville*.

On the other hand, Rossini enthusiasts claimed that the arrival of *Le Siège de Corinthe* at the Opéra was a red-letter day for French music: Rossini was going to work miracles, he was going to give us tunes and, thanks to the power of his genius, was even going to teach Dérivis how to sing.[2] According to these gentlemen, there were no tunes in Sacchini, Gluck, or Spontini, nothing but noise and plainsong.

In between these two extreme opinions was a third, which did not choose to declare itself, which waited for the event, which did not declare itself even after the first night, but which, when all is said and done, represents the dominant position among Europe's musical intelligentsia. The small number who took that line still take it today. After the appearance of Rossini's first French opera (I say 'French opera' bearing in mind the important changes his Italian opera *Maometto II* underwent when its name was changed for performance at the Opéra), found that the composer of the Gondolier's song and the Willow romance in *Otello*, together with other fragments of melancholy, was perfectly capable, if he was so inclined, of writing a serious opera that obeyed all the diktats of common sense and artistic nobility, diktats that he had often ignored, no doubt deliberately in order to accommodate the dominant taste of his fellow Italians.

After the performances of *Le Siège de Corinthe*, the moderates' opinion was that, as well as whole scenes that were entirely admirable, the work did contain a large number where the emotion was false and the character ignoble. The pure Rossinists proclaimed these passages to be 'inimitable masterpieces', while the anti-Rossinists roared with rage, insisting that the whole score 'didn't contain as much as two bars that made sense'. The former declared that thanks to his training in Rossinian melody, Dérivis was starting to sing (that's to say, manage roulades); the latter maintained that, while his singing was satisfactory in the old masters, with their simple, broad-brush

---

2   Henri-Étienne Dérivis (1780–1856) was a principal bass at the Opéra from 1803 to 1828. This apparently brutal aside needs qualifying; Berlioz generally admired Dérivis's performances, although in August 1834 he noted retrospectively that Caroline Branchu, despite her tiny stature, had outsung the imposing Dérivis; in a letter of 4 September 1824 he wrote, with underlining, that in Piccinni's *Didon* '*Dérivis est superbe, magnifique, admirable* dans le rôle d'Iarbe'. Perhaps time had not been kind to Dérivis's voice, though in this review Berlioz was probably being ironic. Alexandrine-Caroline Branchu (1780–1850) created the title role of Spontini's *La Vestale* at the Opéra (15 December 1807). She had made her Opéra debut in 1801 in Piccinni's *Dido*, and her last appearance there was in 1826 as Statira in Spontini's *Olimpie*, when Berlioz wrote that 'she was, if one may say so, more sublime than ever; and at the end, when Talma and Dérivis crowned her, I thought the building would collapse'. (Letter to Édouard Rocher, 15 July 1826, *CG* vol. 1, p. 128).

melodies, he couldn't be other than lumbering and grotesque when attempting cavatinas and *vocalises*. According to the sensible critics (those miscreant moderates), Dérivis had never really known how to sing but, thanks to his gifts as an actor, his physical presence, and his loud voice, he could manage most of the major roles of Gluck, Sacchini, and Spontini, always excepting the violent ones where he could only shout. These severe critics found that, as a result, he was wholly unfitted for those passages in the role of Mahomet that demand lightness of voice, or indeed frivolity. The passage of time has confirmed all their views.

Almost everybody these days admires the beautiful things in *Le Siège de Corinthe*. Nobody contests the splendid verve and brio of the overture, the dramatic character of the introduction, whose martial, melancholy tone sits in perfect harmony with the emotions of this people, ready to die in defence of their homeland and their faith; the touching grace of the trio between Palmyra, her lover, and her father; the impetuous vigour of the Greeks' march; the grandeur and admirably tragic accents in the scene of the Blessing of the Flags; the truly archaic beauty in the Wedding March, etc. But other people also find that certain passages are written in a style that lacks dramatic verisimilitude. As an example, I would cite the chorus with solos for Mahomet, 'Viens, suis-moi dans les déserts' (Come, follow me into the desert), which is very often cut in performance. One also has to admit that the most beautiful orchestral effects are no compensation for the wild and continual abuse of the bass drum which, in at least half the opera, obliterates both voices and violins.

6

Third Conservatoire Concert (The Critic's Life)

RGM, 17 February 1839

The concert took place on 10 February 1839. This description of the critic's life is one of Berlioz's many attempts to engage the reader as an ally, and not to pontificate 'de haut en bas'. Even so, it's not hard for us to read it also as evidence that he would much rather be writing music.

It isn't enough to go to a concert and listen to fine music, you also (at least in my case) have to write down for the public what you think about it. You have to do your utmost to explain to the public, bored and importunate as it is, why a certain piece is beautiful and how it produces that effect. You also have to say why certain other pieces, which are equally beautiful, have made only a small or no impact on the audience. There are just two contrary cases that the critic must not mention, for a thousand and one reasons. If a dreadful composition is badly received, he must not use a wounding epithet, for which the composer and his supporters would never forgive him. If, on the other hand, a bad work is applauded as being good, he will refrain from saying that this applause seemed to him unintelligent and inopportune, which would offend not only the composer, but also the thousand or twelve hundred who made up the critical audience.

Oh! It's a fine trade, being a critic. 'There are no dumb trades' says the proverb, 'only dumb people'. Well, despite the general opinion, I would contend that there are both very dumb trades and very dumb people. Now then, would you like me to tell you once and for all what I really think? … I … don't have the time, they're waiting for my article on the Conservatoire concert. The unvarnished truth climbed out of its well one day, if you believe Florian.[1]

---

1   Jean-Pierre Claris de Florian (1755–94), French poet, novelist, and fabulist and an author much loved by the young Berlioz. This reference is to the first of his fables.

But in any case it quickly went down again – since when, if you really want to consult it, you have to make up your mind to descend into the *dank, cold abyss*, as the Romance in *Joseph* puts it.[2] I once started on a journey down to it, but a thought I had halfway, while the basket was descending, decided me to abandon this splendid project and I came back up.

What's the point, I ask myself? Why? What in Heaven's name comes over these people, that they have to know the truth about musical matters? On the contrary, it's absolutely in their interest *not* to know. If I say to them, 'Mister So-and-So is playing preposterous medleys that I find horribly vacuous' and when this Mister So-and-So is going to repeat his repertoire in another concert, the pure-bred dilettante will refrain from going to hear him, and he will be making a great mistake, because this music would have delighted him. If, on the other hand, leaving truth to slumber in its well, I wrote with a colossal nerve that would raise a blush on the cheek of the most intrepid reader that 'Mister So-and-So performed an air with variations full of charming details, a fine, spirited approach, delightful tunes which an admirable technique made even more interesting, and which the audience greeted with applause. He's a great virtuoso, what more can I say? He's a great musician'. Well, if I wrote that, the ordinary fellow who's read my article meeting another who hasn't, will say to him, 'Yes, it seems this man is a hot number, he's playing his famous air and variations tonight, let's go and hear him'. 'Do you think so?' 'Do I think so indeed! He's a great virtuoso, what more can I say, he's a great musician!' And so, these two gents trot off to the concert, which they wouldn't have done without me, and very much like what they hear and tell all the other gents they know, 'Go and hear Mr So-and-So's famous air and variations; he's a great virtuoso, what more can I say, he's a great musician!'

But this critic's false generosity also has its negative side. Those of his readers who can't claim to be among the initiated (and there may be more of them than you might think), once they've allowed themselves to swallow the bait of his praises, from then on discount them as they deserve, and in their disgust proceed to treat the writer as a poor devil, an ignoramus, a cretin. On the other hand, artists who know that he's totally free of cretinism, but who see him writing dull eulogies of things they know perfectly well he hates, get to the point of no longer believing him when he offers praise with seriousness and conviction and blame him almost as much for his sincere praise as for a biting dismissal – which he hasn't delivered, it's true, but which they imagine to be his real response. The fact is, not everything in

---

2   Three-act opera by Méhul, premiered at the Opéra-Comique on 17 February 1807.

our world comes up roses; and I repeat, there are both very dumb trades and very dumb people.

Never mind! Let's move on to the concert which should be the subject of this article, and here am I a million miles away ... The concert started with Beethoven's Choral Symphony, the soloists being Messrs. Dupont and Alizard, and Mmes Nau and Widman.[3] The performance struck me as still better than the one a year before, which is saying a lot. But the impact on the audience was less noticeable, I don't know why. This symphony has the misfortune to begin with a movement that's so great in form and expression, the following ones to some extent suffer from it – and yet all the rest is colossal.

After this monumental music, we heard a clarinet solo from M. Joseph Blaes. There are a lot of trombones in the accompaniment to this piece, and yet Beethoven wrote six symphonies in which this most formidable of wind instruments does not figure. It's a failing common to almost all virtuosos to engage the whole orchestra to build up the ritornellos and tuttis between their airs and variations as far as possible. However talented they are, it's clearly a false move because (at the Conservatoire especially) it makes one think of the Imperial Guard conducted by a police court magistrate. M. Blaes played very well and was applauded despite the still recent memory of Baermann.[4] Mlle Guelton then sang an Italian aria.[5] This young person, whose name was as yet unknown and who was appearing in public for the first time, possesses a soprano voice that covers a wide range, her lower notes having great presence, and she sings in tune, manages her *vocalises* well, and does not lack style. She deserves to be distinguished in future from the crowd of female singers who coo their cavatinas.

Beethoven's choral piece *Meeresstille und glückliche Fahrt* (*Calm Sea and Prosperous Voyage*) had not been heard in Paris before. The smooth adagio,

---

3   Alexis Dupont (1796–1874), French tenor. Dupont had sung for Berlioz as early as 1827 and took over the title-role in *Benvenuto Cellini* for one complete performance and three performances of act 1. Adolphe-Joseph-Louis Alizard (1814–50), French baritone who made his Opéra debut as Saint-Bris in *Les Huguenots* in 1837 and sang Balducci in some performances of *Benvenuto Cellini*. Maria-Dolorès-Benedicta-Josephina Nau (1818–91), French soprano of Spanish origin who had made her Opéra debut in *Les Huguenots* in 1836. Anna Widman (1815–64), French contralto. Dupont, Alizard, and Widman (named as 'Emily Widemann') sang in the premiere of *Roméo et Juliette* on 24 November 1839.
4   The clarinettists mentioned are the Belgian Arnold-Joseph Blaes (1814–92), and the German Heinrich Joseph Baermann (1810–85), dedicatee of works by Mendelssohn, Meyerbeer, and Weber.
5   Sophie Guelton (1819–41), French mezzo-soprano.

'Calm Sea', is of great harmonic beauty, and the rapid idea the cellos then develop before passing it on to the violins well expresses the wind that gets up and rustles the surface of the waves before engulfing them.

The *Guillaume Tell* overture ended the concert. The Société des Concerts has never so far dreamt of putting Rossini's instrumental music alongside that of the leaders of the German school. It would have been more tactful to have abstained from doing so here. After the lyrical marvels of the Beethoven symphony, Rossini's balletic phrases, with his great whacks on the bass drum on every downbeat, could only produce a very strange effect … And that's enough.[6]

---

6   Berlioz here put a longer row of dots and ended with 'et voilà'.

7

Théâtre-Italien, *Le nozze de Figaro*: Benefit Performance for Lablache

RGM, 10 March 1839

Luigi Lablache (1794–1858) was an Italian bass of French origin. He made an immediate impact at La Scala in 1821, as Dandini in Rossini's La Cenerentola. *At the Théâtre-Italien he had also had a great success in Cimarosa's* Il matrimonio segreto. *He was a great favourite of the young Queen Victoria, who took lessons with him when he came to London. The concert reviewed here took place on 10 February. The cast for the performance of Mozart's* Le nozze di Figaro *included Albertazzi as Cherubino, Persiani as the Countess, Grisi as Susaana, Tamburini as Count Almaviva, and Lablache as Figaro.*

It was a good idea of Lablache to choose this masterpiece for his benefit performance; apart from a few evenings of [Mozart's] *Don Giovanni*, one can say that we have not heard at the Théâtre-Italien for a long time music as pure, expressive, lively, skilful, and natural as this. I have never admired to such a degree the creative power of Mozart's genius, nor the unfailing lucidity of his intelligence. There's something heart-breaking, I was going to say 'provoking', in this unvarying beauty, always calm and sure of itself and demanding incessant homage from beginning to end of this lengthy opera. Even so, most of the audience were saying on the way out, 'it doesn't make an impact, it's cold'. Our Paris public has the wretched habit of taking its lead from the applause in the parterre, in many cases the most misleading and least trustworthy of sources.[1] A host of blatantly mediocre offerings, to put it mildly, can certainly stir them to excitement without the applauders really caring that much about what they are apparently turning into a success. On the other hand, masterpieces can be played before an audience that is calm but attentive, displaying a profound, measured admiration far superior to shouts and handclapping.

I think this is how we should interpret the religious silence in which [Mozart's] *Le nozze di Figaro* was heard last Monday. I merely take as proof the enthusiastic exclamations quietly voiced by my neighbours to the left and right of me, who barely clapped more than once or twice the whole evening. In fact, nothing in this perfect score is made to excite violent outbursts: the story does not contain any of those *coups* that move and excite the masses. It's a lyrical comedy, a genre that is by nature cold, and treated by Mozart in a manner dictated by every artistic habit and feeling for beauty and truth. Every character says in their music what they ought to say, nothing more, nothing less. Each scene begins, continues, and ends in a way that's clear, simple, and natural, and the orchestra contains none of those noisy instruments we've got used to hearing these days, uncalled for by this kind of opera and even forbidden by it.

But despite all these hindrances to applause (seeing as we're forced to discuss this matter with those who are obsessed by it), it's necessary to mention the warm reception given to seven or eight of the numbers, which is certainly something. The famous aria 'Non più andrai' was encored; another very vigorous encore was given to the letter duet 'Che soave zeffiretto' ('What a delicious breeze'); the act 1 finale, Tamburini's aria 'Vedro mentre io sospiro' ('Must I forego my pleasure?'), and Figaro's second aria were likewise all applauded – what more can one ask? If other more beautiful numbers left the audience unimpressed, the performers must take the blame. Madame Albertazzi is dreadfully cold, and Cherubino's aria, that charming number in which the love-struck agitation of the adolescent is painted in such a piquant and truthful way, couldn't help suffering greatly from this total lack of warmth.[2] I may say much the same of her other aria, 'Voi che sapete', in which she sang the right notes but without letting us believe, through any sound that came from the heart, that she had realized the composer's intention, sympathised with his feelings, and understood in the slightest what he had in mind. This is not how Mozart, or any other dramatic composer worthy of the name, should be treated. Madame Persiani deserves the same

---

1 Parterre or stalls; Berlioz refers to the seats nearest to the stage, which were not expensive.
2 Emma Albertazzi, née Howson (1814–47), English mezzo-soprano.

reproach to some extent.³ However, given the character of the Countess's role, I shall be less severe on her; it does not demand as much movement for the most part, and it can indeed allow the singer to appear somewhat bored.

We were mortally afraid that Madame Persiani might give in to the current custom of demonstrating the extreme agility of her voice and allow herself to embroider Mozart's melodies. I must immediately do her the justice of saying that nothing of the sort occurred, and that she sang them very simply, but showing her apparent lack of experience of music in the majestic genre – the most difficult of all, it's true. As a result, her great aria in act 2 ('Porgi amor') came over as monotonous and cold, entirely due to a sort of constraint and uncertainty which she failed to disguise, appearing not to appreciate the weak resignation and deep melancholy this number demands. At any rate, she sang her role perfectly in the letter duet with Mademoiselle Grisi, who undertook the role of Susanna with delightful grace and finesse.[4]

Tamburini is an excellent Almaviva, although to me it seemed that his voice lacked fullness of tone.[5] Perhaps this stemmed from being close to Lablache, whose sonorous voice overwhelms those of the same timbre who have the misfortune of appearing in an ensemble with it. Lablache is still the great actor, the great singer, the great musician we know. Nothing is more deeply felt or more intelligently realized than his performances: he enters into the very heart of the work he's interpreting, he identifies with his role, and brings it alive with such vivacity and warmth that his animation communicates itself more or less to the other singers when they are on stage with him. He manages his vocal resources with rare skill, engaging them with reserve at the beginning of pieces, allowing the intensity to grow as the musical interest quickens, and letting it go at the climax with a power, a beauty of sound, a dramatic relevance and energy, that endow the singer and actor in Lablache with the long-held superiority that nobody would dream of denying him.

---

3   Fanny Persiani (1812–67), Italian soprano, daughter of the tenor Nicola Tacchinardi and married to the composer Giuseppe Persiani. In 1835 she created the title role in Donizetti's *Lucia di Lammermoor* in Naples and made her first appearance at the Théâtre-Italien on 7 November 1837 as Amina in Bellini's *La sonnambula*.

4   Giulia Grisi (1811–69), Italian soprano, celebrated for her beauty as much as for her voice. In 1831 she created the role of Adalgisa in Bellini's *Norma*. She was the companion of the tenor Giovanni Mario (1810–83); together they formed the most famous singing pair of their time.

5   Antonio Tamburini (1800–76), Italian baritone, one of the greatest singers of his era. At the Théâtre-Italien he sang in the premieres of Bellini's *Il puritani* (25 January 1835) and Donizetti's *Don Pasquale* (3 January 1843).

The chorus were extremely feeble, even though this time their task was light; the orchestra on the other hand, conducted by M. Tilmant the elder with an intelligent care that speaks of his admiration and respect for Mozart, left almost nothing to be desired.[6] After the curtain came down, Lablache, called back, returned to the stage at the moment when a crown, as large as a carriage wheel, landed at his feet. If it was a sincere homage (as I imagine), it was of an extremely clumsy kind. If it was a joke, it could not have been more out of place or in poorer taste. In the interval, Rubini sang his favourite *cavatine*, from Pacini's *Niobe*; that's to say he was encored with shouts and wild gestures.[7] The theme of this aria is excellent, but it's certainly not the accompaniment that makes it worth hearing: worst of all is a piccolo that every now and then doubles the voice two octaves higher, an extremely vulgar idea whose effect is supremely disagreeable.

---

6   Théophile-Alexandre Tilmant (1799–1878, known as 'Tilmant l'aîné'; his younger brother was a cellist), French conductor employed at the Théâtre-Italien, and from 1849 at the Opéra-Comique. Berlioz's approval may owe something to the fact that Tilmant had directed two concerts mostly of Berlioz's works (4 and 25 June 1835) at the Gymnase musicale in Paris.

7   Giovanni Rubini (1794–1854), Italian tenor who first appeared at the Théâtre des Italiens in 1825. He sang in four Bellini premieres: *Bianca e Fernando* (1826), *Il Pirata* (1827), *La sonnambula* (1831), and *I puritani* (1835). Giovanni Pacini (1796–1867), Italian composer; his *Niobe*, premiered at the Teatro San Carlo, Naples on 19 November 1826, is perhaps best known through Liszt's *Divertimento sur une cavatine de Pacini*, which he played at his pianistic duel with Thalberg in Paris on 31 March 1837.

8

Second Concert of the *Gazette musicale*: Mlle Pauline Garcia – Gluck's *Orphée*

JD, 17 March 1839

The concert on 3 February also included a Mozart quartet, a cantata by Porpora, and songs and Schubert's 'Trout' Quintet. These were dealt with in summary fashion in the first two paragraphs, so that Berlioz could expand on what interested him most; the translation starts at the third paragraph.

Then came the duet from act 3 of *Orphée*, sung by Duprez and Mlle Pauline Garcia, accompanied by M. Dietsch.[1] You can imagine the audience's curiosity. For my part, never having heard the young singer whose name has attained a reputation that might have its dangers, I took a double interest in hearing her for the first time in a work of the great dramatic school. Singing Gluck as she did, Mlle Garcia overcame an immense difficulty, if one takes account of the musical milieu in which she has lived so far.[2] It is not

---

1   Pierre-Louis Dietsch (1808–65), composer and teacher, became chorus-master at the Opéra from 1840 and later for a short time its chief conductor, directing the infamous Paris premiere of *Tannhäuser*. The Opéra presented his *Le Vaisseau fantôme* (*The Phantom Ship*) in 1842; Wagner believed, wrongly, that his libretto for *Der Fliegender Holländer* had been plagiarized. Dietsch also directed the music at Saint-Eustache (see articles 37 and 57). Duprez: see below, article 9, note 3.

2   Michelle-Ferdinande-Pauline Garcia (1821–1910), better known under her married name Pauline Viardot, was a pianist, composer, and mezzo-soprano. She and her elder sister Maria Malibran were daughters of the famous tenor and singing-teacher, Manuel Garcia. This may be why Berlioz suggests that she was taking a risk in embarking on a singing career. Her stage debut was as

the *cavatinas* and flatulent duets – equally false in their expression, taken from most contemporary Italian operas – that could put her on the path to what counts, in my opinion, as the highest summit of art. It's not by singing music one really likes every evening, if not to hear oneself, at least to give them a hearing in the frivolous salons of almost every European capital, that she would acquire the absolute intelligence and passionate feeling of the grandeur of Gluck's genius. And if we were to express a final judgment on her singing, we should have to say she remained well short of the target she was aiming at. In this music, whose sublime simplicity is so demanding, every bar, whether in aria or in recitative, is an obstacle for anyone who is not accustomed early on, in ear and heart, to the true accent of feeling. To *sing* a note by Gluck is nothing, to *shout* it is vulgar, to *embellish* it is monstrous. Mlle Garcia does not embellish it, I give her that, even though at the end of one recitative she made a short excursion into the lower registers of her voice, introducing us to their sonority in depth, but at the cost of the fidelity she owed to the musical text and to the truth of the character [Eurydice] she was charged with portraying. This is what I mean: Gluck's characters are not ones whose vague physiognomy allows us to be unsure of their true nature and of the feelings and passions with which the composer has wished to animate them; they are types that copy the finest models that a deep study of human nature, together with all the powerful sensitivity of genius, has revealed to him: Eurydice, then, is a young woman who is still timid and straightforward, as she was on the day when, trembling with a vague anxiety, she dared to accept Orpheus as her husband. Her character has retained something of the innocence of that earlier period, veiled by a gentle, resigned melancholy that childhood does not know. She loves Orpheus, but with a passive love that has not survived beyond the tomb, does not intrude on the calm of her home in the underworld, and which is reawakened rather feebly when life and light are given back to her.

Such a character does not favour great vocal outbursts, nor signs of ambition, nor anything too harsh, too forcefully aligned with passion. The most suitable vocal timbre is that of a flexible, smooth soprano. Eurydice sung by a low voice would clearly be a nonsense. And that is why Mlle Garcia, by replacing Gluck's high notes with contralto ones (which she delivers very capably) immediately abandoned the role of Eurydice, negated the charm that supported it, destroyed the truth and consistency of the composer's conception and, in place of Orpheus's wife, she merely gave us a present-day

---

Desdemona in Rossini's *Otello* at the *Odéon* (6 January 1839), and not, as is often stated, in London in the same role later in 1839. She created the role of Fidès in Meyerbeer's *Le Prophète* (1849). Ten years later she scored a triumph in the title role of *Orphée*, in an edition prepared for her by Berlioz.

soprano with a very wide range. We can see how easy it is to go astray in performing compositions of such an exquisite kind, how the flower of emotion can rapidly fade, and why the singers who venerate Gluck must be careful to change nothing of the form in which he has clothed his inspiration.

As for those virtuosos who have neither respect nor admiration for him, I have nothing to say to them: they are more-or-less-competent mechanics who can excel in the exercise of certain artistic products, but who generally fight shy of this monumental style, which is not made for them. Mlle Garcia is not of their number, and the enthusiasm she has shown for singing Eurydice proves, on the contrary, that she respects Gluck and seeks to admire him. This excellent young singer has too much taste and too good a technique for anyone ever to accuse her of shouting. My criticism of her performance of great music in general is therefore directed only at the absence of that intimate, warm, lively feeling which, passing from the singer to her audience, puts them in direct communion with the composer, exhibits it to them in its entirety, and gives birth to impressions that are all the stronger because the performer too has really felt them. In the recitative Mlle Garcia was excellent in the phrase 'Quoi! je vis, et pour toi! Ah, grands Dieux, quel bonheur!' ('What, I live, and for thee! Ah! Ye Gods, what bliss!'). The lines that followed, however, were enunciated in a way that didn't really convey the composer's meaning: 'Quoi! tu fuis ces regards que tu chérissais tant! Ton cœur pour Euridice est-il indifférent? La fraîcheur de mes traits serait-elle effacée? Par ta main ma main n'est plus pressée!' ('But you no longer hold my hand! What! You're turning away from the beauty you once cherished? Has your heart no more feeling for Euridice? Will the brightness of my looks now fade?'). In the duet she considerably weakened the fine effect of the obstinate insistence on D natural over three bars on the line 'Quels tourments insupportables! Quelles rigueurs!' ('What unbearable torments! What hardship!').

[*Here Berlioz interposed some lines on the rest of the recital.*]

Following my thoughts on the duet from *Orphée*, here are a few words about the rest of the score. It's well known that this celebrated work was the only one by Gluck to be popular in Italy. Until then 'the German master' had had only lukewarm successes, and when his plans to destroy the abuses and reform the ingrained habits of the opera world were publicised in certain important passages of his music and in a number of writings explaining his ideals, the *furia italiana* – which has no reason to envy the *furia francese*: far from it – descended on Gluck persistently and brutally. He was insulted in public, and they even went as far as marching a placard through the streets of Bologna representing a turkey-cock with the words 'glu! glu!' on its base, as a parody of the composer's name, imitating the call of that most stupid of birds.

Around that time Gluck had written, among other things, Caffarelli's aria in *Antigono*. This wonderful aria, later reused as 'O malherueuse Iphigénie!' in *Iphigénie en Tauride*, drew the ageing Durante to reply to criticisms from musicians in Naples: 'You may say the strange harmonies in this piece are mistakes, but I have to say I don't know a living composer who can match them'.[3] Gluck also composed *Telemaco* and *Paride ed Elena*, and probably most of *Alceste*. Despite the Italian public's hostility he decided, together with the poet Calzabigi, to force their approval with a highly dramatic and poetic opera, namely *Orfeo*.[4] Maybe the talent of a popular singer was the main reason for the success of the enterprise, but in any case it was a triumph, and performances made Parma rich through the numbers of foreigners they attracted.[5]

This opera, short compared with those composed nowadays, contains seventeen numbers, of which the only failures are the aria of Amore 'Gli sguardi trattieni' ('Avert your gaze'), the final *airs de danse*, and an overture whose emptiness is beyond question. Everything else is, in my view, utterly beautiful. At its first appearance on the stage of the Opéra the score was enriched by the addition of several excellent items, including the second *air de danse* in the Champs-Élysées, Eurydice's aria with chorus 'Cet asile aimable et tranquille' ('This lovely, peaceful resting place') in the same scene, the trio 'Tendre amour', and the Andante in C Major in the Temple of Love.[6] It also unfortunately acquired an utterly ridiculous grand aria, like all those of the type, which Gluck was forced to write for Legros; also a pale, trivial arietta added to the role of Amour and an interminable chaconne

---

3   Gaetano Majorano, known as Caffarelli (1710–83), one of the most celebrated castrati. The aria Berlioz refers to is actually from *La Clemenza di Tito*, premiered in Naples (1852). Francesco Durante (1684–1755) was a Neapolitan composer of sacred music.

4   Berlioz's account is misleading; Gluck wrote all of *Alceste*. The French *Orphée et Eurydice*, performed in Paris on 2 August 1774, was revised from the Vienna (Italian) *Orfeo ed Euridice* (1762), which preceded the Italian *Alceste* (1767) and *Paride ed Elena* (1770). These operas (but not *Telemaco*, which dates from 1765), had librettos by Raniero de' Calzabigi (1714–95), who certainly influenced Gluck's reforming ideas.

5   *Orfeo*'s second production in Parma (1769) was shortened and merged into *Le Feste d'Apollo* to celebrate a royal marriage; this may explain the influx of foreigners.

6   The second 'Air de danse' is the famous flute solo in D minor (mentioned below); the Trio was recycled from *Paride ed Elena*.

of an emptiness almost matching that of the overture, which he had to provide for the final *divertissement*.[7]

The composer also had to exchange the fine poetry of Calzabigi for the rhyming prose of M. Moline, and the delightful contralto of the castrato Gaetano Guadagni for the powerful but cold voice of Legros.[8] In the choruses he had to mutilate the alto line, so gentle and useful for binding the harmony together, in order to turn it into one for high tenor, piercing and rough, as was always the case with what were then termed *haute-contres*. Vocal textbooks of those days insisted that there were no longer contraltos in France. Now that we've learnt to ignore this theory, as we have so many others, contralto voices have become, if not common, at least plentiful enough to make it easy to fill out the Opéra choruses by using them.

Gluck also had in many places to upset the make-up of his orchestra, not being able to find in Paris the instruments he'd employed originally. For instance, he entirely removed the *cornetti*, which are thought to have been a recent discovery.[9] In the Italian version of *Orphée* [*Orfeo*] they formed a four-part band with the three trombones, the *cornetti* doubling the choral sopranos at the unison and each trombone doing likewise with the voices whose names they share [alto, tenor, and bass]. This instrumental quartet, whose effect is so remarkable in the *piano* nuances of the opening chorus, was therefore ruined by the absence of the top line. There is also an accompaniment given to two cors anglais in the romance of act 1 which had to be cut, this instrument being hard to find in France at that time, in the same way as the basset-horn and contrabassoon are today: that's to say, pretty well unknown.

The difference between the [castrato] contralto and the high tenor for which Gluck adapted the part of Orpheus entailed a host of transpositions, key-changes, and other alterations, so that it was astonishing that the melodic lines didn't suffer more than they did. Indeed, on at least one occasion the

---

7   Joseph Legros (1739–93) was an *haute-contre*: a tenor who took high notes in head voice (not the type of falsetto of those now called counter-tenor or male alto). It's unclear why Berlioz called him 'cold'. The aria composed for him, 'L'espoir renaît dans mon âme', ends act 1 of *Orphée*. The additional aria for Amour (the love god) is earlier in the same scene.

8   Gaetano Guadagni (1729–92), Italian castrato. On his visit to England, the music historian Charles Burney called him 'a wild and careless singer'. In London he had studied acting under David Garrick and his performance of Gluck's Orpheus was widely admired for his acting as well as his singing.

9   Berlioz may have assumed that *cornetti* were brass instruments, but they were wooden and leather-covered, a treble equivalent to the serpent, and were not a new invention in Gluck's time. The cornets Berlioz used are chromatic brass instruments (*cornets à pistons*), a recent invention in his time.

effect was positive: at Orpheus's descent into hell, the line 'Deh placatevi con me' ('O be merciful to me!'), which is in E-flat in the Italian score, was transposed up into B-flat in the French one. As a result, all the chorus voices were also raised up a fifth so that the famous 'Non!' of the demons became incomparably more terrifying.[10]

On the subject of this overwhelming interjection, which the whole world has admired, still admires, and will go on admiring as long as the human race retains a spark of imagination, I shall allow myself to criticise the nonetheless intelligent and thought-provoking analysis which Rousseau made of an outstanding passage in this immortal scene.[11] I refer to the response of the infernal spirits to Orpheus's third entreaty. The key is B-flat major; to the word 'spectres' on the two notes E-flat and C the chorus replies with 'non' on an F-sharp in the first orchestra, while the second orchestra is playing a G-flat. Rousseau thinks he discovers the reason for this cry's amazing effect in the difference between the G-flat and the F-sharp, and in the fearful discord thought to result from their conflict. The argument is specious; and experience, that engine of disillusion, is there to prove it so. It states first that the discord does not exist for the listener since the second orchestra, which is playing the G-flat, is made up of a small number of strings offstage playing pizzicato merely to reinforce the sound of Orpheus's lyre. Meanwhile the first orchestra is sitting as usual in the main theatre and is far more numerous, made up not only of violins, violas and lower strings, but also of cornets and trombones which, playing the F-sharp as loudly as possible together with a hundred-strong chorus, make the plucked G-flats of the second orchestra totally inaudible. Furthermore, experience proves that discords have never produced musical effects of that kind. Beethoven has written a similar discord in the Ninth Symphony and Martini a far more striking one at the dénouement of his opera *Sapho*.[12] This causes surprise, like any loud, unexpected noise, but carries no emotional message, while Gluck's F-sharp is hair-raising. Although it's probably impossible in any case

---

10   Nevertheless, when Berlioz prepared a performance with Pauline Viardot as Orpheus, he transposed this and other numbers back to their original keys.

11   Jean-Jacques Rousseau, 'Extrait d'une réponse du petit faiseur à son prête-nom', in vol. 16 of *Collection Complète des Œuvres de J J. Rousseau, Citoyen de Génève*. Geneva, 1782, 386–94.

12   The Beethoven reference is presumably to bar 169 of the second movement, where woodwind play a chord of F-flat major over a string chord of E major. Jean-Paul Martini, real name Johann Paul Aegidius (1741–1816), was a German composer who lived from 1764 in Pari; he is best known for his pastoral *romance* 'Plaisir d'amour', which Berlioz orchestrated for a performance in 1859. Martini's *Sapho* was performed in Paris in 1794.

to have two instrumental groups of exactly equal strength, or placed at equal distances from the singers; but if that could be arranged, then no doubt at the moment of the simultaneous emission of the two sounds close together (and for that reason, so discordant), the mass of the chorus would necessarily combine with one of the two and would therefore destroy the equilibrium of one and obliterate the other entirely.

One could audibly produce the effect Rousseau mentions using two instruments with fixed pitches, such as two trumpets, for example, one in D playing an E and producing an F-sharp, the other in G-flat playing a C and producing a G-flat. If the two players didn't alter the tuning of their instruments using lip or wind pressure, then undoubtedly the G-flat would not be perfectly in tune with the F-sharp, a torture the deafest ear could not endure. If someone were to ask me at this point why this note (G-flat or F-sharp), belonging here to a diminished seventh and therefore to the minor mode but here employed in the middle of the major one, is so peculiarly striking so that, at the moment it reaches the ear, imagination instantly creates around Orpheus new monsters of gigantic size, and the eye seems to see ever taller and paler flames shattering the dark recesses of Hell, I would answer that it is in the nature of the diminished seventh to conjure up such impressions when it is employed on such occasions by genius – in other words, I have no idea. And if someone were to question me about the reason which might have induced Gluck to write it so pointlessly in this dual fashion, I should be forced to admit I don't know that either. But it's sublime, and that's enough.

The scene of the Elysian Fields is less well known than its predecessor precisely because of its beauty, the gentle calm of which makes less impact on the crowd. It is a miracle of inspiration from start to finish, and its colours are so fresh, so smooth that even the absurd staging seen in Paris fifteen years ago could not entirely destroy the effect of the music, which touched the heart despite all the efforts of the ballet master and the scene designer to prevent it.[13] Just imagine: at the moment of a scene change, the footlights go up, and instead of a bluish, crystalline light which should bathe everything in the fields of repose, we see a sharp, brilliant light engulfing the whole stage like the sun beating down on the African desert. But that's not all. After the first *air de danse* that radiates a religious perfection so full of divine peace, comes a profoundly melancholy number whose sighing melody is given to the muted notes of a flute in the middle register, while below it the soft

---

13   *Orphée* was revived in May 1824 in a period Berlioz was frequently attending performances at the Académie Royale de Musique (the Paris Opéra) but not yet writing formal reviews, although he often refers to operas he has seen in family letters.

agitation of strings express exhausted, resigned suffering, the last and lasting murmur of a heart to which death itself has been unable to bring peace. Were it not for the anachronism, one could imagine that Gluck wanted to describe the endlessly tormented shade of the queen of Carthage, that Dido whom Virgil depicts for us as 'indignata sub umbras' ('indignant through the shadows') and who, on seeing Aeneas, the source of all her woes, flees into the dark depths of the forest to hide her wounds and suffering.[14] Well! Instead of the touching pantomime demanded by such music, which had been observed in the original production under the eyes of the composer, a dancer entered stage left, made her way on point to the opposite side, then devoted herself throughout the number to producing what the art of pirouettes and entrechats has to offer at its most brainlessly prosaic and shocking. And the audience clapped ... What crass imbeciles! ... Try telling me again that music is made for everybody!!!

The rest of the scene was managed much better, and the moment when Eurydice, holding the hand of her bewildered husband, appeared out of Elysium, greeted from afar by the harmonious chorus of happy shades, provided, I confess, one of the most delightful tableaux I can remember. Words indeed escape me when I consider how wonderful the music of this chorus is in its depth, delicacy, antique colouring, expression, tunefulness, harmony, orchestration, everything. Listening to it, one forgets the platitudes of Moline's translation and barely feels the loss of Calzabigi's adorable poetry. Instead of the *rhymes à la Pompadour* of the Frenchman, 'Near the tender person one loves, one enjoys supreme bliss; rejoice in the happiest of fates', the Italian gives his hero these words: 'Turn back, O beauteous one! to your husband who does not wish the sky should any longer be deprived of you!'. In saying this, Orpheus is not impatient to restore 'the light of the sky' to Eurydice, as any hack poet might have claimed: on the contrary, it is to the welcoming sky that Orpheus, out of gratitude, wants to restore the enchanting sight of Eurydice. What a picture these few charming words conjure up of her beauty! The author of that was a poet. M. Felice Romani is the only contemporary Italian who has at times found such happy expressions.[15] But as I've mentioned, Gluck says all that and more in his music. And people have dared to say that the gift of simple, tender expression was denied to this complete genius! I should like to know who, among the scribblers and even of the great composers of his time, ever produced a graceful song worthy to

---

14   The last line of Virgil's *Aeneid*. Surprisingly, given Berlioz's worship of the author, it refers to Dido (in Elysium) whereas the last lines refer to the death of Turnus.

15   Felice Romani (1788–1865) wrote around a hundred librettos, including those for Bellini's *La sonnambula* and *Norma*, and for Donizetti's *Anna Bolena* and *L'elisir d'amore*.

be compared with these flowers of melody, whose scent still intoxicates us today? I don't know of any. It may be counted a great sadness for a man to have such ideas at his disposal and to have the task of bringing them into the light, unless, like Shakespeare, he has arrived at the immeasurable scorn for public opinion which leads him to write a *Hamlet* and then to be content to remain in the world without seeing it at his feet nor being its king.

9

Adolphe Nourrit

JD, 22 March 1839

Adolphe Nourrit had taken his own life on 8 March by jumping out of his hotel window in Naples. Despite his successful showing in Bellini's Norma *in that city, there were criticisms that his voice was not loud enough, which he took very much to heart; and he was in some despair at having been eclipsed by Gilbert Duprez in major roles at the Paris Opéra.*

The sad death of Adolphe Nourrit has filled our whole artistic world with grief and shock, and it's the third catastrophe of this kind we have had to mourn in the last few years. But if the deaths of Louis Robert and Antoine Gros were tragic examples of the power imagination can exercise on unbalanced, unworldly minds, the suicide of our celebrated singer has shown also how the noblest and most legitimate pride can prove fatal when it has developed and grown without any outward sign, until the moment when the shield that was protecting it is removed.[1] Nourrit embarked on his career without encountering any of the difficulties of initiation which have proved daunting and persistent for so many others. He was to know them, however; but too late, when his soul had lost the moral strength to resist them and to emerge from them sharper and stronger. Sadly, he was well aware of the dangers of his mentality, leading to a struggle the outcome of which could be predicted in advance. An unbalanced person who recognises his lack of balance accentuates it by thinking about it. Once he learns that he's liable to feel fear, he fears the fear, and at the first storm reason deserts him. This lack

---

[1] Louis-Léopold Robert (1794–1835) was a Swiss painter and engraver. Desperately in love with Princess Charlotte Bonaparte, he took his own life in Venice. Baron Antoine Gros (1771–1835) was a French painter and designer and a pupil of Jacques-Louis David who committed suicide by throwing himself into the Seine.

of energy was the sole cause of Nourrit's retirement. He said so himself to me and explained it most lucidly.

It was the evening of his final recital. I was in his dressing-room with him during an entr'acte with the intention of trying one last time to change his mind, and I talked about all the artists who, in the course of their careers, had to weather the conditions he was determined to avoid himself. I enumerated for him the endless list of obstacles of every kind that we all have to face. I reminded him of the continuing signs of affection, esteem, and admiration the public were showing him every day, and of which he was at that moment receiving such glowing testimony. Nourrit wept bitterly ... then, finding his voice once more, interrupted me:

> Of course, dear friend, everything you say is true in general, but it's not applicable to me. I'm not made for this sort of life. When, at a very young age, I joined the theatre, while my father was occupying one of the top positions there, I found, thanks to a combination of lucky circumstances and my father's support, all avenues welcoming, all difficulties ironed out.[2] After my father's death I remained in the front rank at the Opéra and got into the lazy habit of doing pretty much what I like, as I like. Now everything's set to change. A new talent has arrived with new qualities.[3] The public is fickle and often unjust: I should be forced to retain my place by fighting, every day, every hour ... I'm absolutely incapable, not only of managing it, but of accepting it. I have to leave ... I shall leave, let's not talk about it anymore.

Moving to Italy with no clear plan of campaign and with an unfounded mistrust of his own talents, it was not without difficulty that he made up his mind to reappear in public, and the encouragement of Rossini and Barbaja

---

2   Nourrit made his Opéra debut in the role of Pylade in *Iphigénie en Tauride* on 10 September 1821, when he was nineteen (Berlioz attended a performance on 26 November). Nourrit's father Louis (1780–1831), also a tenor, made his Opéra debut in 1803, retiring in 1826. He was especially successful in works by Gluck, Grétry, and Spontini.

3   This was the French tenor Gilbert-Louis Duprez (1806–96), with his sensational high C in chest voice that Nourrit could not match. Berlioz heard Duprez in Florence in 1832 and wrote to Ferdinand Hiller (13 May 1832) 'He's not an actor like Nourrit, but he sings better [...]. He will make a splash in Paris in the next few years, I'm sure of it'. In 1838 performances of Berlioz's *Benvenuto Cellini* were interrupted when Duprez abandoned the title role. Although Berlioz had good things to say about Duprez in this and other reviews, his behaviour then surely rankled.

very nearly failed to convince him.[4] He would undoubtedly have done better to stick with his refusal because, if he had abruptly abandoned his Paris career to avoid a battle, in Naples he was going to engage in another one, still more dangerous because it was unexpected.

He was going to sing before a public who were secure in their knowledge of all that was marvellous in the way of singing and unwilling to extend to him any support on account of his qualities as an actor, which for us had been so fine a constituent of his art. He was going to discover that the parterre barely applauded anything except vocal tours de force, and that they never applauded at all when the king was in the house, which happened very often.[5] Nourrit was going to find censors who were nitpicking and intolerant when it came to banning from the stage several works on which he had placed his highest hopes, and with whose message he was greatly in sympathy. Maybe he was really considering his time in Naples just as a temporary exile, one that would soon usher in his triumphant return to the theatre of his earliest successes, when a loss of vocal tone, every day more apparent, brought on serious anxiety and persuaded him that he was putting his faith in a dream. If that was the case, then this despair, this terrible suicide are all too easily explained in an artist as impressionable and vulnerable as Nourrit.

The unfortunate reception of his performances in *Norma* only hastened an inevitable outcome. His religious beliefs couldn't act as any more solid counterweight than they have for others who have come to such a sad end. His enthusiasm in this area pushed him to proselytise. He had an idea of 'religious teaching' that would bring about 'religious reform through the theatre' and wanted to set out his system in a work he told me about and which perhaps he had already sketched out on paper. His preoccupation with this type of theology meant that it took over every conversation. He indulged in endless, pointless discussions, even with those of his friends whom he knew to be lacking in faith and even antipathetic to it. One day I was forced to say to him, 'Why involve us in these topics, where the disadvantage is all yours, since I listen to you without interest, as I would listen to the dreams of someone ill, given that every one of my answers causes you terrible pain'. 'Yes', he said, 'I agree, they do make me suffer'. We can't judge Nourrit's literary education by the handful of poems we know of his, but he had a deep understanding of art in the widest sense of that word, and he concentrated endlessly on developing it.

He did not always understand immediately anything that took him out of his habitual concerns, but when he allowed himself time to absorb a new

---

4   Domenico Barbaja (1778–1841), Italian impresario who ran theatres in Naples, Milan, and Vienna.
5   Parterre: see article 7, note 1.

idea, he then came to appreciate it and to judge its importance with unusual perception. For instance, his first reading of Shakespeare's *Hamlet* left him with the impression merely of a bizarre work, lacking order or clarity. 'I can understand Macbeth and the serious lesson to be learnt from his growing ambition', he said, 'but *Hamlet* has no effect on me because everything there is a muddle'. A year later, *Hamlet* was a cult for him; he was reading it endlessly and regarded it as the masterpiece of the human spirit.

In my view, his musical enthusiasms were slightly too inclusive. His earliest was for Gluck, and I have never been able to see how, without losing an iota of his respect for that hugely powerful genius, he later came almost to have a passion for works which ought to have inspired his horror and pity if, as had previously been the case, he would have considered the reasons why he also admired the composer of *Alceste*. Be that as it may, never did Gluck have a more faithful interpreter. The roles of Renaud, Pylade, and Orphée, which he often took, give an idea of what he could have made of Achille and Admète, which he never attempted – I don't know why not.[6] The moving restraint of his singing in the famous aria 'Plus j'observe ces lieux' in *Armide*, in the duet 'Aimons-nous' in the same work, in the aria 'Unis dès la plus tendre enfance' in *Iphigénie en Tauride*, and in the romance from the first act of *Orphée* gave extra weight to the energy, the overwhelming enthusiasm, the pride and tragic distress with which he imbued the other parts of the three roles I've just quoted. In particular he gave an extraordinary impact to the opening of Renaud's 'J'aime la liberté, rien n'a pu me contraindre à m'engager jusqu'à ce jour'. Nor have regulars at the Opéra forgotten the heroic passion he brought to Pylades's aria 'Divinité des grandes âmes', nor the new and ingenious manner in which he rendered the aria 'Ô transport! Ô désordre extrême!' from *Echo et Narcisse*, which he [Nourrit] added at the end of the first act of *Orphée*.[7] As for the numerous roles he created for the modern repertoire, they are so present in our memories, there's no need to emphasize the debt their composers owe him.

It is to Nourrit too that we owe the popularity of Schubert in France, and who knows whether without him, without his continual efforts, without his warm and winning affection for these wonderful songs, without his translations of them, without his exquisite sensibility and the profound

---

6   Roles in Gluck's operas: Renaud in *Armide*; Pylade in *Iphigénie en Tauride*; Achille in *Iphigénie en Aulide*; Admète in *Alceste*.

7   This aria comes at a critical point in act 2 of the opera, as Echo is believed to have died and Narcisse is in mental confusion; there is a clear parallel with Orpheus's feelings at the end of act 1. Presumably Nourrit didn't sing *two* arias at this point but sang the one from the later opera instead of the one written for Legros (see article 8, note 7). Berlioz remembered the words wrongly: 'transport' should be 'combats'.

intelligence with which he sang them, French publishers might never have dared bring out collections of Schubert's music that otherwise would probably never have been appreciated beyond a few artists, the general public being deprived of such thrilling delights.[8]

Ah! It's terribly sad that Nourrit, with his eyes firmly fixed on a painful present, never dreamed of a future that could have given him a position in France even more illustrious than the one he'd lost! His expertise in everything to do with dramatic music, his energy and his honesty were valued, and who knows whether, in a few years' time, he would not have been given some important task worthy of his ambition, the fulfilment of which might have redounded as much to his own fame as to the fame and progress of the art he loved! ... It is a great sadness also for those French artists who were looking forward to this enticing possibility, since they see now the consequences of the marriage between art and industry, and the experience is teaching them, in fairly brutal fashion, that the children born of it, thanks to the domination of the latter, are not slow to waste away.

---

[8] Nourrit was introduced to Schubert's songs at an 1835 concert in Lyon in which Liszt played his piano transcription of *Erlkönig*. See Frits Noske, *French Song from Berlioz to Duparc* (translated by Rita Benton). New York: Dover, 1970, p. 28.

10

Musical Instruments: Exhibition of Industrial Products

JD, 28 May 1839

Berlioz's general unwillingness to accept the status quo in any field is manifest in this review, emphasising the useful improvements orchestral instrument makers were introducing to their products. While we today may marvel at the expertise he displayed in his Grand Traité d'instrumentation et d'orchestration modernes *(1843), his surprise was that so many composers should be so ignorant of the tools of their trade.*

Among instruments of the orchestra, the only ones to have called for and received technical improvements recently are the woodwind. The flute, the clarinet, and especially the bassoon had long suffered from serious faults of intonation and tone which the skill of virtuosos had only managed to disguise up to a point. Boehm's invention for the flute, consisting of a new way of boring the holes for the player's fingers but which unfortunately alters the conventional fingering, has led to important improvements for bassoons and clarinets. We've already had an opportunity to mention this excellent development, thanks to which these instruments, whose sound was the most unsatisfactory, will soon boast one that's perfectly in tune and absolutely equal through all registers.[1] As for the violins and lower strings, there's nothing left to say: you don't find Stradivariuses round every corner. Only the piano continues to make progress, sometimes in one direction, sometimes in another. Érard has got them to produce a volume of sound which means

---

1   In the *RGM*, 1 April 1838.

that, at least in Liszt's hands, they can compete with a standard orchestra.[2] Pape has produced them in various shapes to suit amateur tastes, so that this instrument, which is growing in popularity the world over, from London and Paris as far as the Philippines and the Indies, can cater simultaneously both to every musical need and to the dictates of fashion and luxury.[3]

Pape's console pianos are ever more popular, as much thanks to their elegant shape as to the quality of their sound, which is smooth in the extreme.[4] His grand pianos, since he has decided to place the strings at the back of the soundboard and the hammers above them, are much improved. I shall turn to M. Pleyel shortly. But first, a few words about the invention of MM. Roller and Le Père.[5] By means of a mechanism that allows one to judge the tension of metal strings *visually*, it's possible to tune one's piano accurately and swiftly. Thanks to the *ocular tuning regulator*, even a deaf man can do it easily. Pianists who live in the country and can only organise the visit of a tuner with some difficulty and at long intervals will appreciate the usefulness of this discovery. M. Boisselot, from Marseille, also deserves a special mention for his screw for tightening the strings.[6]

You can hear M. Leclerc's *mélophone* by going to see *Guido et Ginevra*.[7] This instrument blends the sounds of the flute, horn, clarinet, and

---

2   Pierre Érard (1794–1855), son of Jean-Baptiste (1745–1826) and nephew of Sébastien (1752–1831). He continued their work and made useful improvements to the piano and the harp.

3   Jean-Henri Pape (1789–1875), German piano maker who arrived in Paris in 1811 and was responsible for 137 inventions. Friedrich Bechstein was one of his pupils.

4   A console piano is a large type of upright but differs from a grand piano in that the hammer on string action is set vertically rather than horizontally. Most console pianos are between 40' to 44' tall, so are compact and space-saving.

5   Jean Roller (1797–1866) specialised in the manufacture of upright pianos. Jacques-Marie Le Père (1763–1841) was a civil engineer who worked with Roller in 1839 on improvements to the mechanism of the piano.

6   The piano-making firm Boisselot was established in Marseille in 1831 by Jean-Louis Boisselot (1785–1847) and his sons Louis-Constantin (1809–50) and Dominique-François-Xavier (1811–93). Liszt acquired one of their instruments in 1846. Xavier, as he is usually known, took over the management of the firm when his brother died. He was a composer, winning the Prix de Rome in 1836, and also a critic, writing an appreciative review of *Benvenuto Cellini* 1838. Berlioz in turn wrote kindly about his opera *Ne touchez pas à la reine* (1847).

7   Pierre-Charles Leclerc was the co-inventor, with Jean-François-Adolphe Brown, of the *mélophone*. Halévy's opera *Guido e Ginevra* was premiered at the Opéra on 5 March 1838, but soon lost its appeal (last performed there, 15 October 1841).

basset-horn (we're unable to explain its inner workings since M. Leclerc has so far kept the secret to himself). M. Pâris's *harmoniphone* or keyboard oboe is intended to replace, in provincial orchestras, the oboes and cors anglais which, outside Paris, are badly taught and in short supply.[8] From this point of view the invention is very useful. The keyboard of the harmoniphone has thirty keys from C below the G-clef stave to the E on the third ledger line above it.[9] It's played by means of an elastic tube whose mouthpiece fits between the teeth, and into which one blows while the fingers operate the keys. It should be noted that the movement of the keys merely directs the sound outwards and that the shaping of these is all done by the mouth. It's the player's breath that controls dynamic nuances such as *piano*, *forte*, and *crescendo*, unobtainable on all other instruments of this kind. From here we move naturally to the organ.

Organ building in France has recently undergone an extraordinary development, coinciding with the interest and care that have been rekindled in the conservation of ancient religious monuments. People are busying themselves these days with the repair of all the fine, ancient organs built before the Revolution. They are also building new ones, and in this way the benefits of harmony are reaching tiny villages. Pupils of primary and secondary schools are currently studying music, the piano, and the basics of harmony in order to become organists. We can therefore hope for widespread results from all this for the propagation of music in France. Unfortunately, what are missing are experts to respond to this enthusiasm, this taste for the organ which is apparent everywhere. Because of this shortage, provincial churches are being invaded by ignorant workmen to whom the blind confidence of the clergy entrusts the repair, or rather the mutilation, of the finest instruments. In Nevers the cathedral organ has been mutilated by the bishop's janitor. In Orléans the cathedral organ is in the care of a blind man, and the interesting old organ of Saint-Paterne is being repaired by a prison gaoler. Elsewhere workmen from Lorraine and Alsace, who are everywhere in France, have destroyed organs of exceptional merit.

Today there are no more than three or four organ builders at best who can be trusted with repairing or manufacturing an organ of any standing. Among these M. Callinet and M. John Abbey are the best.[10] Both of them have exhibited a large organ; we may therefore mention them separately.

---

8   Presumably Claude-Joseph Pâris, the composer who won the Prix de Rome in 1826, the first year that Berlioz competed.
9   This range requires only twenty-nine keys.
10 John Abbey (1785–1859), English organ builder, was invited to Paris by Sébastien Érard in 1826. He went on to build his own instruments, including that for the Opéra in 1831, destroyed in the fire of 1873.

The organ exhibited by the firm Callinet et Daublaine and built under the direction of M. Danjou, the capable organist of Saint-Eustache, is one of the most remarkable to be completed for a very long time.[11] Apart from that of Beauvais, which we owe to a magistrate, M. Hamel, and the one M. Érard made for the Chapelle royale, there is no organ superior to that of MM. Daublaine and Callinet for quality of sound, variety of stops, and the layout of the manuals and pedal. We may note several new stops: exact imitations of the bassoon and clarinet, and a viola da gamba stop, unknown in France, which makes a delightful sound.[12]

This organ is especially notable for the purity of its sounds and the variety of its stops. Such variety is really necessary in France, where the organist alternates with the choir and plays a large number of different pieces in the course of a Mass, while in Germany and England the organ accompanies throughout and plays only a few preludes on its own. Also, the best known organs in Germany and England may be extremely powerful, but there's very little variety of colour.[13] The organ exhibited by M. John Abbey is also a very fine instrument but suffers from this lack of variety.

The other organs exhibited do not deserve mention and indeed are all fairly poor in their sound quality. Some from Mirecourt, in the Vosges, are notable for their good layout, but their sound is raucous and disagreeable. The jury has not been strict enough, and many of the instruments do not seem to me worthy of inclusion in this exhibition of what's best in our industry. One invention, called an *orgue Milacor*, seems ingenious at first sight but could lead to very unhappy results. It consists of a keyboard placed over the organ keyboard on which a newcomer to music can, by touching numbered notes with one finger, produce chords. Applying this method to plainsong produces a sequence of chords which are often outrageous and always monotonous, and which cannot in any event replace the fingers of the organist. It would be better not to have any organ at all in a church, rather than make use of such a thing. It's vital to forewarn priests against this invention, which people are energetically planning to take up.

---

11 Jean-Louis-Félix Danjou (1812–68), French organist and historian of plainsong, who was also organist of Notre-Dame from 1840 to 1847.

12 Marie-Pierre Hamel (1786–1879), French magistrate and passionate advocate of the classical organ, deploring the 'fashionable mutilations' suffered by some instruments. He built the organ in Beauvais cathedral.

13 Berlioz had yet to visit England or Germany, so he must have obtained this information from others.

11

Théâtre de la Renaissance, First Staging of *Lucie de Lammermoor*: Music by Donizetti, Libretto by Alphonse Royer and Gustave Vaez

JD, 9 August 1839

This review needs to be read in the shadow of the disastrous failure of Benvenuto Cellini *at the Opéra the previous year, and of Berlioz's caustic letter to the Opéra director Duponchel of March 1839, informing him that 'I withdraw my opera* Benvenuto. *I am perfectly convinced that you will receive this news with pleasure'.*[1] *The director of the Théâtre de la Renaissance, Anténor Joly (1799–1852), had planned to open a new Paris opera house, something until then forbidden by a decree of 1807. This plan was widely supported by the intelligentsia, including Meyerbeer. The final boost came from Victor Hugo, who persuaded the relevant minister to expand 'la petite salle Ventadour' into a theatre that would accommodate his recently completed drama* Ruy Blas, *which ran for some fifty performances. The French version of* Lucia di Lammermoor *followed. The phrase 'lively intelligence, courage, and patience' is surely as much a dig at Duponchel as a tribute to Joly.*

---

1 Henri Duponchel, director of the Paris Opéra 1835–9, during which time he treated Berlioz's *Benvenuto Cellini* with scant respect, and again from 1847–9 as co-director with Léon Pillet (the sole director from 1842–7).

The administration of the Théâtre de la Renaissance has made great efforts to supply us with a third opera house.[2] For a long time, I must confess, these efforts seemed to me futile, but the striking success of their last attempt is beginning to soften my conviction. An enterprise which, without a grant or active, powerful support, has managed to reach the point where we find it, must possess a greater vitality than one imagined, and secrets of success one hadn't expected. They consist to a considerable degree in the lively intelligence, courage, and patience of the director. I have heard him reproached, it's true, for having chosen an Italian opera as the first major score to be performed in his theatre. But we need to take account of the difficulties of his position. A major opera cannot be improvised (in France, at least), and long works are frightening to people when they have no assurance that such works will lead to glory and financial success.

Now what *serious* composer could decide to take on a task of such importance with resources as slim as those the Renaissance could command, and despite the prejudices (only too well founded, we may say) with which this theatre had to contend? What's more, to add to the chances of success for his new company the still more daunting ones of the success of a newly composed opera would have been too much. It was necessary therefore, in order to proceed with caution, to find a work which, while not being hackneyed, had at least been generally accepted; and whose subject, while conforming to the tenets of grand opera, did not make it necessary for the administration to dispense extravagant sums. M. Donizetti's *Lucie de Lammermoor* filled the bill perfectly. The storyline, well known from Walter Scott's novel even by those members of the public who never set foot in the Théâtre-Italien, as well as the principal arias and duets performed in any number of concerts at the Opéra and the Odéon in various benefit appearances by Duprez and other singers, had all been enough to accustom the probable audiences for this enterprise to the idea that the success of *Lucie de Lammermoor* was not to be doubted.

Regulars of the Théâtre-Italien, with their memories and prejudices, were probably harder to persuade, given the often-unjust severity with which they judge everything that does not belong to the club whose patrons they have become. But these very prejudices could serve to reassure M. Donizetti's new performers that the lofty aristocracy of the *dilettanti* would not do them the honour of tearing them to shreds; and indeed, they dispensed with it. Furthermore, like most Italian operas, this one doesn't call for a lavish production, and if M. A. Joly decided he should go to some trouble over the costumes and a really delightful set that was entirely new, he exceeded expectations and certainly did more than anyone would have dreamt of asking from him in the

---

[2] Berlioz means a third house performing opera in French, as there were already three opera theatres (Opéra, Opéra-Comique, Théâtre Italien).

present state of things. All that was left to wonder about was whether we could finally hope for an opera house that was true to its name: designed for music and nothing but music, as foreign to the dancing and painting of the Opéra as to the corrosion with dialogue of the Opéra-Comique; that is, a theatre where finally the composer could really be *master* in the true meaning of that word.[3]

The question thus asked was answered very nearly in the affirmative, and the results obtained allow us to have great hopes for the future. M. Joly has, by his researches, care, and sacrifices, managed to bring together a charming prima donna, a good leading tenor, a bass who will go on to do well, a second tenor who is useful if not pleasing, a chorus which, surprisingly, is quite passable, and an orchestra which it is easy to make excellent. And all these sang, accompanied, played with an impassioned accuracy deserving the highest praise. The chorus were astonishing in the vigour of their entries and in the sonorous timbre of the men's voices. It's not a large chorus, but in all the numbers they all sing in tune, and as well as they can: qualities much rarer than you might think. The depth of the stage also is not enough to dampen the effect of the voices by keeping them too far from the audience. With the addition of four first and four second sopranos, three high tenors, three colourful basses, and serious rehearsals over several months under a capable teacher such as M. Strunz – who, I believe, is charged with this important task – the Théâtre de la Renaissance will soon certainly possess a cohort of excellent chorus singers, capable of giving good accounts, if not of all the vocal combinations in the operatic repertoire, at least of those that are mainstream and indispensable.[4]

Before this run, the orchestra, it has to be said, did not exist. Its lack of musicians was obvious, especially among the strings; now additions have been made to the violins, violas, and basses. But I can't claim that this addition has completely solved the ensemble's main problem. The trumpets, trombones, timpani, and bass drum dominate throughout to a horrible degree, to the point that in *forte* passages the violins are inaudible. The brass players probably belong to a military band, and their experience of playing in the open air leads them to blow in such a way as to continually 'blare' the sound, producing a noise that destroys all harmony.[5] The horns, among whom I noticed one of our most capable players, M. Rousselot, are

---

[3] The French term 'maître', beyond meaning 'man in charge', carries overtones of high artistic standing.

[4] Jacques Strunz (1781–1852), born in Bavaria, chorus master, flautist and composer. He was one of the witnesses at the wedding of Berlioz and Harriet Smithson.

[5] Berlioz writes 'cuivré' which means 'played with a forced, strident tone' – something he occasionally asked of horn players in his own work (but only for a special effect).

excellent.[6] But, as I say, the orchestra still lacks violins, lacks violas, lacks cellos; it's the violins and cellos who sing and carry the melody and who mark out the form of the accompaniments in the treble and bass. It's the violas who tie together the various parts that are often a long way from each other; it's they who, when properly used, produce those half-tints by which, in many cases, the imagination is so easily stirred.

And while we're about it, why is it that the violins in small orchestras so rarely play in tune? Because the tuning of several string instruments playing the same part is never perfect, we can only hear the resultant mean of the tuning of the majority. When this number is enough to cover the imperfection of whoever is playing most quietly, the whole ensemble *seems* to be playing in tune; when this is not the case, the whole string body seems to be playing out of tune. If there are fifteen violins, two or three can easily play out of tune without being noticed; if there are only five or six, the error of just one will be perfectly audible. There's nothing so harsh, wrong, shabby and miserable as the consort of two or three violins. Baillot, Artôt, and de Bériot, faced with playing the same part in unison, would send me running for cover.[7] This problem is less apparent in the lower strings; even so, since M. Joly has such good intentions for the musical future of the theatre he's running, he should, as soon as possible, add four or five cellos to the six he already has. But the orchestra pit is full, someone will say, and there's no more room. So, take some space from the parterre; the hall is big enough, and you may be sure that this expense on the one hand and the loss of receipts on the other are actually economies. Nothing is so costly as bad music-making, and good results won't accrue without the sacrifices I've just mentioned.

If it was merely a question of playing ancient scores by Grétry, Monsigny, Philidor, Dalayrac, Paisiello, Sacchini, etc., the Renaissance orchestra could, at a pinch, stay as it is.[8] But as soon as you turn to modern operas where the brass are dominant, where the bass drum is used (ninety-nine times out of a hundred meaninglessly so), where you find, over and above the wind instruments used previously, two cornets, a third and fourth horn, and an ophicleide, you need to call to your aid an army of strings, not merely to smooth out and sweeten the harshness of these rough voices but also so that the violin part, which is really the principal one, can make itself heard and retain, in the musical hierarchy, the place which composers of every era have ordained. It

---

6   Joseph-François Rousselot (1803–80) won first prize for horn at the Paris Conservatoire in 1823.

7   Pierre-Marie Baillot (1771–1842), Alexandre-Joseph Artôt (1825–45), and Charles-Auguste de Bériot (1802–70) were three of the greatest violinists of their day.

8   The lives of these six composers covered nearly a century, from 1726 (birth of Philidor) to 1817 (death of Monsigny).

would perhaps be difficult at the moment, and I dare say beyond that, to find enough good players in Paris to complete the Renaissance orchestra: the concerts of the Champs-Élysées, the Casino, and the Jardin-Turc call on almost all the best of them. But in any case, by the end of the summer these purveyors of bourgeois music, where the audiences, while they chat and walk around, come to listen to overtures mixed with quadrilles, will have closed down, and the new opera house will face an embarrassment of orchestral riches.

As for the singers, I have nothing to say to M. Joly. He knows perfectly well that artists blessed with voices that are sonorous, wide-ranging, and flexible, and who know how to use them with feeling and technique, are of all the features of his enterprise the most precious and most rare, and we are certain that he's stopping at nothing to find them. Let us congratulate him for the principals he's acquired already on this front. Mme Anna Thillon, a young English lady from that fine city London, has devoted herself for only a few years to the study of singing, and she has made rapid progress.[9] Her voice is a true soprano, ranging from d' to d''', therefore encompassing two octaves, and its lower register lacks nothing in sonority or quality of sound. Her voice lends itself easily to light vocalising and grace notes, but her childlike, gentle timbre is less good at rendering accents of sadness or passion. Even so, it fits naturally with the notion one harbours of the timid fiancée of young Ravenswood, and the role of Lucia brought Mme Thillon well-deserved success, which will lead to others. In the first cavatina she sometimes mismanaged the ends of her phrases; perhaps she still doesn't always know how to manage her breathing; emotion and nervousness probably played a large part in this uncertainty in her phrase endings when she first came onstage. She very quickly regained her assurance and in the quartet with chorus and especially in the mad scene.[10] The latter she played in a very new and dramatic manner; her voice took on a brilliance and colouring of which one would not have thought it capable. Applause, flowers, nothing was lacking in her success.

The tenor Ricciardi, who was playing Edgardo, had not been heard in Paris before.[11] He has a voice, feeling and technique. He forgets occasionally that passion should never prevent a singer from *singing*, and one can tell from his sudden cries that he's spent time in the French provinces after leaving Italy (to be fair, they were infrequent). He'll soon return, no doubt

---

9   Anna Thillon (1817 or 1819–1903), née Anna Hunt, born in London or Kolkata, went on to fulfil Berlioz's hopes for her and became a soprano with a worldwide reputation, creating a number of roles in Paris and London.
10 'Sur sa tête qu'il relève'; 'Mon nom s'est fait entendre'. The 'quartet' Berlioz mentions is actually the famous sextet.
11 Achille Ricciardi (? – ?), an Italian tenor who had made his debut in Milan and came to Paris by way of Bordeaux. His benefit concert at the Théâtre de la Renaissance took place on 3 February 1840.

about it, to sensible traditions. His voice is a little veiled, but it's touching and moving; it's powerful but has difficulty rising to the a' in chest voice. Ricciardi makes almost no use of head voice, and his mixed notes would be excellent and full of expression if he had worked on them enough to assure total mastery. Unfortunately, one can sense that he's reluctant to use them, leading to a painful trembling and some uncertain sounds. He enunciated with great verve his duet with Ashton, his asides in the finale, and especially the first part of his final scene; there the Andante in triple time, suiting his voice perfectly, brought him in the opinion of the audience to a level of which the rest of his role hadn't suggested he was capable. Beyond that, let us leave him time to recover from the terrors of a first appearance; now he's been accepted, applauded, encored, let him forget the provinces, let him give up those unfortunate half-spoken words in the challenge to a duel, let him put a little more gravity into the tempo of his last aria. That way he'll place the sound better and the emotion can only gain by it (Duprez, for whom the role was written, sings it more slowly). And: let him have confidence in himself and in us, and all will be well.

The role of the chaplain was taken by a tall young man, eighteen to twenty years old, a Spaniard, I gather, who was promoted from the ranks of the chorus and charged at short notice, almost against his will, with this task, in which he did not acquit himself at all badly.[12] He has a very beautiful bass voice, but the bottom notes A, G, F are entirely absent. He's still too young. Hurteaux (Ashton) is a Frenchman (there are even Frenchmen in this company), recently a pupil at the Conservatoire.[13] He wasn't in good voice the day before yesterday, so I'll say more about him when I next hear him and he's on better form.

M. Donizetti's score is too well known today for me to feel obliged to make a detailed analysis of it. I say only that it contains very beautiful numbers, that the dramatic action is in general far better respected than in most of the serious operas by the Italians of today, and that its faults are those for which the French and Germans reproach most of the works by Rossini's successors. These are: a lack of melodic distinction; regular pauses at the end of each phrase, interrupting the passage of the music in an unfailingly similar manner, in order to give the singer space in which to give his full weight to a final cadence that is itself always the same; bursts of orchestral noise for no reason; excessively prolonged cadenzas, successive chords of dominant and tonic or of tonic alone in perorations; melodic appoggiaturas on the violins doubled two octaves below by a bass

---

12 The performer of this role is reported to be a certain Zelger. A baritone or bass by this name was announced as singing at the Royal Italian Opera in London in 1855, with Pauline Viardot and other luminaries.

13 Auguste-Hyacinthe Hurteaux (1808–?), French baritone who trained at the Paris Conservatoire and abroad before returning to Paris; he also sang for the Société des Concerts du Conservatoire.

singer; lively passages on piccolos in a scene that's sad or dignified; in a word, faults that too often stem from hasty work, and the use of patterns (one might be obliged to call them mechanical) which encourage it.

What I do find beautiful is the great quartet that follows the arrival of Edgard [see note 10]. The overall effect is excellent, extremely dramatic, the voices are cleverly placed, and the final explosion, held back for some time during a high, held sixth under which different harmonies pass, produces a powerful impression. The finale exhibits energy and passion, but I find it ends precisely at the moment when the musical interest is beginning to grow and the style to be coloured with unexpected ideas. The mad scene is cleverly managed, even if it's probably not all that could have been made of such a crisis. But above all the rest I much prefer the final scene, in which the despairing Edgard, waiting to fight Ashton surrounded by the tombs of his ancestors, learns of Lucia's madness and death. The two arias that make up this scene are of a heart-rending sadness, without exaggeration or bombast, full of melody and absolutely true in feeling and expression. The last phrase in particular, in which the voice of the dying lover rises painfully on the beautiful Italian expression, untranslatable into French ('O bell'alma innamorata'), has always seemed to me sublime.[14]

But why, in the midst of this poetical melancholy, does the chorus interrupt and disenchant the listener with such deadly banalities! This phrase for the tenors, consoling Edgard, clearly comes from the repertoire of Italian barbers: it reminds me of my hairdresser on the Piazza di Spagna, his ancient guitar, the waiter in the café Grecco, and the porter of our own Académie.[15] Truly, a composer must have been abandoned by his guardian angel to sully his score like this at its finest moment.

MM. Alphonse Royer and G. Vaez have made their translation cleverly and conscientiously.[16] The Italian libretto has undergone only slight modifications, all to its advantage, and M. Donizetti has composed new music for them.[17] It doesn't often happen that foreign composers see their music adapted to such elegant translations, so faithful and so comfortable for the singers.

14　A literal translation is 'O beautiful, sweet beloved'; in the French score, 'O bel ange ma Lucie'.

15　These references are memories of Berlioz's time when as winner of the Prix de Rome he stayed in the Villa Medici (early 1831 to spring 1832).

16　Alphonse Royer (1803–75), French librettist and playwright who later became administrator of the Opéra, frustrating some of Berlioz's projects. Gustave Vaez (1812–62), Belgian with the same interests. The two men often collaborated in making French translations and adaptations of librettos, including two others by Donizetti, Rossini's *Otello*, and Verdi's *Jérusalem*.

17　A new small role was added, but Lucia's maid Alisa was eliminated, Raimondo's act 2 aria was cut (https://en.wikipedia.org/wiki/Lucia_di_Lammermoor).

12

Letter to Liszt: Music in Paris and London

RGM, 11 August 1839

The length and content of this open letter make clear Berlioz's respect and affection for Liszt without need of further commentary other than to mention that they met in 1830 and corresponded less formally over many years.[1]

Paris, 6 August 1839

I should really like, my dear friend, to be able to tell you *absolutely everything* that's going on in our musical world, or at least everything I know about: the deals that are being done, the business that's being contracted, the underground passages and mines that people are digging, the platitudes being committed; but I doubt very much whether my tale would have any chance of interesting you. It would tell you nothing new: the study of Italian musical habits has made you blasé about all their delights, and what happens in Paris *horribly* resembles what you've seen going on in Milan. In any case you wouldn't have the heart to laugh about it. You're not one of those people who find all the outrages suffered by the muse we serve to be subjects for joking, you who would prefer, at any price, to keep secret the besmirching of its virginal robe and the sad injuries done to its divine veil. So let's say nothing about horrors that would irritate you as well as me, and against

---

[1] This letter is published in *CG* vol. 2, pp. 565–74. Liszt was one of few with whom Berlioz used the familiar 'tu' form of address. He performed at some of Berlioz's concerts and premiered his Piano Concerto in E-flat in Weimar with Berlioz conducting. The letter is also available in Franz Liszt, *An Artist's Journey: Lettres d'un bachelier ès musique, 1835–1841* (translated and annotated by Charles Suttoni). Chicago: University of Chicago Press, 1989, pp. 227–35.

which we cannot even protest freely, for reasons you know and which M. de Balzac's terrific recent novel would explain if necessary.[2] I'm merely going to try and give you a superficial idea of what's going on in our concerts, our opera houses, with our instrumentalists, our singers and our composers, and to do so without commentary, without excitement, without blame or praise, in a word with the flat calm of a member of that famous philosophical school we founded in Rome in the year of grace 1830, and which had as its title *School of Total Indifference on Every Subject*.[3]

This attitude has the advantage of dispensing me from theories and developments and allows me to let the *plain fact* drop heavily, brutally, without bothering about consequences. I begin, in no particular order, with what's most recent.

The day before yesterday, while I was smoking a cigar on the boulevard des Italiens, as I do, someone grasped me firmly by the arm: it was Batta, just back from London.[4] 'What's happening there?' I asked him. – 'Absolutely nothing; everyone ignores music and poetry, and the stage, and everything except the Italian opera, where the presence of the Queen draws the crowds; all the other music societies have been abandoned. I reckon myself lucky not to pay for my lodgings and travel, and to have been applauded at two or three concerts: that's all the British hospitality I got. But I arrived too late, and so did Artôt.[5] A violinist called David had attracted all the attention of London's small musical public; he was "fashionable" and there were no concerts without him.[6] As a result, Artôt, despite his success at the Philharmonic

---

2   *Un Grand Homme de Province à Paris*, the sequel to *Illusions perdues*, was published on 15 June 1839. Berlioz's 'terrible', here translated as 'terrific', has no negative implication; if anything, it implies admiration.
3   Chapter 42 of the *Memoirs* contains the following: 'The painter Bézard, the landscape painter Gibert, the architect Delannoy and I formed a society called "The Four", whose aim was to develop and round out the grand philosophical system of which I had sketched the outline six months earlier. Its title was "A System of Complete Indifference of Universal Application"'. Berlioz was parodying the philosophical language of Kant and the Abbé Lamennais whose famous *Essai sur l'indifférence en matière de religion* had been published in 1817. The four were winners of the Prix de Rome and this mock-society was founded there; besides Berlioz, they are Marie-Antoine Delannoy (1800–60), winner in 1828, and two winners from 1829, Jean-Louis Bézard (1799–1881), and Jean-Baptiste-Adolphe Gibert (1803–83).
4   Alexandre Batta (1816–1902) was a Belgian cellist and composer. Much of this article purports to record a conversation with him.
5   Artôt: see article 11, n. 7.
6   Berlioz writes 'fashionable' in English, as he was wont to do. Ferdinand David (1810–73) was a German violinist and composer, a pupil of Spohr and friend

Society and despite the uncontested beauty of his playing, was considerably annoyed'. – And Doehler?[7] – Doehler was also annoyed. – And Thalberg?[8] – He plays in the provinces. – And Benedict? Encouraged by the success of his first score, he's writing another English opera.[9] – And Madame Gras-Dorus?[10] – Madame Gras quickly became fashionable; she created a balance to the Italian vogue, she was singing everywhere, and her name never appeared unless accompanied by the epithet SINGER WITHOUT EQUAL, in huge letters. I'm told she was whistled at when she came back here to sing in *Guillaume Tell*? – It's true. – Strange. Why? – Fancy a beer [*grog*]? – No, I'm off. Come to Hallé's this evening and we'll drink and make music – Good'.

Hallé is a young German pianist with long blond hair, tall and thin, who plays the piano wonderfully and conjures up the music rather than just playing it; that's to say he's rather like you [Liszt].[11] With him I saw his compatriot M. Heller.[12] A major talent, a tremendous musical intel-

---

of Mendelssohn, he taught at the Leipzig Conservatory from its foundation in 1843. That year he played Berlioz's *Rêverie et caprice*, and in 1845 he gave the first performance of the Mendelssohn concerto.

7 Theodor Döhler (1814–56), German pianist and composer. A child prodigy, he studied composition with Benedict and Czerny.

8 Sigismund Thalberg (1812–71) was an Austrian pianist and composer. His first Paris concert in 1836, while Liszt was away, had been a sensation. His rivalry with Liszt meant that initially relations with Berlioz were troubled, but they eventually became friends. In 1845 Thalberg wrote a *Grand Caprice* on the 'Apothéose' from *Symphonie funèbre et triomphale*.

9 Julius Benedict (1804–85) was a pianist, conductor, composer, and critic of German-Jewish origins. He studied with Hummel and Weber and came to England in 1835. The operas mentioned here were *The Gipsy's Warning*, premiered in 1838, and *The Brides of Venice* (1844).

10 Julie Dorus-Gras (1805–96) was a Belgian soprano who sang in the Brussels performance of Auber's *La Muette de Portici* which may have sparked the 1830 Belgian revolution. Among premieres in which she sang in Paris were Meyerbeer's *Robert le Diable* and *Les Huguenots* (1831 and 1836), Halévy's *La Juive* (1835), and *Benvenuto Cellini* (1838).

11 Charles Hallé (1819–95), originally Karl Halle, was a German pianist and conductor, who came to Paris in 1836, where he met Berlioz, Chopin, Liszt, and Wagner. He left for England because of the 1848 Revolution, going first to London, then to Manchester where in 1857 he founded the orchestra that bears his name.

12 Stephen Heller (1813–88) was a Hungarian pianist and composer. In 1838, at Kalkbrenner's instigation, he left Augsburg for Paris, where he lived until his death. Almost all his compositions are for piano. In later years he became one of Berlioz's closest friends.

ligence, quick in thought and a wonderful technique, these are the qualities, as composer and pianist, that are attributed to him by those who know him well, and they include me. Hallé and Batta played a Sonata in B-flat by Felix Mendelssohn.[13] The general response was to admire its clever construction and consistent style: 'It's the work of a great master', said Heller. We all agreed while drinking beer. Then came Beethoven's A-major [Cello] Sonata [op. 69], the first movement of which drew exclamations, expletives, and enthusiastic cries from the audience. The minuet [scherzo] and finale only increased our musical exaltation, even though the champagne bottles were already circulating. Talking of which, someone observed that good beer was good, but champagne was better.

You tireless vagabond! So, when are you coming back to restore those musical evenings over which you used to preside so splendidly? Between ourselves, there were too many people at those occasions, there was too much talk, not enough listening, and there were philosophical speeches. You dispensed a terrible amount of inspiration which would have given *some people* vertigo, but not *all the others*.[14] Do you remember our evening at Legouvé's?[15] And the C-sharp minor sonata, and the lamp that had gone out, and the five listeners sitting on the carpet in the darkness, and our feeling as if mesmerized, and Legouvé's tears, and mine, and Schoelcher's respectful silence, and M. Gouaux's astonishment?[16] My God, my God, how sublime you were that evening! Come now, I'm forgetting I belong to the school of *indifference*. I return to it.

The exhibition of industrial products this year brought us quantities of music criticism. There were lots of disputes, arguments for and against the pianos, for and against the organs, I saw the moment when someone offered to go to law over a flute stop, and there was nearly a punch-up over a pressure screw. I didn't really understand all this uproar, because after all we actual artists have to soak up criticism at least as unjust and ridiculous as any the instrument-makers have to put up with, and we let the dogs bark without breathing a word. Even so, we don't lack self-belief and our sensitivity

---

13 Mendelssohn's Cello sonata, op. 45, composed in 1838.

14 Berlioz's 'sans tous les autres' probably means that others in room were not intent enough on the music to be so much moved by it.

15 Ernest Legouvé (1807–1903) was a French writer who emerged in the 1830s as Berlioz's patron and confidant; he cheerfully relieved Berlioz's most pressing money worries in the 1830s by judicious loans, generosity that earned him the dedication of the *Benvenuto Cellini* when it was separately published by Schlesinger in 1839. He later supplied the text for Berlioz's *La Mort d'Ophélie*.

16 This refers to Beethoven's Piano sonata in C-sharp minor, op. 27, no. 2 ('Moonlight'). Prosper-Parfait Goubaux (1795–1859) was a dramatist and educationalist.

hasn't been extinguished; we could defend ourselves, and we don't. On the other hand, when, amazingly, a critic displays benevolence, we thank him on the spot but don't tap on his front door about it, and too often we show lack of politeness to the point of forgetting to send him a card. Far from that, those whose exhibits have been praised show exemplary gratitude: visits, letters, presents, they haven't lost a single opportunity to express themselves. Those, on the contrary, about whom few or only negative comments have been made don't consider themselves forbidden from hurling themselves at the critic, cornering him and killing him like a mad dog. We can all say what we think, and even what we don't, about the greatest artists, about the most magnificent works, as well as about those recognized as being mediocre, without anybody paying much attention. But not to appreciate the value of a double contrabass peg or praise a viola's bridge, those are matters whose reverberations are immense and extravagantly prolonged.

I've finally had the puzzle explained to me. '*Your products*, you actual artists', I was told, 'are not sent out *en masse*, you sell them one by one whenever you can. If you don't find any buyers, your work *lacks a reasonable outcome*, because after all a talent which doesn't produce anything *is worthless*, quite obviously. Instrument-makers are *more serious* people, their works are *far more important* because they send out millions onto the market. And you must understand that a newspaper article which might, or might not, advertise 100,000 francs worth of goods or keep them in the shop can't be treated as if it were a Beethoven symphony or a Gluck opera'. – 'Ah! yes, yes, it's all about the money; I hadn't realized'.

On the subject of money, a way has been found to save a bit by not building a new theatre for the Théâtre-Italien. The company of singers of our great Opéra is going to find itself in a direct struggle with singers from the south [Italian], because the plan is to unite the two companies in the theatre on the rue Lepelletier. The battle will be serious: Lablache versus Levasseur; Rubini versus Duprez; Tamburini versus Dérivis; la Grisi versus Mlle Nathan; and everybody versus the bass drum. We shall be on hand to pick up the dead and the dying. The director will probably also be administrating the London opera house, and maybe he'll make a lot of money and it will be a splendid scandal; I don't care ... I belong to the indifferent party. It's up to the money men to calculate how much the musical goods, exploited in this way, can bring in, taking one year with another. They are the ones who ought to be worrying about the longevity of their singing instruments. As for me, if I weren't *indifferent*, I'd say just the same as you: 'I prefer music to all that'.

Duponchel will still be the costume supremo, so don't worry; art and artists will be *beautifully arrayed*.[17] Meanwhile, Mme Stoltz was on the brink of leaving, which was regretted by everybody except the cabal that wanted to force Duponchel to let her go.[18] Alizard, a young singer who has come to notice during your absence, makes an ever greater name for himself every day among connoisseurs and even among the public; from time to time he takes very minor roles in which he always finds a way to impress the audience.[19] He was hugely applauded this winter at the Conservatoire concerts – he'll go far. Mlle Nau has improved greatly; she's charming in the role of a fairy which M. Auber has just written for her.[20]

Many people are saying that the orchestra is tired, or negligent, or has lost interest in its task. The other day I was listening to audience regulars complaining that the instruments were out of tune and claiming that the half of the orchestra on the right tended to play a quarter-tone higher than those on the left – a claim hard to substantiate, my dear sirs. 'So you suffer in silence?' one of them asked me. 'As for me, I didn't say I suffered: first, because I didn't say anything, and second, because …'

Don Giovanni gets an airing every now and then, when they've run out of ideas. If Mozart came back into the world, maybe he would say, like the president Molière mentions, that he shouldn't be played.[21] Spontini on the other hand does want to be played, and he was. Nobody at the Opéra wants to hear talk about reviving his old masterpieces. Ambroise Thomas, Morel, and I were saying the other day that, even so, we'd give a good 500 francs for a fine production of *La Vestale*.[22] As we know this score by heart, we

---

17   The Opéra director Duponchel (see article 11, note 1) was also a costume designer, architect and silversmith.
18   The mezzo-soprano Rosine Stoltz (1815–1902) was recommended by Adolphe Nourrit and made her Opéra debut on 25 August 1837 as Rachel in Halévy's *La Juive*. During the ten years she sang there, she created fifteen roles, including Ascanio in *Benvenuto Cellini* and the title role in Donizetti's *La Favorite*.
19   Alizard: see article 6, note 3.
20   Nau: see article 6 note 3. Failing to land major roles, she left Paris in 1842, but her success elsewhere brought her return to the Opéra, where she insisted on tripling her previous salary. The role mentioned was Zeila in Auber's *Le Lac des fées*, premiered on 1 April 1839.
21   The Italian company had staged *Don Giovanni* at the Théâtre de l'Odéon on 19 and 26 February and 29 March 1839. Performances of *Tartuffe* were forbidden by Lamoignon, president of the Paris Parlement, in 1667.
22   The French composer Charles-Louis-Ambroise Thomas (1811–96) won the Prix de Rome in 1832. He is best known today for works that have been revived, such as *Mignon* and *Hamlet*. He was also the teacher of Massenet.

sang it till midnight (we missed having you as accompanist). Spontini's cause has been defended in a pamphlet by one of our friends, Émile D... [Deschamps] and various newspapers have joined in.[23] The cause was on the point of succeeding when Spontini felt he had to publish a letter, already printed two or three years ago in Berlin, on modern music and musicians. Spontini's enemies would have paid 1,000 crowns to have this letter published, and he gave it to them for free. This doesn't prevent *La Vestale* from being a masterpiece, but it does mean that we'll never see it again. Madame Girardin has written a trenchant article about it which has upset the Opéra's administration.[24]

You've seen in the last article by our wise collaborator Henri Blanchard that the post of composition professor at the Conservatoire left vacant by the death of Paër was to be given to M. Carafa.[25] I'm assured that my embrace of indifference is becoming appreciated in the ministry. The orange trees in Musard's garden are already bearing fruit.[26] Théophile de Ferrière was assassinated last week by someone unknown as he was coming out of the Opéra-Comique; he's feeling much better now.[27] Heine still spells his name with an 'e'. Someone has stolen his charming book on Italy from me. He's living on the rue des Martyrs. Have you seen his Bains de Lucques?[28]

Auguste-François Morel (1809–80), French composer and conductor; he was a friend and collaborator of Berlioz who assisted in making piano reductions of some of Berlioz's orchestral scores.

23 Spontini had been recently elected to the Académie des Beaux-Arts. Émile Deschamps (1791–1871) was a French poet. He co-wrote the libretto for *Les Huguenots* and, having already translated Shakespeare's play, he provided the text for Berlioz's *Roméo et Juliette*.

24 Mme Girardin had pointed out that Rossini had been sent packing by manifestations of ill-will, and that Spontini seemed to be going the same way; so the public should make its feelings known.

25 Michel-Henri-François Carafa de Colobrano (1787–1872) was a Neapolitan musician who had studied with Cherubini and Kalkbrenner in Paris. He remained at the Conservatoire until 1870. He was considered to be absolutely without talent by Berlioz and his friends.

26 Philippe Musard (1792–1859) was a dance music specialist, composing numerous waltzes and more than 150 quadrilles; Berlioz's comment is laden with irony.

27 Théophile de Ferrière Le Vayer (? – 1864) was a critic and diplomat, at one point ambassador to Belgium.

28 French speakers would pronounce the surname 'Heine' like 'haine' (hate'). Heinrich Heine, German poet whose words were set by Schubert, Schumann, and many others. By this time, he was exiled and living in Paris; his article 'Les Bains de Lucques' appeared in the *Revue des Deux Mondes* (15 December 1832). His 'charming book' is the French translation of *Reisebilder*, published by Renduel in 1834.

We're being promised Venetian Nights at the Casino: there'll be an orchestra of 140 players whenever sixty of them aren't needed concurrently at the Champs-Élysées concerts. A gas-fuelled microscope now exists: through it I saw lemons looking as big as melons. I'm telling you all my news as it comes to me. F. Hiller has sent me from Milan some extracts from his *Romilda*.[29] The rumour is that Rossini is selling the sort of fish you hardly ever see. I bet he's as bored in his villa as his enormous fish are in their pond. His standard remark is 'Why should I bother?' If he weren't so fond of his enormous fish, he might perhaps qualify as a proponent of *total indifference*, etc. But I doubt it! One of our enemies recently decided to throw himself off the Vendôme column. He gave its keeper forty francs to allow him to climb it, then changed his mind.

They're going to stage an opera by Mainzer at the Théâtre de la Renaissance.[30] What a good idea! A young tenor called Ricciardi has just made a successful debut at this theatre in Donizetti's *Lucia di Lammermoor*, excellently translated and staged by A. Royer and Vaez. The Renaissance's director is making untold efforts to produce music and musicians, with very little support. The Opéra-Comique is preparing some important debuts, from two tenors and a soprano who are said to be remarkable – I shall pay close attention.[31] Girard always conducts his little orchestra admirably.[32] One only hopes that in the new building promised to the Opéra-Comique

---

29 Ferdinand Hiller (1811–85), German pianist, conductor and writer, came to Paris in 1828 and marked himself out by playing and conducting Bach and Beethoven. Berlioz, Liszt, and Chopin all became close friends. Hiller's opera *Romilda* was premiered at La Scala, Milan, on 8 January 1839.

30 Joseph Mainzer (1801–51), German critic, theorist, and composer. He led the critical mauling of *Benvenuto Cellini* even before it was performed (though there were also friendly reviews). Mainzer's opera *La Jacquerie* was premiered at the Théâtre de la Renaissance on 10 October 1839, and three days later Berlioz reviewed it in *JD*, complaining of a surfeit in one number of the key of D and sarcastically noting borrowings from Rossini (*Otello*) and Meyerbeer (*Les Huguenots*).

31 Claude-Marie-Mécène Marié de l'Isle (1814–79) was engaged by the Opéra as a tenor from 1840 to 1844, then from 1848 to 1851 as a baritone. Nicolas-Jean-Jacques Masset (1811–?) was a French violinist and tenor of Belgian extraction. Eugénie Garcia (1815–80) was married to Manuel Garcia the younger and was therefore the sister-in-law of Pauline Viardot. The press dubbed her 'the Malibran of the Opéra-Comique'.

32 Narcisse Girard (1797–1860), French conductor and composer, had directed several works by Berlioz from 1833–5, including the first performances of his overture *Le Roi Lear* and *Harold en Italie*. As director at the Odéon theatre, he permitted his musicians to play in Berlioz's Messe solennelle in 1827; and in 1849, having succeeded Habeneck as conductor of the Société des

there'll be a room for the players, because at the moment in the Théâtre de la Bourse, before the curtain rises, the poor fellows have to tune up in the hearing of the audience, the result being that while oboes and violins are giving an A, the trombones growl out their B-flat; in which case, truth be told, *indifference* is not an option, it's terrible.

Kastner remains hard at work. He's just finished a book on instrumentation considered from the point of view of harmonic and melodic expression, which will appear shortly; I'm very keen to read it.[33] Last month M. Wilhem gave two public concerts.[34] His five hundred singing pupils were loudly applauded; I didn't find that their performance boded well. All these young people have a desperately vulgar attitude to rhythm. They bang out every downbeat, turning everything, more or less, into a march. Certainly, the result is very fine if you compare the previous ignorance of the popular classes with what they know now; but *knowledge* isn't everything: one has to have *feeling* as well, and I think the Parisian public's too fond of vaudeville and drums. They've been rehearsing Ruolz's opera for two and a half months, with the result that the actors don't know a note.[35] But the costumes are ready and Duponchel wants it to open next Friday. Chopin isn't back; they say he's very ill, but that's not so.[36] *Dumas* has written a delightful play, but that's not my domain.[37] I'm done, I don't know anything.

Adieu; my indifference doesn't extend to covering your long absence, so come back, come back. We miss you; we hope you also miss us [literally 'It's time for us, and for you too, I trust'].

    Concerts, he performed extracts from *La Damnation de Faust*, a rare appearance of Berlioz's music at the Société's concerts in his lifetime.

33 Georges Kastner (1810–67) was a composer and musicologist. In addition to several operas, he wrote a *Traité général d'instrumentation* (1837) and a *Cours d'instrumentation considéré sous les rapports poétiques et philosophiques de l'art* (1839). Berlioz reviewed the latter; see article 13.

34 Guillaume-Louis-Bocquillon, known as Wilhem (1781–1843) was a French teacher and composer of choral music. The concerts mentioned were given at the Sorbonne on 24 February and 30 June 1839 by pupils from Parisian primary schools.

35 Henri de Ruolz (1810–87), French composer and chemist. His *La Vendetta* was premiered on 11 September, exactly a month after Berlioz's letter. In his review of 14 September Berlioz finds Ruolz's orchestration less brilliant than Rossini's, the admitted influence, and finds fault with endless text-repetitions and the composer's unwillingness to modulate. Ruolz had been Berlioz's partner in their unsuccessful effort to become directors of the Théâtre-Italien in 1838.

36 Chopin returned to Paris on 11 October. He lived for another decade.

37 *Mlle de Belle-Isle*, premiered on 4 January 1840.

13

Review of Kastner's *Treatise on Instrumentation*

JD, 2 October 1839

Cours d'instrumentation considéré sous les rapports poétiques et philosophiques de l'art. Par M. Georges Kastner.

Writing this review of Kastner's Instrumentation treated according to poetical and philosophical aspects of the art *may have inspired Berlioz to write his own treatise; in places the review reads almost like a preliminary draft.*[1]

M. Kastner, whose compositions deserve to be better known in Paris, has already made a place for himself among competent, conscientious theorists through his *Traité général d'instrumentation*, a quite different work which is the indispensable introduction to the work under review. In the *Traité général* indeed, the author has confined himself to explaining clearly the *range* and *capacities* of each instrument, and if the Conservatoire has been quick to adopt it for classes in composition, this has been entirely reasonable, given that not only pupils but many justly celebrated teachers needed to learn from it facts of which they were unaware.

I should never have believed, if experience had not furnished me with unarguable proofs, the curious ideas several great composers harboured in this area barely a decade ago. One of them, whom I knew well, was so ignorant that he was wholly unaware of the range of the flute. I'd already noticed several times that his parts for wind instruments were cut short in the treble, when their upward movement would have meant the flute part going above g^3. When I asked him why, he replied that he stopped there because the instrument couldn't play any higher. I took the liberty of pointing out that flutes went up not only to a^3 but without difficulty to b-flat^3 and b^3, and

---

1 See article 12, note 33.

that these days people were even using, in certain cases, c^4. He refused to believe me, and it would obviously have distressed him for me to insist on rescuing him from an error to which he had clung for so long.[2]

It regularly happens that harpists have to arrange accompaniments for their instrument which are perfectly written by the composer for piano, and hence laid out ineffectively and awkwardly for harp even when they aren't actually unplayable.

There is a much admired, and admirable, opera which starts with a pedal on a low E-flat for the third trombone. This note exists on the bass trombone used in Germany, but not on the tenor trombone which is used in Paris for the lowest part. Happily, the ophicleide can play it and, assisted by a moment's inattention, the composer can benefit from the illusion that he's hearing what he wrote.

Hummel, in his magnificent septet, has given the horn a low E. This note, the dummy of dummies, which very few horn players can manage to make acceptable by means of notes descending chromatically from G at a slow tempo, is very nearly impossible, and in any case it's dull, out of tune, and ridiculous in the descending arpeggio (c–G–E–C) written by Hummel. One would have thought such a masterly composer would be free of such distractions; also, his example has misled several young composers.[3]

Talking of horns and trombones, I have to reproach M. Kastner for not giving in his *Traité général* all the details about their true range. Also, he says nothing about the horn's low notes, the A-flat, F-sharp and F-natural, which sound very well when prepared by a G, and from which Weber and Beethoven have produced such fine effects. He has also omitted, in the tenor trombone's scale, the low so-called pedal notes B-flat, A, A-flat, G below the bass clef. They are included in some text books for the instrument and, before using them, I often had the opportunity to appreciate their beauty when I sat in on the lessons given with such intelligence by the Swedish expert M. Dieppo to his Conservatoire pupils.[4] It's understood that these pedal notes cannot be played like other notes, and that they have to be prepared well in advance in a slow tempo, the B-flat by a leap of a fifth or an octave from the F or B-flat above, the other three notes by stepwise motion; and taking care, as one descends in pitch, to leave the player room to breathe, because to get the

---

2   In his *Grand Traité* Berlioz calls the flute c^4 'dure' (hard).
3   The E is the only note in this arpeggio that must be 'stopped', the others being open. Even if it can be played, its timbre would differ from the other notes; in his *Grand Traité* Berlioz calls it 'very bad' ('bouchée, très mauvaise').
4   Antoine-Guillaume Dieppo, the trombonist Berlioz engaged for the solo part in *Symphonie funèbre et triomphale* (*CG* vol. 9 [*Nouvelles lettres*], p. 190); he was actually from the Netherlands.

instrument to vibrate in this case requires a considerable volume of breath.[5] One should also avoid giving the trombone high notes in the passage before the one using pedal notes. Otherwise, the player's lips will be unprepared for the embouchure needed to produce sounds in the bass register. I also ask M. Kastner, for the next edition of his *Traité*, to remove the low D from the scale of the two-valve cornet, which our best players are careful to avoid, declaring that it can't really be included among the true notes of this instrument.

After these observations, which will prove to M. Kastner that I have read and studied his book carefully, I can only repeat what has already been said by M. Meyerbeer and the music section of the Institute: 'This treatise will be of immense help to young composers. By having laid out in front of them all the resources of the modern orchestra, they will easily learn what normally can be acquired only after long experience and any number of failed attempts'. This book also shows us how *young* composers could still find fellow students among those of more advanced age.[6]

I turn now to the new *Cours d'instrumentation*, in which the author teaches the art of treating each instrument sympathetically in matters of harmony, character, and expression. This book is divided into three main categories.[7] The *first* contains the exposition of general rules for the good writing of accompaniments and the use of instruments in the orchestra. The *second* contains various analyses of notable fragments by the greatest composers in different genres. In this method the author has been particularly successful, and it is indeed the best way of explaining to pupils how distinguished composers have combined the elements of the orchestra, why in such and such a case they have chosen such and such an instrument or combination, why they have acted differently in another case, and how these various procedures are always, with them, directly connected with the type of harmony and the expressiveness of the melody. Finally, the *third* part gives some useful advice over military music.

One also finds, in the opening chapter, a brief history of instrumentation from its origins to today, and it's of more than middling interest for a musician to follow the progress of this art, so simple in the early years of civilisation, so bizarrely linked to religious ceremonial and the art of oratory in antiquity, and finally so complex and so powerful with the Europeans of today.

---

5   Berlioz had used these tenor trombone pedal notes in the 'Hostias' of his *Grande Messe des morts* (Requiem) of 1837.
6   Berlioz is quoting from the report issued by the Académie des Beaux-Arts, printed at the front of Kastner's 1836 volume, and from the facsimile of a letter from Meyerbeer to the Academy, dated 2 December 1836, also printed at the front of the volume.
7   From here to the end of the paragraph Berlioz is citing the book's preface.

For a century now, new instruments have been invented, others have been perfected, and performers have reached a degree of competence that our fathers never imagined. Even so, while taking note of these uncontested improvements, we have to admit that the art of music, before displaying them, ought to have been able to progress more rapidly, and that these recent developments have almost been matched by the unspeakable excesses and disorders they have brought in their train. Of all the arts, however, that of instrumentation is the freest by its very nature; supported by experience and guided by it, it ought to have developed in a more agile and effective way. But it's been infected by routine, which for a long time has paralysed its growth, aided as it has been by the naïve ignorance of some, the preoccupation of others, and by the calculated prejudice of various learnèd egoists.

When a teacher says to a pupil, 'You mustn't use this layout of instruments' – 'Why not?' – 'Because it's never done' – that teacher is a fool. You can never forbid the use of a technique without establishing that this technique is faulty or less good than another one, and yet that's what we see happening every day. For example, in writing for wind instruments the first thing we teach is to dispose them as follows: the flutes at the top, the oboes under them, then the clarinets and bassoons. Certainly, there's a logic to this pattern, determined as it is by the ease with which each instrument moves from the treble to the bass, but why tell the pupil, 'You must always do it like this', when experience can regularly tell you you're wrong? What, for instance, is bad about giving the oboe the top line while the flutes fill out the harmony underneath it? Does this reversal of the established order produce a poor result? Certainly not, far from it; the low sounds that today's players draw from their flutes have a special character, which blends very well with certain others on oboes, and whose use can in this case be extremely satisfying. Might one also go further in destroying the instrumental hierarchy by making the cellos sing out in the treble, leaving the bass to clarinets in their *chalumeau* register? Any intelligent artist will, after a moment's thought, reply in the affirmative; others will say it's a crazy idea, like walking on one's hands or planting the branches of a tree in the earth and its roots in the air etc. etc. Weber, in the delightful and poetic Andante of his *Oberon* overture, decided to woo us with the curious charm of this mixture of timbres and happily took no notice of usage or dull routine.

This is certainly not to say, as people are bound to interpret it, that I'm proposing the pointless destruction of all instrumental balance, and that I'm seeking the new or the bizarre in putting the lambs with the wolves. Certainly not. I'm merely thinking that with instrumentation, as with harmony, melody, and rhythm, one must never adopt anything without first making a careful study; never do anything without a reason; but also never reject anything without a purpose, and never recognize any authority except that of experience, and experience that's *thorough*. This opinion, which has guided M. Kastner in his work, seems to have been that of many of the great composers; and if, with some of them, it has not, in the realm of instrumentation, been especially productive, that can be attributed to the fact that they were preoccupied with some other branch of music. Gluck discovered prodigious orchestral effects by instinct and, absorbed as he was by the search for dramatic expression, didn't realize that in the accompaniments to his recitatives the strings were bumbling along in a tiresome way, and that he more than anyone was better advised to change the wretched system he'd inherited. He gave the clarinets in their middle register tones of irresistible tenderness, but never, for reasons unknown, in the numerous infernal scenes he had to set did he turn to their lowest register, the *chalumeau*, which would have suited them so well. On the other hand, he was especially successful in using both registers of the flutes, as we can hear in the D-minor dance in the Champs-Élysées section of *Orphée*, all written *in the middle and upper registers* of the instrument, and in the religious march in *Alceste*, where the two flutes in unison are playing in their lowest register. Apart from Charon's famous call in the same opera, he gave the horns only a rather minor role; like his predecessors and contemporaries, he contented himself with using only their unstopped notes. From the trumpets however, he obtained effects which had never been thought of before him, and which have barely been used after him: not brilliant or warlike, but soft and calm, like the long, held dominant in the Andante of the introduction to *Iphigénie en Tauride*.[8]

As for the trombones, who has made them speak better than Gluck? Whether he's asking them for a ceremonial fanfare, or is joining them in a terrifying unison, or making them deliver a threat of menace, or groan with the ghosts of Tartarus, every one of their notes, as he himself used to put it, 'draws blood'. Also, more often than anyone else he has made the moans of oboes and bassoons pathetic and heart-rending. He never managed to do anything with the timpani. No one in those days foresaw the importance they would acquire much later in the hands of the German school. For him, as for the Italians of his day and ours, the timpani were there simply to produce a more or less loud noise. It was left to Beethoven, Weber, and Meyerbeer to turn them into musical instruments. Composers then were so unsure whether the timpani could be deemed acceptable, that most Italian composers didn't bother to indicate whether they wanted them tuned in fourths or fifths, contenting themselves with indicating tonic and dominant, and never supposing that anyone would think of tuning them otherwise. These days they're used in pairs or groups of three or four, or even more, and they're tuned in fourths, fifths, major and minor thirds, sixths, sevenths and octaves (in the key of F).

---

8 This introduction represents the calm before the storm that brings Orestes and Pylades to Scythia.

Beethoven, in two of his symphonies, produced charming contrasts by using that last effect with two timpani. Gluck never used the bass drum, and only once did cymbals and triangle figure in his orchestra, and with the success we know: nobody will ever forget the chorus and ballet of the Scythians. If his passages for violins are dull and too unvarying, if he never singled out the cellos, and if he only once (in the sleep of Orestes) gave a prominent role to the violas, very probably the reason was the incompetence of players.

Soon after him, Mozart arrived to perfect every branch of instrumentation, which he applied to the accompaniment of voices with that admirable intelligence and that exquisite taste which are the principal elements of his genius. If Gluck turned certain instruments into inspired voices, Mozart, without ever elevating any one of them to be heard over the rest, brought civilisation to the orchestra. The inhabitants of his harmonious city don't include many men of genius, but overall they possess a more cultivated spirit: the richness and purity of the language are, with them, shared out among the greatest number. Beethoven went further than Mozart, along the same road. Weber's spirited, variegated, dreamy, tender, passionate orchestra is merely a development of Gluck's.

Meyerbeer's orchestra is slightly indebted to those of Beethoven and Weber, combined and assimilated with superior intelligence, but even so with various concessions to modern habits of which neither Beethoven nor Weber wished to avail themselves. His resurrection of the nuns in *Robert le diable* and the whole of the fourth act of *Les Huguenots* are incomparable, masterly examples of instrumentation. This naturally leads me to question the complete accuracy of one of M. Kastner's definitions. Instrumentation, he says, is *the art of suitably applying the different kinds of instrument to a given melody*. True enough, but it's also something else: it's the art of using them to give colour to the harmony and the rhythm; even more, it's the art of rousing emotion through the choice of timbres, independently of any effect of melody, rhythm or harmony. I would also include vocal music in instrumentation, since certain very striking vocal effects are solely due to timbre, or else depend wholly on the choice of register.

Some examples will help explain my point. In *Robert le diable*, at the moment when Robert approaches one of the tombs to pick the magic branch, a horn in the orchestra plays an unaccompanied A-flat in its middle register. There's no singing, since this A-flat is on its own; likewise, there's neither harmony nor rhythm. But even so there is a musical effect, there is emotion produced by sound. And none of all that would exist if, from among the innumerable varieties of timbre offered by an orchestra, the composer had not chosen precisely this stopped note on a horn, which sounds harsh and painful like the rattle of a dying man and strikes the listener's imagination all the more powerfully because the opportunity of hearing it unaccompanied like this usually never arises. This belongs truly and solely to the art of instrumentation. I make the same claim for the isolated note, sung offstage by the sopranos of the chorus in the first act of *Le Lac des fées*.[9] This follows the pattern of the previous example. And M. Auber, in choosing this note for the sopranos in preference to any other, a note well chosen to engage instant attention, is clearly availing himself of the art of instrumentation. It's the same in the case of Rubini when, in a totally mediocre phrase, he combines the mixed sounds of his wonderful voice with head notes and chest notes. The same happens when Paganini, treating his violin like a real orchestra, and with one of those bold inspirations that have astonished the whole of Europe, combines, in one of his pieces, staccato and legato bowing with legato and staccato notes pizzicato, together with sounds of plucked open strings or sustained as a pedal with the bow on the G string together with a melody above them in harmonics on the D string, which is accompanied by pizzicato chords in the middle register on the two other strings.

Now, while we may appreciate the graceful unfolding of melody in these passages and the harmonic richness of the arpeggios, it's equally true that the astonishment produced by these vivid, engrossing colours is also due to a marvel of instrumentation.

To sum up, this art is therefore that of inspiring emotion, whether by combining different instrumental and vocal timbres in order to bring out and colour melody, harmony and rhythm; or by impressions directly generated, or produced without the assistance of the three other great musical powers. But I don't need to stress that this art is as hard to learn as that of inventing beautiful tunes, beautiful chordal progressions and rhythmic patterns that are original and convincing. It remains only to point out the general results obtained in certain given circumstances, but which the strength or weakness of the composer's genius may nevertheless then modify in a thousand ways for better or worse. This is what M. Kastner has done with considerable care and talent in his new book. He has enumerated the various instruments, while indicating the composers who have contributed more or less successfully to their usage. He has put together a comparative table of the make-up of almost all the good French and German orchestras, and another table of how to lay out a score, as found in the most famous masters. He has offered several excellent ideas on the art of writing accompaniments and on symphonic music in the true sense of that word and, finally, the series of examples we have already considered, and a critical view of them. He is also going to publish shortly a *Grammaire musicale* and a *Théorie abregée du contrepoint et de la fugue*.[10]

---

9 Auber's *Le Lac des fées* was premiered at the Paris Opéra on 1 April 1839.
10 Kastner's *Musical Grammar* and *Brief Theory of Counterpoint and Fugue* were both published in 1840.

14

Théâtre de la Renaissance

JD, 13 October 1839

This article opens with a long review of the opera La Jacquerie *by Joseph Mainzer, premiered at the Théâtre de la Renaissance three days earlier. The concluding paragraphs on other subjects are translated here as being of more interest to modern readers.*

One of the most distinguished members of the Théâtre de la Renaissance orchestra, M. Coche, professor of flute at the Conservatoire, has just published a handbook for Boehm's new flute.[1] This publication is very useful: it will be helpful to professionals and amateurs who want to familiarize themselves in a short time with the new fingering, made necessary by the changes that Boehm and Gordon have so successfully brought to the ancient flute, which almost all younger players have now abandoned.[2] M. Gouffé had previously written a work for the four-string bass that was similar to M. Coche's for the Boehm flute.[3] The system on which his treatise is based could lead players of this important element of our orchestras to achieve an even more desirable level of execution because, while making the fingering of the instrument easier, it extends its range by two notes at the bottom, whose value will not escape composers.

---

1   Jean-Baptiste Coche (1806–81), French flautist and composer. In fact, he was professor of the preparatory class from 1831 to 1841. Theobald Boehm (1794–1881), German flautist, goldsmith and ironmaster who had published his new mechanism for simplifying flute fingering in 1832. From 1833 to 1846 he was in charge of reorganizing the Bavarian steel industry.
2   Captain William Gordon (? –?), flautist and Swiss army officer of British stock. He worked with Boehm from 1833.
3   Achille-Henry-Victor Gouffé (1804–94), French contrabass player.

I don't presume to talk about Doelher's great études, which have just been published.[4] As compositions, they could be appreciated last winter in all the concerts given by that marvellous pianist, and connoisseurs were quick to recognize the musical merit of several among them, quite independently of the composer's prestige as a pianist. As to the admirable promotion these études represent of the new art of pianism, that art at the pinnacle of which Liszt has seated himself with such brilliance, it would be ungracious of me to say nothing, I who have never managed to play on the piano a progression of two chords or the simplest scale; but I have heard M. Zimmermann speak of these études as being 'an excellent, admirable work', a judgment that permits me to stay silent.[5]

We're told that Chopin is to arrive shortly from his long travels. He's bringing several new manuscripts, already talked of with the lively interest always aroused by his poetically original compositions. M. Stephen Heller, another composer-pianist of rare abilities who has lived in Paris for a short time, may be compared with Chopin for his rhythmic inventiveness as much as for his sophisticated grasp of harmony.[6]

What activity, what life, what a fever of productivity of every kind there is in our musical world! Singers both male and female turn up from who knows where and most of our opera houses rival each other in their enthusiasm (only the Opéra seems to be asleep, and I'm afraid news of the success of its latest female arrival won't wake it up).[7] Performers daily push back the boundaries of the possible, and teachers see their schools overloaded, witness M. Pastou who has just been obliged to double the space in which he's beginning his winter lectures.[8] The instrument makers themselves are making important discoveries every day. Take M. Vuillaume, for example.[9] This fine violin maker, whose instruments obtained the most excellent reports at the recent exhibition, has gone back to the traditions of the school of Cremona. As a consequence, he's resolved the following problem: how to make violins and lower instruments whose sound quality is exactly what one finds in a Stradivarius, an Amati, or a Guarneri etc., and which, moreover, in

---

4   Döhler (see article 12, note 7) had just published his *Grandes Études de concert pour le piano.*
5   Pierre-Joseph-Guillaume Zimmermann (1785–1853), French composer, pianist, and teacher. He was one of the most influential piano teachers of his time, his pupils including Franck, Bizet, Thomas, Massenet, Alkan, and Gounod, who became his son-in-law.
6   Heller: see article 12, note 12.
7   Claire-Célestine Nathan-Treillet (1815–73), French soprano, attached to the Opéra from 1839–44.
8   Étienne-Jean-Baptiste Pastou (1784–1851), French composer and teacher.
9   Jean-Baptiste Vuillaume (1798–1875), French violin maker.

the overall shape, detail and even varnish and marks of age, are such faithful copies of those famous instruments that the most experienced judges are fooled. He can therefore charge 100 crowns for a perfect imitation of an original violin that would cost at least 10,000 francs.[10]

I don't want to finish without saying a few words about the great and real success of Mlle Pauline Garcia at the Théâtre-Italien. I'm all the more determined to do so since the young singer probably found me unduly severe when I covered her performance last winter of excerpts from Gluck and Weber.[11] Without in the least discounting the superiority of her talent and the liveliness of her musical intelligence, she seemed to me to lack certain qualities that are indispensable for catching the spirit of these two masters, and I would be saying the same today if she had sung Rossini in the same manner. But my admiration for her Desdemona is as sincere as my discontent with her Eurydice and Agathe was total. I had been expecting something wholly different, given the brilliant qualities, both natural and acquired, which I knew Mlle Garcia to possess, so that what I felt on listening to her was close to rage. She will understand me, I trust, when she thinks of the violence of some musical idolatry, which she too knows about, towards various great geniuses with whom she is in sympathy, and, I'll warrant, with no less intensity than me. This adoration of mine for particular works makes for excessive severity towards performers, especially when they bear an illustrious name in their field, and when they also possess talent of the highest order. So … weighing the value of these diverse influences, I shall repeat to Mlle Garcia that in singing the great scene from *Der Freischütz* as she did eight months ago, she entirely missed the character of her role and was far from doing justice to the sublime feeling so wonderfully expressed by Weber.

To judge from the way she sang and acted in the third act of *Otello*, and despite the clear difference between the two opposite styles, I now think that if Mlle Garcia is willing, without taking advice from anyone, to reflect further on this masterpiece [*Der Freischütz*], to study it in all its aspects and to penetrate its essence, not only will she recognize where she fell short of expressing all its passion and beauty, but she will perform it with the inspiration and fidelity she brought to the role [Desdemona] that has won her this more recent triumph. Never indeed, apart from Mme Malibran herself, has Desdemona's melancholy character been more perfectly understood.[12] Mlle Garcia's voice, of virginal purity, equal through all registers, in tune, vibrant, agile, doesn't cover three and a half octaves, as one of our best critics

---

10 An *écu*, or crown, was worth three francs.
11 Pauline Viardot, née Garcia; the review is in article 8 above.
12 Maria Malibran, née Garcia (1808–36), sister of Pauline.

has wrongly claimed: it ranges from a low F to a high C (two octaves and a fifth), a range that's already immense, since it unites the three voice types which are almost never united: contralto, mezzo-soprano, and soprano.

Her style is perfect: she's very sparing with her ornamentation and ends her energetic phrases with poise and firmness. The ending of her final aria, 'Intrepida morro', was greeted by the audience with wild enthusiasm. As for the slow and sad arias, one needs to hear her 'Willow Song' to have any idea of the melting charm with which she invests them. And in this scene the beauty of her gestures, as simple as they are expressive, and the grace of those attitudes of a wounded dove, almost equal the pathos of her singing.

This voice will, in a few years' time, acquire fullness and power, and acting experience will provide her with means that are at the moment lacking so that, whenever she is onstage, she will never let the action falter. But as things are, one can say: for the Théâtre-Italien at least, Mlle Pauline Garcia is plainly the singer who has the most promising future, and on whom rest the dearest hopes of those who love music.

15

First Conservatoire Concert: A Few Words on Early Music (I)

RGM, 16 January 1840

Berlioz's immersion in the music of his own time and in its performance didn't prevent him from having strong views about its relationship with that of the past and the problems this presented to audiences.

At last we have something new! To be frank, it was about time! A repertoire intended for listeners who are always much the same has more need than any other of being renewed. It's not that I share in the slightest that viewpoint which tends to see music as a frivolous art, a pastime, a fashionable plaything, a flower whose scent and colours don't last beyond a day. Certainly not. Our idea of the art is far loftier; but our impressions, whatever their source may be, are they not always in the process of fading?

Enthusiasm wanes bit by bit. A warrior who, twenty-five years ago would have punished a slur on Napoleon's memory with death, today is content to shrug his shoulders and treat the blasphemer as an imbecile.

One day in 1830 I heard one of my friends say calmly that there are 'some quite nice things' in Gluck's *Iphigénie en Tauride*. 'If you'd let slip such naivety six years ago', I said, purple with shame and fury, 'I wouldn't have spoken to you again in my life'. But if he said it again today, I'd go as far as biting my lower lip a bit, grinding my teeth quite quietly, and saying to him with a sideways smile, 'Do shut up, you *dilettante* blockhead!'

If you announce public readings of a great poet's latest work, their success won't extend to the audience for the first reading turning up for the second, and the hall, full the first day, will be completely deserted by the weekend. Shakespeare himself doesn't attract British audiences. All those directors who count on the drawing power of his masterpieces go bankrupt in a flash. In Paris, just try and put on [Molière's] *Tartuffe*, and you'll see what huge receipts accrue to M. Védel.[1] As to the vogue for Racine and Corneille, it's quite clear that, if indeed it has been growing, the *new* talent of Mademoiselle Rachel and a reaction against the modern school are the reasons.[2] Without her and MM. Hugo, Dumas, and Soulié, Andromache would be weeping on her own and Hermione would be lamenting in a desert.[3]

One day, at a performance of *Othello*, translated by A. de Vigny, a male member of the public whistled at one of the finest moments in the fourth act.[4] 'Come here!' shouted the celebrated poet in a fury, 'Come on! Yes, you! Animal! Come over to me and I'll give you FORTY WHACKS!' Today, if that sublime drama were to be revived, I can well believe that the man would whistle; but the poet, instead of staying in his seat immobile with fury, would go and find the great miscreant and give him only twenty whacks.

Three years ago, there were crowds in the École des Beaux-Arts to admire Sigalon's copy of Michelangelo's *The Last Judgment*; now the huge picture gets one visit a week at best.[5] I went to sleep in a confessional in St Peter's in Rome, reading Byron's *The Corsair* for the third time. Since I've just mentioned Michelangelo and St Peter's, I should say that, in order to erect his marvellous edifice, the great architect used debris from a monument more famous, more imposing, and more respectable still from the victorious battle it had waged with time, a monument consecrated by history and painted with the blood of martyrs, and from which even so he had a façade removed in order to use its materials. Do you not tremble at the thought of Michelangelo demolishing THE COLOSSEUM? He'd admired it for sixty years!!! That's the reason.

Poetry doesn't age, painting is not a matter of agreement, statuary and massive architecture are not subject to fashion, and yet we get tired of their most marvellous examples. So what's surprising in the fact that musical

---

1   Alexandre Poulet alias Védel (1783–1873) was the director of the Théâtre-Français from 1837 to 1840.
2   In January and February there were performances of Corneille's *Horace* and Racine's *Bajazet* and *Andromaque*. Élisa Félix alias Rachel (1820–58) was a French actress much admired by Berlioz and famous for her clear diction and economy of gesture. At various times she was the mistress of Napoleon III and other males of that family.
3   Frédéric Soulié (1800–47) was a French novelist and playwright.
4   Alfred de Vigny (1797–1863), French poet and dramatist, was among Berlioz's literary friends. He contributed to the libretto of *Benvenuto Cellini*. His adaptation of Shakespeare's *Othello* appeared under the title *Le More de Venise*.
5   Xavier Sigalon (1788–1837) was a French historical painter. His full-size copy of *The Last Judgment* had been exhibited in March 1837.

masterpieces undergo the same fate? We're the ones who grow old, it's our sensitivity that becomes blunted, our imagination that fades. But the power and vital spark of music never diminishes; on the contrary, it grows day by day. The music that we're hearing is a very young art, on the brink of adolescence, and its demise will not come for a long time. In any case, once its weakening and decay can no longer be doubted, it will have to come to a stop and definitely not be added to. But its collected repertoire will always be beautiful, and mankind's admiration for it will be transmitted from generation to generation.

In the view of some people, what is old no longer charms or has any effect, and as a result is worthless. Certainly, there is a lot of old music that was admired in its time and which today strikes us as terrible, but that comes chiefly from the fact that art has progressed on certain fronts, and with it the public and the critics. Yet one could say that in some cases we have wrongly blamed our ancestors, in the sense that maybe the experts of the past found great fault with the music we decry today. That is, people say such and such a work is ridiculous because it's *old*, and in reality because it both is and was bad: this music was old the day it was born.

Another work may appear boring because the great public isn't in the right mood, or not yet up to date enough to appreciate it, to understand and feel its beauties. From this we're led to conclude that those of the composer's contemporaries who lauded it to the skies, for reasons that have as little to do with a feeling for art as those whose current influence is so patent on failures and successes, did not in fact understand it as well as we do, because their education was not as complete as ours.

To my way of thinking, compositions like the aria 'Ô malheureuse Iphigénie' or the chorus of happy shades in the Elysian Fields in *Orphée* bring together all the necessary material for eternal beauty; that will always be beautiful and even more greatly admired as the years go by, because of the progressive development of music education. These pieces were very famous sixty years ago and were praised to the skies. It's absolutely true that Gluck was treated as a god, it being stated in print that he 'had rediscovered the sadness of antiquity'.[6] But how many awkward individuals were then repeating, as they no doubt would today, the quip made by the marquis de Caraccioli: 'I prefer modern pleasure!'[7] The Caracciolis are still with us, praise be! I go further and claim that a host of the *litterateurs* of the last

---

6 A *mot* of Abbé François Arnaud (1730–98), author of a Gluckist manifesto 'La soirée perdue à l'opéra' and other writings in the Gluck-Piccinni controversy which are among those reprinted in François Lesure (ed.), *Querelle des Gluckistes et des Piccinnistes* (2 vols.). Geneva: Minkoff, 1984.

7 Domenico Caraccioli (1715–89), Italian ambassador, dubbed by Berlioz a 'bad inventor of *bons mots*'. After seven years as envoy extraordinary to London, he

century who wrote either for or against Gluck and Piccinni were, when it came to it, wholly unaware of the true qualities of those two great artists.[8] There's so little to choose between the paths trodden by each of them that their supporters, in being so one-sided, displayed the most ridiculous prejudice. Certainly, Piccinni's style is generally flabby, inconsistent, breathless, often vulgar and unvarying. But if the Gluckists had felt the profound beauties of *Alceste* and *Orphée*, they could not have remained insensible to those of [Piccinni's] *Didon* and *Atys*. The true admirers of the scene in the Elysian Fields and the monologue of Admète's wife would have wept tears over the aria 'Ah! que je fus bien inspirée' ('Ah! what great passion I felt') and the funeral march, 'Apaisez-vous, mânes plaintifs, mânes irrités d'un héros!' ('Calm yourselves, plaintive spirits, unhappy spirits of a hero').[9]

On the other hand, the Piccinnists who denied Gluck the ability to express feelings of tenderness and moods of peace and gracefulness were a thousand times more narrow-minded. For if the sleep chorus in *Atys* and Didon's phrase 'Ô digne fils de Cythérée' ('O worthy son of Venus') had moved them profoundly, could they not have realized – poor wretches! – that even in this area of beauty Gluck was incomparably richer and more inspired than his rival? Ah no! No prejudice could have held out against these; they would have fallen to their knees when they heard the arias of Clytemnestre and Iphigénie, 'Que j'aime à voir les hommages-flatteurs' ('How I love to receive the flattery of men') and 'Les voeux dont le peuple m'honore' ('Praises with which the people do me honour'), Orphée's romance, the chorus of Naïades and Armide's gavotte, the minuet in the fifth act of the latter opera, the religious march in *Alceste*, the finale of *Écho et Narcisse*, and any number of miraculous, poetic melodies that I could name. But men possessing the qualities without which one cannot appreciate the masterpieces of music are rare in any age, and idiots discussing its value are everywhere. The extravagances and nonsense collected by M. de La Harpe about Gluck and Piccinni are enough to ensure his *Cours de littérature* undying ridicule.[10]

---

took up another posting to Paris where he made his mark by arranging excellent parties.

8   Niccolò Piccinni (1728–1800), one of the leading Italian opera composers of the day, was invited to Paris by those hostile to Gluck, arriving in 1776. Although his opera *Iphigénie en Tauride* (1781) lost the battle with Gluck's, the revival of *Atys* and the triumph of *Didon* (both in 1783) marked the high point of his career. The latter was revived in the 1820s, when Berlioz saw it with Caroline Branchu in the title role.

9   Both items are from *Didon*.

10 Jean-François de la Harpe (1739–1803), French man of letters and playwright who had the temerity to prefer Lully's *Armide* to Gluck's. The sixteen volumes of his *Cours de littérature* (1799–1805) were generally well received.

To sum up, in early music there are many fine thoughts which today seem colourless because of the progress of instrumentation or because we're accustomed to more thorough developments. There are sublime pieces which need not fear time, which the mob doesn't understand, but which were no better understood in the past, whatever people may say and write on the subject. And there are feeble offerings and a vast quantity of detestable rubbish, which were neither stronger nor weaker when they first appeared.

Someone will ask: what about melodies, and formulas? – To which I say: a beautiful melody doesn't grow old any more than a beautiful harmony. As to formulas, I see them as the real cause behind the short life and vulgarity of a great number of works whose initial inspiration contained both value and a means of survival. It's thanks to formulas that melody, harmony, rhythm, and instrumentation all grow old, and I think that every musician who respects his art should banish them totally. The formula (as its name indicates) is a small form whose charm survived briefly, but which, through being copied endlessly to no purpose, by laziness or mediocrity, has become tiring and unbearable. Its adherence to nobler and larger forms dishonours and destroys them, in the same way as plants and animals are invaded by parasitic growths and mites whose names are bywords for shabbiness and dirtiness. The fine pages of the great masters don't contain formulas, and that's why they will always be fine. Gluck avoided them carefully and continually; Piccinni, on the other hand, had one that was the death of seven-eighths of his output. Beethoven didn't have formulas, but Mozart was not a total stranger to them. The current Italian school is covered with them, to the point that if there still seems some part that's flourishing, the formula's the only reason, like those tropical creepers that put out thousands of branches, having choked the tree that supports them.

Among the old school, Marcello was totally free of such formulas; the Abbé Clari is not so fortunate, and if something can weaken the expressive power or sully the grace of his madrigals, you can be sure it's an obstinate formula that's the reason.[11] The musical flea is easy to see however, and the composer could as easily have prevented it from multiplying: it clings to the end of every phrase, where it imposes the same sudden movement on the melody, the same unexpected contraction which is unmotivated and, in many cases, wholly out of place and close to ridiculous. Without the Abbé

---

11 Giovanni Carlo Maria Clari (1677–1754), Italian composer; master of the music of Pisa Cathedral from 1736. His *Duetti e terzetti da camera* were reprinted in Paris (1823). Benedetto Marcello (1686–1739), Italian composer, theorist, and writer, was best known for his *Estro poetico-harmonico* (1724–6), settings of Italian paraphrases of the psalms, and for his satirical essay *Il teatro alla moda* ('The fashionable theatre', 1720). Berlioz included works by Clari and Marcello in some of his concert programmes.

Clari's unique formula, his madrigals for two and three voices – extremely beautiful as they are – would have no greater reason to fear the passage of time than Marcello's psalms do.

I'm not talking about the theatrical – so-called dramatic – works of that period. With very few exceptions, the formula has gnawed at, poisoned, and destroyed them all. Today, in Italy, a successful opera lasts six months, a year, two years at the most. After which the formulas are repeated and used in a different order to compose another score, and the operation is smartly despatched. It reminds one of those little coloured pebbles, the particles of glass in a kaleidoscope; are you ever tired of seeing them turn into a rosette, a star? Rotate the tube containing them as minimally as you like, and at once you'll have a cross of Saint Louis, a wheel, or something else as charming as it is novel.

This view as to the longevity of what is beautiful in music, as in every other art, would seem to have a firmer foundation if the public were more often allowed to compare contemporary compositions with those of the past. Criticism would soon learn to distinguish between what comes from differences in the means of performance and what comes from knowledge, taste and genius. One would no longer sum up by saying, 'This is bad because it's old', but rather, 'Here's something that's old, here's something that's dead, because it was bad the day the composer wrote it'. The Société des Concerts can perform important services in this respect by continuing to follow the path it has begun this year. It will also provide a great boon in renewing a repertoire that was beginning to become hackneyed; and when it decides to give the public only works able to offer real musical enjoyment, independently of any historical interest, instead of music to study. That will open up an inexhaustible mine. The audience at the Conservatoire is almost always the same: it's made up of the most talented Paris music-lovers, a scattering of artists and, basically, the public from the Théâtre-Italien. Out of these 900 people (the hall doesn't hold any more), there are at best twenty who are familiar with, or who have ever heard masterpieces from the three schools – the Italian, the German, and the French. So, for the vast majority Palestrina, Marcello, Clari, Porpora, Durante, Scarlatti, Pergolesi, Cafaro, Leo, Paisiello, Cimarosa, Salieri, and Sacchini will be new composers. Of the Germans, the same will apply to Sebastian and Emmanuel Bach, Handel, Gallus, Graun, Telemann, Vogler, Gottfried Weber, Naumann, Winter, Benda, Weigl, and Mayr; and of the French, Rameau, Grétry, Dalayrac, Philidor, Lesueur, and Catel.

Even among the works of composers most often heard at the Conservatoire, there are admirable things which they have never performed. Why, for example, has there been only a single excerpt from [Weber's] *Oberon*, two from *Euryanthe* and none from *Preciosa*?... Why have we not heard even once the great finale of [Beethoven's] *Fidelio*, or the grave-digging duet and the quartet from the same opera? ... It's true, we have heard fragments from the first acts of [Gluck's] *Alceste* and *Iphigénie en Tauride* and from the third of *Armide*; but till now no one has taken anything from *Iphigénie en Aulide* or *Écho et Narcisse*, not even the delightful chorus 'Le Dieu de Paphos'. Nor does today's public know anything of the beauties in the score of M. Cherubini's *Médée*, even though, in the opinion of all Europe, it's his masterpiece!

I realize that several of these works demand a performance style that's not familiar to the Conservatoire's artists, but that's precisely another reason to attempt them. An institution like the Société des Concerts should not fall short in any part of its task, which is to *conserve* life for all the fine products of musical art, by performing them with a fidelity and intelligence worthy of such a gathering of virtuosos and of the public who listen to them.

16

First Conservatoire Concert: A Few Words on Early Music (II)

RGM, 19 January 1840

The argument I put forward in the preceding article will no doubt attract many to contradict it; I fear it will be very hard to demolish a generally held opinion, and all the more deeply so because it has been agreed without reflection or reasoning. Experience must be more powerful than anything I could say, and I write only to provoke it. While waiting until experience has given rise to conviction, quotations and examples could not be adduced too generously: it's vital, by every possible means, to shine a light on this question and destroy a prejudice that has, for many artists, been a cause of discouragement, and whose influence is still so damaging for the direction of musical studies in general, and for the taste of the public.

So I shall now add to what I have said about works whose power has survived the passage of time, choosing my examples only from the most familiar compositions: What is fresher or more beautiful in its calm majesty than Palestrina's madrigal *Alla riva del Tebro*?[1] It's clearly a lasting piece, and thousands of years will in no way alter the purity of its form or the charm of its expression. People will say, 'It's not tuneful enough, and its effect stems really just from the chordal sequences and the successive voice entries. No one is denying that its harmony will ensure its survival, it's just the melody that's the problem'. – Very well. In that case, proofs will not be lacking. Half a century has not diminished the melodic nobility of the aria 'Elle m'a prodigué' ('She has lavished upon me') in [Sacchini's] *Oedipe*, or the dramatic impact of 'Ô Richard, ô mon roi!' from [Grétry's] *Richard*, or the simple melancholy of the romance 'Une fièvre brûlante' ('A burning

---

1 A four-part madrigal from 1586 that Berlioz included in some of his concerts, sung by a large chorus.

fever') in the same opera.[2] Time has not weakened the terrifying energy of the chorus 'Jurons sur nos glaives sanglants' ('Let us swear on our bloodied swords') from Philidor's *Ernelinde* and, among cheerful, graceful melodies, the F major *air de danse* in [Gluck's] *Armide*, Tarare's song 'Ainsi qu'une abeille' ('Like a bee'), the couplets in Paisiello's *La Molinara* the romance 'Dans l'asile de l'innocence' ('Under the protection of innocence'); in *Les Visitandines*, the aria 'Aimable et belle', in *Adolphe et Clara*, the romances in *Nina* and *Gulnare*, the aria 'Songe enchanteur' ('Enchanting dream') in *Anacréon*, the biblical choruses in Lesueur's *Noémi*, the trio 'Ô doux moments' in *Oedipe*, the aria 'Dis-moi donc, quand tu me quittes' ('Tell me then, when you leave me') in *La Colonie*.[3] These and a quantity of others by various composers have retained all their charm and make the job of today's melodists immensely difficult. And the national tunes and those songs from Scotland and Ireland with their picturesque atmospheres and delightful lilts, what date do they go back to? God alone knows.

We should consider also various odd styles which superficial judges are likely to regard as old simply because they offer a striking change from what we hear these days. The same applies to those that have been much imitated. Ancient tunes that served as models are also always beautiful: we've had enough of them, it's true, but whose fault is that? The plagiarists and imitators. We shall undoubtedly be putting these ideas to the test when we examine the works in the programme of the first Conservatoire concert and those we shall be hearing in the ones that follow.

The music programme this year was opened by a Beethoven work previously unknown to Parisians, the C-major *Leonora Overture*. *Leonora* was the first title of the opera we know today as *Fidelio*, for which the composer wrote three overtures: this was the first, which the theatre director and the orchestra found incomprehensible.[4] It is perhaps the most beautiful, and

---

2   *Oedipe à Colone* (a post-Gluck tragic opera, 1785) by Antonio Sacchini (1730–86) and Grétry's *Richard Cœur-de-Lion* (an opéra comique, 1784); both works were revived well into the nineteenth century.

3   Philidor's *Ernelinde, princesse de Norvège* (1767) has been called a Gluckist opera *avant la lettre*. Salieri's *Tarare* (1787; libretto by Beaumarchais) was his greatest success in Paris and was revised for Vienna, with an Italian libretto by Lorenzo da Ponte, as *Axur, re d'Ormus*. *La molinara*, opera by Paisiello (1788). *Les Visitandines*, Opéra-comique by Devienne (1792). *Adolphe et Clara, ou les Deux prisonniers*, and *Nina ou la Folle par amour*, opéras-comique by Dalayrac (1786 and 1799). *Anacréon ou l'Amour fugitif*, opéra-ballet by Cherubini (1803). *La Colonie*, opéra-comique (1776) arranged from an Italian opera by Sacchini.

4   The overture *Leonora no. 3* was played at the Societé's concert on 12 January 1840.

without question the greatest of all Beethoven's overtures. Then, the one containing the three main themes of the opera was likewise refused because of its quiet ending which didn't provoke any applause; and lastly the one in E major, whose brilliant character can fit any sort of opera regardless, and which has been definitely adopted under the name *Fidelio* overture.[5]

The instrumental masterpiece we're considering here is not excessively difficult for the players; the *Coriolan* overture makes much greater technical demands. The four-bar phrase that makes up the subject of the Allegro is very simple. Its impact derives from the prodigious skill with which the composer has developed it, the ever-growing complexity of the rhythms, their extreme variety, the exquisite choice of the modulations, the unexpectedness of certain details, the tender expression of another episodic melody, and an instrumentation of marvellous richness and sonority. The audience was overcome, and three bursts of applause bore witness to their enthusiasm. There is, however, a flute solo whose presence, in the middle of this magnificent composition, is totally inexplicable. One does not have to have very severe tastes to find this passage vulgar and its effect paltry and ill-judged. It's a phrase that's *old*, resembling a hundred others that were no longer used in Beethoven's time owing to their generally recognized puerility. It's also doubly old as being an imitation of something that was never good in itself.

The aria with chorus in Bach's *St Matthew Passion* had never been performed in France and is the only item from this famous work we have heard until now. It's a work of admirably antique colouring and of profound and true expressivity. The recitatives of the Evangelist and Jesus, well sung by MM. A. Dupont and Alizard, seemed to me to present considerable difficulties of intonation.[6] The beautiful melody of the C-minor aria [no. 26] given sometimes to a solo oboe, sometimes to the tenor accompanied by a counter-melody on oboe and bass, and split up by choral passages, breathes a feeling of infinite sadness and mortal dejection, expressed by Christ in his cry, 'My father, take bitter cup from me'. Why do we have to experience harmonic clashes and false relations, all the more distressing to the ear in that the passages where they occur are written in only two parts? The one in the seventh bar, where the bass rises via D natural to the E-flat that supports

---

5   Berlioz has understandably not quite got his facts right. The first and second to be composed were *Leonora no. 2* and *Leonora no. 3*; then the less demanding *Leonora no. 1*. The opera was first presented under the name *Fidelio* in 1805, to differentiate it from earlier operatic versions of the same story. It was named *Leonora* in 1806. For the 1814 revised version the title reverted to *Fidelio*.

6   Dupont and Alizard: see article 6, note 3.

a dominant seventh – that is, with a D-flat – without any preparation, is extremely painful, not to put it more strongly.[7]

The Andante of the Bach violin concerto was no less well received than the vocal music before it.[8] The melody is similarly imbued with that religious melancholy one finds in many slow movements of the time. It begins with a really strange ritornello, made up of heavy notes on every beat in the bar and played by basses and violins in alternation. This phrase recurs several times, played by strings with all their force, in between each short solo by the principal violin, and finally brought back in the form of an accompaniment. It finishes the Andante with an unexpected diminuendo, producing a delightful effect.[9] M. Habeneck, for whom the performance of such a violin solo was mere child's play on the technical front, phrased it with soul and faultless purity of tone. He could not escape widespread and long-lasting applause.[10]

Marcello's psalms would be known to us only by repute but for the intelligent efforts of the excellent Choron.[11] The acclaim accorded last Sunday to the first of these to be heard at the Conservatoire concerts shows a desire to know more of them and testifies that they have lost nothing of their power or majestic beauty. This music is very difficult to sing well and needs special training to succeed. The choirs of the Chapelle Saint-Marc, the Conservatoire des Pauvres-Filles, and the Casino des Nobles were, in Marcello's day, at the height of their excellence, and these institutions undoubtedly smoothed out for him difficulties that are pretty much insurmountable today. The art of choral singing was in fact so highly cultivated then that, in some chapels, the habit was to sing a new composition on every ceremonial occasion which, being performed only once, was nonetheless sung *at sight*. Scores that were often highly complex and written in eight to ten parts passed, to the composer's satisfaction, a test which these days would undoubtedly be disastrous.

---

7   Few modern listeners are likely to be disturbed by this progression within a 'circle of fifths' (F–B-flat–E-flat –A-flat).
8   Bach's Violin Concerto in A-minor, BWV 1041.
9   The copy in the Berlin Stadtsbibliothek, stemming from Bach and his assistants, actually marks the ending *forte*.
10 François-Antoine Habebeck (1781–1849), principal conductor of the Opéra (1821–46) and founding conductor of the Société de Concerts from 1828 to 1848. He conducted several Berlioz premieres, including *Symphonie fantastique* and *Benvenuto Cellini*.
11 Alexandre-Étienne Choron (1771–1834) was a child prodigy, speaking fluent Latin, Greek, and Hebrew at the age of fifteen. In 1812 he was charged with reorganising the church choirs of France, and he went on to found the École de musique classique et religieuse, where he gave the first Paris performances of Palestrina, Bach, and Handel. He was encouraging to Berlioz.

The main merit of singers did not, as nowadays, consist of brilliant vocalisation, in the same way that the theatre alone did not absorb the public's entire interest. A composer could make a reputation without submitting his head to the yoke of the cabaletta and without becoming the lackey of a castrato – as we can see from Durante who wrote nothing for the stage.[12] Things have now changed so much that if Marcello were our contemporary, his admirable hymns would have great difficulty in finding, in Italy, a tiny number of intelligent interpreters capable of capturing their sense and spirit; and even in the case that the delights of a good performance were accorded him, the public, in its preoccupation with frivolity, would always prefer, instead of his noble harmonies, the vulgar products of the most wretched cavatina merchant.

Even in his own day, and for a man of noble family favoured by fortune, like Benedetto Marcello, the career of opera composer was nothing easy and honourable from certain points of view. We can judge everything his dignity as man and artist had to suffer in his dealings with the theatre by the bitterness and brutal irony that made a bestseller of his famous pamphlet (*il Teatro alla moda*).[13] He didn't hold back with the ridicule he piled on directors, poets, composers, singers, conductors, prima donnas, their mothers, their protectors, the quarrels, the backstage plots, the responses of the stalls, etc. He turned the whole of that world into a terrifying bloodbath, leaving not a stone unturned in the temple of fashion. His fury was directed especially at *l'orso* (the bear), whose conceit struck him as the rudest and hardest to tolerate. He returns continually to the necessity for those composers who want to succeed to insert themselves into the good graces *del signor orso*, and to the profound respect with which they must treat him on every occasion. It seems that there was then, in the Venetian theatre, an individual whose job was to represent the bear in the intermezzos, ballets and even operas, and that this man, thanks to the delight the public took in his capering, had become someone of the highest importance, making the greatest artists aware of his *superiority*. Imagine M. Meyerbeer being obliged to pay court to the back legs of the camel in *La Caravane* and to stroke the front ones with his hands.[14] So let's not be rude about our own times, the reign of the bear is over; we no longer have those beasts at the Opéra.

---

12   Durante: see article 8, note 3.
13   In a letter to his father (31 August 1824), who deplored his son's intention to abandon medical studies for music, Berlioz tactlessly used Marcello as an example of a composer who was remembered, whereas his father (of the Venetian nobility, although not Doge, as Berlioz supposed) was forgotten. *CG* vol. 1, 64–5.
14   Grétry's opéra-ballet *La Caravane du Caire* (1783).

The style generally employed by Marcello in his psalms is fugal, and he uses it with marvellous ease, always choosing excellent themes, never sacrificing expressiveness to childish combinations, but on the contrary using the varied resources of counterpoint merely to accentuate the main theme in all its guises and always to its advantage. The entry of the subject is always managed in a way that favours the voice; it is only strange when, in a work as careful as the psalms are with regard to harmonic correctness, one finds parts entering on unresolved fourths, as on page 159 at the start of the Allegro: 'Non avvi popolo con tanto barbaro'. Here the first tenor starts on a D at the same time as the contralto ends on a G, while the second tenor starts two bars later on the A, a fourth down from the unresolved D on which the first tenor ends. In a chorus of rough, fierce nature such harmonic treatment would not perhaps be out of place, but here it seems to me hard to justify and, in any case, the effect is not good. Beyond the beauty of the vocal shaping, one must also admire, in general, the ingenious craft with which Marcello makes the simple instrumental bass that forms the accompaniment interesting. The chorus mentioned above is itself a good example, and it would be easy to quote others that are still more remarkable.

The psalm performed recently at the Conservatoire is one of the few where the composer has used a three-part accompaniment: two violas and a bass. The character of these low instruments, which one does not usually hear in such a light texture, is energetic and sad and perfectly matches the religious tone of the voices.

As for melody as such, it's true that, in the psalms, it has little to do with what the Parisian dandy honours with his esteem: its physiognomy is essentially simple and even austere. Sometimes one feels that its shapes are subordinated to the dictates of the contrapuntal combinations in which it finds itself, in which case it recedes slightly into the background to leave more room for its noble sister Harmony, who is not slow to return the compliment, allowing it to dominate in its turn. There are even entire psalms (and they contain at least six or seven different sections) written for a single voice. The Largo of number twenty-one, 'E pur tu quello sei, che nell' eccelso monte a te consagrato, hai ferma sede' ('And yet you are the one who has a firm seat on the lofty mountain') is a sublime example of what in the way of grandeur pure melody can achieve in this style. The Conservatoire certainly ought to let us hear this piece, which is also accompanied by the three parts of two violas and a bass.

Rameau's aria of the savages did not cause any great excitement in spite of some very interesting harmonies. The character of this work's instrumental part is clearly contrasted with that of the voices. The aria's words 'Forêt paisible, jamais un vain désir ne trouble ici nos coeurs' ('Peaceful forest, here no vain desire troubles our hearts') do not, it seems to me, justify the heavy rhythms and rather grotesque jokiness of the orchestra. Compare this with Gluck's chorus 'Jamais dans ces beaux lieux' ('Never in these lovely places') and see how truth and beauty can be combined.[15] Maybe during this chorus of savages (savages like you and me, what's more, who reason 'sur les dangers des faveurs de la fortune' ('on the dangers of fortune's favours') and on 'les faux attraits des grandeurs' ('the false attractions of greatness') ... maybe, I say, another group of these philosophical Hurons danced during the staging.[16] In that case, the activities of the orchestra would be perfectly relevant and my criticism would be beside the point. We should now be allowed to hear the Fates' trio, the aria 'Tristes apprêts' ('Scene of sorrow'), and the chorus, 'Que l'enfer applaudisse' ('Let Hell applaud'). These fragments from *Hippolyte et Aricie* and *Castor et Pollux* are even stranger than the one from *Les Indes galantes*.[17]

M. Dorus played an air and variations on the flute with great success and astonishing perfection.[18] This young virtuoso is unmistakably one of the most skilful to be found in Europe, and he plays in tune. The concert ended with Beethoven's Seventh Symphony, about which all I can say is sublime! sublime! sublime! sublime throughout. The performance was worthy of the work.

The Conservatoire orchestra will shortly lose an excellent artist whom it will be very difficult to replace: M. Dieppo has obtained leave during which he will give concerts in Germany, Sweden, and Denmark.[19] We have no doubts as to the success in store for him, but we seriously trust that they won't be enough to persuade him to stay a long time away from Paris. If we were to lose our principal trombone, what would we do? That sort of quality is hard to come by.

---

15   This solo with chorus is from *Armide*, act 4. The 'aria of the savages' is from Rameau's opéra-ballet *Les Indes galantes*.
16   Hurons were native North Americans living along the banks of the St Lawrence River, and consequently formerly in French Canada; *Le Huron* was Grétry's first opera to be premiered in a Paris theatre.
17   On the aria from *Castor et Pollux* see article 30.
18   Vincent Joseph van Steenkiste, known as Louis Dorus (1813–96), French flautist and composer.
19   Dieppo: see article 12, note 4.

17

Paris Opéra: Revival of *Fernand Cortez*; Liszt and Batta in London

JD, 21 June 1840

Berlioz was fairly unusual among European composers of the time in finding the English in general musical, well organized, and willing to pay for their enjoyment.[1] *He might have been pleased had he been able to read a passage in Thackeray's* Vanity Fair (1847) *describing a ballad sung by his anti-heroine Becky Sharp: it is 'not, be it said, very brilliant, in a musical point of view, but contains numberless good-natured, simple appeals to the affections, which people understood better than the milk-and-water* lagrime, sospiri, *and* felicità *of the eternal Donizettian music with which we are favoured nowadays'. This article begins with a review of the first appearance of the tenor Claude Marié de l'Isle, omitted here.*

The revival of *Fernand Cortez*, which in any case would have caused a stir quite apart from the strange legal incident that it provoked, drew a large, attentive audience to the Opéra, curious to test the persistence of its one-time admiration.[2] If the composer could have heard, after the second act,

---

1   Berlioz's first visit to London was not until 1847, when he was engaged to conduct operas by Donizetti, Mozart, and Balfe, and, ironically, had difficulty obtaining payment.

2   Spontini was unhappy with the revival, although this might seem a small issue about which to institute legal proceedings. He had his solicitors request that the revival of *Fernand Cortez* 17 June 1840 be cancelled because (as they claimed before the Tribunal de commerce de la Seine on that day), the carelessness preparation of the opera 'threatened to damage the honourable reputation of its author' (*Le Droit*, 18 June 1840). The last-minute request came

the explosion of bravos that filled the hall and the exclamations of praise that were heard in the corridors, in the public foyer, in the wings, in the dressing-rooms of the singers and chorus, in the orchestra, and everywhere, I doubt he would have persisted in his opposition. M. Spontini may be assured (I am at least profoundly convinced of this) that the Opéra's administration may perhaps have staged this revival at rather short notice, but also out of total loyalty and with a sincere desire to promote its success. The costumes had, in fifteen years, never been so colourful or varied; the scenery was restored and the roles learnt with real alacrity by those actors most capable of filling them, given the present voices available.

Mlle Nau lacks power in some of the items, but she sang her aria 'Je n'ai plus qu'un désir' ('I have only one wish') very gracefully, as she did her solos in the duet 'Dieu du Mexique', in which F. Prévost gave her firm support.[3] Massol is an excellent Cortez, the best we've ever heard.[4] His strong, vibrant voice suits the electrified steel of this music. He dominated the scene of revolution magnificently. What's more, his voice has been sweetening and softening for some time: he showed this in several recitatives of a tender expressiveness he would not have managed some years ago. If he restrained his indignation at the beginning of the great revolution scene, it would later break out with more force. He should, as far as possible, observe in his singing the gradation that the composer has so cleverly written for the orchestra, and reserve his metallic notes for the ending. Even so, as it is, his execution of this immortal scene is irresistible: he seizes it, carries it along, and if the chorus and orchestra follow him just as they did last time (perfection here would be easy to attain), he is sure of his part, the audience is with him.

One has to say that it's astonishingly beautiful, that it burns with enthusiasm, that the inspiration is overflowing, and that even so it is directed by reason: there are sounds of undeniable truthfulness, of those great sweeps of their wings that only eagles can make, flashes of light that illuminate a whole world. Oh! don't mention to me 'grinding toil', or supposed 'harmonic errors', or the numerous faults for which Spontini is blamed by people who are all rationality. For, even though they're true, the effect made by his

---

too late to prevent the revival but was honoured by the court. Later performances were delayed until the end of the month, when the court, taking into consideration Berlioz's positive review among other evidence, determined that the Opéra had the right to proceed.

3   Mlle Nau: see article 6, note 3 and article 12, note 20. Pierre-Ferdinand Prévost (1800–79) was a French bass who sang at the Opéra from 1824 to 1857; he sang Bernardino in *Benvenuto Cellini* (1838–9).

4   Eugène Massol (1802–87) joined the Opéra as a tenor and sang Fieramosca in *Benvenuto Cellini* in 1838. The tessitura of this role is low for a tenor, and Massol was to become the Opéra's principal baritone from 1850 to 1858.

music, and my emotion and that of a hundred other musicians who are not easy to dazzle, are just as true in their turn. If you add that, in our excitement, we have lost the faculty of reasoning, it's the greatest compliment you can pay this music. Ah! Good Lord! I'd like to see them there, all those who deny the superiority of such a power. Come now, I'd say to them, apparently you don't insist that musical and dramatic works have, as their unique role, to speak only to the audience's reasoning, leaving them absolutely calm and cold in their methodical contemplation? Well then! Since you agree that art can also, without degrading itself, tend to produce in certain characters those emotions they prefer, namely of large, well-trained choruses, a young French orchestra, the best singers that can be found, a libretto full of striking situations, verses suitable for setting to music; go to it, then! Try to move us, to make us lose the power of reasoning, as you put it. It'll be very easy, according to you, since after an act of *Fernand Cortez* we are seen to be fevered, pulsating. Don't worry, we offer ourselves to you without defences. Abuse our impressionability; we'll bring smelling salts, there'll be doctors in the house to judge the point to which musical drunkenness can be taken without endangering human life.

Ah! Poor people, we should soon have proved to you, I fear, that your efforts are in vain, that we still have our reason, and that our hand doesn't tremble when it wields the scalpel on every part of your work to prove that there's no heart.

I know that in Germany especially, to judge by certain popular opinions, this profession of faith will be very badly received. Never mind; I make it because it's mine, and because it would almost be cowardice not to make it today.

But that man, someone will say, has such numerous enthusiasms and scattered over such different objects; he prostrates himself before the fourth act of this opera, before the third of that, he adores German, French, and Italian masters. Does he then like everything? – Ah well, wait a little until the day I decide to tell all, and I'll very soon be justified, when I explain to you that there are unfortunately more things I find perfectly abominable, far sillier things, fantasies, platitudes, and absurdities, than there are masterpieces or merely works that are estimable or worth the slightest attention. Be warned against people who are naïve: there's nothing worse when you come down to it.

Even so, the score of *Cortez* has proved, as it did before its exile from the stage, to be rich in fresh melodies, in fine recitatives (too long in the first act, but that's not the composer's fault), in original ideas that are noble and elevated, always dramatic in its essence, and orchestrated, if not with great finesse, at least with a feeling for expression whose truth never fluctuates.

The Queen sings, Prince Albert sings, the gentlemen and maids of honour sing, Lablache himself sings, it's not just Rubini who deigns to sing in the concerts of the British court. Hurrah, they seem to be paying attention to music in that country. If this craze for Italian cavatinas could leave some doubts as to the reality of the developments that musical education is promoting every day in England, the welcome accorded to Liszt and Batta would be enough to dissipate them.[5] Both played at court in the Queen's private soirées, I've no need to say with what success. After London's applause, Batta sought that of the provinces: his concerts in Manchester and some other large towns succeeded brilliantly. He made a *furore* in the true sense of that Italian word.

As for Liszt, I don't know how to describe the charmed astonishment of that whole milieu. The amateurs and professionals were dumbfounded by his concerts, and the critics' magnetic needle was thrown at least ten minutes out. The North is no longer the North, and the enthusiasm of the *midi* [the South] has been surpassed. To cut a long story short, an entrepreneur has booked Liszt to tour England, Scotland, and Ireland for the middling sum of *twelve thousand francs* a month.[6] I told you the English really value music … we like it well enough in France, but we pay badly for it. As to the other side of the Channel, I won't say: but they like it and they pay well, when they do pay.[7]

---

5   The cellist Batta: see article 3, note 4.
6   The entrepreneur Louis Henry Lavenu (1818–59) was also a cellist and composer of light music. The tour lasted from 19 August to 23 January, with a loss to Lavenu of over £1,000 (over £130,000 in today's money).
7   Berlioz presumably received these details from an informant, perhaps Batta.

18

Third Conservatoire Concert

RGM, 11 February 1841

The concert on 7 February included Haydn's Symphony no. 102, two choruses from Handel's Samson *and* Alexander's Feast, *and two arias from* Rinaldo *and* Scipione *sung by Pauline Viardot, who also sang an aria from [Mozart's]* Così fan tutte. *It ended with Prosper Dérivis and the chorus in the excerpt from [Gluck's]* Iphigénie en Tauride.

Hunters know how distressing and irritating it is to walk on ploughed land in pouring rain, when you've already gone twenty miles, when your game bag and your stomach are empty after you've had the stupidity to miss a deer; and when water has seeped into your gun barrel, the dogs insist, despite this concatenation of daunting circumstances, on finding the scent of any number of game. You come and go, up to your knees in mud, stumbling with every movement. But a dog has stopped dead, you must keep going; a hare breaks cover, you fire, the gun jams! The rain falls even more heavily! And not a tree to shelter you, not a drop of brandy to warm you up; the flask broke when you fell in the last ditch! And you think of the jokes waiting for you when you get back: 'Some hunter! He covered thirty miles on foot and brought back a chaffinch!' etc., etc.

Well, all that's nothing compared with the trouble critics have with various concert notices, the most positive and instant result of which is to upset everybody. You have to say something about a work, new or old, about a singer or an instrumentalist. You make yourself small, you curl up into a ball, you sheathe your claws, you close your eyes like a good tomcat dozing by the fire. Wait a bit for the publication of your elegant article and you'll hear loud cries. 'Oh! Useless coward!' some will be saying, 'he didn't dare attack this platitude, this balderdash! If he's going to run with the hare and hunt with the hounds, who is to be trusted? There's no longer any criticism; it's all back scratching. Because he met this man in a café two years ago, he feels obliged to treat him as a close friend! Because this woman's husband said something really awful about him, he imagines he absolutely must declare her to be sublime, feeling it's in poor taste to do otherwise! It's a question, dear me, of those evangelical virtues, that ridiculous business about returning good for evil! It's a matter of truth! It's a matter of saying what you think and giving just a little thought to the people who read what you write. To hell with it! This piece is very bad, he knows it as well as we do, why pretend it's almost good? This lady singer has very little voice, her F is wobbly, she made hardly any impact, why talk about a triumph?'

The complaints that come from the opposite side are more violent still. Nothing compares with the anger of those people who find they aren't praised enough, either for their own personal virtues, or for those of their friends or protégés. One is a horrible man for saying 'it's very fine!' If the critic contents himself with saying 'fine' without a superlative, clearly he has committed an act of treachery. Has he thought best to confine himself to 'it's certainly good', he's nothing but a wretch; but if he descends to just 'good' on its own, then he's a miscreant who deserves the utmost contempt.

I come now to the Conservatoire concert, which I'd almost forgotten, since the foregoing reflections have certainly not been prompted by this excellent afternoon event – I'm sure that wouldn't be in anyone's mind, and if I thought it was, I'd be truly sorry. It's just that the occasion seemed a little long, a little monotonous, a little cold, a little boring. There's the proof that I don't flinch from the danger of calling things by their names.

We started with Haydn's B-flat Symphony [no. 102], in which the first movement, the minuet, and the finale are extremely jolly. The Adagio, on the other hand (it's true that a majestic tune can't really be jolly) is magnificently and imposingly serene. The instrumentation, which is slightly uniform in the other movements, is here full of variety, of charming contrasts and above all of an exquisite gentleness. As has been remarked, among other striking passages there's a timpani pedal that seems to me superior to most of the effects of this kind which have been tried since Haydn. It came over very well and was appreciated, thanks to the care M. Poussard takes to tune his timpani perfectly, at the Conservatoire especially where the break between the different items gives him the time he doesn't always have at the Opéra to make the minute adjustments that lead to a tuning which, in general, one thinks barely possible on this instrument.[1]

Nothing can match the freshness and grace of the finale's capricious character. In the first movement of Beethoven's Symphony [no. 4] in B-flat but

---

[1] Charles-François Poussard [?– ?] was a French timpanist whom Berlioz elsewhere praised for 'the precision and rapidity of his rolls and the finesse of his nuances'. He introduced sponge heads for drumsticks, instead of leather or cloth, making drum rolls easier. Berlioz praises him twice in his *Memoirs*.

over a gigantic harmonic progression of his own invention, he copied almost note for note the sprightly dialogue between first and second violins, moving from right to left the same group of notes repeated at the unison.[2] Rossini in his turn recalled the theme of the first movement in one of his *airs de danse* in *Guillaume Tell*; he didn't succeed quite as well with it as Haydn [in his finale]. I won't say anything about the minuet because I have the misfortune to be absolutely unable to tolerate the character of ninety-nine per cent of these dances, and this one is no exception. What can I do? I detest gross musical jokes. As it's a question of my feelings and not of anyone else's, I need to confess it.

Haydn wrote an enormous number of symphonies and we all ask why, in the fourteen years it's been in existence, the Société des Concerts has programmed only four or five at most.

We then had a chorus from Handel's *Samson*, an aria from Handel's *Rinaldo*, a chorus from Handel's *Alexander's Feast*, and an aria from Handel's *Scipione*. The first chorus is the one already done in the preceding concert, so we heard again the little trumpet solo whose naivety appeared so striking. Despite Mme Viardot-Garcia's rare talent, the two Andantes she sang could not dissipate the audience's torpor. As I didn't know either the words or the dramatic situation of these arias, it's impossible for me to judge their expressiveness, which was perhaps very meaningful. I'll say the same of the chorus from *Alexander's Feast*; maybe there were words or a situation that could justify an accompaniment like the one boomed out at length by violins and violas, and which recalls by its form, as much as by its somniferous effect, the famous canon *Frère Jacques, dormez-vous*.

The sextet by M. Bertini was the only modern piece included in the programme, and it would doubtless have upheld the honour of contemporary art had the audience been properly awake.[3] I, who had more or less maintained my full attention, should like to mention the excellent structure of the first movement, several passages full of delicacy in the final one, and in general the remarkable way in which this composer has handled the role of the piano; to the point that, even when balanced against the mass of the five string instruments, it retains all its brilliance and maintains its predominance. One knows that M. Bertini occupies an important place among the most technically able players of the modern school; it is therefore almost unnecessary to add that in his new work he played the piano part with a verve, a

---

2 This reference could be either to bars 65–76 or to bars 261–80. Orchestras prior to the last century placed the second violins opposite the firsts, on the right of the conductor.

3 Henri Bertini (1798–1876) was a French pianist, teacher, and composer. In 1828 he was joined by Liszt and two others in a performance of Beethoven's Seventh Symphony, arranged by him for eight hands.

precision and a brio that would have been enough, independently of the work's merit, to stimulate applause.

Finally, Mme Viardot-Garcia was able, in a Mozart aria, to display all the resources of her great talent. It is impossible to place and manage the voice better, to articulate a phrase more clearly and to sing with more nobility. Sadly, this fine instrument has for some time lacked a little in the way of strength. From this comes a greater difficulty for the singer in expressing those outbursts whose warmth communicates itself, and which are the only elements that profoundly move the masses. This aria, although admirably designed and perfect in its characterisation, like everything that Mozart wrote, is not highly coloured or with a meaning that the public can easily grasp.[4]

The great scene of Thoas and the Scythians from *Iphigénie en Tauride* stood alone in totally dispersing the general somnolence.[5] Ah! It's terrifyingly beautiful! It's sublime! And one finds it sublime and beautiful not, as some people do, because the composer is long dead, because one wants to make use of it for a kind of bitter reaction against the present. No, one bows down, one trembles with emotion before such music, because the heart, the senses, the spirit, the imagination, and thinking, all tell you that its beauty is true, great, poetic, strong, eternal. In the same way, there are things we find ugly, not because of their advanced age, but because of their essential ugliness, which always was repulsive.

---

[4] The aria is not identified but is likely to have been one of Fiordiligi's from *Così fan tutte*, either 'Come scoglio' of the Rondò 'Per pietà'; it could have been identified had Berlioz mentioned the orchestration, which is striking in both arias.

[5] The Scythian (barbarian) king Thoas makes two appearances in *Iphigénie en Tauride*, but this must be from the first act, in which there are choruses and dances for the Scythians after Thoas's aria 'De noir pressesntiments'.

19

Paris Opéra: Revival of *Don Giovanni* (I)

JD, 23 April 1841

This review is followed by another on Ambroise Thomas's Carmagnola, *ultimately premiered on 19 April, but this latter is not included here.*

The new work [*Carmagnola*] would have been staged much earlier if the numerous rehearsals of [Mozart's] *Don Giovanni* had not caused its postponement for several weeks. It's annoying that these prolonged sessions delayed the performance of the new opera without any advantage to the ancient masterpiece; we know that twice in a few days *Don Giovanni* was announced to no avail as Barroilhet, feeling hoarse during the first performance, which was consequently abandoned, was replaced by the overture and a trio from *Guillaume Tell*.[1] He was then indisposed shortly before the second performance, which did not take place at all.

If Barroilhet doesn't give up this celebrated role, which seems to terrify him, it's worth making some observations about the way he seemed to me, on the basis of a few scenes, to understand the Mozartian style. Barroilhet clearly belongs to that class of singers, so abundant in Italy, for whom the music, words and the plot of an opera are merely more or less plausible vehicles for his personal success. Everything, if we are to believe these people, must lend itself to the demands and even the characteristics of their talent. If they're dealing with a living composer, they oblige him to change a host of passages in their roles according to their own ideas. If the composer's dead, then they make the changes themselves. And since in general great singers don't exactly possess as much knowledge and taste as great composers, their corrections of masterpieces often lead to extremely unhappy results. For example, the feeling for melodic distinction, for beauty of style, for dramatic convention and for accuracy of expression that Barroilhet possesses is not exactly equal to Mozart's; at least

---

[1] Paul Barroilhet (1810–71), French baritone who after a period in Italy sang at the Opéra from 1841 to 1847, after which he retired to become an art dealer. In 1845 Berlioz dedicated the orchestral version of his song 'Le Chasseur danois' to him.

it's permissible to express some doubt in this respect. In this case, is it certain that he is not mistaken, grossly mistaken, in correcting phrases by the master of whom he should be honoured to be the faithful interpreter? …

That notes beyond the range of certain voices should be changed, that's understandable; that a singer, giving way to the need for applause that torments them all, should allow himself, against all reason certainly, to add a pause the composer didn't ask for, but which is bound to set those with bad taste into paroxysms of admiration, that too is understandable. But is it not truly regrettable to have to reproach Barroilhet with sins against Mozart that nothing can justify? To quote just a single instance, the theme of the duet 'Là ci darem la mano', such an exquisite melody, ends simply and tastefully with the notes G-sharp, F-sharp, E, E, F-sharp, G-sharp, A. Barroilhet prefers A, G-sharp, F-sharp, E, C-sharp, B, A, which here form a dull, vulgar ending, and would undoubtedly not win him even the most anodyne support, the most feeble applause. On the contrary, most audiences for *Don Giovanni* know the main themes extremely well, wait for their appearance, and become rightly indignant when they don't find them. The performer, it's true, can prefer one kind of style to another, but certainly Mozart also had the same right, and the public without question has that of preferring the preferences of Mozart. Also, in this same duet, Barroilhet introduces his favourite exclamation, the least objection to which is that it spoils the rhythm of the verse and corrupts the purity of the musical setting without any reason. The least we can do is to think of his habit as one of those tics that make some people tap their forehead, twist their head from side to side, stroke their eyelids, scratch their nose etc., because in fact, without a tic (a tic we find distressing), what can make Barroilhet say 'Là ci darem, AH!, la mano!' The words aren't hard to pronounce, the melody is straightforward, natural, written in the middle of the voice, nothing is hard for the singer, and his AH! will not earn him any bravos or bunches of flowers, any more than the corrections I mentioned earlier. Ye Gods, this is ah! ridiculous, it's even ah! shocking, and it has to be agreed that if one forgives ah! Don Giovanni his bad treatment of ah! Donna Anna, it is less forgivable to violate ah! the Fren ah! ch language.

In any case, it's very unfortunate, because Barroilhet is a singer of merit whose voice is beautiful, flexible, nuanced, expressive, and melodious. He's loved by the public, who would love him all the more if he could abandon the faults I've just mentioned, that's to say if in his singing he would stop destroying both music and text.

In this revival of *Don Giovanni*, Dérivis was remarkable and justly applauded in the role of Leporello, which he was taking for the first time. Mme Gras-Dorus, in that of Donna Anna which she had learnt at short notice, displayed an energy of which one barely thought her capable, since a comparable occasion had not previously presented itself.[2]

---

2   Prosper Dérivis, French bass (1808–80), son of the elder Dérivis (see article 5 note 2). Dorus-Gras: see article 12, note 10.

20

Liszt's Concerts

JD, 23 April 1841

The two concerts reviewed here were given in the Salle Érard on 21 March and 13 April 1841.

No one had ever dared put on these kinds of concert in Paris, and at such a price; to wit, seven pieces by Liszt filled the whole programme, with tickets at twenty francs. It makes one tremble! Many people found this project unseemly, extravagant, overweening! But the public came, not once but twice, and with even more eagerness the second time than the first. It found the seven pieces short, to the point of encoring one and demanding another which was not in the printed programme. His marvellous talent casts such a spell on people who are not particularly musical, his prestige is so great, he charms, he dazzles, he sweeps along with such grace, brilliance, and energy, that even those artists whose attitudes are almost hostile to him nevertheless go to hear him, applauding him with all their might, leaving the hall convinced of his vast superiority, regaining their settled opposition two hours later, and rushing again to hear him and applaud at the next opportunity.

It would certainly be pointless to look to an analysis of mechanical procedures for the secret of his power; even if in the domain of difficulty and the astonishment he engenders by his victories over it, Liszt is truly unrivalled, it seems obvious that the greatest power does not lie there. I find it in an intelligence that one might call divinatory, in an exquisite sensitivity, carried sometimes to excess, and which, if not kept under control, can, it's true, damage the rigorous performance of certain works which merely demand firm, broad-based, rectilinear execution, but which is also unique in lifting the artist to the heights of great, poetically inspired works. The performer who sings as Liszt does, who is able to dream and lose himself likewise in the secret affections of the heart, to lend so much beauty to the expression of suffering, in a word, to interpret with such superiority one of Schubert's masterpieces, his *Ave Maria*, is alone capable also of making the gloomy passions of *Robert le diable* thunder with all their infernal might, and follow the frantic ride of *Mazeppa* without pausing for breath.[1] These two pieces, out of all those Liszt has played in public so far, are the richest in their impact on the masses, in new impressions and irresistible charms. The episodic structure of *Mazeppa* is magnificent, and its character of savage grandeur comes across all the more strongly because the cruel agitation, the fear, and the desperate efforts of the fierce rider are at the same time most minutely described. The idea so cleverly managed by Victor Hugo to crown his poem has unfortunately not made enough of a mark on the composer. I refer to the famous line 'Il tombe et se relève roi!' ('He falls and rises up a king!') which lent itself, even so, to a splendid musical peroration.

As to the fantasy on *Robert le diable*, nobody has ever written anything for the piano in this genre that comes near it. This great piece contains passages that are bold as well as ingenious, the general layout is skilful, the effect as powerful as it is variegated. The passage that strikes listeners most forcibly, even though other pianists have accustomed them to more or less successful tactics of this nature, is the theme of Bertram's aria in the third act, where one finds it, together with that of the *air de danse* written for Mlle Taglioni in the scene of the nuns, first played together and then in reverse order, the first time high on the keyboard, then separately low down.[2] This harmonious union of two such different melodies is extraordinarily successful. There's no need to speak of all the miracles of the performance, the overwhelming staccato of the left hand octaves, the microscopic embroidery in the extreme treble, those diatonic phrases as swift as lightning, etc, etc. Nothing I could say would give the slightest idea of them. These two concerts will be crucial events in the history of the piano.

---

1   Liszt's fantasy on Meyerbeer's opera *Robert le diable* (1841). *Mazeppa* is one of his *Études d'exécution transcendante* (revised in 1840); it was later reconceived for orchestra as a symphonic poem (1854).

2   Bertram's aria 'De ma gloire éclipsée' ('Of my obscured fame') and the *air de danse* 'Jadis filles du ciel' ('Long ago, daughters of heaven').

21

Paris Opéra: Revival of *Don Giovanni* (II)

JD, 16 May 1841

Don Giovanni has finally been revived [24, 28, and 30 April], played complete, and very well received. Barroilhet no longer goes ah![1] In the first two performances the trio of masks was encored, as was Don Giovanni's aria in the third. There's nothing to say about that except that it's very good!

It is good indeed that *Don Giovanni,* having been promised so many times, has been played, as it's a masterpiece; we can also be glad about the reception it's had from the public, as the performance, although better than what it generally was in the last performances before the revival, was not absolutely beyond criticism and was noticeably inaccurate in several respects. It's easy to find examples. Mozart's orchestration and melodies have been altered. Trombones have been added in several places, with moderation, but wrongly, since it is to misunderstand the intention and thought of the composer to treat this instrument as we do now.[2] Mozart was sparing in his use of trombones, reserving them exclusively for scenes of terror and to accompany the funereal voice of the Commendatore. In any case, my main point is to ask: Who has the right to correct such a master? What composer today is placed so high that he dares give an orchestration lesson to Mozart and treat him *de haut en bas*?

Barroilhet has, it's true, given up his favourite interjection, but certainly not a host of extremely irritating decorations with which he believes he is

---

1 Barroilhet's 'Ah!': see article 19. The Opéra had staged *Don Giovanni* in 1834, and Berlioz reviewed the production (*JD,* 15 November 1835; translation in Julian Rushton, *W. A. Mozart. Don Giovanni.* Cambridge: Cambridge University Press, 1981, pp. 131–7). The encored aria was probably 'Fin ch'an dal vino' (sometimes misnamed the 'champagne aria').

2 Mozart confined trombones to scenes in which the statue of the Commendatore appears (the graveyard scene and the second act finale).

rejuvenating melodies that are a thousand times fresher than the shrivelled grace notes daily imported from Italy. His little arpeggio, his appoggiatura on the D-sharp in his duet with Zerlina, and his pause at the end of his serenade are so many examples of unspeakable licence, clashing what's more, and affording the most pitiable contrast with Mozart's style.³ Mlle Nau, in her turn, has a number of peccadillos of this kind to reproach herself with, especially in her duet. Mme Gras makes a change at the end of the trio of masks: where the second section of the final phrase is f^2–e-flat^2–d^2–c^2–b-flat^1–a^1–b-flat^1, she sings a^2–g^2–f^2–e-flat^2–g[?]–a^1, b-flat^1.⁴ All this is serious, extremely serious. You only take such liberties with very docile, humble, and stupid schoolboys. I must do Mlle Heinefetter the justice of saying that she doesn't offer Mozart any of her own inspirations; she sings the difficult role of Elvira with care, and I didn't notice that she modified her part at all.⁵ Exposed to the contagion of imitation, Mlle Heinefetter has the rare merit of having agreed to resist it. I, for my part, will remain infinitely grateful to her. Marié has merely made some small attempts [*velléités*] at ornamentation: he makes a cadence of the high A in Ottavio's aria, but at least it is written by the composer in the violin part.⁶ Dérivis does not allow himself any liberties in the role of Leporello, any more than Alizard does as the Commendatore. 'I can well believe it', you will say; 'putting musical affectations into the marble mouth of the Commendatore's statue would be the last straw!' You can never tell with monstrosities of this type! There are singers capable of anything. As for Ferdinand Prévost (Masetto), I don't have anything to justify: he's all attention, enthusiasm, and respect for the master, allied with a perhaps excessive modesty and the most invulnerable integrity.⁷

---

3   There is no D-sharp for Giovanni in the duet with Zerlina ('Là ci darem la mano'). Barroilhet may have approached e^1 from d-sharp^1, before the change of metre to 𝄴 where the tempo could be stretched to accommodate this license.

4   Berlioz does not make clear whether she rose to g^2, descending a seventh to a^1 or, which is more plausible, went down to g^1 and ascended to the tonic.

5   Kathinka Heinefetter (1820–58) was a German soprano. She made a very successful debut at the Opéra despite her German accent and nervous disposition. She retired from the stage in 1853.

6   This refers to Ottavio's act 2 aria, 'Il mio tesoro'. No doubt Marié was emulating the great Rubini (see article 7, note 7), who sang Ottavio at the Théâtre-Italien; he is reported to have made a trill from a^1 to b-flat^1 in this aria, presumably breaking off the sustained f^1 at bar 67 where these notes appear an octave higher in the violins. The final fermata a few bars on invites improvisation – there is a suggestion to that effect in the New Mozart Edition – but doesn't otherwise fit Berlioz's description.

7   Alizard: see article 6, note 3. Prévost; see article 17, note 3.

As I'm currently revealing the errors that spoil the performance of *Don Giovanni*, I cannot forget to point out that the tempo of the serenade ['Deh vieni alla finestra'] is much too slow. It is no doubt impossible to prove mathematically to conductors the clear difference between the dragging pulse adopted by the Opéra for this piece and that indicated by the sprightly gait of the accompaniment, Maelzel's metronome not having been invented when Mozart was composing. But I can say, setting aside my personal feeling, that several accomplished musicians – used to hearing *Don Giovanni* in German theatres where the Mozartian tradition is best respected – have made the same observation and feel, like me, that this speed is nearly twice too slow. It leads to a loss of colour in the whole scene, a breathless, extenuated, flabby rhythm, a desperate loss of ardour which makes the singer's job still more difficult by slowing down the vocal line, prolonging the silences, and by increasing the natural temptation he has to embellish, seems to justify him if he succumbs to it.

One further word: Mozart wrote the charming accompaniment of this serenade for a *mandolin*, so why play it at the Opéra on *two guitars*? Perhaps someone will say, 'Mandolin players are rare!' But they can soon be taught. I remember very well that this problem arose some twelve or thirteen years ago, at the rehearsals for *Don Giovanni* at the Odéon.[8] M. Seghers, then the theatre's assistant conductor who had never touched anything but the neck of a violin, offered to save the theatre from embarrassment: he took the music away to look at it, and at the end of a week he was a consummate mandolinist.[9] The thin, metallic sound of this instrument is nothing like that of *two guitars* in unison! In any case the basic fact, as ever, is that there's no room for discussion: Mozart wrote the part for a mandolin, it's a special instrument, so this absolutely what must be used, because he's the composer, because he's Mozart and that's what he wanted.

Barroilhet brings fire and brimstone into his aria 'Fin ch'han dal vino' but doesn't articulate clearly enough all the notes of the tune: the movement from the third to the fourth bar ('calda la testa') lacks sonority and precision, the interval of a fourth from F to B-flat being almost inaudible. One would think, because of the speed of the phrase, one was hearing F–G. instead of F–B-flat. He seems less at ease in the simple recitatives than in those of the modern school, which demand more of the singer; but still, he's an excellent Figaro!

---

8   A version of the Don Juan story based on Molière's play and E.T.A. Hoffmann's essay, but using Mozart's music, had been played at the Odéon on 24 December 1827.

9   François-Jean-Baptiste Seghers (1801–81), French violinist and conductor. The tuning of the mandolin strings is the same as the violin's.

22

Liszt's Concert at the Conservatoire

JD, 16 May 1841

The programme on 25 April consisted entirely of works by Beethoven: the overture Die Weihe des Hauses *(The Consecration of the House); the 'Emperor' Concerto [no. 5] in E-flat, played by Liszt, who followed it with a transcription of the song* Adelaide; *the 'Kreutzer' Sonata in A played by Massart and Liszt; and the Pastoral Symphony conducted by Berlioz. Three lines about a singer that end the review are omitted.*

This concert had a fine and noble purpose! It was a homage rendered to the greatest modern composer by the leading virtuoso of the day. Liszt is busy, as we know, putting together the sum needed to complete the Beethoven monument.[1] He has already given several concerts in Germany for this cause, so he could not fail to invite the Parisians to add their belated offering as well; and they have responded with the best will in the world! The hall was full, the audience brilliant, full of enthusiasm and supremely intelligent.

The overture [*Die Weihe des Hauses*] op. 124, which opened the concert, was still unknown to the French public, but its fine qualities were immediately recognised, at least to judge by the warmth of their applause. It's one of six overtures in C by Beethoven, who had a particular affection for this key. The imposing, majestic introduction contains a theme of great beauty for the wind instruments. Then comes a trumpet fanfare whose style, despite its glitter, could be more distinguished; a very odd passage for bassoons is heard beneath, the tempo increases bit by bit to lead gradually from Andante maestoso to Allegro, as a way of passing from the first part of the work to the second without interruption. This Allegro is a fugue whose subject lacks

---

1   This inauguration finally took place in 1845, in Beethoven's birthplace, Bonn. See article 38.

the exquisite freshness found especially in the overture to *The Magic Flute*; it offers, on the contrary, something of the gothic roughness of themes by Handel. But it advances, marches and bounds along with such energy in its various transformations that, like it or not, one has to be swept along by its momentum. The interrupted cadence [*cadence rompue*] on A-flat in the final bars causes surprise, and an admiration that might be hard to explain, given that this cadence is so common; but here it is made fresh by the charm and novelty of the composer's way of introducing it.

But it was the Piano Concerto (in E-flat) that roused the greatest enthusiasm. Never indeed has such a player performed such music with the accompaniment of such a magnificent orchestra. Those long stately passages in the first movement, those cheerful melodies the piano shares with oboes and flutes, the religious song of violins in the Adagio, those dialogues of such originality during which the piano seems at times to caress the music, to be guided by it, to efface himself and to grovel like a slave before it; those piercing notes descending from the keyboard in slow octaves, like pearls in a golden vase, while wind instruments, conversing mysteriously among themselves, seem to be telling each other tender secrets, all that, evoked as Beethoven was able to imagine it, but not hear it, held the audience spellbound for three quarters of an hour. We were afraid to applaud, but applauded nonetheless; we interrupted a passage, only to repent having done so. Liszt surpassed himself in an interpretation of this work that was as poetic as it was faithful; he demonstrated all the depth and power of his talent, even while refusing to trade on the fame of his exceptional technique. He was sublime![2] I can't add anything to what I've already said about his fantasy on *Robert le diable*, which was requested with such insistence that, despite his stated intention that no music should be heard at this concert except Beethoven's, he had to give way. This brought cries of astonishment and delight, the first signs of which came from the orchestra which was momentarily at liberty. Then came the torrent of flowers flooding the stage, and bravos from the ladies who never clap, and everything that these days goes to make up great, fashionable triumphs, so wonderful, so rare, and imitations of which are so cold and ridiculous.

Massart happily overcame several of the terrible difficulties in the A-major Sonata, difficulties made still worse by the tempi Liszt took in the Allegros, so fast that they made the violin part almost impossible to manage.[3] He sang

---

2   According to D. Kern Holoman Berlioz conducted the concerto as well as the symphony; see *Berlioz*. Cambridge, Mass.: Harvard University Press, and London: Faber & Faber, 1989, p. 615.

3   Lambert-Joseph Massart (1811–92), by origin Belgian, was a fine violinist who also performed with his wife Louise-Aglaé Massart (1827–87), an excellent pianist whose Beethoven playing Berlioz also admired. The couple were

the theme beautifully in the variations (Andante), which allow the player more freedom and let him breathe a little amid the manifold dangers the composer was pleased to scatter in his path. The orchestra completed this excellent concert with the 'Pastoral' Symphony, performed with its customary majesty and skill.

As an entr'acte, M. Geffroy of the Comédie-Française gave a simple but touching recitation of some beautiful lines by M. Antony Deschamps on Beethoven.[4]

Chopin's concert took place a few days after Liszt's.[5] The superiority and originality of his pianistic talent cannot be contested. But his compositions, in their naïve and curious character, the boldness of his rhythms and harmonies, and a melodic style that is capricious, fleeting, and hard to grasp, are more remarkable still. Sadly, it requires a combination of extreme musicality, developed by study furthermore and with the closest attention, to catch this multitude of delicate, understated thoughts as they pass: all these go to make up Chopin's style, and several of them must necessarily go unnoticed in big halls and before the public at large. This, undoubtedly, is why opportunities to hear this marvellous player are so rare. He shuns overwhelming, motley crowds; he doesn't feel he can dominate them or hold his own against them, so the silence and composure of a select audience are, for him, indispensable.

He must have been satisfied in every particular with the audience assembled in Pleyel's salon; never was a musician listened to more carefully or better understood. Several pieces were encored, among which I should mention two études in an entirely new form and ravishing style.

---

    friendly with Berlioz, especially in his later years. Massart had studied with Rodolphe Kreutzer, after whom Beethoven's Sonata in A, op. 47, is named. Massart's own pupils at the Conservatoire included Wieniawski, Sarasate, and Kreisler.

4   Antoni Deschamps (1800–69), French poet, younger brother of Émile (see article 12, note 23); he wrote the words when Berlioz added a chorus to the finale movement ('Apotheosis') of his *Symphonie funèbre et triomphale*.

5   Chopin's recital was given on 26 April 1841.

23

Paris Opéra: Poultier's Debut in *Guillaume Tell*

JD, 19 October 1841

Placide-Alexandre-Guillaume Poultier (1814–87) was a French tenor at the Opéra from 1841, when he took over the role of Arnold in Guillaume Tell *on 4 October, to 1851. He was particularly successful in Halévy's* La Juive *and in Auber's* La Muette de Portici.

The arrival of a new tenor on the stage of the Opéra is an event whose musical importance becomes greater by the day.[1] It's easy indeed to think ahead to a time not so far in the future when the staging of most of the great works in the repertoire will be impossible unless some young singer, with talent and a voice, with a figure and a voice, with sensitivity and a voice, with energy and fire and a voice, comes to the aid of the theatre, the composers, and the public – who after all have a stake in this, even if in these areas they seem sometimes to have gone into retirement. We need a tenor made for the music and not a virtuoso for whom the music must be made: an artist who sings his roles and can avoid *accommodating* them to the needs of his organ. We need a tenor whose strong, vibrant, beautiful chest voice goes from at least e to b′ flat[1] (an octave and a half), whose low notes are truly acceptable and sonorous, whose head notes are pure and achieved without effort, who can sing at speed without losing energy, and can hold a g′ and even an a′ without fear in an Andante. These various vocal qualities are not often allied in the same individual with those of an actor. But we must not despair of finding them: we know that M. Pillet has his eye on a young man

---

[1] When Berlioz wrote this review, it was not long after three articles from the *JD* (22 September 1839, 17 March 1840, and 10 January 1841) that formed a satirical account of the rise and fall of operatic tenors. He reprinted them in *Les Soirées de l'orchestre* (sixth evening).

whose musical and dramatic studies are in the hands of capable teachers, and for whom Nature has done her best.[2] We've heard him again recently in one of the most difficult roles in the repertoire, that of Robert [in Meyerbeer's *Robert le diable*], and we share the hopes that this event has raised in the Opéra's director. There remains the great test before the public, without which one can harbour only more or less well-founded conjectures, and which alone is decisive.

Poultier undoubtedly possesses some of the qualities we look for in a tenor. But what he lacks seems to me to restrict him necessarily to specialist roles. His voice is gentle and at times touching, but it lacks those sympathetic vibrations which move and sweep the masses along. It's consistent, even if without much strength, from e to a^1; his b flat^1 and b natural^1 in chest voice don't sound without effort, or without detriment to beauty of sound. His head voice is agreeable, but he must be careful not to force its production, as currently it sounds a good quarter of a tone sharp, and that's the worst way in which to be out of tune. As for agility, it's totally lacking and we would be very surprised if the range and strength of his voice allowed him to sing only in the grandest operatic style, in roles of pathos and passion. Sadly, this is not the case, and the exalted, lyrical style is the one that, out of them all, is least suitable to his delicate vocal reserve. Maybe, given extended practice, it will develop by changing in timbre and expression: the unique example of Duprez is there to prove, if need be, that it can be done.

Poultier's diction is good, even if he has a problem that smacks of the inflexibility of his recent studies and the minute care with which each word is articulated. It's plain that MM. Michelot and Ponchard, his two capable teachers, have taught him a certain way of opening the mouth, of closing the jaws, of extending the lips in order to produce certain vowels or consonants, all of which reminds one unwittingly of M. Jourdain's philosophy lesson in which that excellent fellow learns, by watching a demonstration, the correct way to pronounce an O.[3]

Despite the profound terror that tightened his throat at his first appearance, Poultier was very persuasive in the way he phrased several passages of the famous role of Arnold, so full of tenderness, despair, and enthusiasm. It's exclusively in the accents of tenderness that he succeeded, as we can

---

2   Raymond-François-Léon Pillet (1803–63) was a Parisian who studied law before becoming a journalist. In 1838 he was appointed royal commissioner for the Opéra, became associate director with Charles-Edmond Duponchel in 1840, and was in charge of the direction of the theatre from 1841 to 1847.

3   The reference is to act 2 scene 4 of Molière's *Le Bourgeois gentilhomme*, in which his teacher, the Master of Philosophy, explains that 'the vowel O is formed by opening your jaws and bringing your lips together by the two corners, the upper and the lower: O'.

easily hear. So it was that in the first act duet, the phrase 'O Mathilde!', sung slightly sharp at its first appearance in G-flat, was performed better and perfectly in tune when transposed up into A-flat when repeated. The final exclamation of 'Haine, malheur à nos tyrans!'('Hatred, disaster to our tyrans!') entirely lacked the character it forcefully demands. He was successful in the andante of the second act duet, 'Doux aveu' ('Sweet avowal'), but had completely ruined the recitative by singing sharp. In the trio, his voice's lack of power was obvious: placed between Bouché and Barroilhet, in the ensembles he could barely be heard and his phrase in the allegro, 'Vengeons-le, ne le pleurons plus' ('Avenge him, weep for him no more'), disappeared completely.[4] He had the good sense not to attempt the impossible by trying to use chest voice for the dangerous passage 'Ô ciel, Ô ciel, je ne te verrai plus' ('O Heaven! I shall never see you more') on g-sharp', a-sharp', b'. Why did Duprez accustom us in this passage to those three impassioned notes which, all of two years ago, gripped the whole house, and which the loveliest sounds of head voice could never replace?[5] He made a good showing faced with the danger one feared for him in the final aria, 'Asile héréditaire' ('Refuge of my fathers'). On the second evening especially, this magnificent andante brought the debutant a real success; but the following allegro, including the famous 'Suivez-moi!' ('Follow me!'), is not really within his powers; it requires a different voice to give full weight to this passionate call to arms, and to make this great cry of fury ring out, of a son who must avenge his father, of a lover who must win his beloved, and of a furious slave who is breaking his chains. So it's to roles of graceful second tenors that Poultier should be laying his claim.

This latter position, left vacant by Alexis Dupont's retirement, would have suited him on several fronts.[6] The embarrassment of the director is quite clear since, a few months ago, he engaged Wermeulen and Octave, who naturally will not give up their rightful posts to make way for a newcomer.[7] So there would be only one way to find Poultier a place at the Opéra, and that

---

4   Étienne Lucien Bouché (1807–91) was a French bass whose voice, according to Berlioz, was 'of unusual power when he has time to breathe'. Barriolhet: see article 19, note 1.

5   Duprez took these high notes in chest voice, an accomplishment he first displayed in this same role in the Italian premiere of Rossini's opera (Lucca, 1831).

6   Alexis Dupont; see article 6, note 3. Retirement from the Opéra left him free to sing in smaller spaces, more suited to his voice; there he proved highly successful.

7   Charles-Victor Wermeulen (?–1853), French tenor, made his debut in 1838, and pursued a career mainly in Rouen and Marseilles. He substituted for Mario at the Opéra (17 May 1840) in the title-role of *Robert le diable* and directed

would be to write roles specifically for him, as was done twenty-five years ago for a young singer called Roland, who appeared in Catel's *Sémiramis* and in the disjointed, barbarous *pasticcio* brazenly produced under the name *Don Juan*.[8] But as new operas don't follow each other that hastily in our main opera house, Poultier would have a long time to wait if he didn't use this time to appear in public by going round the main provincial cities. This is what he should be encouraged to do, for his benefit, as for ours.

---

the Théâtre du Havre from 1848 to 1851. Jean-Baptiste Octave sang in *Guillaume Tell* at the Opéra in 1842.

[8] A *pasticcio* is an opera put together from several pre-existing works. The Italian word means 'pie' or pastry; or, which would perhaps have been Berlioz's choice, 'mess'.

24

The Saint-Denis Organ

JD, 19 October 1841

Between 639 and the nineteenth century the Basilica of Saint-Denis was the burial place of forty-three kings and thirty-two queens of France. Cavaillé-Coll's initial proposal was for an organ of eighty-four stops, to be built over three years at a cost of 80,000 francs. Delays in the rebuilding of the cathedral allowed him time to reduce the stops to seventy-one.

The magnificent instrument M. Cavaillé has installed in the Église Saint-Denis has received unanimous approval. Even the maker's rivals are agreed in praising it, and organists can't stifle the regret that such a fine piece of work does emphatically not belong to Paris. It is indeed an admirable organ which combines, together with the finest qualities of the best organs of its kind, others which are unique to itself, thanks to details invented beyond doubt by M. Cavaillé. Its *diapasons* are very powerful, the *reeds* very strong and sonorous, and the cor anglais stop has a delightful timbre. There is a slight fault in the sixteen-foot stops in that the pedals are slow to speak. A remarkable new effect is that of the crescendo achieved by a mechanism placed under the feet but above the pedals, and which allows the organist to add as many stops as he likes *without taking his hands off the keyboard*.[1] This is truly splendid, and you have to hear the build-up of these choruses, these accumulating orchestras, to have a real idea of this invention's merits. The *vox humana*, which seems to have been made in imitation of that in Fribourg, is far from being as perfect. But I hasten to add that, if the Saint-Denis organ is inferior to the Fribourg one in this particular, it is superior in all others. The bellows alone are a masterpiece.[2]

---

1   These couplers are known as 'jeux de combinaison', in English 'ventils'.
2   Berlioz never visited Fribourg (Switzerland); he may have read about its cathedral organ in *La France musicale* (25 January 1840), but it is more likely that he had already heard about this remarkable instrument, constructed by Aloys Mooser, from Liszt, who visited the cathedral and played its organ in September 1836, and from George Sand's account of her visit there with Liszt, in the tenth of her *Lettres d'un voyageur* (published in the *Revue des deux mondes* in 1836 and in book form in 1837).

25

Fourth Conservatoire Concert

RGM, 27 February 1842

The programme on 20 February included Mendelssohn's overture The Hebrides ('Fingal's Cave'), *Pauline Viardot-Garcia singing scenes from Gluck's* Orphée, *and Beethoven's Seventh Symphony.*

Before M. Habeneck began, he several times expressed his desire to exact from the audience a more serious, profound silence. He succeeded, not without some readily understandable gestures of impatience, in finally quelling the confused rumble circulating in the hall, and his insistence seemed to be saying to the public: 'Now listen, you pitiless gossipers, frivolous cavatina fans, be finally, totally, completely, absolutely quiet! No moving about, no breathing (no point asking you to stop thinking!). My task is to perform an incomparable work of art in your presence. It's a work of *new* music, of fresh, poetic inspiration, which will remain an enigma to you, but to which we musicians, together with various intelligent amateurs, need to listen with all the respect it deserves. Silence!' And in fact there was silence, and Mendelssohn's overture *Fingal's Cave* began.

In the Orkney islands there's a cave well known for its natural colonnade and for the strange noises the sea makes there.[1] When Mendelssohn visited this strange palace, raised above the waves by some volcanic explosion and nowadays traditionally dedicated to Fingal, he was struck by the mysterious harmonies with which the breaking waves surround the listener, multiplied by echoes resounding from the crags of these numberless pillars, and the idea came to him of turning them into a musical composition. That's why

---

1 'Fingal's Cave' is not in the Orkneys but on Staffa (Inner Hebrides), a small island near to the Isle of Mull. The Scottish tribal leader Fingal is legendary. The overture (1830) is properly called *Die Hebriden*; Mendelssohn conceived its opening on the ferry to Tobermory (on Mull), where no crags are to be seen, before he took the boat-trip to Staffa.

this overture is called *Fingal's Cave*. It's already been played several times in Paris in between two quadrilles, and before the bored strollers in the Salle Saint-Honoré. But it's not in conditions like these that a work of this nature should be played, so until now we've resisted our desire to hear it. It needed performance in the hall of the Conservatoire.

I was saying just now that the music's new; in fact, it struck me as something unknown, recent, and freshly blossoming. It's verdant, radiating youth. One feels that only a choice spirit, all-seeing and of an extreme lucidity, could have created it: the form resembles no form, the style is comparable with no other; it's a pure invention. The theme has something naïve about it, like the ancient melodies of Nordic peoples, which lends a supreme quality to all the undulating movements that the composer's fantasy lays upon it; the song of the cellos, then taken up by the violins, charms by its very vagueness, by its indecisive allure, by its incompleteness; it melts magically, what's more, into the gentle, arpeggiated rustling of high violins, as it also does into the dull murmurs of low cellos. The B minor theme is played first by violas, bassoons, and cellos under a held F-sharp on first and second violins in octaves which, through the modulation of the tune, after being the dominant of the key of B, becomes the third of the key of D and finally the tonic of F-sharp. These successive transformations of a single note, already employed in a different way by some modern composers, here produce the most graceful effect. The nuances of *forte* and *piano*, the *crescendos* and *decrescendos* are never foreseeable; noise breaks out suddenly and likewise dies away; sometimes one hears it coming to life from an imperceptible distance; it grows, and one expects the harmonious rumour to increase and become powerful, formidable; on the contrary, it dies away, it's defeated, the winds have wafted it away, all is calm and silence ... Then the howling of old Ocean rises once more, and this time shakes the echoing grotto to its most unfathomable depths.

Despite a fairly large number of different patterns, either contrasting or combined, in the orchestration of this unusual and charming composition, each part moves at its ease, and the result of the ensemble is one of perfect clarity. As to the overall sound of the orchestration, it doesn't resemble anything known to me; it's an orchestra of crystal, vibrating at the slightest contact. The two clarinets in A, finally echoing together the cellos' tune over a held string chord, blossom and flourish in delightful fashion above the harmony. After a staccato crescendo of great piquancy and a lively development, the overture finishes pianissimo, sharing this type of ending with those of all the Mendelssohn overtures I know. I adore this calm disdain for applause; but on this point shouldn't we remind ourselves of the ideas of most of those disappointed amateurs, who have vainly espoused the banal form of theatrical overtures, run-of-the-mill tunes, foreseeable recapitulations, and the standard noise at the appointed place? In their astonishment, anxiety, and bad temper, they're like a sufferer from catarrh who, having gone to sleep in a feather bed, suddenly wakes up in the middle of a wood on grass wet with dew. What joy, on the contrary, for those with healthy lungs, to breathe the balmy forest air and to escape, if only for a moment, the noxious atmosphere of human habitation! It's for having allowed us to taste, last Sunday, this rare, poetic joy, that today one must sincerely, and with every sort of admiring exclamation, give thanks to M. Felix Mendelssohn. What's more, he would certainly have been delighted with the way the Conservatoire orchestra performed his work; we may doubt whether, anywhere in the world, one could find a performance more perfect and more completely beautiful in every respect.

26

Cherubini

JD, 20 March 1842

Luigi (Carlo Zanobi Salvadore Maria) Cherubini, born in Florence in 1760, had died on 25 March 1842.

The life of this great composer can be offered as a model for young artists in almost every particular. Cherubini's studies were long and patient, his compositions numerous, his enemies powerful. To the inflexibility of his character and the tenacity of his convictions must be added a real dignity that kept him always respectable, and which, sad to say, one does not often find in even the most eminent of artists. He was born in Florence towards the end of 1760, was taught from the age of nine by Bartolomeo and Alessandro Felici, and later by Bizzari and Castrucci, all composers nowadays forgotten.[1] He didn't complete his musical education until around his twentieth year under Sarti.[2] The Grand Duke of Tuscany [later Holy Roman Emperor Leopold II] then took him under his special protection, and Sarti, as payment for his lessons, was happy to get his pupil to write a large number of works which he inserted among his own, unscrupulously keeping all the honour of them for himself. Ultimately however, the teacher had to decide on launching his pupil's career, and Cherubini, finally free to see his music applauded under his own name, wrote several scores for Italian theatres, the success of which soon led to him being invited to London.[3] It was there that he wrote *La finta principessa* and *Giulio Sabino*. A few years later *Ifigenia in Aulide* appeared with great success in Turin. After *Faniska*

---

1   Bartolomeo Felice (1985–1776), Italian organist and composer, and his son Alessandro (1742–72), harpist and composer. Pietro Bizzarri (?–?); Pietro Castrucci (1679–1752), Italian violinist and pupil of Corelli.
2   Giuseppe Sarti (1729–1802), Italian composer, teacher and conductor.
3   Cherubini stayed in London from the autumn of 1784 to July 1786.

was mounted in Vienna, he came back to England to conduct the concerts of the Philharmonic Society.

On his return to France, his friend Viotti, who was very popular, introduced him to elegant society and arranged his entry to most of the capital's salons.[4] Cherubini's sole dream at that time was to write something for a French opera house, and Marmontel gave him the libretto of *Démophoön*.[5] Although this work is very dramatic and made for music, it had already sunk an opera by Vogel, of which only the touching overture has survived.[6] Cherubini's *Démophoön* cannot be called much of a success, but the emphatic beauties one could not miss gave notice of what we could expect from the composer in this grandiose, serious genre.

Shortly after this, he was appointed musical director of the Opéra-Italien and, either to support works that were being staged there or perhaps also quite often to satisfy singers' caprices, he returned to the role of anonymous collaborator which he'd abandoned on leaving Sarti. This led him to insert a quantity of charming numbers into various scores, including the famous quartet in *I viaggiatori felici* and the less well-known but equally fine one in Gazzaniga's *Don Giovanni*; which goes to prove there was an Italian composer called Gazzaniga, who wrote an opera called *Don Giovanni*. Mozart also wrote one.[7]

In the middle of composing these tuneful fragments for the skilful soloists of the Théatre-Italien, Cherubini was looking at the spirit of the French school, and wondering whether, by greater use of a dramatic style, of unexpected modulations and orchestral effects, one could make up for the French singers' lack of skill. The question was answered in the affirmative by his opera *Lodoïska*, whose success would have been longer and greater if Kreutzer's little work, on the same subject and with the same title, hadn't displaced it through being easier to perform and through the graceful lightness of its tunes.[8] We know that, in France especially, large, fine enterprises

---

4   Giovanni Battista Viotti (1755–1824), Italian violinist and composer.
5   The libretto of *Démophoön* was adapted by Jean-François Marmontel (1723–99) from Metastasio's *Demofoonte*. *Démophoön* was premiered at the Opéra on 5 December 1788. It lasted for only eight performances.
6   Johann Christophe Vogel (1756–88), German composer and admirer of Gluck. His opera *Démophon* [*sic*] does survive intact; Berlioz means that only the overture was remembered.
7   Giuseppe Gazzaniga (1743–1818), Italian composer, pupil of Porpora and Piccinni. His *Don Giovanni* appeared early in 1787 and its libretto served as a starting-point for Lorenzo da Ponte's for Mozart's *Don Giovanni*.
8   In a rivalry typical of the Paris theatres (cf. *Iphigénie en Tauride* and *Démophoön*), *Lodoïska* by Rodolphe Kreutzer (1766–1831) was premiered at the Théâtre Favart on 1 August 1791, shortly after Cherubini's *Lodoïska* at the

are often eclipsed by others that are merely pretty. Even so, Cherubini's *Lodoïska* caused a great sensation in the musical world; and the impetus it gave to the art of opera, seconded by the almost identical efforts of Méhul, Berton, and Lesueur, launched an era of glory for the French school, the possibility of whose arrival had understandably been in doubt.

Lodoïska was followed, at smaller or larger intervals, by *Élisa ou le Mont Saint-Bernard*, *Médée*, *L'Hôtellerie portugaise*, and finally *Les Deux Journées*, which rapidly became popular. It's in *Élisa* that one finds the chorus of monks looking for travellers buried under the snow, which has too rarely been performed at Conservatoire concerts, and whose impact is so realistic, one feels like shouting, 'This music makes you shiver!'. In the same opera, it's understandable we should admire the bell scene in which, by turning constantly around a single bell-note that is heard without interruption from beginning to end, the master musician calls on all the harmonic resources at his disposal and on his rare ingenuity in moving from one modulation to another.

Médée is a work that's still more complete. It has remained in the repertoire of a great number of German opera houses, and it is a cause of shame for ours that it's been ignored for so long. The same applies to *Les Deux Journées*, which there was recently a vague notion of reviving at the Opéra-Comique, but which was finally left to moulder on the shelf because it was *impossible* to give the composer, for the role of the water carrier Henri, the singer he asked for. So much for these laughable *impossibilities*, spoken of as seriously as if it was a question of resuscitating Talma.[9] *L'Hôtellerie portugaise* has been less lucky. This score hasn't even been engraved. All that remains of it is a very interesting comic trio (often included in concerts) and the overture, the Andante of which contains a canon on the tune *Folies d'Espagne*, mysterious in colouring and original in effect.[10]

Shortly before the run of *Les Deux Journées*, Cherubini was appointed as one of the inspectors of teaching at the Conservatoire.[11] This post was for a long time the only one he filled, Napoleon having had, as we know, the bizarre affectation – and certainly one that was unworthy of him – of letting

---

Théâtre Feydeau (18 July). The subject-matter is a model for the popular subgenre of 'rescue opera'.

9 Talma: see article 1, note 8.
10 'Les Folies d'Espagne' was the standard French way of referring to 'La folia', a tune (and/or harmonic progression) used by many composers across several centuries.
11 When the Conservatoire was founded in 1795, Cherubini was made an inspector of teaching together with Méhul, Lesueur, Grétry, and Gossec. He remained at the institution, in one role or another and eventually as its director, until the year of his death.

Cherubini know the antipathy he felt for his person and his music. The reason generally given for this estrangement was a number of rude replies Cherubini gave to some fairly unmerited remarks Napoleon made about his music; it's claimed the composer said to the First Consul one day, with a vivacity quite understandable in the circumstances: 'Citizen-consul, you stick to winning battles, and let me get on with my job about which you know nothing!' On another occasion, when Napoleon had confessed his predilection for music that was *monotonous*, that's to say gently lulling, Cherubini responded, if with more finesse than humour: 'I understand, you like music that doesn't stop you thinking about affairs of state'. Such repartee, as will be seen later, certainly fitted Cherubini's character and turn of phrase. In any case it's certain that Napoleon constantly found ways to damage his *amour-propre* by lauding Paisiello and Zingarelli in his presence every time there was an opportunity, leaving him out in the cold like some mediocrity, and obstinately pronouncing his name in the French fashion to make clear he didn't think him worthy of an Italian name.[12]

It was only in 1805 that Napoleon, after his victory at Austerlitz, and knowing that Cherubini was in Vienna working on his opera *Faniska*, summoned him and was good enough no longer to pronounce his name in the French fashion. He even entrusted him with organising private concerts but never failed, when they took place, to criticise their arrangement and ask Cherubini for the most ridiculous things. For instance, he wanted the aria for the father of Paisiello's *Nina* (an aria for bass) to be sung by the castrato Crescentini.[13] When Cherubini pointed out that the poor fellow could only sing it an octave higher, 'Well then', replied Napoleon, 'let him sing it, I'm not insisting on an octave!' Which was just as well, because if the great man had *insisted on an octave*, and demanded the singer produce a deep voice, despite all his goodwill it would have been impossible for him to manage.

It was in Vienna too that Napoleon had the endless discussion with Cherubini, which he'd initiated so many times with Paisiello and Lesueur, about orchestral nuances. The giant of battles, the virtuoso of the cannon, didn't like it when musical instruments took it upon themselves to raise their voices: *forte*s and noisy *tutti*s made him impatient. He would claim that the orchestra was *playing too high*, and once he'd made his poor conductors understand that he actually meant *playing too loud*, they were forced to abandon any thought of obeying the composer's intentions, let alone the

---

12 .The 'French fashion' means saying 'Ch' like 'Sh'; ironically, Berlioz in his *Memoirs* (chapter 9) satirized Cherubini's *Italian* accent!
13 Paisiello's *Nina o sia la pazza per amore* (*Nina or the Girl Mad with Love*) was premiered at the Royal Place, Caserta in 1789. The subject is the same as Dalayrac's *Nina*.

meaning of the music, and tell the players to bring the sound level down to *pianissimo*. The music then lulled the great man, and he could *dream of affairs of state*. In the place of choir and orchestra, Napoleon would have been happy with an Aeolian harp. Certainly nothing is less like the harmonious sighs of that instrument than Cherubini's orchestra. But the Emperor's exclusive taste for music that was gentle, calm and dreamlike, did perhaps contribute, by alerting the composer to this side of his art, to his discovery of the curious type of *decrescendo* of which he left such admirable examples in some of his religious works. No one before Cherubini and no one after him has possessed to this degree the technique of *chiaroscuro*, of the half-tint, of the progressive fading of the sound; when applied to certain essentially melodic passages of his masses, it inspired him to veritable marvels of religious expression, and to discovering exquisite delicacies of instrumentation.

On his return from Vienna, Cherubini suffered from a nervous illness that caused his family serious anxiety and made all musical work impossible for him. Composition being forbidden him, he turned, in his profound melancholy, to a passionate love of flowers; he studied botany and was never happier than when working with plants, making herbaria, reading Linnaeus, Jussieu, and Tournefort.[14] This passion even seemed to outlive the illness that had caused it, and when, fully recovered and supported by the prince de Chimay, he was able to get back to his long interrupted work, it was only in obedience to the firm entreaties of his hosts that he decided to write a solemn mass for three voices, one of the masterpieces of the genre.[15]

Back in Paris, full of health and confidence in the strength and brilliance of his genius, he wrote *Pimmalione* for the Théâtre-Italien, *Le Crescendo* for the Opéra-Comique, and *Les Abencérages* for the Opéra. I know nothing about the first two of these, but we have heard various fragments of the third which give a good idea of its merits. Especially the aria 'Suspendez à ces murs mes armes, ma bannière' ('Hang on these walls my arms, my banner'), so often sung by Ponchard, is surely one of the most beautiful things that dramatic music can boast of since Gluck.[16] There is nothing simultaneously more true, more deeply felt, more noble or touching. One doesn't know which to admire most: the recitative, so full of despondency, the melody of the Andante so desolate and tender, or the final Allegro in which the return of misery provokes cries of anguish from Zoraïde's unhappy lover.

---

14 Carolus Linnaeus (Carl von Linné, 1707–78), Swedish naturalist; Antoine Laurent de Jussieu (1748–1835) and Joseph Pitton de Tournefort (1656–1708), French botanists.
15 Cherubini's Mass in F was premiered on St Cecilia's day, 22 November 1808.
16 Louis-Antoine-Éléonore Ponchard (1787–1868), French tenor.

Cherubini improvised, one might say, two occasional operas, together with three other composers: *L'Oriflamme* and *Bayard à Mézières*.[17] I know of only one item from *L'Oriflamme*, a chorus based on the *decrescendo* pattern mentioned above: it was performed eight or ten years ago in the Conservatoire concerts and never failed to produce there the strongest impression by its exquisite delicacy and its complete originality. Given the truly delightful effects Cherubini has been able to extract from voices and orchestra in their pianissimos, the distinction of his melodic style, and the finesse of his orchestration that never deserts him, and the grace with which his harmonies and modulations follow one another, one is allowed to regret that he has written far more in the contrary style. His energetic pieces don't always shine with the qualities that should be natural for them, the orchestra sometimes, even in his masses, making brusque, inelegant gestures that don't conform with the religious style.

The Restoration finally did Cherubini justice; the Bourbons set their hearts on making him forget his problems with Napoleon, and promised him the post of superintendent of the King's music in the future. On his return from the island of Elba, the Emperor however finally felt he should appoint him Chevalier of the Légion d'honneur. In addition, around the same time, the number of members of the Académie des Beaux-Arts having been increased, Cherubini entered the Institute. On Martini's death, he succeeded him and shared with Lesueur the post of superintendent of the King's music. From then on Cherubini devoted himself almost exclusively to sacred composition.[18] For Louis XVIII's chapel and that of Charles X he composed a number of prayers, motets, and masses, of which the two main ones are known and admired by every European musician – I'm talking of the mass for Charles X's coronation and the first Requiem for four voices parts.[19] It's true, several passages in the Coronation Mass whose style evinces the fault I mentioned just now, contain more violence than vigour, and display little in the way of religious feeling. But so many others are beyond reproach, while its Communion March is an inspiration of such quality that it should make us forget its few faults and immortalise the work to which it belongs.

---

17   *L'Oriflamme*, one-act opera by Berton, Kreutzer, Méhul, and Paër, premiered at the Opéra on 1 February 1814 (Cherubini is not credited as a contributor); *Bayard à Mézières*, one-act opéra-comique by Boieldieu, Catel, Cherubini, and Nicolò (Nicolas Isouard), premiered at the Opéra on 12 February 1814. Cherubini wrote only a trio, an ensemble, and the concluding warlike song.
18   Martini: see article 8, note 12.
19   Cherubini's *Messe de Requiem* in C minor, dedicated 'à la mémoire de Louis XVI', was premiered in the Basilique Saint-Denis, the traditional resting place of French kings, on 21 January 1817. It is for mixed voices, unlike Cherubini's second Requiem, for male voices in three parts.

Here is an expression of the mystical in all its purity, Catholic contemplation and ecstasy! If Gluck, with his decisive instrumental melodies, imbued with a kind of passion that is melancholy but not dreamy, found in the march from *Alceste* the ideal of the antique religious style in the march from *Alceste*, Cherubini with his melody, likewise instrumental, vague, veiled, elusive, was able to reach the most mysterious depths of Christian meditation. Gluck's march, passionate in its very gravity and from time to time emitting reproachful sighs from a suffering heart barely resigned to the will of the gods, distresses the listener and draws burning tears; the march bears the character of a religion that is poetic, yet sensual. Cherubini's work breathes only of divine love, a faith without clouds, a soul's calm and infinite serenity in the presence of its creator; no earthly clamour disturbs this celestial peace and, if it draws tears from the eyes, they fall so gently, and the reverie it produces is so profound that, listening to this seraphic chant, one is carried beyond thoughts of art and memory of the real world, is unaware of his own emotion. If ever the word *sublime* was rightly and truly applied, it refers to Cherubini's Communion March.

The [C-Minor] Requiem is, in my opinion, its composer's masterpiece in every respect; no other work by this great master can bear comparison with it for the abundance of its ideas, the majesty of its forms and the unfailing loftiness of its style and, were it not for the violent fugue on the meaningless phrase 'quam olim Abrahae promisisti' ('which once you promised to Abraham'), one would have to say also for its constant truth of expression. The 'Agnus' with its decrescendo surpasses everything that's been attempted in this genre: it's the gradual collapse of the sufferer, we see him fade and die, we hear him expire. The technique of this score is also beyond price: the vocal parts are closely packed but clear, the instrumentation is colourful and powerful but always worthy of its subject. There's no need to mention that this *Requiem* is far superior to his later one, which Cherubini composed three years ago for his own funeral and which, following his last wish, was performed at Saint-Roch this morning.[20] The overall plan of this is much less imposing, and the breath of inspiration less evident: that kind of brusqueness, or tendency to anger, which manifests itself too often in some of Cherubini's works, is more evident, and the ideas are not always of the highest distinction. Even so, it contains entire movements that are generously apportioned and of the greatest beauty, among them the 'Lacrimosa'.

Cherubini wrote some string quartets in a fine style, which are too little known. His last opera *Ali Baba* was removed from the Opéra stage after ten

---

20 Cherubini's *Deuxième Messe de Requiem* in D minor was premiered by the Société des concerts on 23 March 1838 and replayed in the Église Saint-Roch on 19 March 1842.

or twelve performances, for one of those financial reasons that have seen off so many other excellent works ever since the Opéra became a private enterprise, an industrial company.[21]

Nothing was more total or more unvarying than Cherubini's convictions. In matters of harmony especially, he did not admit the possibility of any modification or even a mere extension of the established rules. On this subject he often had very lively discussions with the knowledgeable professor Reicha and with Choron.[22] And one day, when a systematic theorist, less well known than those two masters and wholly absorbed in the strange doctrine of musical theology of which he is both disciple and founder, insisted on arguing with him, Cherubini, boiling with fury but not willing to show the door to his obstinate opponent, shouted, 'Out of the house! Out, I say, or *I'll throw myself out of the window*! And everyone will say it's you who pushed me!'

The tendency of his spirit was eminently caustic, and his conversation was full of mordant expressions, laced with piquant and incisive abruptness.

One day, passing by the courtyard of the [Salle des] Menus-Plaisirs at the moment when a concert was to be given by a young composer I knew, somebody wanted to take him into the hall to hear the new symphony which was then the subject of very animated musical controversy: 'Leave me be', said Cherubini, 'I've no need to know how not to compose!'[23] On another occasion, at a rehearsal of Beethoven's great *Missa solemnis*, I was complaining about its D-major fugue with a frankness that my admiration for the composer could, I think, excuse. A pianist, no doubt a man of some merit,

---

21 *Ali Baba ou les Quarante voleurs* (*Ali Baba or the Forty Thieves*) was premiered at the Opéra on 22 July 1833. It partly used music from an unperformed opera *Koukourgi* (1793) and had only eleven performances. (Alfred Loewenberg, *Annals of Opera*. London: John Calder, 1978, column 753.) Berlioz excoriated it in chapter 47 of his *Memoirs*. Berlioz's remarks about the Opéra perhaps require some context: 'While, for 150 years, everybody had gone bankrupt directing the Opéra, [Louis] Véron, thanks to his subvention and the successes of Auber, Rossini, and Meyerbeer, retired in 1835 having made his fortune, leaving the post to the architect Duponchel, who had less success. His successor Léon Pillet (1841–47) renewed the series of failing directorships: he resigned ... leaving a debt of half a million francs'. (J.-G. Prodhomme, *L'Opéra*, 1669–1925. Geneva: Minkoff (reprint), 1972, p. 37).
22 Anton Reicha (1770–1836), French composer, theorist, and teacher of Czech birth. As well as Berlioz, his pupils included Liszt, Gounod, and Franck. Alexandre-Étienne Choron (1771–1834), see p. 104, note 11.
23 The Salle des Menus-Plaisirs is another name for the Salle du Conservatoire in the Rue Bergère. The young composer in question was Berlioz, at the first performance of *Symphonie fantastique*.

especially in those days, and one who's written a lot of music, took up the cudgels on behalf of Beethoven's fugal, anti-religious racket. Cherubini appears in the lobby in the middle of the discussion and, despite my signals for my adversary to keep silent, he continues, on the contrary, in a manner to attract the attention of Cherubini, who turns round and asks, 'What's going on here?' 'It's Monsieur', replies the pianist shamelessly, 'who doesn't like fugues'. 'That's because fugues don't like him'.

Cherubini was pitiless even to his pupils, when his wit saw the chance of a put-down. One of them was going to have a new opera performed, and Cherubini attended the dress rehearsal in a box. After the second act, the young composer, full of anxiety, comes to the box and waits in vain for some of those kind words one needs so much in situations like this: 'So, dear maître', he finally says, 'you're saying nothing to me!' – 'What in God's name do you want me to say to you!' replies Cherubini with a laugh; 'I've been listening to you for two hours and you still haven't said anything to me!' The taunt was all the more hurtful in that it lacked accuracy or justice. The pupil's work was a great success.[24]

---

24   This pupil is not identified but cannot be Berlioz. In general, this obituary is more tactful than the frank personal reminiscences of Cherubini in Berlioz's *Memoirs*.

27

Sixth Conservatoire Concert

RGM, 27 March 1842

The items in this concert of 21 March were Mozart's Symphony no. 40 in G minor (K.550), two movements from Mendelssohn's oratorio Saint Paul, *a concertino by Vogt for oboe and orchestra, played by Verroust, the 'Dies irae' from Cherubini's Requiem in C minor and Beethoven's Second Symphony.*

Mozart's Symphony in G minor, as usual, gave the greatest pleasure, and the minuet was encored. The excerpts from Mendelssohn's oratorio *Saint Paul* were as yet unknown to me, and I'm at a loss to understand why there's been such a delay in bringing this fine work to Paris when England, Germany, and even some cities in regional France have given complete performances of it some time ago. Whatever the reason, the two extracts brought to us last Sunday are admirable compositions. The first chorus in E-flat, accompanied by a repeated pattern on the first violins, is couched in a calm and a purity that are truly angelic; if this is not religious music, then such a thing has never existed. The harmony is silky, the style of the melody, tender and suave, lends a further charm to the timbre of the cellos, and the incessant accompaniment of the first violins decorates the ensemble, without disturbing its gentle gravity. The form of the work is also highly distinguished: the orchestra and choir are not always combined, sometimes the orchestra is silent, allowing the voices to sing unaccompanied, and sometimes on the contrary it's the orchestra that's heard on its own. Then there are those effects of half-tint and pianissimo which only the greatest composers know how to obtain from such large forces. In a word, this choral work is, in my view, a true masterpiece, a product of inspiration and technique, beautiful, irreproachable, complete.

If the Conservatoire public deserved the reputation of connoisseurship that it currently enjoys, although it aspires to no such thing, then no doubt that public would have greeted this first movement of Mendelssohn's celebrated oratorio with the liveliest enthusiasm; instead of which we had at best fifteen or twenty people applauding. The public seemed to find the work fairly agreeable, but as for being moved, as for admiring and comprehending ... as I live and breathe, the oysters which half-open at midday on the seashore offer as much admiration to the sun!! The second extract, in an excellent style and for solo bass and chorus, had less success than its predecessor: its mood is full of sadness and, if it seems rather long, only the persistently heavy rhythm in the basses should be held responsible. Nothing tires us more quickly than such heavy, continual down-beat accents in the bass, particularly in a slow movement when they're not aiming at any brilliant effect that's part of the work's overall plan. It's one of the details of Handel's style that I think it's not good to imitate. Alizard sang the bass solo very well, and without deviating at all, at the ends of phrases, from the style adopted by the composer. This is how to be a faithful interpreter; this is how a singer can be a true artist.

But now listen! The orchestra is lit up from port to starboard, the trumpets and trombones are blasting away! The composer however – idle fellow – hasn't used either the bass drum or ophicleides!! As long as there's M. Verroust to come and play us an oboe solo! This instrumentalist is first class, he has all the resources of the instrument at his command, drawing from it sounds remarkable for their fullness and sweetness, and he's a wonderful 'singer'. But there's no need for those great blasts from the brass to introduce him. Even so, this concertino by M. Vogt, apart from its rather cautious instrumentation and its excessive length, contains passages of true merit.[1] M. Verroust had a great success.

The 'Dies irae' from Cherubini's first *Requiem* replaced the aria from *Euryanthe* initially announced on the poster. The audience understood that the Société des concerts wanted to pay homage to the great master we have just lost, and this terrible text of the dead, with its vocal parts so grandly imagined, so full of terror and shudders in the orchestra, was loudly applauded by both public and musicians. The concert ended with Beethoven's noble, proud Symphony [no. 2] in D major.

---

1   Louis-Stanislas-Xavier Verroust (1814–63) and Auguste-Gustave Vogt (1781–1870), French oboists.

28

Thalberg's Concerts

JD, 26 April 1842

Sigismond Thalberg made triumphant tours round Europe between 1837 and 1848.[1] For some musicians he was 'the greatest pianist', but for others Liszt was 'the only pianist'.[2] For the first concert on 12 April, his contributions were three of his own Fantasias on themes from Mozart's Don Giovanni, *Donizetti's* Anna Bolena, *and Rossini's* Mosè in Egitto. *For the second, on 21 April, he played Fantasias on Donizetti's* Lucia di Lammermoor *and Rossini's* Semiramide, *and a 'Grand Duo' for two pianos on themes from Bellini's* Norma.

After a three-year absence, Thalberg has returned both powerful and calm, as in the days of his earliest triumphs and, if possible, even happier. He in fact belongs to the small number of artists for whom everything succeeds, even success. It's not held against him that he has great talent, that he is favoured by glory and fortune; and were he to possess, together with Beethoven's genius, the name of Napoleon, and the wealth of the Banque de France, he would not be loved any the less. Does he take the trouble to become famous and rich? Not in the slightest. Before leaving for Paris, he writes to a friend (he has them) to announce his forthcoming arrival and a concert. The friend duly hires the Théâtre-Italien, orders a printer to put up notices: 'Tuesday … April, first concert by M. Sigismond Thalberg' and organises a wretched little orchestra, rickety, knock-kneed, peevish, made for playing overtures no one will listen to and accompanying singers who will hardly be heard. The day before the concert, the virtuoso arrives, puts together his programme in a few hours, looks in at the theatre for a few minutes to reassure himself that

---

1   See also article 12, note 8.
2   Berlioz would have chosen his friend Liszt as 'the' pianist; he said of Thalberg that he played his own music better than other people's, which he would not have said of Liszt.

the beautiful ladies who dream of him will be there on his return, and next day, hey presto!, the house is *full* of them.

First concert: he makes his entrance, huge applause; he plays, enormous applause; he walks off, immense applause. He comes across the cashier: 'How much? – Twelve thousand francs! – Perfect!' And off he goes, smoking his cigar like a simple man. Second concert: he makes his entrance again, applause; he bows to the audience, uproar; he plays, coronation! Even flowers and laurel wreaths aren't enough, someone throws him a crown of *gold*, or at least 'gilt', according to a new process invented by M. de Ruolz, which is both delicate and utterly deserved, as there's no doubt this great pianist plays the piano magisterially. Crown of gold apart, the entirely satisfied Thalberg again meets the honest cashier: 'How much – Thirteen thousand francs! – More than perfect!' And the emperor Sigismund on the way out picks up a cigar from one of his enemies (he has them; there's nothing this devil doesn't have!) who was enjoying a serious smoke in the theatre entrance and goes back to the Hôtel des Princes as cheerful as an ordinary citizen who's just won a game of dominoes in a café.

That's what it's like to have a colossal talent, lots of common sense, a graceful simplicity of manners, then more talent, a marvellous talent, and happiness.

Must I now speak to you about the compositions that are entirely by Thalberg, and about his compositions on pieces composed by Donizetti on compositions by Rossini? Oh! You wouldn't want that! Does one talk about beautiful sunshine, a scented breeze, a summer night on the Posilippo peninsula, a firework display on the Bosphorus?? ... All I can say is that Thalberg has written an étude not composed on anyone else's composition, and that it's always encored, first of all because it has an effect as delightful as it is original, and secondly because when he plays it, he goes through so many notes that even Poussard, with his best drum-sticks and his best drums, couldn't exceed their astonishing speed.[3]

---

3   Poussard: see article 18, note 1.

29

German Theatre: First Performance of *Jessonda*, Opera in Three Acts by Spohr

JD, 30 April 1842

Every now and then Berlioz let fly with his armoury of denigration and sarcasm, when he felt especially strongly that his subject had shown laziness, incompetence or poor taste.[1]

This Jessonda belongs to the family of the Coras and Amazilys and the rest, who love a handsome stranger, almost always Spanish or Portuguese, whom a cruel priest wants to murder, and who, at the moment of climbing the stake or lowering themselves alive into the tomb, are rescued by their faithful lover. Jessonda has in addition a sister, whose charms have inspired a culpable passion in a young Brahmin; and he, moved by the prayers of the girl he loves, joins forces with the Portuguese and gives them the wherewithal to save Jessonda from the stake. Add some dancing girls who pretend to dance, some soldiers and priests who pretend to sing, and you'll have a reasonably good idea of the interest and details of this drama, in which we find echoes of *Fernand Cortez, Le Sacrifice interrompu*, and *Die Zauberflöte*.[2]

The score of *Jessonda* enjoys a certain reputation in Germany, but it's far from being Spohr's best work. On the whole, the Paris audience found it

---

1 *Jessonda* was premiered in Kassel on 28 July 1823. Paris had no German theatre; although the opera was sung in German, the venue was the Théâtre Italien. *Jessonda* was one of Spohr's most successful operas (Alfred Loewenberg, *Annals of Opera*. London: John Calder, 1978, column 688).
2 *Fernand Cortez*: see article 17. Spontini's *Le Sacrifice interrompu* was premiered at the Odéon theatre on 21 October 1824. On Mozart's *Die Zauberflöte* (*The Magic Flute*), see below, article 43, note 11.

dull, lacking in character, short on excitement, contrast, and variety, short on ideas that are fresh, grandiose, or out of the ordinary, short on what ultimately gives life to music, especially to musical drama. The structure of scenes here often seems indecisive and truncated; we don't know when they start or when they stop; voices are frequently overpowered by the orchestra, and we especially find, to an irritating degree, the fault (with which Spohr has so often been taxed) of piling up disparate harmonies in the shortest space possible, in such a way as sometimes to place four or five different harmonies under a single note of the melody. The instrumentation, albeit careful, is monotonous and bland, a textural fault clearly caused by the violins generally playing in their low or middle register, and by the frequency of held notes from the whole string section. It's strange that Spohr, one of the most capable violinists in Germany, has managed to extract so little from the violins here.

The overture proceeded almost unnoticed; the vague Andante that serves as introduction is followed by an Allegro barely relevant to the subject of the work, and its main theme offers little interest. The introduction which follows is extremely short; the vocal part here is set over a canon at the octave, played by the [cellos and] basses and violins, from which it naturally transpires that the chorus, in between these imitative instrumental lines that echo each other without one knowing why, becomes mere harmonic filling. The § Allegretto of dancing girls is quite graceful, but the way the chorus accompanies it, by giving little taps now and then on tambourines, is puerile and provoked laughter. The priest's solo 'Brama nahm ihn von der Erde' ('Brahma took him from the earth') survives as best it can over a continuous orchestral figure whose meaning is unclear, and it also gives the vocal line the air of being a second trombone part taken by the singer. One has to accord a certain pomp and straightforwardness to the chorus 'Lasst uns Brahma, Brahma loben' ('Let us, Brahma, praise Brahma'), even if the tune doesn't stand out for its novelty. The composer's habit of trying to cram in as many chords as possible under each note in the voice parts is particularly evident in the duet between Dandau and Nadori: the Allegro here is better than the Andante, despite several awkward phrases and enharmonic modulations that produce a fairly cold and uncouth effect. One can say the same about the trio that ends the first act; what's more, the voice parts here are written in such a way as to give the singers a great deal of unnecessary work and difficulty, while nothing is as gauche and unsingable as the brief phrase of the middle section.

In the second act, the chorus of Portuguese, in triple time, must be noted as one of the better passages; it's written simply, in a style that's compact and sounds well. The orchestral march, to which the Portuguese go through their warlike drill, contains only the beginnings of phrases; it's empty, feeble and cold, making no impression. The *airs de danse* that follow seemed quite pleasing but are not sufficiently developed and are always more or less affected by the kind of somnolence that reigns even over the sections by Spohr that aim chiefly at gaiety. Tristan d'Acunha's aria 'Des Kriegeslust ergeben' ('Devoted to the love of war') is animated and deserves praise, despite the unusual instrumentation of its opening, where the theme of a bass aria is played by the highest instrument in the orchestra, the piccolo. This theme, what's more, is close to being a bolero, which is hard to justify. We may note a § section full of grace in the duo between Jessonda and her sister, despite some awkward, abrupt modulations. The duet between the lovers Nadori and Amazilli is still better, offering a feeling of true passion. The E-major rondo in triple time 'Dass mich Glück mit Rosen krone' ('Though good fortune may crown me with roses') is fairly insignificant, and its vocalizations are in somewhat doubtful taste. The layout of the libretto has obliged the composer to break up the beginning of his second finale unduly into dialogues; but he could have written more spacious and beautiful music in the stretto, where nothing stood in the way of an expansion, and where we're waiting for him to unleash a long, dramatic ensemble.

Jessonda's great aria of despair in the third act certainly gives the singer the opportunity to shine. We may however be surprised that this role, written in a style that tends toward the expressive, descends suddenly into the exorbitant vocalisations it has avoided so far, and which only become all the more shocking because they militate against the scene, the character's situation, and the sentiments of misery it was trying to express.[3] Mme Walker sang less well than on the first evening I attended, her voice not having the same steadiness of intonation she normally shows, and which she will undoubtedly recover in the performances to come. The baritone was several times applauded in the role of Tristan: the actor given the role of Brahma doesn't have a deep enough voice, his low notes – B, A, G – lacking timbre and volume. The chorus had barely any opportunity to shine in this sad opera, but they gave proof of enthusiasm and concentration. The orchestra was even more scanty than in *Der Freischütz*; at some moments it was so difficult to know which instruments were playing that we quite understand the two or three uncertain entries by the chorus at the back of the stage: they couldn't hear the orchestra's interventions.[4]

---

3   This complaint is like one Berlioz often made against Donna Anna's aria 'Non mi dir' in *Don Giovanni*.

4   Berlioz had written a critical review of the performance of Weber's *Der Freischütz*, also at the Théâtre-Italien, together with his article on Thalberg (*JD*, 26 April).

This production of *Jessonda* has had very little impact. The director should do his best to see it's forgotten, by putting on some work that can allow the singers he's supporting to show what they can do, and whose merit, which we're told is considerable, we're impatient to experience. [Beethoven's] *Fidelio* is announced for Sunday; may one say, 'so much the better?' ... Who then will sing Leonora? It can't be Mme Walker: her figure does not lend itself to the demands of male attire.[5]

---

[5] Nor to heavy work; see article 1, note 5.

30

Castor et Pollux; the Score

RGM, 13 November 1842

Berlioz had published an article on Pierre-Joseph Bernard's libretto for Rameau's Castor et Pollux *in the* RGM *on 4 September. Although this work was given at the Opéra no fewer than 254 times between 1737 and 1785, very little Rameau was played in the early nineteenth century, and it is unlikely that Berlioz had heard it, although he had heard extracts from the opéra-ballet* Les Indes galantes *in 1840.*

It seems to me that this study of Rameau's score comes rather late: it should have followed far more closely the analysis I made of the libretto that gives it its name. But *the wish to see* and *the restless spirit* carried the day even over the respect every contributor to the *Gazette musicale* owes to his readers (we all hope we have readers).[1] I travelled to the banks of the Rhine, leaving Castor and Pollux on the threshold of Olympus, on the point of being made gods, without saying a word about the music sung by these two interesting twin heroes.[2]

Let me repair this serious omission. The opera in question is not like the great lyric dramas of today; it has an overture, and that's one of its most undeniable faults. Like 999 operas out of a thousand from that period, we can say that it has an overture, as we can say of a man who's otherwise smart that he has a wart on his eye or a lump on his forehead, or some other deformity. This overture consists of a Maestoso which seeks to express heroic strength and pride, and a kind of fugal minuet that seeks to express nothing whatever, and which perfectly succeeds in this. All that goes to make up an

---

1 La Fontaine, *Les deux Pigeons*, book 9, fable 2: 'Mais le désir de voir et l'humeur inquiète / L'emportèrent enfin'.

2 In September and October Berlioz had made his first concert tour, in Brussels, after which he travelled to Frankfurt to prepare the way for the concert he gave there in December.

ensemble of utter uncouthness and insignificance. People say, in an attempt to justify the overture makers of that time, that instrumentation was still in its youth, that performers weren't very skilled, etc., etc. And the reply to that is: that even so these masters possessed, as we do, violins, violas, [cellos and] basses, flutes, oboes, bassoons, trumpets and drums; that these instruments suffice for the composition of excellent examples of instrumental music; that instrumentation, in most cases, is no more than the colouring of the picture; that it was possible to write extremely beautiful music even for the harpsichord; also that Beethoven wrote sonatas for the piano that are perhaps superior to his wonderful symphonies; that the instrumentalists of that time were no less skilled than the singers; and that if composers have found ideas when it was a question of presenting tragic scenes in sung music, it was because the words inspired them while, left to themselves in composing for instruments and deprived of the guidance of words, they stumbled at every move or found nothing but platitudes and puerile nonsense. It should be added that it's probably far more difficult to write a good overture than to outline a beautiful piece for singing, since we see so many operas being admired, and so few admirable overtures.[3] Let's move on.

The chorus of Arts and Pleasures 'Vénus, ô Vénus!' is rather dull, and so is Minerva's aria, 'J'implore, Amour, le secours de ta mère' ('I beg, Love, your mother's help'), which seems to me to lack character and falls back into the terrible style of the powdered minuet, the besetting sin of melody at that time. It also contains a standard bit of vocalising on the word 'trait' in the phrase, 'Lance tes *traits* vainqueurs' ('Let fly your conquering arrows'), a musical pun which composers then felt obliged to respect, and which wasn't regarded as any kind of blunder.

In writing about this work, may I be allowed to say frankly what I think? ... the Rameau fanatics won't cause too much trouble ... and whether they do or not, I dare go on. I find Amour's recitative very heavy and ungraceful, but on the other hand Minerva's aria far too playful; the little duet for Venus and Amour, with its vocalises on the word 'gloire', strikes me as not very interesting. The instrumental gavotte in duple time, in A major, is graceful, tender, and imbued with a gentle melancholy; this melody, one of the best in the score, returns after the ballet, sung by Amour to the words 'Renais plus brillante, / Paix charmante!' ('Be reborn more brilliant, charming peace!'), with which it fits beautifully; but the first note is held too long for the first

---

3   The overture introduces only the Prologue, not the actual drama; French opera prologues were not directly concerned with the opera's plot. The fugal section is marked 'Vite' (fast), so is certainly no 'Minuet'.

syllable, causing a shocking fault in prosody. One can't say '*re*... nais'. The minuet, initially for instruments, then vocal, is likewise very graceful.[4]

The chorus 'Que tout gémisse!' ('Let everything bemoan!') is finely coloured; it contains successions of chromatic notes to good effect; the doleful, plaintive character could not be bettered. The scene between Phébé and Télaïre, 'Où courez-vous?' ('Whither are you running?') seems to me very feeble; its movement is sluggish and sounds unnatural. There's an infinite distance between such recitatives and those Gluck wrote a few years later.

On the other hand, Gluck himself wrote few pages superior to Télaïre's celebrated aria, 'Tristes apprêts, pâles flambeaux' ('Sad preparations, pale torches'). Here harmony, melody, rhythm, and expression combine to move the listener. Each note has its value because it is precisely the one expression demands; and the final explosion, 'Non, je ne veux plus que vos clartés funèbres' ('No, I now want nothing more but your funeral torches') has long been prepared with equal skill. What is there of sadder nobility than the lines 'Toi qui vois mon coeur éperdu, / Père du jour, ô soleil, ô mon père, / Je ne veux plus d'un bien que Castor a perdu'. ('You who see my tormented heart, Father of light, O sun, my father, I no longer want a blessing Castor has lost'). And the reprise of the theme, and its plagal movement of the A over the tonic E-flat, even though A, the diminished fifth of the scale, should resolve diatonically onto G; and that bass line, equally sad in its bleak immobility as in its slow, downward progression![5] Everything combines to make this aria one of the most sublime conceptions in all opera.

The chorus that follows, 'Que l'enfer applaudisse!' (Let Hell applaud!) does not lack energy, and the slow movement inserted for the lines 'Qu'une ombre plaintive en jouisse' ('Let a melancholy shade rejoice') also makes for a welcome contrast with what has preceded it and what follows. The ballet and chorus of athletes is not at all on the same level and, still pursuing truth, I have to say that the recitative in which Pollux declares his love to Télaïre is still worse. It's false, turgid, badly constructed, in short almost ridiculous. After several pages of filling, in which the same lack of truth and distinction declares itself, we come, in the role of Pollux, to a kind of rhythmical recitative, slow and full of expression and nobility. I'm referring to the prayer to Jupiter: 'Ma voix, puissant maître du monde, / S'élève en tremblant jusqu'à toi!' ('My voice, O mighty master of the world, rises trembling towards you!').

---

4   These movements are all part of the Prologue; the drama proper begins with the chorus 'Que tout gémisse!'; they are mourning Castor, who has been killed in battle.

5   Télaïre's aria: this is odd since an A-natural in the key of E-flat would normally resolve up to B-flat, as indeed it does in bars 21–2. The bass descent follows (from f down to low E-flat).

Among the mediocre items we can include the chorus and ballets of Hébé's followers; if this is the music of the heavenly realm, then one feels Pollux may not be making a great sacrifice in leaving it.[6] It's in one of these choruses that we again find one of those words that habit or, to speak plainly, long-lasting routine used to condemn inevitably to more or less grotesque roulades and vocalises – that is, the word *chaîne*. In those days one couldn't sing *traits, flamme, chaîne* or *volez*, without introducing *enchaînements* of notes, which would make the voice *voler* like a *trait* or undulate like the *flamme*. There's much movement and harmonic richness in the ensemble with chorus, 'Sortez, sortez d'esclavage!' ('Escape from slavery!'), and still more in the chorus 'Brisons tous nos fers!' ('Let us all break our chains!').

The scene in the Elysian Fields cannot in any way whatever compete with that in Gluck's *Orphée*, but it has merit nonetheless, and Castor's monologue 'Séjour de l'éternelle paix' ('Abode of everlasting peace') is deeply imbued with that vague melancholy with which the memory of his earthly love clouds the hero's happiness. But it's a long way from that to the sublime beauty of the chorus of happy shades 'Torna o bella al tuo consorte!' ('Turn, O beauteous one, to your husband!'), to the magnificent description of the Elysian Fields by Eurydice's husband, and above all to that aria depicting a suffering shade, all of which make that passage in Gluck's *Orphée* a veritable ancient poem to rival those left to us by Homer and Virgil.

The rest of the score of *Castor et Pollux* offers nothing more than a rather uninteresting mixture of choruses and *airs de danse* which are only indirectly connected with the plot. There's a certain majesty in Jupiter's aria 'Descendez des sphères du monde!', however ludicrous this may seem from the king of the gods, ordering the stars to come and dance a chaconne before him.

The voices in this opera are generally written for in their high registers, which perhaps meant that the singers had to shout, often and loudly. They are also tied in with parts of the accompaniment, with the result that a good deal of their freedom is necessarily denied them, leading to an inevitable heaviness and roughness in their delivery.[7]

The wind instruments are merely employed according to the pattern of the time, underlining certain fragments of melody or doubling the strings, without ever being asked by the composer to produce any effect through

---

6   Pollux has not yet arrived in Elysium; rejected by Télaïre, who loves Castor, he asks his father Jupiter to let him change places in Elysium so that his twin, Castor, can return to life.

7   Pitch at the Opéra in Rameau's time was probably lower than a hundred years later. Pitch levels varied between performing venues in Paris, at least prior to the standardization commission on which Berlioz served in 1858.

the individual resources each possesses. Rameau's melodic style is in general morose and discreet. As to his harmony, it does often display character, but even if the system of the fundamental bass had been entirely unknown, such character would not have been less in evidence. That's to say there is not a single chord in this opera which is not supported by all the theories of harmony, and that if there *are* beautiful chords, the composer would certainly have found them, even if he had been ignorant of those so-called laws of nature so sporadically observed, about which he has made so much noise.[8]

---

[8] In *Le Traité de l'harmonie réduite à ses principles naturels* (1722), Rameau held that a fundamental bass might, 'as a general rule, proceed only in fourths and fifths upwards and downwards'. Before coming to Paris, Berlioz had struggled to understand Rameau's theories; see chapter 4 of his *Memoirs*.

31

Théâtre de l'Opéra-Comique: Revival of *Le Déserteur*, libretto by Sedaine, music by Monsigny

JD, 12 November 1843

This three-act opera by Pierre-Alexandre Monsigny (1729–1817) was revived on 30 October with new orchestration by Adolphe Adam (1803–56).[1]

I could have bet on it! No sooner is *Mina* declared a success than along comes a counter-success which threatens to steal public attention from that charming score.[2] Is it a good thing or a bad thing for the theatre? I don't know. In any case, it's extremely awkward for the composers.

There's no way round it, *Le Déserteur* has had a huge success; it has pleased everybody, the young, the old, the Germans, the French, and the Italians. I saw an Italian voice teacher, the man who normally hates French opéra-comique more than anything else in the whole world, and he was moved, thrilled, and enthused by this old music which he'd never heard mentioned. He declared that all its charming melodies were so written *that you couldn't adapt them to other words without barbarism*, and that it really was *the ideal of truth and expressivity*. For a master of Italian singing, a modern one, to

---

1 Monsigny's opéra-comique *Le Déserteur* was premiered at the Opéra-Comique on 6 March 1769. Adolphe Adam (1803–56), French composer and occasional writer. His output was mainly in opéra-comique, but he is now best known for his ballet *Giselle*; he was generally hostile to Berlioz's music.

2 *Mina* by Ambroise Thomas, premiered at the Opéra-Comique on 10 October, had been given an excellent review by Berlioz in the *JD* (17 October).

bend the knee before such qualities! It's enough to make one cry out with Molière's *malade imaginaire*: 'O Nature! Nature …'[3]

I believe indeed that in no musical work destined for the stage has the sense of dramatic structure and the expression of feelings and characters been taken to such lengths. Monsigny is as true to his genre as Gluck to his. He is as unsophisticated as Grétry, with musical forms that are more developed and spacious. What could be more touching than Louise's aria 'Peut-on affliger ce qu'on aime?' ('Can one hurt what one loves?')? The young peasant girl's couplets 'J'avais égaré mon fuseau' ('I had lost my spindle') are piquant and original, and have lost nothing, absolutely nothing, of their original freshness. Alexis's great aria, without being as intrinsically melodic as those two pieces, shines by means of its considerable dramatic impact, and the same goes for the aria that follows, when the young soldier, learning of what he thinks is Louise's infidelity, throws his cap in the air, tramples his *épaulettes* with his feet, and declares himself a deserter.

In act 2 we find yet more delights. Here the comic, the farcical, the grotesque, and the truly musical grotesque combine with proclamations of passion and the wittiest jokes. Montauciel's aria 'Je ne déserterai jamais' ('I shall never desert') is a well-structured piece, with a tune that's good and natural, splendidly developed and with an admirable conclusion. As for the double song which sends the entire audience into paroxysms of laughter every evening, I confess to regarding it as a stroke of genius: no more, no less. The idea of giving a ridiculous air to the opera's idiot, then another of an open, jolly character to the drunkard Montauciel, and finally to combine them with each singing a different tune together, is one of the cleverest applications of counterpoint to the progress of the drama.[4] In the scene where Montauciel spells out his letters and goes through his reading lesson, melodic interest finds itself naturally transferred to the orchestra. One can see it was impossible, without resorting to ridiculous vocalisations, to sing a tune when spelling out 'V-o-u-s-ê-t-e-s-u-n-b-l-a-n-c-b-e-c' ('Y-o-u-a-r-e-a-n-o-v-i-c-e'), letters out of which Montauciel manages to make the two words 'trompette blessé' ('wounded trumpeter'). But on the other hand, the violins play some very pretty phrases over this and the drama doesn't suffer.

In the third act we have a trio it's impossible to admire or praise too highly. The situation is dramatic and the composer has made it sublime. Alexis, condemned to death as a deserter, has managed to separate himself

---

3   Molière, *Le Malade imaginaire*, act 1, scene 5. Berlioz seems to be emphasizing the capriciousness of human nature: even an Italian voice teacher may come to appreciate a French opera.

4   Such a combination of arias, heard separately and then together, was later effected by Cherubini in *Lodoïska* and Berlioz in act 4 of *Les Troyens*.

from Louise and be alone with the ancient invalid Jean-Louis, to whom he intends to tell this grisly news and confide his last wishes. But, with one of those surprises Sedaine is so good at inventing, the young girl learns elsewhere what her lover wants to conceal, and enters in distress, crying out and almost dead with fear and horror.[5] Immediately there sounds a tune that's almost barbaric in its oddity, which the three singers latch onto successively in fifths, as in a fugal exposition. The style is wonderfully apposite: one is surprised and terrified to hear such a progression of sounds: it strikes at the soul and the senses, and when the female voice, dominating the two male ones, lets fly with lamenting cries on a succession of dissonant harmonies, the listener is consumed by the most terrible illusions, really experiencing what the singers must be feeling, his heart rent in tune with theirs. Here is something remarkably fine in the combined action of dramatic truth and musical inventiveness. I know of nothing like this trio, it's unlike anything else.

It's pointless, I think, to say at this juncture that the soldier's aria, 'Le roi passait, / Et le tambour battait aux champs …' ('The king was passing by / And the drum was beating in the fields …') is also well designed, written and invented as naturally as the rest. But the merit of a piece like this can't be compared with that of the dramatic power I've just identified. Still, one has to admire, and profoundly, Alexis's farewell to Louise, who has fainted. Overall then, there's not a weak moment in this score by an old French master who possessed almost nothing of what's called musical 'knowledge'; who wrote before Grétry; whom we fail even to acknowledge as one of the adornments of our art; and whose name most of our young musicians, composers, singers and instrumentalists living in Europe today may not even have heard. O the fickleness of fame!

Now let's tackle the burning question of the arrangements and corrections M. Adam – like us an admirer of Monsigny's art – has decided to make changes to the score of *Le Déserteur*. He has been bitterly blamed and insulted and made the butt of nasty poems distributed all over Paris. Was he mistaken to expose himself to such outright calumny? Has he, in fact, succeeded in the dangerous task he's undertaken? Can this freedom to retouch works from the past be allowed as innocent in the religion of art?

First, it is never wrong, in my view, to brave complaints in order to bring about what one believes to be useful, appropriate, and beautiful. Moreover, I have to recognise the talent and intelligence of which M. Adam has given further proof by transposing some items in this score that were badly arranged for voices, by completing the accompaniments to various others,

---

5   Michel-Jean Sedaine (1719–97), French author who wrote librettos for some of the most successful operas of time, including works by Philidor and Grétry.

and also by adding instructions the composer hadn't even indicated. There's no doubt the score gains by these, and as a result so do we all. But can one admit in principle that it should be allowed to change, modify, and destroy the physiognomy of old composers in order to give them, if not a modern flavour (which clearly would be absurd), but at least more energy, more vigour, and a kind of youth that they've lost? I have never thought so, and my conviction over this remains the same.

The consequences of this principle are too serious and too easy to foresee, and I don't mind appearing to contradict myself when I say that I reject them with all my might. If I've decided to orchestrate a piano piece by Weber, I have merely transferred it from the piano to the orchestra, in the opposite direction from the usual practice these days, of transferring operas and symphonies from the orchestra to the piano, in the same way one translates poems and plays from one language to another.[6] Now translation, *when it is faithful*, allows no additions, suppressions or alterations of any kind to the author's ideas. Unfortunately, in the present instance it's not a question of translation but of *corrections* and, therefore, of a doctrine whose deplorable consequences we see today in English literature. People have retouched and corrected Shakespeare!!!! Now, doesn't common sense indicate first of all that such liberties could only be taken with great artists (if indeed that's what they are) by people who are exceptional and greater still? And who was greater, who is greater, who will ever be greater than Shakespeare? ... To which someone may retort that it isn't necessary to be superior to Shakespeare in order to have a good idea. No doubt Garrick invented the most sublime dénouement possible to *Romeo and Juliet*, and substituted it for Shakespeare's, whose version has less impact! ... [7] But on the other hand, who is the wretch, the cretin, the bizarre busybody who thought up the dénouement to *King Lear*, which is substituted sometimes, even very often for the final, pathetic scene chosen by Shakespeare for his masterpiece?

---

6 In 1841 Berlioz had orchestrated Weber's *Aufforderung zum Tanz* (Invitation to the Dance), in preference to inserting music of his own for the ballet in the Opéra's production *Der Freischütz*, for which he also provided the recitatives required by that theatre. His own reputation had been assisted by Liszt's transcription of *Symphonie fantastique*.

7 In the version by the English actor David Garrick (1717–79), Romeo drinks poison but is still alive when Juliet wakes up. Garrick justified this by regretting that Shakespeare 'did not work up a scene from it of more nature, terror and distress'; his new lines were 'an endeavour to supply the failure of so great a writer'. Berlioz made Garrick's version an exception to his indignation at those who tampered with masterpieces and used Garrick's dénouement in his dramatic symphony *Roméo et Juliette* (1839), as did Gounod in his operatic version (1867).

Who is the tasteless, brainless poetaster that put into the mouth of Cordelia. – the simple, straightforward Cordelia, the heavenly creation of a superhuman genius – these brutal tirades, expressing vulgar passions so far from her chaste, noble heart? Where is he? So that the whole company of poets, artists, father, and lovers can come and whip him, and tying him to a pillory of indignation, say to him, 'Revolting idiot! You have committed a foul crime, because it destroys that utmost faculty of mankind we call genius! Be jeered at, spat at, be cursed! Despair, therefore, and die!' [8]

Haven't people also added characters to *The Tempest*, turned *Richard III* upside down, condensed *Hamlet*, etc.? That's what Garrick's example has led to!

To return to music; haven't you groaned, you, Adam, at the mutilations inflicted on the music of *Der Freischütz*?[9] This time the corrections came not from above to below, but *vice versa*, and *perpendicularly*, what's more! Don't we see sonatas and trios by Beethoven published today, under our very eyes, with bars added to certain phrases which the editors don't find regular!! Heaven preserve us! And they still live!!! Don't we hear every year a Beethoven symphony, the greatest of all [the Fifth], deprived in the scherzo of the contrabass parts written down by the composer!! And if the conductor dares to suppress this part, what's to stop the leader removing another one? The timpanist too can say, 'I don't want to play this note whose sound *displeases me*; I'd rather play this roll *forte* instead of *piano* as marked, I like it better that way'. And the timpanist, the leader, and the conductor will have as much right as each other to correct Beethoven. Correct Beethoven! Correct Shakespeare! My hand shakes as I write these abominable words! The cult of genius must truly be unknown in our conceited, imbecilic world for such words to have any meaning.

No, no, no, ten million times no. Such artistic immorality cannot be justified by exceptional results. No, no, no, a thousand million times no, no man has the right to force another man to abandon any physiognomy in order to take on another one, to express himself in a language he has not chosen, to become a mannequin operated by a stranger's will and galvanised after his death. If this man is a mediocrity, let him be buried in his mediocrity! But if on the contrary he is by nature one of the elite, let his equals, let his

---

8   Berlioz is citing Shakespeare's *Richard III*; the ghost of Prince Edward addresses the King (act 5, scene 3). Berlioz reproduced this passage in chapter 16 of his *Memoirs* but did not identify the 'busybody' who interfered with *King Lear*: Nahum Tate, librettist of Purcell's *Dido and Aeneas*.

9   Adam wrote criticism for a number of journals and had expressed dislike of both the Castil-Blaze arrangement of *Der Freischütz* as *Robin des bois* and the version of Weber's opera prepared in 1841 by Berlioz himself.

superiors indeed respect him, and let his inferiors prostrate themselves humbly and trembling before him.

I have nothing more to say about *Le Déserteur*. It remains only for me to do justice to the artists involved. Roger has warmth and true sensitivity, Mlle Darcier is a nice little idiot, Mme Thillon is pretty as always, and we note that in her run across fields, to ask for Alexis's help, she carries her satin slippers *in her hand*, because they are *entirely white* and fresh and delightful, as though they came from a shop on the rue Vivienne. Mocker has a huge success in the role of Montauciel, which he plays marvellously; as for Sainte-Foy (the tall cousin), he makes you laugh as you haven't for twenty years, as nobody laughs any more, as I didn't think anybody *could* laugh any more.[10]

---

10   Gustave-Hippolyte Roger (1815–79) sang Faust in the premiere of Berlioz's *La Damnation de Faust* in 1846; moving to the Opéra, he created the title role in Meyerbeer's *Le Prophète* (1849). Charles Louis Pubereaux, known as Sainte-Foy (1817–77), French tenor. He was prized as much for his comic acting as for his voice; it was said that 'the Opéra-Comique without Sainte-Foy is a dinner without wine'. Célestine-Hyacinthe Darcier (1818–70), originally named Lemaire, sang at the Opéra-Comique from 1840 to 1852. Mlle Thillon: see article 11, note 9. Toussaint-Eugène-Ernest Mocker (1811–95), jack of several trades (baritone/tenor, timpanist, producer).

32

M. Berlioz's Concert at the Théâtre-Italien

RGM, 12 May 1844

The concert, which took place on 4 May 1844, included Liszt playing a concerto by Weber, his own Réminiscences de Don Juan *(Mozart's* Don Giovanni*), and his transcription of 'Un Bal' from* Symphonie fantastique. *The orchestra played the overtures* Le Carnaval romain *and* Les Francs-juges, *and the symphony* Harold en Italie. *The concert ended with Liszt and Döhler playing Liszt's* Hexaméron, *variations on the duet 'Suoni la tromba!' ('Sound the trumpet!') from Bellini's* I puritani. *Berlioz reported to his sister Nancy Pal on 19 May that 'Liszt was marvellous, and the takings (12,000 francs) astonishing'.*[1] *At the end of the article, by way of thanking them, Berlioz singled out orchestral players whose work he especially appreciated.*

I can't abide that man! He's one of the weirdest characters, one of the most unlovable people, one of the most absurd intelligences anybody could meet in this world of ours, so lacking as it is in decent folk, happy beings and cheerful spirits. And it's yet it is I who have been chosen to write about him. – 'Go on! Go on!' I'm told, 'it'll be acceptable to one person and disagreeable to another, and all the more original because you both have the same name. People will think he's reviewed his own concert, there'll be complaints and arguments, it's exactly what's needed'. All very fine and generous! So all it needs is for me to speak enthusiastically about it in order to wreck it and cover it with ridicule. But as there are people simple enough to take my praises seriously, and also as I'm unable to say much against it and

---

[1] *CG* vol. 3, p. 181. *Hexaméron* is a set of variations originally composed in 1837 by six composers; the others were Thalberg, Pixis, Czerny, Chopin, and Herz.

have just declared someone to be profoundly antipathetic to me, the best I can do is to say nothing about it at all.

Liszt was playing in this concert: he played the Weber concerto with the orchestra, and without it his *Fantasy on Don Juan* [*sic*], the 'Ball' from *Symphonie fantastique*, and his Hungarian melodies. Huge enthusiasm, huge applause from both audience and orchestra, as expected. But really you couldn't anticipate the way Liszt performed Weber's admirable, charming concerto: there are no points of comparison with any other pianist to give an idea of the speed and grace, allied to such grandeur, strength and resounding sonority! It's the arrow that flies, the lightning that strikes, the diamond spark from a jet-black eye that shines and thrills the heart! And what ravishing interplay between piano and orchestra! The former sometimes turning all small and modest in order to expand later and intertwine with the latter, to dominate it, hold on to it, and submerge it under a deluge of harmonious pearls! Poor Weber, never to have been able to hear one of his masterpieces played like this!

As for the *Don Juan* fantasy and Hungarian melodies, everything's been said, I think, and I can only repeat the expressions of admiration from our friends in the major and minor newspapers. I'll merely add that no one has sufficiently profited from the multiple inventions these pieces contain, from the point of view of both composition and keyboard technique. These are works that harmonists will need to study as well as pianists; and to choose just one passage at random, I'll ask the *experts* to tell me whether anyone had previously heard, with a similar result, the flattened supertonic sounding in the bass and often repeated without detracting from the power of the tonic key. This harmony is magnificent and entirely new.

In his playing of the ball scene from *Symphonie fantastique* after the orchestral performance, Liszt performed a tour de force, not at all in the sense one might suppose, that's to say drawing from the piano handfuls of orchestral sound, but by singing the melodies with a grace, an abandon, and a voluptuous caprice that the most supple, professional orchestra, united in its complexity, could never attain. Another struggle, no less curious, was that between Doehler and Liszt in the final duet, the *Hexaméron*. To say that Doehler acquitted himself valiantly, isn't that praise of his talent which makes any other redundant?[2]

As Mlle Zerr was not yet known in Paris, she could not have found a finer or worthier occasion to announce herself.[3] She was the only female singer in the concert, in which she was heard to succeed three times. It was therefore possible to study her voice and technique at one's leisure. Her voice is pure,

---

2   Döhler: see article 12, note 7.
3   Anna Zerr (1822–81), German soprano and composer.

with a wide range, if not of great volume. She has taste, her vocalisation does not lack agility, and her style uses ornaments with restraint. She was applauded in an Italian aria written by Ch. Bériot for Mme Viardot.[4] The 'Lied' by Lachner, very well accompanied on the cello by M. Cossman, left the audience a little cold.[5] No doubt the reason is the inability of a French audience to appreciate the expressive merits of this kind a piece when sung in German. True, Agathe's aria from *Der Freischütz* was also sung in German, but everyone knows the subject of this immortal scene, and it was easy to recognise the emotion with which the singer imbued it.[6]

Let's talk now about the orchestra, that poor orchestra which M. Berlioz habitually crushes, twists, blasts, explodes, and punctures in so many deplorable ways. It was made up of the cream of Parisian instrumentalists, a total of seventy string players, with all the wind in groups of four: that is, four each of flutes, oboes, clarinets, bassoons, horns, trumpets, and trombones, together with four percussion instruments, two cornets with valves, two harps, and an ophicleide. I firmly believe this orchestra is the most admirable you could find in Europe; it's one the pitiless composer has been happy to torture for ten years in his Conservatoire concerts, moulding them to the thousand extravagant caprices of his bizarre compositions, and whose various commitments, operating only in the winter months, prevent him from always having a full complement.[7] This time they were complete, with no foreign bodies. One saw there the flower of our young violinists led by Tilmant the elder, the cellos and contrabasses headed by MM. Desmarets, Chevillard, Tilmant the younger, Rignault, and Duriez.[8] For the wind instruments one would have to name them all, while the brass players in particular are unrivalled. They are both energetic and agile, their sound is powerful but pure and lovely, and their ensemble is strong without being harsh, while leaving nothing to be desired in the way of tuning and precision. The entry of the

---

4   Charles Auguste de Bériot (1802–70), Belgian violinist and composer.
5   Franz Paul Lachner (1804–90) or his brother Vinzenz Lachner (1811–93), both German conductors and composers. Bernhard Cossman (1822–1910), German cellist, in the Théâtre-Italien orchestra from 1840 to 1847.
6   Agathe's scena in act 2 of Weber's *Der Freischütz*; the aria is 'Leise, leise, fromme Weise'.
7   By 'Conservatoire concerts' Berlioz means concerts he has organized that took place in the concert-hall of the Paris Conservatoire; not concerts given by the Société des Concerts du Conservatoire, which hardly played any of Berlioz's music in his lifetime.
8   Jean-Émile Compagnon, known as Desmarets (1804–66), also a composer; Pierre-Alexandre-François Chevillard (1811–77), Belgian cellist and composer; Alexandre-Théophile-Joseph Tilmant 'the younger' (1808–80); François-Émile Rignault (1812–95); Armand Duriez, also a composer.

trombones and ophicleide in the introduction to the *Francs-juges* overture was wonderfully played, evoking the terrible majesty of the secret court. The violins could have done with more careful rehearsal over uniformity of bowing in the F minor Allegro of this overture; elsewhere they were excellent.

M. Vény played the cor anglais solo in *Le Carnaval romain* with exquisite feeling and taste. MM. Dufresne and Forestier played the introductory theme in *Harold* with a broad cantabile [bar 73]; and the other brass (cornets and trombones) nowhere played with as much energy as in the orgy with which the symphony concludes.[9] This movement, possibly the most difficult there is for the orchestra because of the chromatic style of certain sections, of the rhythmic pitfalls, and of the violence and suddenness of its accents, was played as never before. The orchestra here showed itself to be *sans peur et sans reproche*.[10]

M. Berlioz owes profound gratitude to his viola soloist, M. Urhan, who, always faithful, always attentive and careful, also always gives to this difficult piece so much melancholy poetry, a colouring that's so gentle, a reverie that's so religious.[11]

As for him, as for M. Berlioz the conductor, he always looks as though he's in a temper, and we noticed the moment when he was about to hurl his baton at the heads of two entirely respectable ladies who were chatting rather noisily in the second stage-box during the performance of 'The Pilgrims' March' [in *Harold*]. Surely a prime occasion for a show of temper! And may one not demand absolute attention from the whole house when it's not a question of listening to a ballet? Anyway, for more than ten minutes these good ladies then said nothing and the silence was profound everywhere else.

The theatre, hermetically sealed by a double row of flats, piled one on the other, was very well organized for seeing and listening. Altogether it was a splendid evening in which everybody was satisfied, the artists, the audience, the attentive listeners, the gossiping old ladies, and the flower sellers.

As for the compositions of my closest enemy, I've already said I'll say nothing. Even so ... Ah, no! Too bad, the devil take it!

---

9   Berlioz singles out three players: Louis-Auguest Vény (1801–?), on cor anglais, and two horn-players: Louis Dufresne (1800–66) and Joseph Forestier (1815–82).

10   'Fearless and beyond reproach', epithet applied to the 'Seigneur de Bayard', the French knight and military leader Pierre Terrail (1473–1524).

11   Chrétien Urhan (1790–1845), German violinist and composer who settled in Paris as a teenager and studied with Le Sueur. He also played viola, including the solo in the first performances of *Harold en Italie*.

33

Théâtre de l'Odéon: Premiere of *Antigone*, the Tragedy by Sophocles, Translated by MM. Meurice and Vacquerie, Music by Mendelssohn

JD, 26 May 1844

This first French performance of the tragedy with Mendelssohn's incidental music was on 21 May. As this is a play, not an opera, the characters spoke their lines, sometimes accompanied by the orchestra; the music is almost entirely for double chorus and orchestra.[1]

It was an excellent occasion, whose literary value I leave to a more expert pen than mine to assess. I will allow myself merely to say that I was, like all the artists in the audience, profoundly moved by the powerful ideas of this Shakespeare of antiquity. I found it beautiful, noble, and touching and wept as much as is permitted without making oneself ridiculous. I applauded Bocage and Mlle Bourbier with all my might, as well as Mendelssohn's music, the choir, and the innovative, imposing stage production.[2] Certainly

---

1 Mendelssohn's music for Sophocles's *Antigone* was premiered in Berlin in 1841. The French version was prepared by François-Paul Meurice (1818–1905) and Auguste Vacquerie (1819–95).

2 Pierre-Martinien Tousez, known as Bocage (1797–1863), French actor; Virginie-Marie-Catherine Bourbier (1804–57), French actress. Bocage delivered the important speaking role in the premiere on 9 December 1832 of

the director of the Odéon, by giving new life to Sophocles, has done our culture a favour by demonstrating, by way of this famous example, that those men of today gifted with dramatic genius have simply been following the path of the classical playwrights in portraying nature and truth. This upsets certain people, it's true, who had different views about Sophocles and who now find him as vulgar as Shakespeare because he uses the right words. But why worry? Most audiences these days are quite happy that Tiresias should talk of 'dogs' and 'crows', and that when Creon learns of Eurydice's death he responds simply 'O my poor wife!', instead of following classical practice, as janitors do, with 'O my unfortunate spouse!'

What shocks most people over this production is the intervention by the chorus, singing in response to the actors' dialogues.[3] For example, in the magnificent scene in which Antigone, condemned to death, pleads amid sobs and tears with the Theban elders, who respond to her pathetic supplications with majestic, sombre singing, a man in the audience, quite near to me, made a typical joke, saying, 'They're always a bundle of fun, that lot!' Singing, to the vulgar mind, is invariably a sign of gaiety. Even so, this *Antigone* is one of the greatest successes we've had for some time. The whole house was shaken and aghast at the terrible moment when the king of Thebes [Creon], with moans of misery, carries onto the stage the body of his son Haemon, who had just cursed him, and throws himself at the feet of Eurydice: the sobs of the distraught father embracing the young corpse; the icy silence of the queen who, learning of her son's death, leaves the stage without a sound, without a word, but goes indoors and kills herself; the scene in which the soothsayer Tiresias comes to intercede for Oedipus's daughter and, predicting for the king an impending, fearful denouement, finally breaks his stubborn will; Ismene's touching weakness compared with her sister's noble determination, a determination which nonetheless does not prevent the virgin heroine from turning her back on life and abandoning herself to the most harrowing despair when, at Creon's orders, the soldiers come to drag her from Jupiter's altar to take her to her death. All that is overpowering, moving beyond words.

The staging is also new: a double stage, with one level occupied by the main actors, which the populace never enters, and another, lower one for the chorus to which the actors can sometimes descend to join the populace. The tableaux formed by the chorus, sometimes stationary, sometimes moving

---

Berlioz's 'mélologue' *Le Retour à la vie* (also known as *Lélio*, and a sequel to *Symphonie fantastique*).

3   This follows the pattern of Athenian theatre, as understood since the Renaissance.

slowly round Jupiter's altar, give this staging of *Antigone* a special quality I hadn't experienced before.

Mendelssohn's music is deeply imbued with the serious, restrained melancholy that suits the subject. The composer has succeeded in his use of recitatives sung in unison by massed voices. Several of the choruses are extremely beautiful in both expression and harmony, and the orchestral music accompanying some of the spoken passages contains some truly dramatic, even poignant effects. The hymn to Bacchus is a masterpiece: towards the end there's a kind of vocal crescendo which sends shivers down the back, and the second chorus's repeated exclamations, 'Hear us, Bacchus!' on descending octaves strike me as a most remarkable idea.

On this occasion Mendelssohn owes much, first, to the director who has spared no pains in finding skilful interpreters and succeeded, as the choir is excellent; and secondly to M. A. Morel, who rehearsed the score over a period of eighteen days, and who conducts these performances with the care and talent he brings to every musical occasion.[4]

---

4   Auguste Morel: see article 12, note 22.

34

Large-Scale Concert at the Opéra: 'Le Droit des pauvres'

JD, 29 October 1844

Berlioz takes the opportunity of a large-scale concert to complain about one of his major bugbears, the poor tax (literally 'right of the poor') which varying in amount over the years, taxed the takings (not just the profits) of concerts and other entertainments. It had been introduced by Louis XIV, to be used for the maintenance of the poor. It was reduced to a mere 1 per cent in February 1848 at the outset of the revolution. The bracket [...] in the third paragraph marks the omission of an anecdote whose relevance Berlioz himself questioned.

The Opéra is currently preparing a ceremonial concert of the greatest interest conducted by M. Habeneck: a large-scale performance of the famous oratorio *The Creation*. Haydn's masterpiece will be heard this time in its entirety; the five hundred performers, ranged on an amphitheatre built on the stage, cannot fail to make a colossal impact in the acoustic of the Opéra, whose dimensions, although vast, are not excessive.

The solos will be sung by Mme Gras-Dorus, Mme [Cinti]-Damoreau, Mlle Dobré, and MM. Duprez, Barroilhet, Roger, and Hermann-Léon.[1] The concert will conclude with Weber's lovely overture *Oberon* and with the

---

1   Normally *The Creation* requires only three soloists. Laure Cinti-Damoreau (1801–63), French soprano, the most highly paid singer at the Opéra, where she created roles in operas by Rossini, Auber, and Meyerbeer, before transferring the Opéra-Comique; she taught at the Conservatoire. Marie-Rosalie-Claire Dobré (1818- ?), French soprano. Duprez: article 9, note 3. Barroilhet: article 19, note 1. Roger: article 31 note 10. Léonard Hermann, known as Hermann-Léon (1814–58), French baritone who sang at the Opéra-Comique. He was Mephistopheles in *La Damnation de Faust* in 1846.

'Song of Triumph' from Handel's *Judas Maccabeus*. The takings from this splendid evening are to be given to the Association of Musicians, a recently formed, really useful institution, which already includes most Paris musicians, as well as a large number of foreign ones.[2] The five hundred performers are giving their services entirely free, but even so there's fear that the sum intended for the support of destitute musicians will be rather small, considering that the costs come to nearly 10,000 francs, including hire of the venue, the construction of the amphitheatre onstage, posters, copying, stamp duty, personnel, and the 'droit des pauvres' – this terrible tax which is destroying theatres and concerts in France.

It's true that the administrators and committee of the almshouses do their level best to soften the dictates of the law. They could take a quarter of the gross receipt but only ask for an eighth and often still less. But even so, it's arbitrary, and the smallest upset can change the authorities' attitude. [...] Whatever one may say, this law, proposed in a spirit of thoughtless philanthropy, has led to the ruin of a host of theatrical institutions which are short precisely of the sums they've had to pay. Moreover, it's also reduced to penury hundreds of artists and functionaries who earned their living from the theatre. The existence of many musicians, who were living honourably from the product of their talents without this heavy burden, is thus made difficult and precarious. It renders any large-scale musical production almost impossible, because it doesn't take costs into account, and because, if the bold man whose life is dedicated to promoting a beautiful idea is unlucky enough to receive takings that merely cover the cost of his enterprise, then, to meet the deficit which the *droit des pauvres* leaves in his budget, he either has to sell his furniture or be dragged off to prison. This law is iniquitous, cruel, and in plain contradiction to the morals of our nation. It does not exist elsewhere. In Germany, for example, where a tax on concerts would bring in a tidy sum, the *droit des pauvres* is unknown. That may be, it's true, because there are no poor people in that country: I didn't see a single beggar in the whole of Prussia, nor in the northern states I passed through. But in Paris just recently, after an expensive concert, on the very day when, under the law protecting the poor which seems designed to reduce their number, I had to

---

2   Baron Isadore-Justin-Séverin Taylor (1789–1879) was a French dramatist, artist, travel writer and philanthropist, closely involved with the development of French theatre and a pioneer of Romanticism. He founded the Association des Artistes-musiciens in February 1843; his 'mutual societies' for professional artists continue to this day. He was a supporter of Berlioz, who served on the board of directors of the association from its inception until 1857; some of his own concerts were arranged to benefit the association. Its aim was to reduce poverty among working musicians, who were in a more serious plight than other artistic groups.

pay a tax of four thousand francs, I also had to take out my purse twice in the same street and (voluntarily, at least) give money to some poor women with half-naked children crouched up against a post.[3]

But all this, I know, is a pointless complaint. Only the Chamber of Deputies has the power to rescind this law, which is so alien to our traditions, and to recognise and remove this odious imposition which, in our country and in defiance of the Constitution, causes suffering and despair to precisely those people who cultivate the liberal arts. The Chamber alone can do this; unless all the theatre directors, all the musicians, all the singers and all the instrumentalists choose to play a nasty trick on the administration and club together in closing all their venues and, by instantly depriving Paris of shows and concerts, apply their own violent but unassailable remedy to the problem.

Meanwhile, we must go on paying.

---

[3] This must refer to the concert in the Palais de l'Industrie on 1 August 1844, with approximately one thousand performers and music by several composers (D. Kern Holoman, *Berlioz*. Cambridge, Mass.: Harvard University Press, and London: Faber & Faber, 1989, pp. 617–18).

35

Michel de Glinka

JD, 16 April 1845

The Russian composer Mikhail Ivanovitch Glinka (1804–57) had received a note from Berlioz three weeks earlier asking for details of his musical background. He evidently responded in some detail.

We French are rather inclined, in Paris especially, to base our reception of foreign composers of an unfamiliar type on a kind of prejudice, the injustice of which is always recognised too late to have any impact. Our opinion of them is settled in advance, an opinion that's either friendly or hostile, according to our surroundings, habits, and ideas, and we go along with it initially without any reasons to justify it, though with the possibility of changing it if we absolutely have to. So that if we mention a new Italian composer to the vast majority of Parisian artists, they'll think, even if they don't say so, that he must be some mediocre cavatina merchant, unable to string three chords together properly, the servile copyist of copyists who imitated the imitators of Rossini, unaware of what's happening in the great musical world, as though it were some tune sung around Juggernaut's pagoda and that experiencing it was best avoided by anyone not wanting to be dubbed a stick-in-the-mud.[1] As a result, the greatest Italian composers could suffer this kind of unwarranted stigma if they arrive here out of the blue. On the other hand, in the world of elegance, that of soirées with singing where the word 'concert' means the more or less grotesque performance of half a dozen Italian arias, duets, trios or whatever, with piano accompaniment, the new arrival would, on the contrary, be presumed a delightful composer, full of tuneful melodies, and deserving of the encouragement and support of everyone who loves and honours music. Then, if he happens to have one of his pieces played to the

---

1   Penitents thronged round this pagoda on the Gulf of Bengal, promising to tie themselves on Jagrenat's feast day to his chariot and be crushed beneath its wheels.

public at large and the work's thought to be dull, you're allowed to let it down gently, and the composer returns to his obscurity.

A German composer would find a totally different reception from the two milieux. Musicians, even if not predisposed in his favour, will at least be willing to give him a hearing and take him seriously. The people of fashion, women especially, will hold him in awe as the academic composer who writes quartets, sonatas, and songs *without singing*. Weber would have been taken for a cold contrapuntist. And Albrechtsberger would have been welcomed as one of the greatest, with due respect for his genius.[2]

If it's a question of a young French composer, he'll find the coldest indifference in the salons and a terrifying impartiality in the orchestras. It's only too true, what the Bible says: 'A prophet is not without honour, save in his own country'.[3]

We're never given to wondering what delights can be produced on the compositional front by people from the North, and we're certainly unaware that they're our superiors in some areas of technique. But I know a number of works from Denmark of exquisite delicacy, full of poetry, and written with a purity and stylistic coherence that are truly rare. The arrival of symphonies by Gade, a Danish composer introduced by Mendelssohn to Leipzig two years ago, was greeted with great excitement in Germany.[4] And now we have M. de Glinka, a Russian composer of considerable gifts, in his style, his grasp of harmony, and above all in the freshness and novelty of his ideas. I'm sure you'd like to know more about him.

Michel de Glinka, two of whose pieces I conducted at the Cirque just recently, has revealed his talent to Parisians for the first time; but he is already celebrated in Russia. Coming from an aristocratic family of considerable wealth, he did not at first consider a musical career. He studied at St Petersburg University, but the success he had in various subjects, including science and languages both ancient and modern, did not deflect him from his favourite subject, music. Even so, he had no thoughts of becoming a professional musician: his tastes, entirely free of any ideas of money or position, made this impossible, as did his social standing. The young musician therefore found himself in the most favourable condition for developing, carefully and with every possible means, the gifts with which Nature had so kindly endowed him. Similar circumstances went into the making of such

---

[2] Johann Georg Albrechtsberger (1736–1809), Austrian composer and theorist, teacher of Beethoven.

[3] Gospel according to St Matthew, chapter 13, verse 57.

[4] Niels Gade (1817–90), Danish composer who impressed German contemporaries such as Schumann.

masters as Meyerbeer, Mendelssohn, and Onslow.[5] In the midst of his composing studies, Glinka did not neglect instrumental practice. In a few years he became an accomplished pianist and also learned the violin, thanks to excellent [piano] lessons from Charles Mayer and Boehm, a talented player from St Petersburg.[6]

Soon being forced, as happens in Russia, to join the civil service, he didn't forget his true vocation for a moment, and despite his youth his name quickly became known through compositions full of grace and naïve originality. But wanting to work at a more serious, professional level, he felt the need to travel, and through the regular input of new experiences to lend his talent the strength and breadth it still lacked. He left the service and went to Italy with the tenor Ivanoff, who owes part of his musical education to his talented friend.[7] At that time, living either in Milan or on the banks of Lake Como, or else travelling through other parts of Italy, Glinka was writing for his favourite instrument, the piano, and the catalogues of Ricordi, his Milan publisher, are there to testify to the young Russian's activity and the scope of his ideas. Even so, the main aim of his stay abroad was to study the theory of singing and the mysteries of the human voice, an exercise from which he would later draw considerable benefit. In 1831 I met him in Rome and had the pleasure, at one of the soirées of our director M. Vernet, of hearing several of his Russian songs wonderfully performed by Ivanoff.[8] I was greatly struck by their ravishing melodies, absolutely different from anything I'd ever heard.

After spending three years in Italy, he moved to Germany, first of all to Berlin. Here he developed his knowledge of harmony and counterpoint under the direction of the theorist Dehn, who was then the librarian of the

---

5   George-Louis Onslow (1784–1853), French composer of English paternity, best-known for his considerable output of chamber music. Like the other composers mentioned, he came from a privileged background with regard to wealth and connections.

6   Charles Mayer (1799–1862), German pianist who settled in St Petersburg and was a pupil of John Field (who also took Glinka for three lessons). Berlioz praised Mayer's playing on hearing him in Germany (*JD*, 16 April 1845). The Hungarian violinist Joseph Boehm (1795–1876), studied in St Petersburg with Pierre Rode and presumably taught Glinka while there; he was later based in Vienna and had many distinguished pupils including Joseph Joachim.

7   Nikolay Ivanoff (1810–80), Russian tenor, was about twenty years old when Berlioz met him in Rome.

8   Horace Vernet (1789–1863), French painter, was the director of the Villa Medici and was supportive of Berlioz when he was there after winning the Prix de Rome.

music section of the Royal Library.⁹ The profound and conscientious studies he underwent there finally made him a master of all the resources of his art, so he returned to Russia determined to write an opera in the style of national songs, an idea he'd long been cherishing. So, he set to work enthusiastically on a score whose libretto, written with his input, was ideally made for bringing out the characteristics of Russian musical feeling. The title of this score, from which we have recently heard a charming cavatina, is *A Life for the Tsar*. The storyline is taken from a history of the wars of independence at the start of the seventeenth century. This truly national opera became a brilliant success. But patriotic fervour aside, its quality is unmistakable, and M. Henri Mérimée was undoubtedly correct when he wrote, in one of his letters on Russia published last year, that the composer had absolutely understood and conveyed the story's poetic nature in music that is at once simple and heartrending.¹⁰ *A Life for the Tsar* was as successful in Moscow as it had been in St Petersburg. Then, to reinforce this double success, and support it with a favour a composer of Glinka's age couldn't aspire to, the Emperor appointed him choirmaster of the Imperial Court Choir.¹¹

It should be said at this point that the Russian Emperor's chapel choir is something marvellous and, if we may believe all the Italian, German, and French musicians who have heard it, words can convey only a very imperfect idea of it. Last year already, on Adam's return from Russia, he published an article on the extraordinary impression this magnificent vocal orchestra had made on him.¹² Other artists too, of a standing that guarantees the value of their response, have spoken on the same lines. And today we cannot doubt that, if the orchestra of the Paris Conservatoire is superior to all known orchestras, the Russian Court Choir is likewise rated above all the current choirs anywhere in the world. It comprises around one hundred men's and children's voices singing unaccompanied: the Russian Church, like the Eastern Church generally, does not allow the presence of female voices, the organ, or any instrument. The singers are recruited mainly from the central provinces of the empire. Their voices have an exquisite timbre and a range, especially in the bass, that's almost unbelievable. Ivanoff is a member, and I recall the modest reply he made in Rome when someone praised the beauty of his voice, saying there were several tenors in the Imperial Choir who were far superior to him in range, power and purity. The low voices are divided

---

9   Siegfried Dehn (1799–1858), German music theorist and critic.
10 Henri Mérimée (1807–70), French archeologist and philologist, cousin of Prosper, the author of the novella *Carmen*.
11 Tsar Nicolas I (ruled 1825–1855), to whom Berlioz dedicated *Symphonie fantastique*.
12 Adolphe Adam; see article 31, note 1.

into basses and contrabasses, these last going down effortlessly and loudly to a low A-flat (a third below the cello's bottom C). In this way they double the fundamental notes of the harmony, giving the texture a solidity we don't find in our own choirs, and turning this one into a kind of expressive, human organ whose majesty and impact on the nervous systems of impressionable listeners are beyond words. Glinka scoured Ukraine to find the children's voices, these 'seraphic voices' as he calls them, only to be found apparently in those half-savage territories. One strange thing, or at least not generally known, is that these children are also blessed with fine musicianship, so that you can't upset them by using a violin to play the most bizarre intervals or the most outlandish, unsingable musical lines.

Three or four years later, Glinka found his health declining and decided to give up the directorship of the Imperial Choir and to leave Russia once again. Nonetheless the choir, which he left in excellent condition, has recently improved still further under the wise direction of General Lvoff, a fine violinist and composer and one of the most distinguished amateurs (or rather artists) that Russia can boast. I often heard his compositions praised during my time in Berlin.[13]

Before leaving Russia, Glinka composed a second opera, *Ruslan and Lyudmila*, based on a Pushkin poem.[14] This work, fantastic and semi-oriental in nature and perhaps doubly inspired by Hoffmann and by the tales in *A Thousand and One Nights*, is so different from *A Life for the Tsar*, you'd think it was by a different composer.[15] His talent here seems more mature and powerful. *Ruslan* is without question a step up, a new phase in Glinka's musical development.

In his first opera, mingling with the melodies so freshly redolent of national colouring, the Italian influence was predominant. In the second, from the importance now assumed by the orchestra, the beauty of the harmonic texture, and the expert orchestration, we can, on the contrary, sense the influence of Germany. The numerous performances of *Ruslan* show it's been a real success, even after the popularity of *A Life for the Tsar*. Among the musicians who have done justice to the beauties of the new opera we should mention Liszt and Henselt, who have transcribed and invented

---

13   Alexei Fyodorovitch Lvoff (1798–1870), Russian violinist and composer. In 1833 Tsar Nicolas I had commissioned him to write the Russian national anthem.

14   The opera had been premiered in St Petersburg on 27 November 1842.

15   E.T.A. Hoffmann (1776–1822), German lawyer, composer, and a writer revered by Robert Schumann whose *Kreisleriana* evokes one of Hoffmann's characters. His *Fantastic Tales* appeared in French as *Contes fantastiques* and may have suggested to Berlioz the word *fantastique* for his symphony in 1830.

variations on some of its most striking themes.[16] Glinka's talent is essentially supple and reactive: his style has the rare virtue of being able to transform itself as he wishes, to suit the demands and character of the subject in hand. It can be simple, naïve even, without ever descending to vulgarity. His melodies are unpredictable and include passages of a strange charm. His harmonies are well chosen and he writes for instruments with care, and a knowledge of their most secret capacities, which makes his orchestration currently the most novel and lively to be found anywhere. The audience at the concert given by M. de Glinka in Herz's hall last Thursday seemed to agree wholeheartedly. The indisposition of Mme Soloviowa prevented us from hearing the vocal items announced on the programme.[17] But his *Valse-fantaisie* and *Cracovienne* were loudly applauded, and if his *Fantastic March* was less successful, that was due merely to its abrupt conclusion, the coda being cut short and finishing in such an unexpectedly laconic fashion that one had to look at the orchestra to be sure that was where the composer laid down his pen. The scherzo is attractive, full of extremely striking rhythmic details, truly inventive, and cleverly developed. The *Cracovienne* and march impressed chiefly through the originality of their melodic style. This is a rare attribute, and when the composer adds to it a distinguished harmonic sense and an orchestration that's straightforward, clear, and highly coloured, he then has a right to claim a place among the best composers of his time. The composer of *Ruslan* has that right.

---

16 Liszt wrote a *March of the Circassians* from the opera in 1843. Adolf von Henselt (1814–89), German composer and pianist who taught in St Petersburg from 1838–48; his friendship with Liszt dated from the latter's Russian visit of 1842.

17 A. A. Solovieva, née Verteuil (c. 1820–?), French soprano attached to the St Petersburg theatre.

36

Conservatoire Concert: Spontini, *La Vestale*

JD, 14 May 1845

It is no surprise that Berlioz, the lover of Gluck, should have been equally enthusiastic about Spontini, who was greatly influenced by his predecessor. In the words of René Dumesnil, Spontini 'was able to create a kind of work that fitted the sensibility of the imperial age; more dramatic than lyrical but, despite the simplicity of its architecture, retaining the passionate accents of Italian opera'. La Vestale, which was accepted by the Opéra only though the intervention of the Empress Joséphine, was premiered there on 15 December 1807.

Spontini's masterpiece, so much admired throughout France for twenty-five years, has become almost a stranger to our present musical generation. Opera houses have not kept it in their repertoire, and concert halls and salons fight shy of programming excerpts. This is a boon for which the composer should be considered very lucky. Performance of this kind of work really demands qualities that are becoming ever rarer. For *La Vestale*, as for Gluck's operas, one needs grand voices trained in the grand style, also male and especially female singers possessing more than just talent. One needs choruses who can sing and act, a powerful orchestra, and, above all, it's vital that all the performers are steeped in the art of expressivity. This feeling is almost extinct these days in Europe, where the most enormous absurdities become astonishingly popular, and where the most trivial, and particularly the falsest style, is the one that has the greatest chance of theatrical success. This leads to extreme difficulty in finding listeners and interpreters for these artistic masterpieces. The degradation of the public in general, its inability to understand matters of imagination or feeling, its love of brilliant platitudes, the lowness of all its melodic and rhythmic instincts, all these have inevitably reacted on performers and led them along the path they now tread. It seems a matter of basic common sense that the public's taste should be formed by the artists, but sadly it's the artists, on the contrary, who are deformed and corrupted by the public.

There's no need to argue in the public's favour that they sometimes pick a fine work to adopt and make into a success. That only proves that 'the smallest seed would have been more to the point' and that the public has accidentally swallowed a pearl. The public's palate is even less refined than that of the cock in the fable, who wasn't taken in.[1] Nevertheless if the public applauds certain works because they are beautiful, there are other occasions when it goes the other way and it responds with outrage and indignation. They can be severely critical of people who have so often insulted art and common sense.

And they are far from having done that. Perhaps something that had no bearing on the work's merit was responsible for its success, or some musical joke amused these great children, or they were fascinated by a performance of outstanding brilliance or unaccustomed visual glamour. Because, in Paris at least, if you catch the public unawares before it's had time to agree on an opinion, with an exceptional performance you can make anything succeed, even a masterpiece. It's clear now that M. Spontini is to be congratulated on the cold shoulder the theatres are offering him because, as the obliteration of the public's sensitivity is total, the only chance of success for a masterpiece of expressivity like *La Vestale* lies in a performance of a standard that's impossible to produce at the present time.

When M. Spontini came to France, the art of decorative singing among female singers was certainly not as advanced as it is today, but undoubtedly large-scale, dramatic, impassioned singing did exist free of all dilution, at least at the Opéra.[2] Then we had a Julie, an Armide, an Iphigénie, an Alceste, and a Hypermestre.[3] There was Mme Branchu, with one of those

---

1   The reference is to the first stanza of La Fontaine's fable 'Le coq et la perle', book 1, fable 20: 'A cock was rummaging about in the dirt when turned up a precious jewel, which he took immediately to a polisher of precious gems. "No doubt", said the cock, "this jewel is very costly, but for me a single grain of millet would suit me better than all the jewels in the world"'. This may be a gloss on Christ's words (Matt 7–6): 'Give not that which is holy unto the dogs, neither cast ye your pearls before swine, lest they trample them under their feet, and turn again and rend you'. It has to be said that Berlioz's complaint of the public being guilty of the deformation and corruption of musical taste is negated elsewhere in his writings, where artists are definitely held responsible for such influence.
2   Spontini arrived in Paris in 1803.
3   Caroline Branchu: see article 5, note 2. Julie is the title role in *La Vestale*, Hypermestre the heroine in Salieri's *Les Danaïdes*. Branchu also took the title roles in the three Gluck operas.

soprano voices that are full and resounding, sweet and strong, capable of riding over chorus and orchestra, and able to come down to the faintest murmur, of hesitant passion, fear, or reverie. She has never been surpassed. I had long forgotten the wonderful way she *spoke* recitatives and sang slow, melancholy melodies, until Duprez, in his debut in *Guillaume Tell*, came to remind us of the power of this art brought to such a degree of perfection.[4] But to these outstanding qualities Mme Branchu added those of an irresistible wildness in scenes of high drama and an ease of voice production that allowed her never to slow down the tempo unnecessarily or add beats to a bar, as happens all over the place today. What's more, she was a tragedian of the highest class, with an indispensable gift in filling the great female roles of Gluck and Spontini. She possessed enthusiasm and true sensitivity and never had to resort to trickery in order to imitate them. I never saw her in the role of Julie that was written for her: when I heard her at the Opéra, she'd already given up the role. But her performances in *Alceste*, *Iphigénie en Aulide*, [Salieri's] *Les Danaïdes*, and [Spontini's] *Olimpie* allowed me to imagine what she must have been like fifteen years earlier in *La Vestale*.[5]

Spontini was also lucky enough, when casting his opera, to find a special actor to play the part of the Supreme Pontiff: the elder Dérivis, with his formidable voice, tall figure, dramatic diction, and well judged, majestic gestures. At the time, he was young and almost unknown. The role of the Pontiff had been given to another actor who could make nothing of it and, as a result, grumbled endlessly at rehearsals about what he claimed were difficulties in music he couldn't understand. One day in the rehearsal room, when his incompetence and impertinence were even more evident than usual, Spontini in a rage snatched his score from him and threw it on the fire. Dérivis was there and, hurling himself towards the fireplace, plunged his hand into the flames and rescued the score, shouting, 'I've saved it, I'm keeping it!' To which the composer responded, 'It's yours, and I'm sure you'll do it justice!' The prophecy was fulfilled: the role was indeed one of Dérivis's best, and maybe even the only one that allowed the inflexibility of his rough voice to show itself without disadvantage.

The style of this fine score is, in my view, entirely different from the one adopted at that time by composers in France. Neither Méhul, Cherubini, Berton, nor Lesueur wrote like this. It's said that Spontini followed on from Gluck. In matters of dramatic inspiration, definition of character, truth of expression, and vehemence of passion, that's true. But in melodic and harmonic style, orchestration and musical colouring, he's his own man. His

---

4   Duprez: see article 9, note 3. He took over the role of Arnold from Nourrit on 17 April 1837.
5   *Olimpie* was first performed at the Opéra on 22 December 1819.

music has a particular physiognomy that one can't mistake. Some (very rare) infelicities of harmony have drawn ridiculous charges of incompetence, aimed in the past by the dullards of the Conservatoire, charges inspired still more by excellent new harmonies the great master had invented and applied with success, before the pedants of the time had dreamt of their existence or the reasoning behind it. That was his great crime. Was he aware of this? Employing chords and modulations that had not yet been cheapened by usage, and before the academics had decided whether it was permissible to include them! ...

There was also, it must be said, another motive behind the Conservatoire's blockade. Apart from Lesueur, whose opera *Ossian* enjoyed a number of well received performances, none of the composers of the time had much success at the Opéra.[6] Persuis's *La Jérusalem* [*délivrée*] and *Le Triomphe de Trajan* had passing successes that leave no mark on the history of art, and which can be attributed to their lavish productions, and to political allusions between the heroes of these operas and the hero of the immense drama that was currently turning the entire world upside down.[7] The basic repertoire of the Opéra was for many years reliant on two operas by Spontini (*La Vestale* and *Fernand Cortez*) and five by Gluck.[8] The only rival in our major opera house to the old glory of the German composer was that of the young Italian. This was the cause of the Conservatoire's profound hatred, nursed by composers whose attempts to shine at the Opéra had proved fruitless.

There were no terms scornful enough when talking about Spontini. He didn't know how to string two chords together! He was entirely ignorant about composing! Any student would have been able to give him advice about instrumentation! His recitatives were unsingable! It would have been impossible to stage *La Vestale* without the corrections made by experts who wanted to help this monstrous score so that it was performable etc., etc.! That's what led to the ridiculous claims of a whole host of people to the glory of having retouched, corrected, and purified Spontini's music. I myself know four composers who are supposed to have had a hand in this. When the success of *La Vestale* was by then an irresistible, undeniable fact, they went further: it wasn't just a matter of corrections, whole scenes had been written by someone or other; one claimed he'd composed the second act duet, another the third act march, etc. It's strange that among the considerable number

---

6   *Ossian*: see article 8 note 2.

7   Louis-Luc-Loiseau de Persuis (1769–1819), French violinist, conductor and composer. Some of the arias in the second opera were composed by Le Sueur at Napoleon's command.

8   Gluck's five: *Orphée*, *Armide*, *Alceste*, and the two *Iphigénies*. In fact, works by Piccinni, Salieri, and Sacchini were also revived into the 1820s and seen by Berlioz.

of duets and marches written by these illustrious masters you can't find any pieces of the same kind, or at this level of inspiration! ... Might these gentlemen have taken devotion to the point of making Spontini a present of their best ideas? Such self-sacrifice goes beyond the limits of the sublime! ...

Finally, this turned into a tale long familiar in the musical limbos of France and Italy, namely that Spontini was not the composer of *La Vestale* at all. This work, written in defiance of common sense, corrected by everybody, on which scholastic and academic curses had been raining remorselessly for so long, this indigestible, confused opus – Spontini wouldn't even have been able to invent it; he'd bought it ready made *from a philistine*; it was the work of a *German* composer who'd died in penury in Paris, and all Spontini had to do was set the tunes of this unhappy musician to M. de Jouy's words, and add a few bars to tie the scenes together.[9]

One has to admit he's made a good job of this *arrangement*; one would swear that every note was written for the word it sets. Even M. Castil-Blaze hasn't managed that![10] From time to time, one asked from which philistine Spontini later bought the score of *Fernand Cortez* which, as we're aware, is not without merit, but nobody ever knew. But there must have been so many people for whom this precious outlet was a godsend, and who'd have been keen to do deals with him! ... It must surely have been the same person who sold his *Orphée* to Gluck and his *Le Devin du village* to Rousseau. (The paternity of both these works, so disparate in quality, has been contested).[11] But enough of these ridiculous follies: no one doubts that raging envy can, in the unfortunates it devours, produce a state verging on imbecility.

One can imagine that such a hostile attitude *after* a success might be deep-rooted, and that it was all too likely to be energetically expressed *before* one. God knows what bizarre tortures Spontini had to endure when putting on the work that was to immortalise his name. First of all, the orchestra, stunned by being faced with instrumental demands that were unheard of at the time and mixtures of timbres that Gluck had never employed, complained they

---

9   Victor-Joseph-Étienne de Jouy (1764–1857), French librettist and playwright.

10 The French critic and composer François-Henri-Joseph Blaze, known as Castil-Blaze (1784–1857), 'arranged' both French and foreign operas (including Weber's *Der Freischütz*), earning Berlioz's sobriquet of 'correcteur universel'. He wrote music criticism for the *Journal des débats* from 1820 until 1832.

11 Gluck was wrongly accused of using an aria by the Italian composer Ferdinando Bertoni (1725–1813) in *Orphée*, and Rousseau of not acknowledging the help of the French violinist and composer François Francœur (1698–1787) in writing *Le Devin du village*. In fact, Francœur didn't know who had written the opera until, in Rousseau's words, 'a general acclamation had established the merit of the work' (Maurice Cranston, *Jean-Jacques. The Early Life and Work of Jean-Jacques Rousseau*. London: Penguin, 1987, p. 264).

were impossible to play. His discouragement increased by leaps and bounds, and as a result rehearsals would undoubtedly have been cancelled had not several scenes from *La Vestale* been performed at the Tuileries, prompting a decree from Napoleon for this cancellation to be reversed and rehearsals completed. So of course the impossible had to be attempted, and was duly achieved. There remained the factions involved with the premiere who were being efficiently organized in various ways. One of them came from the counterpoint students at the Conservatoire. The conspirators had the rather jolly idea of each bringing a night-cap with him and then, at a given signal in the middle of act 2, they would all put them on and go to sleep. I was told this detail by the chief sleeper, who was joined in directing the sleep-in by a young singer of romances who's now become one of our most successful composers of opéras-comiques.[12] Anyhow, the first act went off without a hitch, and the plotters, who couldn't deny the effect of this beautiful music, which according to them was so badly written, contented themselves with saying, in a tone of naïve astonishment free of all hostility, 'It's going well!'. Boieldieu, listening twenty-two years later to the final rehearsal of Beethoven's Fifth Symphony, would also say with the same feeling of surprise: 'It's going well!'[13] The Scherzo had struck him as being so *bizarrely* written that, in his view, *it shouldn't be going well!* Sad to say, there are lots of other things that did, do, and will go well, despite professors of counterpoint and composers of opéras-comiques.

Then came the second act, and the growing interest of the temple scene didn't allow the plotters to dream for a moment of going ahead with the wretched prank they'd prepared. The finale found them joining the impartial audience in enthusiastic applause, for which they no doubt had to make amends next day in class by continuing to abuse this ignorant Italian who, even so, had been able to move them so profoundly. Time is a great leveller! Not a new tag, but the revolution that's taken place in the Conservatoire over the last dozen or fifteen years testifies to its validity. These days, the establishment harbours barely any prejudices or obstinate anti-modern attitudes. The spirit of the place is excellent. I think the Société des Concerts, by familiarizing young musicians with a host of masterpieces by good composers whose determined, independent genius had never found its way into our scholastic reveries, has had a lot to do with this improvement.

---

12 Possibly Giuseppe Blangini (1781–1841), Italian cellist, singer, and composer. He also taught singing at the Conservatoire from 1816 to 1830.

13 Berlioz's teacher Le Sueur was also perplexed by Beethoven's Fifth Symphony; he concluded that 'such music *ought not to be written*' (*Memoirs*, chapter 20). François-Adrien Boieldieu (1775–1834), French composer primarily of opéra-comiques, of which only *La Dame blanche* is remembered. A meeting with Berlioz in 1829 is recounted in the *Memoirs* (chapter 25).

Then there was the performance of extracts from *La Vestale*, given quite recently by the Société des Concerts together with students from the Conservatoire, which proved to be an enormous, unheard-of success, with applause, shouts, and tears that ravaged both performers and audience, to the point that the concert had to be discontinued for half an hour. Spontini, hidden away at the back of a box, was gazing philosophically at this storm of enthusiasm and no doubting wondering, as he pondered the tumultuous reactions of orchestra and chorus, what happened to all those little jokers, all those little contrapuntists, all those little cretins from 1807; then the parterre, spotting him, stood up *en masse* and turned towards him, whereupon the whole house broke out into new shouts of congratulation and admiration.[14] It was a sublime sound, that of affected souls saluting true genius, and his noblest recompense! Might we see the workings of providence in the triumph accorded this great artist in the very heart of the school where, for thirty years and more, the lessons had always been of hatred for his person and of contempt for his music!

Even so, how much the music of *La Vestale* loses, when deprived of the honour of a staging, for those listeners especially (and they are many) who have never seen it at the Opéra! How can one guess, from a concert performance, at the multitude of different effects brought about by the abundance and depth of dramatic inspiration? What listeners can appreciate its truth of character and expression, enclosed in the opening bars of each role; it's the intensity of passion that makes this music luminous through the ardent flame that fills it, and it's the purely musical beauty of melodies and chord progressions; *sunt lacrimae rerum*.[15] But there are thoughts that are summoned only by being staged. There's one, of rare beauty, in the second act. In Julie's aria 'Impitoyables dieux' ('Pitiless gods'), an aria in the minor and full of desperate agitation, there's a heart-breaking phrase of renunciation and tender sorrow: 'Que le bienfait de sa présence enchante un seul moment ces lieux' ('May the blessing of his presence cast a momentary spell on this place'). After the aria and words of the recitative, 'Viens, mortel adoré, je te donne ma vie' ('Come in, beloved, I give thee my life'), while Julie goes to the back of the stage to open the door to Licinius, the orchestra repeats a fragment of the previous aria in which the Vestal's expressions of passionate despair are still dominant. But at the very moment the door opens, letting in the starlight, a sudden pianissimo in the orchestra recalls the phrase 'Que le bien fait de sa présence' ('May the blessing of his presence'), with delicate ornaments in the woodwind. Immediately it seems as though a delightful

---

14 The parterre, or stalls: see article 7, note 1.
15 Virgil, *Aeneid*, book 1, line 462. Aeneas gazes at the ruins of Troy: 'such things call out for tears'.

scent is filling the temple, a scent of love that's in the air; it's the flower of love that's opening, it's the sky that's uncovered, and we sense that Licinius's lover, weakened by her fight against her heart and finally overwhelmed by the memory this melody recalls, staggers and collapses at the foot of the altar, ready to give her life for a moment of passion. I have never been able to watch this scene without being overwhelmed.

But from here on, the musical and dramatic interest continues to grow, and one could say that the second act altogether is nothing less than a giant crescendo, finally reaching its peak in the last scene, with Julie veiled in black. This is not the place to analyse the beauties of this immortal score – a book would hardly be large enough for that. But I can't resist mentioning, among the excerpts recently performed at the Conservatoire, admirable passages like these from the beginning of the duet!

Licinius:	Je te vois!	I can see you
Julie:	Dans quels lieux!	Where?
Licinius:	Le dieu qui nous rassemble	The god who brings us together
	Veille autour de ces murs	Watches over these walls
	Et prend soin de tes jours.	And guards your life.
Julie:	Je ne crains que pour toi!	I fear only for you!

What a difference there is between the tones of voice of the two characters! Licinius's words are forced out between his passionate lips; Julie, on the other hand, can no longer find inflections for her voice, she lacks the strength, she's collapsing. Licinius's character is further developed in his cavatina, with its beautiful melody that goes beyond praise. It begins tenderly, he's consoling, adoring, but at the end, on these words: 'Va, c'est aux dieux à nous porter envie' ('Go; it is the gods who should envy us'), a kind of pride can be heard in his voice, he gazes at his beautiful conquest, the joy of possession even overpowers happiness, and his passion is tinged with arrogance.

As for the duet, and especially at the climax of the ensemble: 'C'est pour toi seul je veux vivre! Oui, pour toi seule que je veux vivre!' ('It is for you alone I want to live! Yes, for you alone I want to live!'), these are lines beyond description. Here are palpitations, cries, desperate embraces unknown to you pale lovers from the North; this is Italian love in all its furious grandeur and volcanic heat. In the finale, at the point where the people and priests enter the temple, the rhythmic patterns grow inordinately; the orchestra, beset by storms, rouses itself and vibrates with a fierce majesty; this is religious fanaticism. 'Ô crime! Ô désespoir! Ô comble de revers! / Le feu céleste éteint! La prêtresse expirante! / Les dieux, pour signaler leur colère éclatante, vont-ils dans le chaos replonger l'univers?' ('O crime! O despair! O climax of disaster! The holy flame has gone out! The priestess is dying! Will the gods, to signal their unbridled fury, again plunge the universe into chaos?').

This recitative is terrifyingly truthful in its musical development, in its modulations and instrumentation, and is of monumental grandeur. Everywhere we feel the powerful menace of a priest of Jupiter thundering. And in Julie's melodic lines, in which dejection, resignation, revolt, and bravery follow one another, there are turns of phrase so natural it seems impossible to use any others, and yet so unexpected that the finest operas hardly contain any of them. These, for instance:

Julie:	Eh quoi! Je vis encore!	But what! I'm still alive!
	Qu'on me mène à la mort! …	Lead me to my death! …
	Le trépas m'affranchit de votre autorité! …	Death delivers me from your power!
	Prêtres de Jupiter, je confesse que j'aime! …	Priests of Jupiter, I confess I love! …
	Est-ce assez d'une loi pour vaincre la nature? …	Can this law overcome nature? …
	Vous ne le saurez pas! …	You will never know it! …

At this last reply of Julie to the pontiff, wild flashes of lightning break out in the orchestra and one feels she is lost, and that the touching prayer the poor woman has just addressed to Latona won't save her. The measured recitative beginning 'Le temps finit pour moi'('My time is coming to an end') is a masterpiece of modulation with respect to what precedes and follows it. The high priest has finished his phrase in the key of E major, soon to be that of the finale. The Vestal's vocal line gradually moves away from this and comes to a halt on the dominant of C minor. The violas then begin a tremolo on the B, which the ear takes for the leading note of the current key. By means of this B, now suddenly returned to its previous role as a dominant, they introduce the explosion of the brass and timpani in the key of E major, now at double its original volume. The effect recalls those lights which, in darkness, appear more brilliant after an obstacle has momentarily blocked them from our sight.

I ask the reader to forgive me these technical details: I needed them in order to cool down, because when I start thinking about this finale, my memory of their effects on me makes me feverish and my hand trembles as I write. Now, for the curse which the pontiff lays on his victim, as much as for the stretto in which the priests' rhythm contrasts so terribly with the tearful song of the vestals, again all description would be as powerless as useless. I'll confine myself again to pointing out, over the layout of the men's voices in this superb stretto, that far from being a misjudgement or a weakness as has been claimed, the balance of vocal forces has been most carefully considered by the composer. The tenors and basses are initially divided into six parts, only three of which are heard at any one time; it's a dialogue for double choir. The first choir sings three notes that the second repeats immediately, so as to produce a continual repetition of each beat in the bar, with the result that there is never more than half the male voices employed at once. It's only with the approach of the *fortissimo* that all of them unite in a single mass. It's the moment when the melodic interest has been carefully graded to achieve its greatest impact, and when the irregular rhythm needs new support to deliver the strident harmonies that accompany the women's singing. It follows from the vast crescendo I've already mentioned, which reaches its apogee only with the ear-splitting chord on which the pontiff covers Julie's head with the fatal black veil. It's a superb combined operation, for which no praise could be adequate, and permission to criticize it granted only to a ten per cent musician, like the one who found it wanting. But it comes naturally to critics from highest to lowest to take exceptional men to task by reproaching them for their good points, and to see as a weakness the most obvious manifestation of their competence and power. When will the Paganinis of the composing world cease to be obliged to take lessons from the blind men sitting on the Pont-Neuf ...?[16]

It remains for me to say something about the performance at the Conservatoire of extracts from *La Vestale*. The performers' enthusiasm for the works they were involved in and their total devotion to the composer meant they were ideally directed. The orchestra was beyond reproach, as usual. I have nothing but praise for the male chorus, and the sopranos sang well in the stretto of the finale; but in the evening prayer 'Daughter of Heaven' the whole body of female voices left a lot to be desired in purity of tone and in intonation. There was even some indecision in their entries, which was excusable given that the first row of singers was unable to see the conductor's beat, placed as he was, at the Conservatoire, immediately behind them.

Massol is an excellent Licinius: he has understood the role, sings it with love, and better than any of the ones he's taken so far.[17] He sings the cavatina 'Les dieux prendront pitié' ('The gods will take pity') with distinction of style and as much intelligence as feeling. Massol only needs roles written to suit the character and range of his lovely voice to render great services

---

16 The Pont-Neuf (new bridge) in Paris gave its name to a genre of musically unsophisticated topical songs, often using existing tunes, that were sung and sold as sheet-music there.

17 Massol: see article 17, note 4.

to composers and music in general. Just recently, a production of *Lucia di Lammermoor* in Rouen, where he sang the role of Ashton, earned him an enthusiastic ovation.

Mlle Dobré had studied the role of Julie with the utmost care, bringing sensitivity to it, particularly in her prayer, and delivered excellently the sublime passage of depression and utter despair:[18]

Ah! Daigne, avant que j'y tombe,	Ah! I pray you, before I lie in it,
Écarter de ma tombe	Lead away from my tomb
Le mortel adoré pour qui je vais mourir.	The beloved man for whom I am to die.

Her delivery of the line 'La fille de Saturne' ('Daughter of Saturn') was even better, but one could see that this style, so different from the that in which she was brought up, still did not come naturally to her. She sang certain parts of the recitative far too slowly, copying the exaggeration popular with followers of Duprez. What's more, she allowed herself the extreme licence, as many singers do these days, of turning verse into prose by removing elisions: for example in the phrase 'Qu'on me mène – à la mort', instead of eliding the second syllable of 'mène' with the following vowel, and likewise 'Mon supplice – au moins'.[19] This is shocking, and could have been no more than tolerated at rehearsal by the composer, who is careful not to write anything of the kind.

Alizard, whom we should be glad to see once more back at the Opéra, sang the Supreme Pontiff superbly. He launched the theme of the finale 'De son front que la honte accable' ('From her forehead overcome with shame') with splendid impetuosity, and in the recitative 'O Crime!' his severity was full of menace. His outburst of indignation 'Sous ces portiques saints, quelle horrible blasphème' ('Beneath these holy porticos, what foul blasphemy!') made a vivid impression on the audience, but he went further still in emulating Mlle Dobré's error by singing 'Le terrible – anathème!' ('The terrible – curse') and by not holding to the end the note on the penultimate syllable, even though he had taken a breath when suppressing the elision. These words, and the long-held note for the final word, absolutely must be sung in one breath, otherwise the effect is lost and the meaning destroyed. Dérivis used to sing this passage as written, and Alizard could easily have done so

---

18   Dobré: see article 34, note 1.
19   Where the final syllable of a word and the first syllable of the next are both vowels, rules of Italian and French prosody elide them, so that 'mène_à la mort' counts as four rather than five syllables. These rules are sometimes breached in musical settings, even by Berlioz.

had he wanted. This observation aside, which I had to make, and whose importance is greater than singers think, Alizard, I repeat, earned nothing but praise, and fully deserved the applause that interrupted his singing several times.

This concert will go down in the annals of the Société des concerts, and our young musicians, for whom the score of *La Vestale* was unknown until now, will remember it for many a year. As for me, I can only repeat what I wrote to the composer some months ago:

Cher maître,

Your work is noble and beautiful, and today it is perhaps, for the artists capable of appreciating its magnificence, a *duty* to say it to you again. Whatever your worries may be at the moment, the knowledge of your genius and of the priceless value of its creations will easily allow you to forget them.

You have stirred up violent hatreds, and because of them some of your admirers seem afraid to admit their admiration. They are cowards; I prefer your enemies. Glory and respect to the man whose mighty imagination, warmed by his heart, created these immortal scenes!

[...]

If music had not been abandoned to public charity we should have in Europe a theatre, an operatic Pantheon, exclusively devoted to the performance of monumental masterpieces, in which they would be produced at long intervals, with a care and a magnificence worthy of them, by *artists*, and heard, as part of special music festivals, by audiences of feeling and intelligence.

But music has nearly everywhere been disinherited from the honour of its noble origins, and is no more than a foundling whom, it seems, they are trying to turn into a fallen woman.

Adieu, cher maître. There is a religion of beauty; I belong to it. And if it is a duty to admire great things and to honour great men, I am conscious, as I shake your hand, that it is also a pleasure.

H. Berlioz[20]

---

20 The letter is in *CG* vol. 2, 695–6; in his article Berlioz omitted one paragraph (at [...]). The letter is dated 27 August 1841 and was inspired by a performance at the Opéra of *Fernand Cortez* on 25 August. See also article 17.

37

Cherubini's *Messe du sacre* in Saint-Eustache

JD, 17 May 1845

Cherubini wrote this mass for the coronation of Charles X in Reims on (29 May 1825). It is generally held to be less successful than his C minor Requiem of 1816. Dietsch had just taken up his post as choirmaster and organist of Saint-Eustache.[1] Although in this article Berlioz asks for Dietsch to be given 'a little encouragement', in the JD *(13 November 1842) he had summed up Dietsch's opera* Le Vaisseau fantôme *as the work of one who 'has carefully and over a long period thought about the various doctrines of the masters, objects of his admiration, but who has not yet made a clear choice between them'. Perhaps he simply thought Dietsch should stick to religious music.*

M. Dietsch is a tireless fighter. He has taken it upon himself to reactivate the fervour of artists, if not of the public, for religious music; and thanks to the intelligent enthusiasm of the parish priest of Saint-Eustache, who's at one with his young choirmaster in his views, we shall perhaps soon see the problem resolved. We've already had the opportunity a few months ago of sincerely praising a mass M. Dietsch had just written and seen performed at Saint-Eustache. Certainly no artist could do more to prove his disinterested love of art than to give, as M. Dietsch has done, his time, his care, his work, his thought, and above all his mass, and all too often his money, without even the certainty of having any listeners, and so without earning the weak compensations of legitimate pride that are so justly his. M. de Gasparin, when he was minister of the Interior, had the excellent idea of using an annual sum from the funds of the *beaux-arts* to encourage religious music.[2] It's a

---

1   Dietsch: see article 8, note 1.
2   Adrien-Étienne-Pierre, comte de Gasparin (1783–1862), minister of the interior from September 1836 to April 1837; his initiative brought about the

matter of regret that this project was abandoned by his successors. Indeed M. Dietsch, despite the influence that accrues to him as *maître de chant* at the Opéra, from his numerous links with singers, the high opinion they have of him and his generally accepted talent, is unable, even with the sacrifices made by the priest of Saint-Eustache, to enjoy the large-scale performances that are more or less demanded by the style of religious music and are, in my opinion, the only ones suited to very large churches.[3] He succeeds only up to a point when, with a little help, he would be able to reach his goal. It's so rare to find a man who loves his task, knows what its demands are, and crowns his talent with the energy and willpower to make it happen! Here we have a choirmaster, charged with the musical direction of one of the most important Paris churches, in itself something amazing and rare! He's a conscientious artist who has made a thorough study of sacred music. He's not an actor, not a stonemason, not a carpenter or a goldsmith. The fact is, I repeat, he's a capable musician, and a musician who loves music. Why not give him a little encouragement? ...

The performance of Cherubini's mass was remarkable for its precision, even if not in its final effect. (The orchestra had only forty-five players, and the chorus fewer than fifty singers.) It's unfortunate that it wasn't possible to include the 'Communion March', an admirably colourful orchestral piece in which the composer has painted religious ecstasy in celestial patterns and with sounds it was not often given him to find.[4] It's still more unfortunate for Cherubini's glory that it's possible to hear pieces like his 'Kyrie', his 'Gloria in excelsis', and his 'Sanctus', all of a very dull, irreligious character, already given the thumbs down by the audience of the Conservatoire concerts on a number of occasions. This mass, on the other hand, contains some good moments in the 'Credo', and an 'O salutaris' of unadorned piety.

---

    commission of Berlioz's *Grande Messe des morts* (Requiem) in 1837.

3   Berlioz showed how to do this, conducting his *Requiem* in Saint Eustache in 1850 and 1852, followed by the premiere of his *Te Deum* in 1855.

4   Cherubini's 'Communion March' is more fully discussed in article 26.

38

Music Festival in Bonn: The Beethoven Statue

JD, 3 September 1845

Berlioz wrote two articles about this occasion in the form of letters to the editor, rather than halfway down p. 1, the usual position for feuilletons. The first (22 August) told something of the project's history, the build-up to the unveiling, and the concert. This is the second article, sent from Königswinter. It concerns the event itself, in which not everything went as planned. Much of the funding came from Liszt and when, with four weeks to go, it was realized that there was no concert hall large enough to hold all those invited, he paid for one to be built. It was completed with two days to spare. Berlioz included a slightly altered version of this article in Les Soirées de l'orchestre *(Second Epilogue); but I hope readers will understand my wish to include such a characteristic piece of writing.*[1]

To the editor of the *Journal des débats* [Armand Bertin]

Dear Sir

I come rather late to tell you again about the festival to inaugurate Beethoven's statue. But please allow me to return to the matter, after everything that's already been said in its favour, in order to mention Liszt's cantata which merits a more extended review on its own than I can offer today.[2]

---

1 Berlioz, *Les Soirées de l'orchestre*. Paris: Michel Lévy frères, 1852. Translation by Jacques Barzun as *Evenings with the Orchestra*. Chicago: University of Chicago Press, 1956.
2 *Festkantate zur Enthüllung des Beethoven-Denkmals in Bonn*. The cantata includes an orchestral arrangement of the Adagio from Beethoven's Piano Trio op. 97 ('Archduke'). Alan Walker, *Franz Liszt, the Virtuoso Years, 1811–1847*. London: Faber, 1989, p. 423.

I must also mention the many distinguished artists who are known in Paris only by name, and whom we should be so happy to see there.

I'm in a village whose calm and peace contrast strangely with the tumult that was still raging a few days ago in the cities round about. Kœnigswinter is on the opposite bank of the Rhine to Bonn. Its peasantry is very proud of the glory that has redounded to it. Several old men claim to have known Beethoven in his youth. Crossing the river by boat, he often used to come, so they say, to dream and work in their fields. In fact, Beethoven had a great love for the countryside; this feeling had a considerable influence on his style and makes itself felt sometimes in those very pieces that have nothing pastoral about them. To the end of his life, he was in the habit of wandering alone through the fields, without worrying about finding somewhere to spend the night, forgetting to eat or sleep, and paying very little attention to enclosures and hunting regulations. On this subject, the story goes that one day, in the environs of Vienna, he was arrested by a gamekeeper who insisted on taking him for a poacher, setting traps for quails in the standing corn where he was sitting. Being already deaf and not understanding a word of the recriminations issuing from this inflexible representative of public order, the poor genius, with that naivety so common to poets and famous artists who never imagine that their celebrity hasn't filtered down to the lower ranks of society, began to puff, repeating, 'But I'm Beethoven, you're making a mistake! Leave me alone! I'm Beethoven, I tell you!' To which the guardian replied, like the one on the Brittany coast when Victor Hugo was on his way back from a paddle in the sea and couldn't show his passport, which he'd left in the nearby town: 'And what's it got to do with me that you're Victor Hugo, a man of letters, and that you're the author of *Mon cousin Raymond* or *Télémaque*![3] You haven't got a passport, you have to follow me, and come quietly!'

I almost didn't get to hear the mass in the cathedral on the second day, thanks to the casual attitude of the committee toward its guests, treating them much as the footmen of the Hôtel de l'Étoile do. It was impossible to get near the church doors, with the crowd blocking every entrance. pushing and shoving without mercy. It was among this rabble that the light-fingered fellows from London and Paris plied their trade most effectively. Finally, thinking there must somewhere be a door reserved for orchestra and chorus, I went on the hunt and, thanks to a kind citizen of Bonn, a member of the committee who, on hearing my name, did not ask me if I was the author of *Télémaque*, I was allowed to enter with my coat in one piece, albeit slightly creased.

---

3   This is satire: Berlioz knew that these works were not by Hugo. *Mon Voisin Raymond* (1822) is a novel by Paul de Kock, and *Les Aventures de Télémaque* (1844) is a vaudeville by Dumersan, Leuven, and Brunswick.

Once in the church, thanks to M. de Marcellus whom I hadn't seen since my time in Rome in 1832 and who turned up at the crucial moment to give me further proof of his great courtesy, I was lucky enough to find a place near the altar.[4] From the other end of the church came dreadful cries, like noises of a city under attack. Even so, the mass duly began; and the performance of the music was really remarkable. The score, less severe in style than the *Missa solemnis* and of smaller proportions, contains a number of admirable movements, and in character resembles the best solemn masses by Cherubini. It's straightforward, vigorous, and brilliant. At times, bearing in mind the tone demanded by the sacred text, there are even passages of excessive vigour, both in speed and impact. But according to a widespread rumour, most of the music in the work had been written by Beethoven for motets and hymns, and had then been adapted, with great skill, it has to be said, to the words of the divine service.[5] The choral sopranos did splendidly and, I thought, were better supported by the male chorus and orchestra than on previous occasions.

The Bonn clergy, happily less rigid than those in France, felt they could allow women to sing in this religious office. I'm well aware that otherwise a performance of the Beethoven mass would have been impossible; but this reasoning could have seemed invalid despite the exceptional nature of the occasion. In any case, it would have carried no weight in Paris, where women are only allowed to sing in church on the express condition that they are not professional singers or musicians, and that they follow the grotesque habit of sticking to tunes from vaudevilles or opéras-comiques. For many years it's been possible to hear music from the repertoire of the Théâtre-Italien at Notre-Dame-de-Lorette, but on other occasions at Sainte-Geneviève I admired a canticle sung by the ladies of the Sacré-Coeur on the tune 'C'est l'amour, l'amour, l'amour'; and it's still forbidden today in our churches for women to take part in performances of a mass by Cherubini or an oratorio by Lesueur. This means that currently it's only in theatres and concert halls that you can hear fine performances of religious music.

You could say that in France, when it's a matter of our musical institutions or of the influence we should allow to be exercised regarding our morals in this domain, we feel it's a real boon to be short on common sense.

Immediately after the mass we had to go and watch the inauguration of the statue in the nearby square. It was here especially that I had to make

---

4 Marie-Louis-Jean-André-Charles de Martin du Tyrac, comte de Marcellus (1795–1865), French diplomat and writer.
5 The performance was of Beethoven's Mass in C major op. 86 (1807), composed for Prince Esterházy; the rumour Berlioz mentions seems to be without foundation.

continuous use of fist power, thanks to which, and by bravely leaping over a fence, I managed to secure a little place in the reserved enclosure. So, when all's said and done, the invitation I'd received from the committee to attend the Bonn festivities had not actually prevented me from seeing them. We stayed there cooped up for a very long hour, waiting for the arrival of the King and Queen of Prussia and of the Queen of England and Prince Albert, who were to attend the ceremony from the vantage point of a balcony duly reserved for them. Finally, Their Majesties arrived and the cannons and bells resumed their fanfares while, in a corner of the square, a military band did its best to give us bits of the *Egmont* and *Fidelio* overtures. Once silence had been gradually restored, M. Breidenstein, the president of the committee, made a speech which affected its audience in probably much the same way as when, in antiquity, Sophocles read out his tragedies at the Olympic Games.[6] I apologise to M. Breidenstein for comparing him with the Greek poet, but the truth is that only his immediate neighbours could hear him, and that for 99 per cent of his audience his speech was inaudible. The same went more or less for his cantata. Even if the square had been quiet, I certainly wouldn't have heard much of his piece. We know how vocal music can suffer in the open air; the wind was blowing strongly over the choir, and so my helping of M. Breidenstein's harmony was unjustly removed to the spectators at the other end of the square who, gluttons as they were, found it feeble in the extreme. The same fate befell the German *chanson*, which had been entered for a prize and was crowned by a jury who had probably heard it.

How could the composers of these pieces have had even a momentary illusion as to the response that would greet them? A score that isn't played can still pass as admirable. There are people whose job it is to magnify the reputation of unknown works, but one that's made public *in the open air*, thereby necessarily making no impact, is always given a bad name and keeps that name until a reasonable performance, *indoors*, allows either the composer to abandon it, or the public to accept it. When the animated conversations of the listeners who weren't listening suddenly abated, this announced the conclusion of speeches and cantatas. Then everybody waxed attentive to see the veil over the statue being removed. When it was revealed, there was applause, hurrahs, trumpet fanfares, rolls on the drums, volleys of rifle and cannon fire, peals of bells; all this hubbub of admiration that is the voice of

---

6   H. K. Breidenstein, described by Alan Walker as 'a musician from Bonn'. Walker adds that the committee 'had never grasped the complexities of the event for which it had made itself responsible'. Walker, *Franz Liszt*, p. 418.

glory among civilized nations broke out once more and saluted the statue of the famous composer.[7]

This is the day when these thousands of men and women, young and old, whom his works have allowed to spend so many happy hours, whom he has so often raised on the wings of his thought to the highest realms of poetry; these enthusiasts whom he has excited to the point of delirium; these jokers whom he has amused by so many witty and unexpected whims; these thinkers for whom he has opened up endless fields for cerebration; these lovers from whom he draws tears by reminding them of the early days of their affection; these hearts in the grip of an unjust fate, to whom his energetic phrases have given the strength to briefly rebel, and who, rising in indignation, find a voice to blend their cries of rage with the furious sounds of his orchestra; these religious souls to whom he has spoken of God; these admirers of nature for whom he has painted with such true colours the calm, contemplative life of the fields on glorious summer days, the joys of village life, the terrors caused by the storm, the damage of the hurricane, and the consoling ray of the sun returning through the scattered clouds to smile on the anxious shepherd and restore hope to the frightened labourer; it's now that all these people, in whom sensitivity is united with intelligence and on whom his genius has shone, either peaceful or menacing; all of them are drawn to him as to a benefactor and a father.

But it's getting late; this bronze Beethoven is insensitive to such homage, and it's sad to think that the living Beethoven, whose memory we are here honouring, may not have received from the city of his birth, in the days of suffering and penury that were numerous during his arduous career, one ten-thousandth of the sums spent on his behalf after his death.

Nonetheless, it's good so to praise the demigods who are no longer with us, it's good not to keep them waiting too long, and we should thank the city of Bonn, and especially Liszt, for understanding that the judgment of posterity has been passed on Beethoven long since. A huge final concert was announced for the last day at nine o'clock in the morning, so one had to be there by half past eight. The departure of the kings and queens, who were to attend the concert and then return to the Château de Brühl later in the day, was the reason behind this unaccustomed hour. The hall was full long before the official time, but Their Majesties didn't arrive. We waited respectfully for an hour, after which it was decided to begin without them, and Liszt conducted the performance of his cantata.

We know what it's about. The orchestra and chorus, with the exception of the sopranos, fulfilled their task with a sloppiness and incompetence that

---

7   Curiously Berlioz, not normally one to miss a joke, doesn't mention that when the statue was unveiled the watchers found themselves gazing at its back.

sounded very like ill will. The cellos in particular played one very important passage in a way that made you think of students lacking either technique or experience, while the tenors and basses made several false entries and others that were ragged and uncertain. Even so, it was possible to judge this work's marked superiority over all the others written for the occasion, and even over what we expected from this composer's great abilities. But barely had the last chord been played, when an unexpected commotion in the doorway announced the arrival of the royal families, at which the whole audience stood. Their Majesties Queen Victoria and the King and Queen of Prussia, Prince Albert, Prince William of Prussia and their retinue, took their places in the huge box prepared for them to the right of the orchestra, and Liszt bravely began his cantata all over again.

That's what we call presence of mind and keeping one's head. He instantly took this decision, which turned out to be the right one: 'The public will think I started again because the King ordered me to, and so my cantata will be better played, better heard and better understood'. Indeed, nothing could be more different than the two performances of the same work ten minutes apart. Where the first had been limp and colourless, the second was precise and lively. The first had served as a rehearsal, and no doubt the presence of the royal families made the orchestra and chorus try harder, and imposed itself over the little outbreaks of ill will that had just begun to manifest themselves in the serried ranks of this musical army. We may well ask why and how ill will could have been directed at Liszt, the eminent musician whose uncontested superiority is, what's more, German, whose celebrity is immense, whose generosity is proverbial, who is regarded with reason as the true instigator of everything that's best about these Bonn festivities, who has been all over Europe giving concerts to raise money to make them possible, and who has even promised to make good the deficit, if there is one. What other feelings could a crowd display than those naturally inspired by such behaviour and efficiency? ... Heavens above! Crowds are always the same, in little towns especially, and it's precisely this efficiency and this noble behaviour that has caused offence. Some people hold it against Liszt that he's enormously talented and uniquely successful, others that he's rich, some that he's young, others that he's generous, or because he had written a cantata that was too good and because the other choral works written for and performed on the occasion weren't successful, because he has hair instead of wearing a wig, because he speaks French too well, because he knows too much German, because he has too many friends and no doubt not enough enemies, etc. One can see that the reasons for attacking him were many and serious.[8]

---

8   'Some measure of the bad feeling generated in Bonn may be gauged by the fact that when, in 1870, twenty-five years after these events, the Beethoven

Be that as it may, his cantata, which was really well played and warmly applauded by three and a half quarters of the hall, is a fine and beautiful work which at a stroke places Liszt very high among composers. Its expression is truthful, its technique correct, its style elevated and novel, its construction intelligently imagined and well executed, and its instrumentation remarkable for its power and variety. His orchestration never includes those passages of unchanging sonority that make some works, for all their quality, so tiring to listen to; he knows how to contrast small and large groups, he never demands too much of instruments or voices; in a word, he showed from the very start that he possessed what one might fear he had not yet embraced, namely *style* in his instrumentation, as in all other aspects of musical composition.

His cantata begins with a phrase that sounds interrogative, matching the meaning of the first line, and this theme, treated throughout the introduction with rare skill, returns in the peroration in a manner that is as successful as it is unexpected.[9] Several very effective choruses lead to a decrescendo in the orchestra which seems to focus the attention on what is to follow. What does follow is in fact very important, as it's the Adagio and Variations from Beethoven's B-flat Trio, which Liszt had the excellent idea of introducing into the final part of his cantata in order to make a kind of hymn to the glory of the master. This hymn, presented initially in its character of melancholy grandeur, finally breaks out into all the pomp and majesty of an apotheosis; then the theme of the cantata reappears in a dialogue between chorus and orchestra, and the piece is at an end. I say again, this new work by Liszt is vast in its size and truly beautiful in every respect. This opinion, which I don't express out of any partiality towards the composer, is also that of the very demanding critics who were there for its performance; its success was total and will continue to grow.

One could say that the contents of this concert were excessively rich; its duration had not been properly taken into account; and realization that it wouldn't be possible to perform it in its entirety came too late. That's indeed what happened. To begin with, the King, realizing instantly that he wouldn't be able to stay for such a long concert, chose the pieces he wanted to hear, after which he would leave. The royal will was obeyed

---

centenary celebrations were mounted there, Liszt was not invited'. Walker, *Franz Liszt*, p. 426.

9   The autograph of the cantata is in Weimar; the cantata was first published by Peters, New York in 1989. The interrogatives occur in the first two lines of text (by the German novelist Oskar Ludwig Bernhard Wolff [1799–1851]): 'Was versammelt hier die Menge? / Welch Geschäft rief Euch herbei?' ('What brings the crowd together here? / What business called you here?'). I am grateful to Professor Walker for sending me this text.

and the programme was reorganized as follows: (1) *Egmont* overture, (2) Weber Piano Concerto, (3) aria from *Fidelio*, (4) aria by Mendelssohn, (5) Beethoven's cantata *Adélaïde* [*sic*].[10]

The King of Prussia well understands how to assemble a programme. The *Egmont* overture was played superbly, and the coda in $\frac{2}{4}$, taken up by the orchestra with enthusiasm, produced an electric effect.[11] Mme Pleyel played Weber's concerto with rare alertness and elegance.[12] Mlle Novello sang the great aria from *Fidelio*, with three obbligato horns, correctly but without much charm; she might perhaps have done better with Hidraot's aria from *Armide*.[13] Mlle Novello wore a black dress decorated with red and gold arabesques, an indication of her taste for sombre, strange things, and which one could easily have mistaken for the costume of a necromancer at the moment he's delivering himself of his spells. This dress seems to have intrigued the Queen of England far more than the aria. Mlle Schloss sang the lovely aria by Mendelssohn admirably, in a relaxed fashion that contained magnificent tone, perfect intonation, and expressivity that was true and authentic. What a pity for opera composers that this singer refuses to have a stage career! At least her French is perfect, and I know one large opera house where she could render invaluable services.[14] I can't say as much for Mlle Kratky: she sang that sweet elegy *Adélaïde*, one of Beethoven's most touching compositions, in a dull, thick tone that was continually flat.[15] And with Liszt at the piano! ... You needed to have heard Rubini, who learned its style from Beethoven himself, to experience all it contains of melancholy tenderness and passionate languor! ...[16]

---

10 Beethoven's *Adelaide* op. 46 is a solo song; it isn't clear why Berlioz called it 'cantate'.
11 The final Allegro ('Symphony of Victory') is in 'c' ($\frac{4}{4}$), not $\frac{2}{4}$; Berlioz's mistake is probably because it would be conducted with two beats in a bar.
12 Marie-Félicité-Denise Pleyel, née Moke, known as Camille Pleyel (1811–75), Belgian pianist, teacher, and composer, who had been briefly engaged to Berlioz in 1829–31. Despite threatening revenge (see his *Memoirs*, chapters 28 and 34), Berlioz seems by 1845 to have regained some respect for her.
13 Clara Anastasia Novello (1818–1908), English soprano, daughter of the publisher Vincent Novello. The aria is 'Komm, Hoffnung'. Berlioz's poor impression is conveyed his reference to Hidraot, a vengeful character in Gluck's *Armide*, who sings bass.
14 Berlioz means services to the Paris Opéra. Sophia Schloss, a mezzo-soprano who had studied at the Conservatoire with Panseron, came for the occasion from Cologne.
15 Elise Schmezer née Kratky (1810–56), German singer and composer.
16 Rubini: see article 7, note 7.

Their Majesties left after these pieces, and then the rest of the programme was played. M. Ganz, principal cello at the Berlin Opera, gave a fine rendering of a fantasia on themes from [Mozart's] *Don Giovanni*.[17] Then young Moeser, whose success some time ago at the Paris Conservatoire we remember, played a concertino of his own composition on themes by Weber. Whatever opinion one might have of his composition, there's no way of improving on the exactness of his intonation, the purity of his style, and the vigour of his commitment.[18] What's more, he deals with difficulties by means of cheerfulness and aplomb; it's beyond doubt that he is currently one of the finest violin virtuosos in Europe. Because he had played the whole piece in the most profound silence, without applause or the faintest murmur of approbation, his success could not be foreseen, and it was sudden and overwhelming; the bravos went on and on, and the young violinist himself was so surprised that, in his joyful stupefaction, he didn't know how to make his exit, nor how to manage himself if he stayed onstage. Auguste Moeser is a pupil of Charles de Bériot, who must be very proud of him; at twenty, he's already a great violinist. M. Franco-Mendès had the unfortunate idea of sticking to his cello solo despite Ganz's which had preceded it, and the still more unfortunate one of choosing arias from Rossini's *La donna del lago* as themes for his fantasia; as a result, his performance was very badly received. Even so, the aria 'O mattutini albori' ('O morning light') is a very delightful, poetical piece; M. Franco-Mendès plays the cello beautifully; but he is Dutch and Rossini is Italian, a double source of fury for the fanatical German nationalists. A wretched business, we have to admit.

That still left an aria from [Spohr's] *Faust* sung by Mlle Sachs, a song by Haydn sung by Staudigl, and several choruses.[19] But the concert had already lasted four hours, the crowd was drifting slowly away and took me with it. It's true I didn't fight it with much desperation. The fact was another concert awaited me that evening. The King of Prussia had been kind enough to invite me to the one he was giving his guests at the chateau of Brühl and, for more than one reason, I was very keen to conserve my strength in order to find my way there and appreciate the concert.

When I reached Brühl amid fairy illuminations and heavy rain, there was another dazzling crowd set to do battle with arms of chivalry: spurs clattered on the lofty staircases, and there was a continuous sparkle of diamonds, beautiful eyes, epaulettes, pale shoulders, decorations, hairdos full of pearls,

---

17 Moritz Ganz (1802–68), German composer and cellist.
18 Auguste Moeser (1825–59), German violinist.
19 Joseph Staudigl (1807–61), Austrian bass who sang opera mainly in Vienna and London; in 1847, in Birmingham, he created the title role in Mendelssohn's *Elijah*.

and helmets made of gold. The black swallow-tail coats, I can tell you, cut a very miserable figure. Thanks to the King, who came to talk with them for a few minutes, treating them like *old acquaintances*, room was now found for them and we were able to hear the concert. Meyerbeer was at the piano. The first piece was a cantata he'd composed in honour of Queen Victoria.[20] This piece, sung by a choir with MM. Mantius, Pischek, Staudigl, and Boetticher as soloists, is candid, fast-moving, nervous, and spare in texture. It's a harmonious huzzah and full of spirit. Mlle Tuczeck then sang a lovely romance from *Il Torneo* by the Count of Westmorland.[21] (I can't get used to the idea of an English music-lover, and an aristocrat, composing such charming music.) Liszt played two pieces, as he does.

I also had my first opportunity of hearing the much-praised Jenny Lind, who is turning all heads in Berlin.[22] She possesses indeed a talent superior to anything you can hear at the moment in French or German opera houses. Her voice has an incisive, metallic timbre of great power, it's unbelievably supple, and lends itself both to half-tints, to the manifestation of passion, and to the finest filigree. Hers is a complete and magnificent talent. But, according to competent judges who have admired her in Berlin, I was able to appreciate only one facet of this talent, which needs the animation of the stage to reach its peak. She sang the duet from the third act of [Meyerbeer's] *Les Huguenots* with Staudigl, the finale of [Weber's] *Euryanthe*, and an aria with chorus that was ravishing in its originality and freshness, full of unexpected effects between chorus and soloist, vibrant and distinguished in its harmony, and smart and poignant in its melody. It was announced in the programme as 'Niobe's aria by Pacini'. Never did mystification have such a happy outcome. It's certainly the case that M. Pacini has made considerable progress and has strangely modified his style in order to write arias now so different from his earliest efforts. Clearly this piece comes from some new opera by Meyerbeer that I don't know.

Pischek and Staudigl sang a duet from *Fidelio*. Pischek's voice is one of undiluted beauty and blended admirably with Staudigl's, the power of which I have already praised. For me, Pischek's voice has the most wonderful

---

20 Meyerbeer wrote it for Princess Augusta of Prussia, but when Queen Victoria heard it, she liked it so much that he gave it to her.

21 John Fane, Lord Burghersh, eleventh Earl of Westmorland (1784–1859), soldier, diplomat, and composer, instigated the foundation of London's Royal Academy of Music in 1822.

22 Jenny Lind (1820–87), soprano nicknamed 'the Swedish nightingale'. She made her debut in *Der Freischütz* in Stockholm (1838). After studies in Paris with Manuel García, in 1842 she failed an audition at the Paris Opéra and subsequently refused offers to sing there. Berlioz admired her acting as well as her singing; see article 47.

timbre of any male singer I know. Add to which that he's young and tall, well-built and sings with unimpeachable verve, and you'll understand the haste with which the King of Württemberg took him from the Frankfurt opera and gave him a place in his chapel for life.[23]

Mme Viardot-Garcia also sang three pieces with her peerless technique and poetic expressivity, both of which seem to have acquired new qualities since her stay in Russia.[24] These were a pretty cavatina by Charles de Bériot, the scene in the underworld from *Orphée* (abominably sung by the choir, be it said in passing), and an aria by Handel, requested by the Queen of England, who knew the superior manner in which Mme Viardot interpreted the Anglo-Saxon composer. Midnight was sounding! (*Suadebant cadentia sidera somnos*).[25] Luckily, I found a place in a railway carriage to take me back to Bonn. I was in bed by 1 a.m. and slept till midday, out of my head on harmony, exhausted with admiration, giving in to an irresistible need for peace and quiet, and already yearning for the thatched cottage in Kœnig's-Winter from which I'm writing to you.

---

23   Jan Křttel Pišek (1814–73), Czech baritone whom Berlioz, having heard him again in London, considered 'perhaps the greatest dramatic singer of our time' and hoped he would sing Mephistopheles in an operatic version of *La Damnation de Faust* that he was contemplating. Pischek spent most of his career as a court singer in Stuttgart rather than pursuing a operatic career.

24   In the autumn of 1843 Viardot was in St Petersburg, where she was admired by Glinka, whose music she sang and who, like most Russians at the time, referred to her as '*our* prima donna'.

25   Berlioz slightly misquotes, no doubt relying on memory, Virgil's 'Suadentque cadentia sidera somnos' ('The declining stars encourage sleep'), from the *Aeneid* (book 4, line 81).

39

New Method of Instrumental Practice

JD, 7 June 1846

Instrumental practice, based on an understanding of the hand's anatomy, approved and annotated by M. Cruveilher, adopted exclusively by M. Thalberg[1]

Berlioz takes the opportunity of this review to state his attitude towards rules in music. His discussion of the New Method involves physiological details that really call for illustrations and is omitted.

The exact sciences have not always made a positive contribution to music when they have decided to offer their help; far from it. In the study of harmony, for instance, the calculations of mathematicians have come up with theories that are, to say the least, strange, producing results which music had little incentive to welcome, and with which the ear had little reason to be satisfied. We may even suspect that quite often it was disgusted, since the calculating harmonists, instead of initially consulting the ear at the start of their experiments in harmonic progression, paid no attention to its feelings and failed almost entirely to consult it. We know what a maze of errors Rameau got himself into with his system based on the resonance of chords. What trouble that great composer gave himself by trying to use a fundamental bass to justify agglomerations of sounds which, regarded as real chords, shocked those of a delicate disposition, or by explaining others that sounded

---

1 *De l'anatomie de la main considérée dans ses rapports avec l'exécution de la musique instrumentale ou Nouvelle Méthode instrumentale raisonnée* by F. Levacher d'Urclé, under the patronage of Thalberg. On 18 December 1846 the authorities of the Conservatoire approved the study as useful.

perfectly good and had no need of such explanations! He even reached the point of denying the evidence of his own ears and rejecting chords incompatible with his system, however good they might be, while in the case of others he remained in a state of total indecision, of absolute doubt. He didn't know if this should be declared good, if that should be included as music, and instead of asking in good faith whether his ear was pleased or not and sticking with that, he would obstinately wonder to what category of resonance the chord in question could be attached. When his musical good sense and his impeccable harmonic instinct told him that music could not reject the chord whose *natural origin* contradicted his research, he wore himself out in hopeless efforts, absurd arguments, and bizarre calculations, trying to invent a formula that could, somehow or other, be reconciled with his theory. Other theorists, who certainly don't accept his ideas, fall every day into similar errors, trying to rationalise a system of their own invention. Music scoffs at their vain deliberations, as it scoffed years ago at Rameau's, at d'Alembert's arithmetical hotch-potch, and at so many others of the same stamp.

40

Inauguration of Rossini's Statue

JD, 9 June 1846

9 June is also the date given for the inauguration itself. The statue was by Antoine Etex (1808–88), whom Berlioz had known in Rome in 1831–2. The concert consisted of the following, all by Rossini: the overtures to Il barbiere di Siviglia *and* Guillaume Tell, *the* Stabat Mater, *act 2 of* Guillaume Tell, *an aria from* Maometto II *(the Italian opera revised as* Le Siège de Corinthe *for Paris), a cavatina and a duet from* Il barbiere, *the final aria from* La Cenerentola, *the prayer from* Moïse, *and the 'divertissement' from act 3 of* Guillaume Tell.

Arguments about the statue had been going on for two years. Decades later, they were reactivated with respect to the plan in 1907 to erect a statue of Saint-Saëns in Dieppe. There were some satirical comments by those who thought a statue to the living composer premature. The monument to Gounod had only recently been put up in St Cloud. In spite of, or perhaps because of the erection of one to Marshal Macmahon in his lifetime, a law forbade the inauguration of statues to the living. But significantly, government intervention enabled the ceremony to take place in the foyer of the Dieppe Theatre. "Since one only puts up statues to the dead, it follows that I am now counted among their number" [Saint-Saëns] remarked. "You will excuse me therefore from making a speech."[1]

There's been much discussion about the expediency of this homage being made to a man who is still alive; the majority are against it. We accept as tolerable statues to men who are dead, while the other arrangement is generally rejected. I confess this is a matter beyond my capacity. In any case, the ancients were not so choosy about honours being done to living people who

---

[1] Brian Rees, *Camille Saint-Saëns, a Life*. London: Chatto and Windus, 1999, p. 379.

had earned recognition from their fellow citizens. Could it be that such enthusiasm was a reality in the great days of Rome and Athens, that it flourished in long-lasting laurels and palms, while all we have is a smelly poppy, which lives the life of poppies, gone overnight? Could it be that envy, that miserable passion of the multitudes, is still stronger and more widespread with us today? It would be a savage blow to our delicate feelings to admit as much.

The most shameful practitioner of these crass idiocies, in which common sense, good style, harmony, melody, rhythm, poetry, and music are all attacked, the most ridiculous merchant of these platitudes that contribute so powerfully, under various titles, to keep France in the state of musical barbarism in which we see it today, these purveyors of liquorice water and adulterated wine who haunt public places and private salons in order to quench the thirst for melodic rubbish felt by our children's titled nurses, our aristocratic men of the people, those producers of romances and quadrilles whose works sell in their thousands – all these people will have their portraits lithographed and framed in every shop where their goods are displayed, and at every cross-roads. Meanwhile, a great composer like Rossini would not be able to cast a living eye on his bust or statue in the foyer of the Opéra! Now there's something odd, to say the least!

What could the reason be? Our morals? Do we have morals? ... So I would agree entirely with those who think it only right and proper that this honour should be offered to Rossini in his lifetime, all the more so since he's not in Paris, despite what anybody might think about the influence of his style and school on the present and future of the Opéra![2] I would agree with them, as I say, if on this occasion the Opéra had reacted to a feeling of enthusiasm or simply of gratitude. But the Opéra no longer feels enthusiasm for Rossini, since of the four works he wrote for this house only one is in the repertoire, and since one of his most famous (*Moïse*) was so foully mutilated more than a decade ago, when it acted as a curtain-raiser, being reduced to part of its fourth act. This was performed by stand-ins of the vocal troupe, by chorus members at least half of whom had never learned the finale, and by an orchestra so incomplete that one day there were no harps to accompany the famous ensemble 'Mi manca la voce' ('My voice fails me'); the violins had to replace them by trying to improvise with pizzicatos that were a hopeless substitute. The Opéra no longer has any enthusiasm for Rossini, since it has allowed *Guillaume Tell* to be altered and shortened to the point where it no longer resembles the printed score; any amount of numbers were omitted without even asking the composer. If that's what enthusiasm leads to, what will indifference and hostility do?

---

2   Rossini had returned to Italy but settled in Paris from 1855 until his death in 1868.

The Opéra's real aim in this present business is to flatter Rossini into writing a new work for it, or at least an old one revised. But the master has his wits about him and a very positive philosophy; it's doubtful that he'll allow himself to be seduced. One knows how he reacts to homage in general. Wasn't it in a similar situation that he replied jokingly one day to people who were talking to him about having a statue cast in bronze to be set up in a public place somewhere in Italy: 'This statue's going to cost you an enormous amount of money; just give me half of what you want to spend and, during the days of the festival, I myself will climb on to the pedestal where, instead of a copy, the whole population will able to gaze at the real thing'. The illustrious composer would undoubtedly be more tempted to write for the Opéra than by all these stone statues, if he were given male and female singers of the first order, driven by the sacred fire that produces artists, an orchestra of young, brilliant, devoted players, choruses who could sing and act, and an attentive, intelligent audience – in a word, if he could count on a performance worthy of him and of the present state of music.

Here we recall an ovation of the same kind that was addressed to one of the fathers of harmony from the very highest source, through truly great enthusiasm: in 1844, at the prompting of the illustrious maestro Spontini, His Majesty the King of Prussia commissioned M. Émile Wolff, a Prussian sculptor living in Rome, to make a marble bust of Palestrina, to be placed with the Pope's approval in the entrance to the Capitol, which now houses the busts of the great poets, artists, and intellectuals that had previously been scattered over the different monuments of that capital of the Christian world.[3] The order came from Rome that this bust of the prince of sixteenth-century religious music, which was missing from the collection, be solemnly inaugurated on 7 March last. On this bust, which does the greatest honour to the already famous workmanship of M. Wolff, is the name of Friedrich Wilhelm IV, learned and generous Patron of the arts, and that of his musical director Spontini, the energetic instigator of this inauguration:

TO PIERLUIGI DA PALESTRINA
BORN 1524
DIED 1594
FRIEDRICH WILHELM IV, KING OF PRUSSIA
THROUGH THE SOLICITOUS CARE OF
CAVALIERE SPONTINI

Well said! Here's a homage that's pure and sincere and, if Palestrina were alive today, Spontini's devotion to him would only strike us as all the more precious and noble.

---

3   Émile Wolff (1802–79), German sculptor, director of the Accademia di San Luca in Rome.

41

Théâtre de l'Opéra-Comique: Revival of *Zémire et Azor*

JD, 18 July 1846

Berlioz's distaste for rules also shows for what he castigates as 'formules', patterns taken off the shelf with no thought for relevance or beauty. In contrast, he has sympathy for composers who plough their own furrow, even if their execution is imperfect. Grétry's four-act opera Zémire et Azor, *on a verse libretto by Jean-François Marmontel, was premiered at the Opéra-Comique on December 16, 1771; the story is a version of 'Beauty and the Beast'. The run reviewed by Berlioz began on 29 June.*[1]

Attempts to restore old compositions to the repertoire of the Opéra-Comique, like the one I'm reviewing today, have so far been successful. Current audiences have never shown a lack of respect for those of the early years of the century by reacting against works that were well received by the previous generation. That's because these works, true masterpieces in some respects, demonstrate expressive qualities unaffected by time: forms change, proportions grow, artistic means become more numerous and powerful, and this necessarily produces a more or less obvious difference between the musical products of varying epochs. This difference does not always work to the advantage of new pieces, especially when it comes to comparing them with some past master whose style is free of formulas. What we call musically 'old' in the negative sense of the word seems old only because of formulas. This is regularly proved by experience. Several times I've showed first-rate

---

1   André-Ernest-Modeste Grétry (from Liège, 1741–1813) was possibly the most successful composer of opéra-comique in his time. He wrote *Mémoires, ou Essais sur la musique* (1789, enlarged edition 1797), recording his early adventures (including walking to Italy to study); the book was, however, cruelly nicknamed 'Essais sur ma musique'.

musicians an aria from Gluck's *Telemaco* (an Italian opera he wrote long before his French ones) without revealing the composer's name; and there's not one of them who didn't take this aria for a fine excerpt from some modern opera he didn't know.[2]

The aria from *Telemaco* doesn't include formulas; it is pure, expressive melody, and for that reason eternally beautiful; a thousand years from now it will sound as good. An abundance of Grétry's pieces are the same, even if the quality of his style is, for me, not as lofty as that of Gluck. (One might say the same of Grétry's predecessor Monsigny).[3] His orchestration is limp, leaden, characterless, often empty and badly balanced, but the vocal lines are beautiful, true, dramatic, and touching, the modulations sometimes highly original, and the dramatic sense is always respected. This accounts for the success of *Richard Coeur-de-Lion*, of *Le Déserteur*, and of *Zémire et Azor*, successes which have in general hinged on the interest of the libretto independently of the music.[4] So [Monsigny's] *Le Déserteur* has been more successful than *Richard* because of the delightful, often hilarious naivety of the storyline, and I'm afraid it'll be the same for *Zémire et Azor*, since Marmontel's libretto is fairly dull. That's how it is: given that music's main job is to be at one with the words and the drama, it must obviously more or less share their chances of success and rise or fall with them. What's more, even when we appreciate the intrinsic beauty of each scene, that's to say the innate value of the score, if the story has only a middling impact on the audience, they won't rush in to support it – and in the theatre, success is all about audiences.

There's been a tendency lately to try reviving the music of Grétry and Monsigny with modern touches and changes in instrumentation. I've given my views often enough on the propriety of such behaviour not to need to repeat myself.[5] My current thinking is, as it's always been, that only a single arrangement would make such retouching tolerable: namely, if a composer could be found who evinced parallel qualities to the one whose work was to be strengthened by the resources of modern art, and who was superior to him in intelligence and genius. Leaving aside for the moment this question so often debated, I'd like to talk about the effect produced by the notes M.

---

2   *Telemaco ossia l'Isola di Circe*, premiered in Vienna in 1765, was not written so long before Gluck produced an opera in Paris (1774), and he had been writing French operas for the Viennese for some years. One of the first-rate musicians fooled by Berlioz in this way was Mendelssohn; Berlioz, *Memoirs*. 'Travels in Germany' I, fourth letter.

3   See article 31.

4   Grétry's opéra-comique *Richard Coeur-de-Lion* was premiered at the Opéra-Comique on 21 October 1784.

5   See article 31.

Adam has added to Grétry's score. Shortly before going to see *Zémire et Azor* at the Opéra-Comique, I had heard it at the Conservatoire, the two main roles being taken by the same singers and the work performed exactly as Grétry wrote it.[6] I must speak plainly and say that I enjoyed it more in its slightly dilapidated condition than when it was presented in new clothes specially made for it, which don't suit it, and which make it less attractive. Several of M. Adam's additional wind parts destroy the singing altogether: introducing trombones seems to me, to say the least, pointless in general, and particularly horrible in the 'La Fauvette' aria. No doubt someone will reply that in this aria the trombones only play twice, at the start of the ritornello and towards the end of the piece. To which I reply: that's far too much. What's the point of this booming brass in a ritornello of this kind of aria – one that's light, fresh, and cheerful? I can't imagine it's to make its characterization clearer and more obvious? It's about a warbler and her chicks, not a lioness and her cubs. Might it be, as one musician has suggested, a violent noise intended merely to warn the public that the famous 'La Fauvette' aria is about to begin? If so, why put it at the end as well, unless that's to warn us that the aria is about to end? Why do we need these warnings? Are we deaf? Are we in Italy, where people chatter in theatres as though they're at a fair, and where it is indeed necessary to advise the assembled company that the favourite cavatina is about to start, so that if the audience would be so extremely kind as to be silent for a few minutes, those people who like the piece can actually hear it? I feel reason and feeling have very little to do with the use of brass in this case. The addition of a harp to the trio 'Ah! Let me weep for her!' at least doesn't clash with the character of the melody, but the only reason for it is the supernatural character of the plot. It's agreed that in ballet music you must have harps whenever there's a magic scene. Even so, I must confess that when the trio was played at the Conservatoire quite simply with the two clarinets and bassoon Grétry asks for, I was deeply moved, really touched, and that in the Opéra-Comique I was left absolutely cold. Honesty compels me to agree that the change in the trio 'Veillons, mes sœurs' ('Let us keep watch, my sisters') is acceptable and perhaps necessary. In Grétry's score, this number is really a duet sung by three voices, the composer having decided, for whatever strange reason, to write for two of the voices in unison instead of three separate parts. M. Adam has added the missing part and now the trio really is a trio.

The score of *Zémire et Azor*, one of Grétry's best, abounds in melodies that are graceful, natural, and memorable, and in passages where his intentions are good even if their execution is not always beyond reproach. This

---

6   The performers on 24 May 1846 were mainly students of the Conservatoire, conducted by Habeneck.

music isn't as easy to sing as is generally thought, and, like all compositions which involve emotion, it makes serious and rare demands on its singers. To say of the artists entrusted with the roles of Azor and Zémire that they've sung them adequately is to award them considerable praise. This is rightly due to Mlle Lemercier and M. Jourdan, both Conservatoire pupils.[7] Mlle Lemercier has agility enough not to be worried by brilliant passages and vocalises like the 'La Fauvette' aria, and her voice has enough character to carry simple passages that demand energy and passion. Unfortunately, it's a rather muted voice and its emission still seems to be difficult and slightly forced. Rémusat was applauded every evening in the flute solo of 'La Fauvette', and deservedly so: he plays it superbly.[8] M. Jourdan enunciated the words excellently in his aria 'Du moment qu'on aime' ('From the moment one loves'), and even better in 'Ah! Quel tourment d'être sensible!' ('Ah! The torment of being susceptible'). His main need is to control his intonation in the highest register, where I noted frequent problems especially in moving from one register to another. His head notes are charming and in tune, but the danger for him is in the transition from chest voice to mixed voice and from mixed voice to falsetto proper. Chaix must be careful, at the start of the magical trio, to listen to the instrumental entry: the evening I heard him, he started a good quarter of a tone flat.[9] Sainte-Foy makes as much as possible out of the sad clown Ali, who gives us a rather poor idea of Marmontel's comic abilities. Marmontel, who was a pupil and admirer of La Harpe, certainly ought to have learned, among other things, a little grammar from the *Cours de littérature* of that great tragedian, the author of *Coriolan*.[10] One cannot say, I think, when talking about the sun, 'Si je le vois coucher avant votre retour' ('If I see it set before your return');

---

7   Maria-Charlotte-Léocadie Lemercier (1827–?), French soprano who sang at the Opéra-Comique from 1846 to 1862. Pierre-Marius-Victor-Simon Jourdan (1823–79), French tenor who sang there from 1846 to 1860.
8   Jean Rémusat (1815–80), French flautist, composer and conductor. In later life he lived in Shanghai, where he died.
9   François-Amédée Chaix (1820–50), French bass. He died of cholera in Rio de Janeiro.
10 Jean-François de La Harpe (1739–1803), minor playwright and fierce opponent of Gluck. Jean-François Marmontel (1723–99), French author and literary critic. La Harpe's verse play *Coriolan* was premiered at the Théâtre-Français in 1784 and was staged eighty-five times up to 1839. Berlioz points out that Marmontel failed to use the required reflexive verb. Marmontel was some years older than La Harpe and certainly *not* his pupil. He wrote or adapted librettos for Grétry and Piccinni; his books include *Contes moraux* and an autobiography, *Mémoires d'un Père*.

'Le soleil ne couche pas, il se couche'.[11] Perhaps this was the example that led the author of a well-known romance in the old Opéra-Comique repertoire to commit the same fault: 'Quand on fut toujours vertueux, / On aime à voir lever l'aurore'. ('When one was always virtuous, One liked to see the dawn break').

When we see works by members of the Academy on the stage, depraved though we may be, we quite like to hear French spoken. But what crown the literary merit of the author of the *Contes moraux* [Marmontel] and of *Coriolan* are all the nice things those two great men had to say against Gluck. They both proved that Gluck was no more than a vulgar German, a sort of Danubian peasant without melody or dramatic inspiration, who could only write brutal collections of chords or military ditties. So it is that this wretched composer of *Alceste*, *Orphée*, *Armide*, and the two *Iphigénies* has barely survived the telling criticisms of those two worthy academics. Today he's almost forgotten, while the works of Marmontel and La Harpe enjoy the full brilliance of their youth and beauty. There are men of genius for you!

What a lovely thing is La Harpe's *Coriolan*! And how intelligent! And how intelligent too to keep it in the repertoire of the Théâtre-Français and not to include Shakespeare's *Coriolan*, that savage, not to mention drunken savage.[12] Ah! We French are a nation of artists! We don't want anything to do with things that are small, tawdry, false, dull, dry, and cold: we love only what's true, tough, sumptuous, splendid, beautiful. We're a people apart among the nations, a people made essentially to understand and love art and poetry, passionate for the noble manifestations of intelligence, devoted to progress, an enemy of routine! The 100-sous pieces are right: God protects France![13]

As I'm digressing, writing about things that are no business of mine, I take the liberty of saying a few words about the music of a new ballet that's just been given at the Opéra with the title *Betty*, with music by Ambroise Thomas, one of our most distinguished composers, continually referred to by one of his more slender claims to the attention of musicians, as composer of *La Double Échelle*.[14] It's common practice among us to refer to artists

---

11 Sainte-Foy: see article 31, note 10.
12 The reference is to Voltaire's comment: 'You'd think this work comes from the imagination of a drunken savage', *Dissertation sur la tragédie ancienne et moderne*.
13 The phrase 'Dieu protege la France' (may God protect France) was embossed on the circumference of the 100-sous coin. Berlioz ironically converts this prayer into a statement: 'God *does* protect France'.
14 Ambroise Thomas: see article 12, note 22. His one-act opera (*The Double Ladder*) was premiered at the Opéra-Comique on 23 August 1837, ran for 247 performances, and was twice reviewed by Berlioz (27 August, at length in

using some unimportant work, even after they've written many other far better ones. This is a sop to the admiration one is forced to express for works of a superior order that set their composers on pedestals. It's a silly little game and everybody plays it without acknowledging the fact. So, among other serious works, Thomas has written *Mina*, a charming score, full length and of the highest calibre. But even if he'd written *La Vestale*, *Iphigénie en Tauride*, *Der Freischütz*, *Oberon*, and *Guillaume Tell*, people would still be referring to him as 'the composer of *La Double Échelle*'. So 'the composer of *La Double Échelle*' has enjoyed himself for a few weeks writing a ballet called *Betty*, and I thoroughly enjoyed listening to this lively, smart, piquant score, always distinguished and always relevant to the plot, orchestrated with a masterly hand, with brilliance, but not to excess; with variety, but not with affectation; and written throughout with taste and technique. For us it's a real stroke of luck, and all the more so as the orchestra, enjoying the music, allowed themselves the luxury of a first-rate performance. Now that commissions for operas are being given to students, at least the good news is that those for ballets are going to professionals.

JD and more briefly in *RGM*). Although Berlioz complained, as he did about Dietsch (see article 37), that Thomas had not yet chosen between two musical influences, German and Italian, he regarded him as 'above the general run of composers', with the added virtue of not using the bass drum.

42

On the Harmonium

JD, 7 October 1846

Despite the heading, the material on the Harmonium itself has been omitted; what appears here is the section on its usefulness. The article is one of several that show Berlioz not only to have been a perfectionist where music was concerned but also to have possessed what we would now call a 'social conscience', a feeling not so widely spread among composers of the time; it could well have come to him, at least in part, from his father, whom he saw 'to be a humane, unprejudiced, sensitive man of liberal outlook and broad intelligence, well read in Latin and French classical literature, and devoted to his work and his fellow-creatures'.[1] As the doctor in the small town of La Côte-St-André, Louis-Joseph Berlioz was, by all accounts, not merely respected but loved.

The popularization of music in small provincial towns, market towns, and even in villages far away from musical centres has often attracted the notice of serious-minded people who take an interest, either in the progress of music itself, or in the civilization of the lower classes, and who regard music as a very powerful means of achieving these ends. Sadly, in very many cases such attempts have, in my view, tended to produce either the opposite result to that intended, or no result at all. For music to exist, there are absolute requirements that must be met. Without these, the noises that are given the title of music must necessarily horrify those of a delicate disposition and encourage the barbarism of those who aren't. I conclude from this that it would be better not to play any kind of music to people who are totally deprived of it, rather than get them used to the sort they're all too often given.

---

[1] Hugh Macdonald, *Berlioz (The Master Musicians)*. London: Dent, 1982, p. 2. Berlioz's 'social conscience' had more to do with education than politics. He supported the 1830 revolution, but not that of 1848, and was never a republican, considering an authoritarian government preferable in that it was more likely to support the arts (although in this he was often disappointed).

It's hard, unless you've experienced it, to get an idea of the grotesque results produced by the so-called philharmonic societies in the provinces. The honking of a gaggle of geese, accompanied by the grunts of several angry pigs give you an idea of their orchestras at full belt, and as for their soloists ... I give up. A fair number of those playing in the middle of the texture, such as the second violins and the violas, have clearly acquired their vocation in answer to the conductor's question: 'Can you play the viola?' To which they must have given the famous reply: 'I'm not sure, I'll give it a go'. The outcome is that violists, like violinists, are divided into three classes. The first class contains those who can't play at all, the second those who play badly, and the third those who play well. The first class sticks to the instrument, believing it has already reached the second class and will soon make it to the third. I even came across one person who passed as first viola in a quite respectable provincial orchestra, but who, in the rehearsal of a ballet from *Armide* I wanted to include in a concert, could never tear himself away from the single note Gluck wrote to accompany the melody. I realized then that if I hadn't had a group of other violas, my concert wouldn't have been like that of the famous Bilboquet, and that 'those who like that note' would have had reason to be outraged.[2] Clearly this fiddler belonged to the first class.

I've lost count of the number of times I've surprised bass players bravely playing an instrument tuned F-sharp–E-flat–A instead of G–D–A, without imagining anyone could find fault with them, and unable to understand the pun aimed at them by the second class players, 'Those guys are going to fall into the dungeons'.[3] I came across something even worse, but it was with a group of Paris amateurs fifteen years ago that the phenomenon manifested itself. At the first rehearsal, it was all to do with one of those wonders unknown to the general public these days, a marvel they might well be introduced to once a year to produce one of those bursts of hysterical laughter

---

2   The reference is to *Les Saltimbanques*, a comédie-parade by Charles Varin (1798–1869) and Théophile-Marion Dumersan (1780–1849), premiered at the Théâtre de Variétés on 25 January 1838. The character Bilboquet says, 'It's easy! All you have to do is blow; also, you'll only play one note, always the same one, and the people who like that note will be thrilled'.

3   'Dungeon' in French is 'basse-fosse'. French players of the time favoured the three-stringed contrabass. Berlioz preferred the four-stringed one, noting that the Italian virtuoso Domenico Dragonetti (1763–1846) agreed, and that he 'has set up a contrabass school in London in which the instrument is tuned in fourths: thanks to this method, English players have acquired an undisputed superiority in this area' (*Le Rénovateur*, 12 October 1835, *CM* vol. 2, p. 310.)

that make us all feel so much better. The work is question was a symphony by Girowetz [*sic*].[4]

From the first bars, a clarinet part that rose triumphantly a minor third above the key of the rest of the orchestra made me think the player had got the wrong part. A check was made, and this wasn't the case. We started again. The piece was in D, and here again was my amateur playing in F with imperturbable aplomb. Someone showed me his part, clearly identifying 'clarinet in A'. But he only had one instrument, in C; hence the error. 'If you haven't got the instrument specified', I said to him, 'you'll have to transpose and play a minor third below what's written'. 'Ah! dear me', he replied, 'I'm not in the habit of transposing'. 'Oh well! In that case, don't play'. But this extreme solution didn't suit the ideas of our amazing clarinettist; he wanted to play, come what may, and nobody could stop him. I remember being so upset by this overweening ambition that in my haste to get out I left my hat behind.[5] Well, the 'philharmonics' of a vast number of French, English, and Italian Societies give these astonishing rackets the name of 'music'. This shows clearly enough not only that they haven't the faintest idea about this art but, more than this, that they have a false idea of it, and that their untutored ears are further stiffened by the frequent exercise given them by these diversions, worthy to be heard by Turks and Moroccans.

Even so, how many famous musicians have come from the provinces, whose feeling for music would never have been awakened without the happy accident of some early musical impression. More than once, it's been the organ that's given birth to this. By and large an organ is in tune, which matters. And then most organists know a bit about harmony and have a rough idea about the keyboard. And even if they only know how to put together progressions of three of four chords correctly, that could be enough to develop musical feelings in people and inculcate them in larger groupings. Wasn't it through listening to an organ that Méhul conceived his great passion for music?[6] Why is it that so many celebrated composers and singers have come from cathedral choir schools? It's not so much, I think, because someone had taught them the rudiments of music in their childhood, more that they were immersed in harmony from their very early years.

In their churches these children had constantly heard music that was serious, harmonious, and which by its nature led to reverie; they therefore

---

4   Adalbert Gyrowetz (1763–1850), Bohemian composer who was once startled to see a work of his own published in Paris under the name Joseph Haydn.

5   Berlioz reused this anecdote in *Les Grotesques de la musique*. Paris: Bourdilliat, 1859; reissue Paris: Calmann Lévy, 1880, pp. 20–21; translated by Alastair Bruce as *The Musical Madhouse*. Rochester: University of Rochester Press, 2003, p. 11.

6   Méhul's first musical study was as an organist.

benefited from excellent conditions towards becoming, if not all of them poets in music, at least stylish musicians and good players. That's why I see the popularisation of the organ and the instruments of that family as being the primary element in the musical civilization of the untutored provinces. But an organ, however small it may be, costs the sort of money many communities can't afford, added to which an organist has to be paid to play it. While the harmonium, an instrument of the organ family, has the advantage of being able to produce crescendos and diminuendos, giving it an expressive character not found in ancient organs, its chief importance is that its moderate cost means it's within the budget of almost every church.[7]

---

[7] Here Berlioz is writing about the harmonium invented and patented (including the name) by Alexandre-François Debain in 1842. In 1844 a similar instrument was devised by the firm Alexandre, but they had to use a different name: 'Orgue-mélodium'. Alexandre commissioned composers including Adam, Meyerbeer, and Berlioz, to write pieces for his instrument. Berlioz's *Trois pièces* ('Rustic serenade to the Madonna, to the sound of Italian bagpipes', 'Toccata', and a fugal 'Hymne for the Elevation') were published in 1844. Édouard Alexandre (who came from a Jewish family) remained a friend of Berlioz and supported him financially; as a quid pro quo, Berlioz contributed publicity for the firm, less by music than by advocacy in writing, including in the second edition of his *Grand Traité*.

43

Paris Opéra: Premiere of *Robert Bruce,* a Pastiche in Three Acts, Music by Rossini

JD, 2–3 January 1847

This premiere took place on 30 December 1846 with Paul Barroilhet as Robert and Rosine Stoltz as Marie. The plot was concocted by two librettists, the Belgian Gustave Vaez (1812–62) and the Frenchman Alphonse Royer (1803–75).

The situation at the Opéra is extremely serious. I shan't deal with the question of money, about which I'm ignorant and which anyway I'm not competent to write about; as I understand it, it's a question over which the government has the right to intervene, rather than any individual. Instead, I'll concentrate on the musical resources still available to this unfortunate theatre, and on the influence of the disastrous condition to which it finds itself reduced upon the state of the art throughout France, to the astonishment of those who visit our country. This ruin of an institution which was, and maybe still is, so beautiful, so much loved by our country in every way – for which it makes so many sacrifices each year, and which it's in the habit of regarding as the focal point of its pretentions to artistic splendour –this ruin is due to causes we can't help wondering about, the reality of which continues to strike everyone who can see clearly and is without prejudice.

    Having failed to acquire a new work from any of the major composers of Germany, Italy or France, the Opéra has found itself constrained to beg Rossini to do them the insulting favour of rummaging around in his paperwork to extract from it fragments of old scores made popular throughout Europe by the best Italian singers – admirable fragments, no doubt, but which, put together more or less competently by someone else, could not by any means, at any time or in any country however barbarous, constitute a true, serious work of art or, whatever the posters might tell us, justify the title of 'a new opera'.

It was six years ago at least that M. Meyerbeer completed a large work called *Le Prophète*.[1] Once he'd put the finishing touches to it, he came to Paris but, finding even then that the Opéra's musical resources weren't up to giving a good performance of his work, he immediately went back to Prussia. Two years later he finished another opera, *L'Africaine*, more suited, he thought, to the state of the personnel in our great opera house. But while he'd been working on it, the destructive forces within the Opéra had been active, and M. Meyerbeer, returning to the theatre after a fairly long absence, had to realise that *L'Africaine* could not, without very considerable risk, accept the hospitality it was being offered.[2]

Finally M. Meyerbeer wrote *Le Camp de Silésie*, which was premiered with great success in Berlin, which he is currently staging in Vienna, and which we are vainly hoping to see in Paris.[3] So the illustrious composer, whose two great works *Robert le Diable* and *Les Huguenots* have played such a large part in the Opéra repertoire over the last sixteen years, has three times provided the example of a hesitation that's found its imitators. Even though he disguised this hesitation with the politest of excuses, he was nonetheless motivated by a real, profound conviction, and one that today's audiences share, namely that trying to put any score like his through the Opéra's mill is a waste of time.

Everybody knows it: music has no existence or impact without a performance. And performance takes its value from the direct interaction between its own qualities, inner powers, and the inner powers and special qualities of the composition. An orchestra and chorus, however good they may both be, are not enough to guarantee the success of a work whose interest is equally divided between mass action and the individual emotions of a greater or smaller number of individuals. The artists charged with representing these characters should normally be both actors and singers; and in order to be both an actor and a singer one needs natural abilities developed by study, and by resources of energy, heart, soul, and intelligence that are rarely found together. If it's ridiculous to give the name 'actress' to a woman

---

1   *Le Prophète* was eventually premiered at the Opéra on 16 April 1849. Berlioz's generally favourable review (*JD*, 20 April) is in *CM* vol. 7, 115–28.

2   *L'Africaine* had not received all the finishing touches when Meyerbeer died; it was first performed at the Opéra nearly a year later, on 28 April 1865, with final revisions by Fétis.

3   Berlioz gave a French title to Meyerbeer's German opera *Ein Feldlager in Schlesien* ('A Military Camp in Silesia'), which was premiered in Berlin on 7 December 1844. A French version, *L'Étoile du nord*, was given at the Opéra-Comique on 16 February 1854.

who, without taking any part in the action, comes to the front of the stage, sings her cavatina and then leaves, it's also unfair to give the name 'singer' to someone whose talent consists merely in firing great blasts of sound, in attempting ambitious vocalises which she can't manage, someone who can't sing two consecutive notes in tune, and who can't hold a candle to the least adept wind player in simple melodic style and tasteful ornamentation. An admirable singer who once had a marvellous voice, a first-rate musician and splendid actor, despite all the sympathetic gratitude with which he is surrounded, despite the splendid shafts of light that his inspired ardour can, now and then, cast on the deep shadows in which he's now forced to live, is no longer an interpreter a composer can use if there's no longer a voice. Another singer whose voice is powerful and with a wide compass, but whose inexperience is blatant, cannot command the confidence of either composers or public. The one whose voice and technique can only operate in a mood of calm and sang-froid that doesn't tally with the mood of the drama is of only middling value, and it can be dangerous to rely even on the mood we credit in him. If some singers learn enough for them to be classed as *useful* mediocrities, if their voice unfortunately has a timbre that's ugly or grotesque, they will inevitably be treated by composers as one of the *terrible* mediocrities, and by the public as insupportable. These propositions seem to me as plain as a pikestaff, and only the necessity of discussing the sad state of the Paris Opéra has forced me to mention them here.

Well now! Without talking about the works that could have been staged but haven't been, so as not to see them fail thanks to an interpretation that's false, heavy, and dull, what works are there in the repertoire whose current performance has more or less stuck to the truth? I'm not talking about Gluck's and Spontini's masterpieces which haven't been in the repertoire for ages, whose sentiment and style are foreign to all the present singers of the Opéra, and not a single role of which could be sung complete except in the most mediocre fashion. Could it perhaps be [Meyerbeer's] *Robert le diable*? But Gardoni, who was happy to sing the principal role as it's written, is no longer at the Opéra (whatever may have been the reasons for his departure, the fact is that he wanted to leave and that he's left).[4] Duprez, in order to tailor the role to suit the imperious demands of his voice, has perverted the work in many places and only sings the rest with efforts that are as painful for his listeners as for himself.

Might it be [Meyerbeer's] *Les Huguenots*? Where is the Valentine? Have you got a truly lyrical tragedienne, a truly large soprano voice like those

---

4   Italo Gardoni (1821–82), Italian tenor, was engaged at the Opéra from 1844 to 1846. After a few months at the Théâtre-Italien, he moved to London in the summer of 1847 to perform with Jenny Lind, before returning to Paris.

demanded by all those passionate roles like Valentine? I may get a reply suggesting half a dozen, but I'm only asking for *one*, and it's precisely this *one* who doesn't exist. This absence is equally obvious in [Halévy's] *La Juive*, in which the fine role of Rachel doesn't respond any better to 'more or less'.

Is it [Rossini's] *Guillaume Tell*? But this score is mutilated in the most dreadful fashion; you could make another opera out of all the bits of music that have been removed since Duprez took the role of Arnold; but do these cuts have the positive effect of making the role of Mathilde possible, since otherwise it's very heavy for the young singer who has the role at the moment?

Could it be [Donizetti's] *Lucie de Lammermoor*? Apart from Duprez, who will always be splendid in the role of Edgard, even if there only remained six notes to support his poetic inspiration, and Barroilhet, who's an excellent Ashton, I don't think that the overall performance of this work at the Opéra could seriously stand comparison with the one at the Théâtre-Italien.[5] Should it be like this?

What about the operas M. Halévy wrote for Mme Stoltz? While admitting that terrible imperfections mar the overall performance of these fine works, can we at least dare to say that Mme Stoltz sings her roles in an irreproachably fine manner? The truth is, we can't. While she is best suited to female characters who are impetuous, strong, and violently passionate, or to playing dashing young men, and possesses undoubted skill as an actress even if it's not always governed by perfect taste, she is not at all suitable to parts that call for naivety, candour or unfeigned tenderness, let alone artless grace or goodness. Whereas she was dramatic in many passages of her role as queen of Cyprus, in *Charles VI* on the contrary she lent Odette traits that were very odd, to say the least, and very different from those that seemed natural to the role.[6] So much for her as an actress. As a singer, Mme Stoltz possesses a bright mezzo-soprano voice that's beautiful and even moving in the middle register, worn and harsh in the upper one, unimpressive in the lower one,

---

5   Duprez and Barroilhet took these roles on eight occasions between 23 March and 8 May 1847. Duprez: see article 9, note 3. Barroilhet: see article 19, note 1.

6   Rosine Stoltz created the role of Catarina in Halévy's *La Reine de Chypre* (22 December 1841), and of Odette in his *Charles VI* (15 March 1843). Berlioz and Stoltz were not always at loggerheads. However, he had advised her not to tackle full soprano roles but to be content with those for mezzo-soprano or even contralto. Not long after her success as Ascanio in *Benvenuto Cellini*, she sang Agathe in the French translation in Weber's *Der Freischütz* (1841), for which Berlioz supplied the recitatives necessary for performance at the Opéra; he was annoyed that she transposed her arias down despite being able to reach higher notes in ensembles.

agile enough to manage various simple *vocalises*, strong enough to be heard against vocal and instrumental climaxes, but lacking control in her tuning, which tends to be flat. Although she is a good musician in general, she lacks style; her treatment of ornaments is in doubtful taste and her placing of vocal accents is often faulty; the resulting combination of notes of varied qualities and tuning, some acceptable, some not, bring to mind those necklaces worn by savages, a jumble of large beans, fragments of coral, flaking pearls, bits of wood, fish-bones, teeth, and gristle. All in all, Mme Stoltz's voice today causes even the least sensitive listener constant anxiety and very often sheer pain. In one role only, that of Léonor in *La Favorite*, her good qualities abound and her faults appear less striking.[7] This score is also, when Duprez is having a good day, one of those less badly performed at the Opéra.

Can we now be surprised that composers are not at all keen to write for a theatre where such terrible possibilities are in store for them, and in which success itself, if by any remote chance it could be promised them, would be accompanied by the vexation of seeing their most heartfelt ideas, their noblest inspirations perverted or wrecked, and a stop put to their search for the truth, the grandeur, and the beauty of music. And how could they avoid being crushed by this trap? There's no talent, no genius that could withstand it. The utmost goodwill, the strongest desire to be equal to the task drives every one of the artists to whom the composer's fate is to be entrusted: the director is full of the best intentions, ready to make every kind of sacrifice; but the day of the performance arrives, the public listens, suffers, and goes away unhappy; they return, suffer again, grumble, and go away even more unhappy; they come back a third time, suffer still more bitterly, express their disappointment with some energy, go away, and this time do not come back. That's what the future inevitably holds now for large enterprises destined for the Opéra, because of the outrageous disproportion between the unyielding demands of the music and the means of execution operated by this theatre; because also of the slow but continual development of the public's musical understanding, which today allows them to appreciate any number of effects they would never have noticed fifteen years ago.[8]

But, someone will say, is there not a single one of the new works that's properly staged and sung at the Opéra? – There's one. Do you know which?

---

7   The principal role in Donizetti's *La Favorite* (1840) was composed specifically for Stoltz.

8   Berlioz's dim view of the Opéra was no doubt affected by the management's poor behaviour over *Benvenuto Cellini* in 1838–9, and he was further maltreated in 1847 when they said that an opera he had started composing on a libretto they had offered him (*La Nonne sanglante*, by Scribe) must be put in rehearsal at once, although the manager (Duponchel) surely knew that even the libretto was not yet complete, let alone the music.

L'âme en peine![9] It's a lovely little character opera, containing some lovely little pieces of music, well sung according to its character by Barroilhet, whose voice and technique always demonstrate really brilliant qualities, and by Mlle Nau, whose grace, languid, gentle, calm, meek and passive, lends the utmost charm to the principal role. Brémond's fine voice also brought the best out of a curiously coloured ballade.[10] I don't know who replaced Gardoni in the tenor role. But when it comes down to it, does the Opéra receives a grant of 600,000 francs so it can produce a reasonable staging of a character opera in two acts?

These opinions, as conscientious as they are severe, cannot, I know, be judged by a mathematical demonstration. One can't use algebra to prove the poor timbre of a voice, a fault in expression, a melodic platitude, etc. But such things can certainly be felt and, on any given point, the opinion of a majority of capable judges counts as certainty. So, I firmly believe that as regards the current state of the Opéra, out of six hundred practising musicians chosen at random in Paris, there are at least five hundred and eighty who agree with me.

In this state of things, and forced by his contract with the state to produce annually so many new acts (or supposedly new), it's clear that M. Pillet, who had no substantial new opera to hand, got out of his difficulties by tapping Rossini's philosophic impartiality.[11] He alone, out of all living composers, has developed such a disdain for his own works that he allows them to be wasted and revised as has just been done to produce *Robert Bruce*. Despite his lack of respect for the elements of music that go to make up expressive truthfulness and respect for character, he nonetheless knows better than anyone what these things consist of, and how far one can go without their support. He'd be the first to say, if he was prepared to speak seriously just for a minute, that a piece conceived and written as well as you would expect and consisting of musical items written fifteen, twenty or thirty years earlier for five or six different operas whose various subjects had been borrowed, one from the poetry of the North, another from that of the Midi, extracts from Tasso or Walter Scott; Rossini, I'm saying, would be the first to confess that this kind of agglomeration of different elements cannot decently claim to bear the title of opera, and still less because of the respect due to serious works of art. It is indeed very irritating that a director of the Académie

---

9 *L'âme en peine* (*The Soul in Torment*) by Friedrich Flotow (1812–83) was premiered at the Opéra on 29 June 1846.

10 The French bass Matthieu-Joseph Brémond (1810–78). Mlle Nau: see article 6, note 3.

11 Léon-François-Raymond Pillet (1803–68) was director of the Opéra from 1840 to 1847. He resigned after an argument with Rosine Stoltz, whose relationship with him had her termed 'la directrice du directeur'.

royale de musique should have been licensed to bring such an object before the musical world and to follow in the footsteps of the compilers. What is now to stop another director doing what was done once at the Odéon and elsewhere, and putting together a pastiche composed not of different works by the same man but by several composers, inventing the most lurid couplings between two antipathetic artists: Beethoven and Rossini, Weber and Verdi, Mozart and Musard![12] There's no shortage of people with vulgar tastes who might enjoy these horrible potpourris. But such outrages against art don't often bring happiness to those responsible. A wretch dared to produce under the name Mozart, in Paris some time ago, an abominable pastiche called *Les Mystères d'Isis*.[13] This was a foul stew of movements torn out of *The Magic Flute*, arias from *Don Giovanni* turned into trios, shreds from Haydn symphonies, an 'Andante' from *La Clemenza di Tito*, mixed up with 'Allegros' composed by the arranger; this miscreant is still alive and is dragging out a painful, obscure old age in Vienna.

I hasten to add that things have not sunk to that level with *Robert Bruce*; this pastiche has been put together with more skill and care, and also with Rossini's blessing. But even so it's still a pastiche, a compilation, the feeble fall-back of theatres which are without true men, and of men who are without ideas. I repeat, it's very sad that the director of the Opéra has been reduced to needing it, and still sadder that he has been allowed to turn to this last resort.

So, what effect did this strange musical object have at its first performance? A terrible one, and the worst of any M. Pillet might have been dreading: namely that of exposing to the public the vast distance separating the singers of his troupe from those for whom Rossini wrote these brilliant passages. Even if you'd made the choice deliberately to advertise this crushing comparison, you couldn't have made a better job of it. I'm tempted to suppose that Rossini, the greatest mystifier in the known world, presided personally over this manoeuvre in order to play a smart trick on the Opéra. And, Heavens above, enough of his operas have been wrecked in this theatre for years on end for such an act of vengeance, by an artist and a man with his

---

12   Philippe Musard (1792–1859), French composer, mainly of dance music, and conductor of the very popular Concerts Musard, mentioned here because Berlioz enjoyed the near-identity of his name (in French pronunciation) with 'Mozart'.

13   *Die Zauberflöte* (*The Magic Flute*), premiered in Vienna in 1791, reached the Paris Opéra on 20 August 1801 in a much-altered form as *Les Mystères d'Isis*, with a French libretto by Étienne Morel de Chédeville and music arranged by Ludwig Wenzel Lachnith (1746–1820). The German original was performed at the Théâtre-Italien on 21 May 1829.

wits about him, to appear not merely excusable, but of an admirable finesse in its cruelty.

Can you imagine Mme Stolz battling against the memories of all those divas who sang in *La Donna del lago*, in *Zelmira*, *Bianca e Faliero*, etc.? And Bettini repeating before us those splendid passages, those floating vocalises with which Rubini enchanted his breathless audiences a few years ago?[14] Both of them sounded like runners-up in a Conservatoire violin competition, struggling with a Paganini concerto. Instead of the enthusiastic shouts that these passages once provoked, there were groans of misery when, twice, Bettini's voice cracked on the same high note Rubini used to sing with such ease. As for the famous cavatina 'O mattutini albori' ('O morning dawn') from *La Donna del lago*, one of Rossini's freshest and most delightful moments, Mme Stolz would not, even in better days, have come close to equalling the poetic renderings of the prima donnas everyone remembers. But last Wednesday, singing flatter than usual, for five whole minutes she made us endure a veritable torture, cruelly accentuated by the solo horn's entry in unison with the voice, but playing it at pitch while the soprano went on with her flat contributions. Despite this, no one in the hall said anything. It was only in the second act, the singer's pitch becoming less and less *arguable*, that the physical pain felt by the audience began to grow and, once the claque had applauded sarcastically, one began to hear widespread sounds of disapproval. Mme Stolz, who was apparently indisposed, waxed indignant; which led to an unusual scene that distracted and absorbed the whole audience.

Mme Stolz could not contain her indignation. She stopped singing and, strutting furiously round the stage and raising her eyes to heaven, she ended by ripping up her handkerchief and strewing the bits over the stage, while shouting, 'I cannot understand how one can insult a woman so viciously!' We're told that after she'd stopped singing, Mme Stolz thought she heard (or really did hear) an insult sent in her direction, in which case her fury is understandable.[15] But I think that at the beginning of the outbreak she reacted badly. If instead of saluting the complainants three times, she had walked up to the footlights and said simply, 'Gentlemen, I'm still unwell, show a little indulgence for my voice, I'll do the best I can!', then the entire audience might not have encouraged her enthusiastically or weathered without complaint her voice's painful imperfections. But instead of

---

14 *Zelmira* was premiered in Naples on 16 February 1822, *Bianca e Faliero* in Milan on 26 December 1819. Alessandro Bettini (1821–98), Italian tenor, had a long and successful career, mainly in London, Paris, and Rome.

15 Following the appearance of Berlioz's article, the *Journal des débats* published a letter from Stoltz to the editor, claiming that she had been forewarned of a concerted display of insults.

this compromise, irritation was shown on both sides and a veritable tempest ensued, one that might have led to even greater trouble had the majority of the audience not shown, as always, an indulgence and a politeness that can hardly be too highly praised in the circumstances.

This unfortunate incident overshadowed the fine finale from *La Donna del lago* that completes the second act of *Robert Bruce*. Even so it was warmly applauded, the staging being extremely beautiful and well-rehearsed. These bards in their white tunics, held in by a belt of iron; all the Scottish clans grouped on the mountain at the back of the stage; the multitude of lances, harps, and claymores [traditional Scottish long swords] make a fine picture. The bards' chorus, mixed with the hunting fanfares and the voices of the Scottish soldiery, was very effective. But the dramatic context of this passage is so simple that, with the means at his disposal, M. Pillet could have conjured up an unusually grand and powerful scene. Under no great pressure, with a week's rehearsal and at very little cost, his task was to make this final piece and its staging strong, unparalleled and overpowering … Instead, this musical ensemble, although, as I say, very fine, does not go beyond previous successes of the kind at the Opéra. The third act lacks excitement, and among the musical items in it there's only the great final sextet that makes any impact. I don't know what opera the chorus of horsemen comes from: 'Buvons, buvons, il faut saisir, / Amis, les heures du plaisir' ('Drink, my friends, we must seize the hours of pleasure'). But it is in every respect a long way from the famous bacchanal in *Le Comte Ory*.

The storyline is taken from an episode in the wars of Robert the Bruce with the English king Edward II. There are marches, contra-marches, ambushes, chases. The Scottish king, surrounded by the English army, is surprised with Marie (daughter of Douglas-the-Black) by Arthur, an English officer in Edward's service and the lover of Marie, loved by her in return. The young man is jealous, not recognizing Robert. The young girl pleads for Robert, appealing to the generosity of her lover. He responds by saving Robert the Bruce, who on leaving gives him an oak twig which Arthur will wear on his helmet during the battle, and which, allowing his noble enemy to recognize him, will allow the two men to avoid fighting each other.

Later on, Arthur, denounced to the English king as responsible for Robert's escape, is condemned, in the midst of a fete, for high treason. He faces death when Edward who, despite several warnings, puts important matters off till the next day, is surprised in his turn by Scots in the midst of his dancers and minstrels: Robert has surrounded his palace, and Edward is a prisoner. Arthur, saved from death, marries Marie. Robert cries out, 'Scotland, to thee independence!' The Chorus, 'To Robert immortality!'

MM. Vaez and Alphonse Royer have worked miracles in constructing a libretto that is logical and serves as a poetical link for so many single items from a variety of scores.[16] They have regularly found words that echo the sense of the music and so have corrected, as far as they were able, the main problem with pastiches, namely the disjunction between the music and the words required for the plot. Honours for the dancing go to Mlles Maria and Adèle Dumilâtre.[17] Barroilhet sang splendidly; Anconi, who has a good technique, also has a voice that's lovely in the middle register, but less pure and slightly veiled in the higher one. Calm, unexcitable roles suit them best. Mlle Nau showed grace in her tiny role; she was wildly applauded and warmly awarded encores. I must not forget to mention several magnificent sets, those of the second act especially which represent a view of the Scottish mountains, painted by MM. Séchan, Diéterlé, and Despléchin; it was greatly admired.[18] The second performance of *Robert Bruce*, which should have taken place last Friday, has again been delayed 'owing to indisposition'.[19]

---

16   Gustave Vaez (1812–62), Belgian playwright and librettist; Alphonse Royer (1803–75), French playwright and librettist.
17   Maria Jacob, known as Maria (1818–?), French dancer, engaged by the Opéra in November 1833; Adèle Dumilâtre (1821–1909), French dancer engaged in 1834.
18   Charles Polycarpe Séchan (1803–74), Éduard-Désiré-Joseph Despléchin (1802–70), Michel Diéterlé (1811–89), painters and set designers at the Opéra.
19   The indisposition, presumably, of Rosine Stoltz. The second performance, initially announced for 1 January, was finally given on 4 January.

44

Adolphe Sax's New Concert Hall

JD, 14 February 1847

The Belgian instrument-maker Adolphe Sax (1814–94) arrived in Paris in 1842. In the first edition of Berlioz's Grand Traité, *of the Sax instruments only the saxophone is considered; others, such as saxhorns, are treated in the second edition (1855). Berlioz's promotion of Sax's work helped get him established in Paris; in another quid pro quo (cf. that with Alexandre; see article 42), Sax in turn offered Berlioz facilities for rehearsal and storing the considerable quantity of performing parts needed for his concerts.*

The size of concert halls is generally proportionate to the love the public are supposed to have for music, and their interior arrangement is in keeping with the kind of music to be performed there. That's why we don't have a large concert hall in Paris. There are halls for banquets, halls for balls, halls for drawing lots for military conscription etc., but we haven't got a single concert-hall worthy of the name that can be hired when you need one. Hence the impossibility of performing certain compositions, if theatres either won't or can't be transformed into concert halls, and especially during the winter when the exclusive use of the furniture repository of the Crown, itself extremely small, is reserved for the Société des Concerts du Conservatoire.

Some years ago, M. Herz had an excellent hall built for medium-sized concerts, that is for those where you can hear instrumentalists and singers accompanied by a piano or small orchestra.[1] But even apart from the fact that the stage is badly placed for even a body of forty performers, it's

---

1   In 1838 the Austrian composer, pianist, and teacher Henri Herz (1803–88) had built a concert hall inside his piano factory at 48 rue de la Victoire. Seating 668, it was one of the largest halls in Paris, together with the Salle Pleyel and the Conservatoire. It was here that Berlioz conducted the first complete performance of *L'Enfance du Christ* in 1854.

impossible for seating the large orchestra of today; from which it follows that one can't even think of adding any kind of chorus. Since the city of Paris is too unmusical to support the construction of a suitably worthy building, we ought to think ourselves lucky to have M. Herz's hall, were it not that any number of cases have proved that, while too small for large concerts, this hall was too large for the small audiences drawn to medium-sized concerts. It holds eight hundred people ... How these days, except for concerts with no entrance fee, is one to attract an audience of eight hundred for a violinist, pianist or singer? ...

This is the problem to which M. Sax was fully alert in putting up his new hall, which is half the size of M. Herz's.[2] Of course it will only hold a tiny orchestra, but at least it holds an audience of only four hundred, which means there's a chance of filling it when a celebrated virtuoso of the highest talent performs there. It has good acoustics, is well decorated, is easy to get to, being in the best part of Paris, and the price of hiring it is reasonable. It had a worthy inauguration last Sunday with the recital by Laurent Batta, an excellent pianist and the brother of the well-known cellist whom we hear too rarely.

Sax is not yet free of the lawsuits brought against him by his rival instrument makers. Claiming that he's unmarried and Belgian, while they are French and the fathers of families, they want to deprive him of the copyrights he has acquired for the improvement of wind instruments. I'm sure these are both good reasons, but it's doubtful that they will prevail with the judges if his opponents don't have any others to offer. Sax's contributions are important for music in general and for military music in particular. Thanks to this artist's talent and perseverance, thanks to the questions he has raised, the discussions he has set in motion, and the outcomes he has provoked, our military bands show clear evidence of progress on several fronts. The regimental orchestras are rather larger than they were; military bands, technically superior and with better instruments, will soon be both better paid and better regarded. The study of the fine instrument he has invented is already on the syllabus of the Gymnase-Musical; a special saxophone class has been created in this establishment. And while people trouble him by contesting his inventions, he goes on making plans and bringing to fruition other projects which will be realized not as far in the future as we might think; not to mention his vast steam organ, destined for public festivals and with a relationship to present organs comparable to that between the pedal

---

2   Situated at 10 rue Neuve-Saint-Georges, Sax's hall was to be used to publicise his instruments as well as being hired out for concerts.

notes of Notre-Dame and hand-bells.[3] Let us also note his instrumental programme for a totally modern orchestra, a programme that would provide a skilful composer with an opportunity for brilliance.

Sax's idea is to provide a very large symphony orchestra with all possible resources, and sounds: combining the various families of wind instruments with a numerous family of strings, made up of violins including sopraninos, sopranos, tenors, altos, baritones, basses, and contrabasses in various sizes and various keys. That's to say, if we take the present violin as being non-transposing in C, there would be other violins both higher and lower in the categories I've mentioned and which, also tuned in fifths, would become transposing violins in F, G, E-flat and B[-flat], like wind instruments; as well as increasing the range, especially towards the bass, the combination of open strings would provide a much richer tone to the instrumental sound. The only drawback might be that careless composers who used all these instruments at once, while they should be used only in groups, could destroy the character that belongs to each key, and thereby could, in some cases, make the sound quality of this new string orchestra extremely unpleasant. For example, in the current orchestra the key of E-flat minor is heavy and lugubrious; clearly, if for a piece which should have this character, the composer uses violins which, through the intervention of open strings, make it less heavy and lugubrious, this change will not help to achieve the desired effect.[4] But a similar problem is to be found in every branch of music, whatever it may be; everywhere one can find abuse, or unintelligent and ill-judged usage, together with ingenious application of the resources that music has to offer. The above inventions will make composing more difficult and taxing but will also lead to more powerful and beautiful effects, so long as the composer has learnt to profit by the various means which I have indicated, and with which M. Sax is working to supply him.

---

3   An article in the *Revue et gazette musicale* noted, 'This monster organ will be used at popular celebrations and inaugurations of railways. Standing on a truck in front of the locomotive that would provide the steam as well as turning its musical cylinder, this grand instrument would overwhelm the howl of pistons and the roar of wheels and thunder'.

4   In the *Grand Traité* Berlioz lists the twenty-four major and minor keys to identify their technical and expressive suitability for violins. E-flat minor is 'Difficile; très terne et très triste' ('difficult; very subdued and sad'). Similarly, he deplored the lazy habit of horn players, once they were equipped with pistons or valves, of playing every note 'open', whereas composers wanted stopped notes to sound different from open notes (he offers examples from Weber and Méhul).

45

To M. Friedland in Prague

RGM, 23 July 1848

The magazine here returned to printing letters from Berlioz which were thought to be of general interest. Ferdinand Friedland (1810–72) was a German industrialist and patron whom Berlioz had probably met in Breslau. The full heading of the article is 'Musical Journey in Bohemia. To M. Friedland in Prague'; the translated part mostly concerns music in London. A personal note reflects Berlioz's attitude to the February 1848 revolution: 'You'll be reading this letter seven months after it was sent to you, but will you actually be reading it, my poor Friedland? Our beautiful Prague has been under attack! You will assure me that you're still alive? They're killing each other with as much enthusiasm as in Paris'.

London, 4 January 1848

You reproach me, my dear Friedland, for the long interruption in the account of my journey in Austria, and you seem to attribute the delay in my article about Prague to some sort of coolness I was feeling towards you. Your reproaches and suppositions are both unfair. I haven't written during the last four months because I've spent all that time in London, where I'm living such a terribly busy life that, far from having a moment for dreams and memories, I've barely got time for my job.[1] To launch a serious opera house in England, with no repertoire chosen in advance, with a troupe of young singers most of whom had never appeared on a stage before, was a dangerous

---

1   Berlioz had been appointed by Louis-Antoine Jullien (1812–60) to conduct operas by Mozart, Donizetti, and Balfe at the Drury Lane Theatre. He left for London on 3 November 1847 and the season began on 6 December. Jullien went bankrupt. Berlioz remained in London, giving concerts with the help of friends and starting to write his *Memoirs*. He returned to Paris in July when the situation had become more settled.

enterprise of considerable difficulty, as the outcome has already proved. As a result, my contribution looms large in such tasks; there are rehearsals every day and performances every night; and when I get home at midnight, having conducted the opera for hours on end, I no longer have the strength to lift a pen, and I'm sure you'll forgive me for spending the rest of the night asleep. All that's needed by the magnificent orchestra I'm in charge of, packed with virtuosos and wonderful sight-readers, is a bit of free time; but, apart from the unending labours in Drury Lane, there's not an important concert in London or its surrounding towns to which these section leaders are not invited to contribute. I really don't know how the woodwind players can stand it.

I see now with my own eyes to what extent the generally accepted ideas in Europe about the English aptitude for music, and about the feeling the great London public has for the art, are bizarre and very far from the truth. More to the point, even fine voices are quite common in England; as proof I need only mention the excellent chorus singers in Drury Lane, whose musical intelligence is also very sharp, and who, instead of being stuck rigid on each side of the stage, as immobile and unfeeling as organ pipes, join in with the action and enliven it with rare aplomb. And with what rapt attention the theatre and concert audiences listen to the most serious works! I experienced this lately in the chorus's performance of Mendelssohn's *Antigone* at the St James theatre, and even more so of his oratorio *Elijah* in Exeter Hall. It was shortly after the announcement of the early demise of this great master, dead at the same age as Mozart, in the fullness of his boundless faculties and in the undimmed power of his genius.[2] There were five hundred in the chorus (all amateurs), accompanied by a large orchestra. An audience of more than three thousand packed the hall, which was draped in black. Printed leaflets had been distributed among them in advance, asking them not to show overt tributes of admiration, so that nothing should affect the religious mourning of the occasion. As a result, there was no applause; but after the final pages of this colossal work, a discreet murmur, passing from one end of the hall to the other, left no doubt as to the audience's profound emotion.

London therefore possesses a very numerous, very intelligent, and very attentive public for serious music.

---

2   Mendelssohn had died in Leipzig on 4 November 1847 aged thirty-eight: Mozart died aged thirty-five. Berlioz wrote to the London critic Henry Chorley on 14 November: 'I partake of your sadness, please believe me. Without being as close to Mendelssohn as you, nevertheless I knew him very well; and even had he remained totally unknown to me, I would be mourning him as a great artist and an utterly superior spirit'. *CG* vol. 3, p. 468.

46

Opening of the Théâtre de la Nation: The Théâtre-National, or Opéra (Old Style)

JD, 26 July 1848

The director of the Opéra pilloried in this article was Henri Duponchel (1794–1868), director between November 1847 and November 1849. He was an architect and stage designer and seems to have had no musical training. After Louis-Philippe's departure, the Académie royale de musique was renamed 'Théatre de la Nation' on 26 February 1848, then 'Opéra-Théâtre de la Nation' on 29 March. Berlioz had recently returned from London.

I always get in a muddle when it's a question of using their new title to mean the Opéra and the hitherto third opera house founded by M. Adam.[1] I dare say other people will have the same problem. It seems to me difficult to work out in what sense 'The Theatre of the Nation' is not 'national', and how 'The National Theatre' can't be the theatre of the nation. Happily, the question is no more serious than knowing whether one should say 'the shape' or 'the form' of a hat; the great thing, at the moment, is to have both a hat and a head; because many people, in theatre and elsewhere, don't have a hat to put on their head, while heads, even in certain places where they're of ultimate necessity, seem to be rarer than hats. As for the Opéra, we shall

---

1   In 1847 Adolphe Adam had launched a 'popular' opera house which he dubbed Théâtre National, intended to give young composers somewhere to make themselves heard. But the 1848 revolution was its downfall and it closed on 23 March 1848.

refrain from deciding whether it's in the same category as those places.[2] We were there at its 'opening'. One unimpressed wit claimed this word should be understood in the sense of 'autopsy'. After the corpse's innards had been examined, the doctors unanimously attributed the cause of death far less to the wounds, dislocations, and contusions it received in the recent catastrophe which is still making Paris tremble, and more to an organic failure that had become incurable through its longevity. It succumbed to a paralysis of the heart; from that stemmed the feeble pulse, the torpor, the malaise, the general weakness that people had been noticing for so long and which gave every indication of decay. The larynx too was threatened with tuberculosis which would shortly have become evident; the limbs themselves had already lost much of their vigour and elasticity. The legs were heavy and stiff, the feet swollen. As for the brain, it was found to be in the usual condition of the brains of this species, that's to say so small it was not worth discussing.

Last Friday, once the autopsy was completed, the next stage was the interesting and difficult one of galvanization. Because the battery sent by the minister of the interior was luckily powerful enough, success was total: the corpse rose up on its support, a prolonged cry emanated from its throat, it smiled the smile of the dead and even briskly closed its right hand; it seemed to be closely gripping something. The witnesses, we have to say (but is this to praise their courage or blame their lack of sensitivity?), did not manifest any great emotion before this strange spectacle. One would have said they'd been used to it for years, that they'd spent their whole life in the amphitheatre, and that Volta's battery was their favourite instrument. For me, even though I've become used to the terrible experiences of which we've seen so many in France and elsewhere, there was no way I could preserve the necessary sangfroid needed to weather a close study of the secondary phenomena of the operation. I was tormented ceaselessly by profound inner suffering all through them; my head was buzzing, there were shooting pains in my ears and especially in my heart, muscular, nervous pangs, extreme anxiety, an inability to stay motionless, a continual tendency to look at the door, and an almost irresistible desire to run away; a desire to which I had to give in before the end of the séance, overcome by a fever that didn't leave me for another twelve hours. So they're not my impressions that I'm describing here, as they were too painful and confused, but rather those of the

---

2   The loss of heads must refer to the failed revolution from 23 to 26 June that aimed to overthrow the administration that replaced the monarchy in February. Arrested insurgents were piled into improvised dungeons; Flaubert wrote, 'Nine hundred men were there, crowded together in filth, pell-mell, black with power and clotted blood, shivering in fever and shouting in frenzy. Those who died were left to lie with the others'. All theatres were closed and artistic life was temporarily abandoned.

other witnesses, whose calmness allowed them to conserve better than me the lucidity of spirit necessary in those circumstances.

I could write here a detailed description of last Friday's performance; but that could perhaps cause the director pain, something I prefer to avoid at all costs. – Is it not the case, dear director, that it could … upset you? I see you don't deny it … Good for you! You're honest, you're not bashful. In any case it's natural; it's a very easy thing to do. I can understand, when you're the director of the Opéra, and when you're not well up with things musical (that's a pleonasm), when you are, I say, the director of the Opéra, when you're surrounded by kind friends ready to say yes to everything you suggest, and 'bless you!' when you sneeze, I can quite see that it's uncomfortable to find next to you, or in front of you, or behind you, an old friend you thought to be out in the Indies, and whom you thought to be rid of for good; I'm sure it must be unbelievably irritating to hear someone telling you over and over: 'Hard to port! Hard to port! Take in the inner jib! She's listing! Take it in! What in God's name are you doing? You're about to sink us!' Yes, that's tiring and irritating, especially when you know that he knows you don't know. I'm very far from wanting to annoy you or exhaust you, my dear director, I don't even want to irritate you. There are people I'm prone to like even so; if I found them on a barricade and they were firing a gun at me, I still couldn't prevent myself from bursting out with laughter and shouting at them: 'Blunderers!' You're one of those.

That said, I can now, freely and in a fraternal spirit, likewise ask you a simple question, less to produce an explanation to me personally than to find out the depth of knowledge you now possess in these matters. Here's my question: What is your view of the state of music in Europe at the start of the current year of 1848, in other words what condition it was in when it died? You're not a scholar, by your own admission; this is stonewalling. You really must have formed some sort of opinion on the matter since it touches on your capacity as director. I'm not asking you whether you play the trumpet or the clarinet or the contrabass or the violin; whether your voice is a bass or a baritone or a tenor (never mind a soprano), whether you understand harmony and counterpoint – coming from me, that would be a poor sort of joke.[3] I simply want to know to what part of musical Europe you would first have turned six months ago to try and find good composers and good interpreters of their music, given that you can't do without either of them. It's a sad necessity, whose importance I'm sure you realize, but it's one you still have to face in the future, no question about it. Tell me, would you have gone to the north, the south, the east, the west; would you have explored

---

3 Berlioz was often said, quite wrongly, not to have a 'correct' understanding of counterpoint and harmony.

Italy, Germany, England, Sweden, or Spain, or just France and Paris? ... Ah! You're cross, you answer me harshly, treating me as an awkward customer, as a cantankerous critic! Me a cantankerous critic! But if I were cantankerous, if I were a critic, if I were even the most easy-going of critics, I'd say that ... Instead of which, I'm a simple artist like you; we're supposed to chat peaceably. You've allowed me, in my role as musician, to give you advice from time to time which could be useful to you, the director of the Opéra, in your role as architect, and it's to make sure this advice was the best that I risked asking you to enlighten me as to your current thinking, that's all. But since you're angry, let's call it a day. In any case I don't have time today to indulge in a consultation, I've got to write a letter to England.

Farewell; buy Fétis's book *Music Explained to the World*. He'll be thrilled, and it won't do you any harm.[4]

To M. Davison, editor-in-chief of Musical World, 106. Great Russell Street, Tottenham [Court] Road, London[5]

My dear Davison,

I enclose herewith an article intended for the *Journal des Débats*, on the reopening of the Opéra, which took place last Friday. Translate it and insert into your column, if you think it's worth the trouble. There's no way of saying here anything with the tiniest element of reason about this great monster, the Théâtre de la Nation. The director or the Nation, or perhaps both, would go purple with fury. The Nation would treat me instantly like a false friend, and the director like a criminal. Even so, I'm deeply distressed by the dreadful state in which I find the music and musicians of Paris after my long absence. All the theatres shut, all the artists bankrupt, all the professors jobless, all the pupils scattered, *poor pianists playing sonatas in the public squares*, historical painters sweeping the streets, architects employed making mortar in the state studios, etc., etc. Ah! You'd have to have a heart of stone not to be moved by such misery, one shared by everybody and whose end no one could foresee. The National Assembly has just voted quite large sums to enable the theatres to be reopened and also to bring some small assistance to the neediest artists. But just think of their long-term prospects (not to mention that of the musicians); there

---

4   The third edition of Fétis's *La Musique mise à la portée de tout le monde* (first edition 1830) had just been published.

5   James William Davison (1813–85), English critic and composer, worked simultaneously for *The Musical World* and *The Times* between 1846 and 1879. He and Chorley held conservative views, Davison pronouncing in 1855 that 'Robert Schumann has had his innings and then been bowled out like Richard Wagner'. Davison, however, was on good terms with Berlioz, whose letters to him use the familiar 'tu' form.

are first violins from the Opéra on 900 francs a year. They had lived as best they could so far by giving lessons; but, *without turning to crime*, you can't imagine they've ever managed to *buy chateaux with their savings*. Now, with their pupils dispersed, what's to become of the poor wretches? ... They won't be deported, although many of them have no chance of making a living except in America, in the Indies or in Sydney; deportation is too expensive for the government; to achieve it you have to have deserved it, and all our artists fought the insurgents and attacked the barricades. Tell me whether, in the midst of this terrifying confusion of the just and the unjust, of good and evil, of the true and the false, by speaking a language in which most words have lost their meaning, there's not enough to send you completely mad!

An association has just been formed to give major concerts in the lovely setting of the Jardin d'Hiver, the takings from which will be shared out among the performers. The price of entry is very reasonable; God grant that the enterprise succeeds! Ten years ago, the French were still willing to listen to music, then they would only listen to what was offered them for free; now I'm not sure you can collect an audience for free, that's to say *without paying them*.

Farewell, my discussion with the director of the Théatre de la Nation had cheered me up slightly, but now gloomy thoughts are assailing me once more with all the power of their black wings.[6]

---

6 'Farewell', as in other Berlioz writings, is written in English.

47

The Opéra: Mme de Lagrange's Debut; Duprez, *Otello*

JD, 5 December 1848

It may initially strike the reader as otiose to follow Berlioz's demolition of Duponchel with another, but this article is crucial in providing chapter and verse for the composer's discontent.

This evening will remain in my memory as the saddest I've attended since the memorable benefit performance given on the same stage for Mlle Falcon.[1] I can't imagine that the public who were present at the musical agony of that young and beautiful singer, whom it surrounded with so much love and passionate admiration, suffered more on that occasion than at the recent spectacle of Duprez's fanatical, ferocious devotion to the theatre of which he was for so long the glory and support. The fact is (and it needs to be said in favour of our Parisian public who are so fickle and ungrateful in general towards its one-time idols) that certain artists enjoy the rare privilege of retaining their unalloyed sympathies for years on end, and as passionately as ever. Duprez is one of these. Here, then, is the position he has come to assume.

The Opéra is sick, the Opéra is dying. It's undeniably easier and more straightforward to regain the interest of a public who are bored, discontented, and discouraged by means of a striking artist, a young talent, original, seductive, and exceptional, who takes control and carries everything before him, than it is by the impact of a fine ensemble, a majestic, faithful and lively production of the great works in its repertoire, a grandeur that can

---

1 Berlioz had written a long article in the *Journal des Débats* (17 March 1840) on this benefit performance, in which Mlle Falcon, 'who had been absent for so long, reappeared before her numerous admirers only to die before their eyes'.

be achieved only through intelligent and constant care, well directed efforts, and dedication that is even painful, supported by a true and deep love of music. As a result, it was decided to turn almost exclusively to this brave singer capable of preventing so many disasters, this diamond who's able to carry so much paste.

Ah! If only they could have Jenny Lind! Yes, but this great artist is earning fabulous sums all over Europe, and especially in London; the Paris Opéra cannot possibly offer her a quarter of what she earns there; and Mlle Lind has no reason to be charitable with her marvellous talent and her worldwide fame as a favour to this same theatre where, despite the notable support of the composer of *Les Huguenots* [Meyerbeer], she was unable to make her debut four years ago. We should not forget that attacks on the self-esteem of certain artists are as serious as they are certain in their effect, and that once artists have finally found outlets for their abilities and made the reputation these abilities have gained for them, they should be entitled to feel, if not hatred, at least profound indifference towards those places where they were disregarded. What effect can Paris's opinion have on Mlle Lind's fame? ... Paris's imprimatur is indispensable, we're told, to celebrities from abroad: it alone has the power to make reputations and to crown the kings and queens of music! Yes, it's Paris that says that. But this certificate of intelligence, feeling, taste, and enlightened enthusiasm, this superiority it modestly grants itself over all the other capitals, is now only a meaningless, puerile boast, insofar as it applies to an appreciation of the finer points of music. It was not always a prejudice; but nowadays, when the great centres of European civilization march along the road to musical progress, leaving far behind them a Paris that's unmoving in its naïve vanity, it's a pitiful, overweening joke.

Mlle Lind is a great actress as well as an incomparable singer; if her double talent has enabled her to add to the adoration of the crowd the plaudits of all intelligent and serious critics, all great minds, and all artists of any standing, in places hallowed by geniuses such as Shakespeare, Goethe, Schiller, Handel, Gluck, Mozart, Weber, and Beethoven, and the splendid company of their inspired interpreters, we may well think that her ambition, which we may suppose to be considerable, has found full satisfaction. When she offered the Opéra her hand, it was ignored, so now it must content itself with hunting for the modest resources that may still be left. Bereft of a gold mine to exploit, now it's forced to scrape the barrel. The current directors of the Opéra, we know, are not responsible for this difficult position; they have merely made fruitless attempts to escape it. But they're in the process of making it worse. I'm fearful.

As part of their anxious scrutiny of the musical horizon in every direction in order to discover a talent capable, by its mere attraction, of bringing crowds back to the Opéra, their eyes came to rest on Mme de Lagrange, a

French singer whose successes in salons and in some Italian theatres captured their attention.[2] A contract for four months has, I gather, been offered to Mme de Lagrange before her debut and she has accepted it. Clearly there was hope that she would be useful during the winter season, until rehearsals for Meyerbeer's *Le Prophète* came to an end. Unfortunately, the talent and voice of the new singer made her particularly suitable to the less manageable works in the Opéra's repertoire. Into this category must go Rossini's *Otello*, which she has chosen for her debut. But manageable or not, this work had to be resuscitated, and the embarrassment was considerable, the Opéra having for many years been organized in such a way that the most famous works of the great composers, from Gluck to Rossini, had become almost unperformable there. The only works given tolerable performances there are modern operas, written for the necessities of the moment and for the resources of the moment. It's impossible, without shaming and mutilating these masterpieces to a disgraceful degree, to put on *Moïse*, *Le Siège de Corinthe*, *Der Freischütz*, *La Vestale*, *Cortez*, *Armide*, *Orphée*, *Alceste*, the *Iphigénies*, not even *Le Comte Ory*, *Guillaume Tell*, or *Les Huguenots*, which appear on the notice boards from time to time.

The music of *Otello* may not be as demanding as the operas of which I've just made a sad recitation, but even so it does call for one other role, as well as for a prima donna, to wit that of Othello, given that we have not yet reached the astonishing bravado I was able admire in the Italiens, when I saw a production of Pacini's *La Vestale* in which the only thing missing was … *La Vestale*.[3] So there absolutely had to be an Othello, without whom Mme de Lagrange felt she could not make her debut. It's crystal clear that I'm not talking about an Othello of Shakespearean magnitude; for sure, there's no one these days demanding enough to voice such a pretention. No, it was just a question of finding a tenor strong enough to sing the Italian arias and duets of the role of Othello in their French translation. The Opéra possesses five tenors on its staff, bound contractually: Roger, who cannot appear before the premiere of *Le Prophète*; Poultier, a light, very light tenor, who couldn't be risked as The Moor of Venice; Paulin, an even lighter tenor, whom they were risking to play Rodrigo; Gueymard, an energetic tenor, but inexperienced and especially unfamiliar with Rossini's ornate style; and

---

2 Anna de Lagrange (1825–1905), French soprano. In a later feuilleton (*JD*, 7 January 1849) Berlioz praised her performance of the title role in *La Fiancée de Lammermoor* (the title translates that of Sir Walter Scott's novel rather than using the name, Lucia/Lucie): 'her success in the mad scene was brilliant and deserved'. *CM* vol. 7, p. 9.

3 Giovanni Pacini's *La vestale* was premiered at La Scala, Milan, in 1823. Berlioz's recollection of its Paris production is intended to draw attention to the superiority of Spontini's opera on the same subject.

THE OPÉRA: MME DE LAGRANGE'S DEBUT; DUPREZ, *OTELLO*

finally, and most of all, Duprez.[4] But Duprez, the fine musician, the capable singer, the fascinating virtuoso, the often admirable actor, has, despite so many qualities, despite his doggedness, his audacity and his indomitable will, has almost entirely lost his voice. We know it, he knows it; it would be crazy to imagine any possible illusion about this. What's more, Duprez has been ill for several weeks. So, despite everything being against him, Duprez, not having resigned but determined to make a necessary effort, allows Mme de Lagrange's performance to be announced and, right up until the last moment, nurses the hope of contributing to it. But at 7 p.m. the public arrives at the Opéra to find a white sheet pasted over the poster: the performance is cancelled. *Otello* was not staged, nothing was staged; the theatre was closed owing to Duprez's indisposition. New hope of recovery, new poster, new disappointment. After this, the second announcement of *Otello* is replaced by a ballet, for the same reason.

Mme de Lagrange's debut was beginning to be highly problematic until finally, last Friday, Duprez thought he really could be counted on. *Otello* is announced for the third time; the public loyally turns up.[5] The opera begins; enter Duprez. I won't try to describe what we all felt: desolation, sadness, rage. I felt my chest tighten, tears overwhelmed me; one turned one's eyes away so as not to witness the convulsive efforts of this fighter against his agony. Raucous sounds … a voice that broke at every moment… feeble notes … lost, imperceptible … a singer with croup! … And the whole audience who, had they dared, would have cried mercy for the devoted artist, trembles in its gloomy silence, unable to imagine how the performance could continue and nonetheless remains immobile, praying with all their heart for a phrase, a run, one single sovereign note that might be the occasion, the pretext for signalling to Duprez, through their warm applause, their vivid, profound sympathy … And the phrase, the run, the note not arriving … What a time we had there! What terrible torment!

By one of those miracles in which Duprez specializes, we were allowed, it's true, to recoup our losses in the third act; his voice suddenly returned, and he was magnificent in the famous phrase 'Il cor mi divide di tanta crudeltà' ('My heart rebels against such cruelty') from his duet with Iago. At which what shouts! What applause! What heartfelt bravos could be heard from the whole house! But on the stage around him earlier there had been a deplorable chaos. Portehaut, playing Iago, missed his entrance; well may Rodergo

---

4   Roger: see article 31, note 10. Paulin, Louis-Matthieu (?–?), French tenor. Louis Gueymard (1822–80), French tenor. Duprez: see article 9, note 3.
5   *Otello* was finally premiered on 24 November 1848.

say, 'I spy Iago', the traitor doesn't appear.[6] The thoughtful Rodrigo thinks he can't do better than go and look for him, so the stage remains empty; the astonished public start to ask themselves, like Beaumarchais's Brid'oison, 'Who are they kidding?'[7] However, Iago reappears and the public in their righteousness take it out on the obliging Rodrigo who, at the end of his tether, nevertheless does his best to sing, with his poor, little, fluting, light (excessively light) voice.

At the end of that terrible first act, you should have seen the agitation and dismay of the audience as they headed for the corridors and the foyer to get their breath back after that prolonged anguish! 'There are three more acts', said someone, 'will they ever get to the end? Also, the other roles don't seem to be well known. Why did Portehaut miss his entrance? Is there no stage manager? It's enough to upset the debutante! Etc., etc.'

Mme de Lagrange did indeed seem to be seriously shaken to begin with, but the obvious enthusiasm with which she was greeted soon restored her confidence. The main quality of her voice, what strikes you immediately, is its exceptional range. You could say that Mme de Lagrange has a high soprano voice that's clear and highly individual above a contralto voice very sonorous in its lower register. Altogether these cover a range of two octaves and a fourth, from the low a to a high d^3. The high sounds are charming and very pure, even if not very loud, and those at the bottom of the scale are not lacking in character. Unfortunately, her medium range, that part of the voice with which *one sings* does not perhaps possess the same qualities and leaves something to be desired over its sonority and expressive power. Mme de Lagrange's talent is above all one of vocalization, her agility being remarkable in diatonic scales. Without awkwardness and with graceful ease she produces ripples of sound that delight those fond of musical pyrotechnics. The tuning of the sounds that make up her most difficult flights is beyond reproach, which can't always be said of that in her calmer offerings.

To sum up the praises she deserves, I'll say that it's a pretty voice, with a wide range, agile, in tune, and made for vocalises of a certain style that's not much in use today. If I'm to turn to the general impression produced by this first performance, given under such poor conditions, I should add this: Mme de Lagrange is weak in singing proper, especially in singing that's calm and steady; her phrasing seems indecisive, and with this her voice seems to lose some of its volume; some notes are hard to hear, and these defects become

---

6   Jean-Baptiste-Florentin Porthéhaut (1822–89), French baritone who made his début at the Opéra in April 1845 in Halévy's *La Reine de Chypre*.

7   Berlioz has confused Brid'oison, the lawyer in Beaumarchais' *La folle Journée ou le Mariage de Figaro*, with Basile, the music master in the same author's *Le Barbier de Séville*; it's Basile who says, 'Who the devil are they kidding here?'

more noticeable when the role calls for accents of passion and spontaneity in her acting. As if she's unsure of her powers, she remains calm at these moments, resulting inevitably in an unhappy frigidity in the effect she has overall. Also, her voice has the defect, so common these days, of vibrato: it undulates constantly like the organ stop known as the 'tremulant', which becomes extremely tiresome for the listener. The advanced state of her pregnancy does not allow her either to indulge in miming or in unduly animated gesticulation. Her partner was continually obliged to take note of this in the most dramatic moments of the opera: Desdemona 'sat' slowly on the ground instead of 'falling' on it, and Othello 'led' her when he should have 'dragged' her. Even so, Mme de Lagrange was applauded in the brilliant moments of her role, and her talent for vocalization deserves the courteous response it received.

After the happy moment vouchsafed by Duprez in the third act, in the fourth his powers again began to fail and diminish. Finally, we reached the dénouement and I might have said, with a sigh, like Shakespeare's hero: 'Othello's occupation's gone!' Mlle Fuoco had a great success with the ballet, and a triple round of applause followed her return to the wings.[8] Now: does it need to be added that the chorus tenors often sang flat to a shocking degree, and that certain nasal voices, which nasalise among them, more than once gave rise to ironic exclamations from the audience? In whose interest? We're told that in Paris good voices can't be found for choruses; and even if they were, could or would the Opéra pay them a decent wage?

'But why are the extras not marching in time?' one of my neighbours kept asking as we watched the irregular progress of the Venetian soldiers. Heavens, I've no idea. I can't understand why the same soldiers who, out on the street, keep step absolutely with the rhythm of the drum, are unable to do so on the stage of the Opéra during a smartly rhythmical march played by an orchestra of eighty people. Perhaps it's because in the street the soldier is controlled by a corporal, who obeys a sergeant, who's under the orders of a sub-lieutenant commanded by a lieutenant who takes his orders from a captain, etc., while at the Opéra, where nobody's in charge and where there's no musical surveillance onstage, the soldier marches at his own pace, without listening to the orchestra or bothering about the rhythm.[9]

---

8   The Italian dancer Sofia Fuoco (1830–1916).
9   This is one among dozens of such comments that indirectly demonstrate Berlioz's political attitude; for musical performance as for the organization of society, he always felt the need for order and authority.

48

Distribution of Prizes at the Paris Conservatoire

JD, 5 December 1848

Berlioz takes the opportunity of this occasion to offer his views on the current state of French music.

In the absence of M. Dufaure, this occasion was presided over by the Directeur des Beaux-Arts, M. Charles Blanc.[1] The speech he made at the start of the meeting was reckoned to be full of sense and relevance; it was notable too for an accurate judgment of the power of modern music and the importance it is tending to have among civilized peoples. M. Charles Blanc did not fail to underline the role played by music in those great political and social upheavals known as revolutions. Unfortunately, he was unable to say – if music has indeed contributed almost everywhere to the progress of those revolutions by stirring up the enthusiasm and the good or bad passions of the populace – whether it is equally the case that those revolutions have contributed to the progress of music. As it is, we have only too many reasons for believing the contrary, and the following passage of M. Blanc's speech, which was applauded by the whole room, explains to what extent the new state of things had given rise to fears for the most precious of our musical institutions: 'I was present, gentlemen, at the Assembly when, considering the Conservatoire, it refused, when the question was raised by one of its members, to discuss your needs. At a time when circumstances demand so many sacrifices, the Assembly has left your funding intact, wishing to prove by that what generosity you can rely on when times become more prosperous'. That is to say, when the revolution

---

1 Jules-Armand-Stanislas Dufaure (1798–1881), French lawyer and politician, twice minister of the interior between October 1848 and October 1849. Auguste-Alexandre Philippe-Charles Blanc (1813–82), French journalist, author, critic and art historian.

is over, when peace, confidence, and financial stability have returned and become durable, when all the revolutionary agitations have ceased. M. Blanc added, 'The national Assembly, gentlemen, has understood that music has now become a French art; that after being regarded for many years as a doubtful French quality, musical genius had restored to us that distinctive character we have so often noted in the visual arts. I refer to the striking role played by intelligence in French music as in painting; I mean the particular sentiment that marks the scores of our masters as a noble, intellectual occupation rather than something just to tickle the ear'.

That's very right, very true, and those French musicians to whom it applies should accept this appreciation of their works as the highest praise. It was already true at the beginning of this century, in that epoch now too often ignored when our opera houses offered works by Dalayrac, Méhul, Lesueur, and Berton, to name only the French composers, and when the French school could be proud of the masterpieces its example inspired in nationalized foreigners, such as Grétry, Cherubini, and Spontini. Yes, France possessed and still possesses great artists who have advanced the art of music, who have defended it with all their might against the attacks of taste that is false, despicable and useless; thanks to them, France possesses an immensely valuable repertoire of dramatic music, which it is still very far from judging at its true value. France founded, and for more than half a century has supported, a Conservatoire of music which, even if the teaching there isn't perfect or all-embracing, is nonetheless incontestably the best in Europe in many respects. Every year France makes considerable financial sacrifices to sustain two opera houses which, if they had been left to their own resources, would have foundered long ago.

But France still has no clear ideas about the power and dignity of the art of music. We think music doesn't exist outside the theatre.

As to style, the most frivolous, the most false, the most mannered, the most empty style is still the one which has the greatest chance of success (in the theatre), and attracts the most numerous followers. Works where *intelligence plays the principal role* are still, with rare exceptions, the least popular, and the slowest to be appreciated (if they are). Those (I'm still talking about dramatic works) which do not include either an interesting plot or luxurious staging or some other extra allurement are, whatever their value, sure to leave the public cold.

A terrible opera whose cast includes an artist of exceptional talent will always be preferred to a masterpiece when the performance, while satisfactory in every respect, doesn't show off a famous star.

There is in France a kind of comedy containing couplets called vaudevilles, in which people sing abominable trashy tunes that no musical ear can stand, out of tune and time, in voices that are cracked, ugly, and horrible. And the French put up with them.

We still have dramas called melodramas in which the action is continually interrupted, and in which the spectator is annoyingly distracted by meaningless bursts of music badly played by orchestras that are discordant, broken down, loathsome. And the French love them. Well, as musicians see it, if there's anything worse about people than not liking music, it's undoubtedly people liking bad music.

France (and we shouldn't be surprised by this) doesn't love and doesn't even suspect the beauty of music on the grand scale. When they include music in national festivals it's always hurried, uncared for, without any real grandeur, without even considering the conditions that are crucial to its development and existence. There, music is treated like those poor female street singers, who are dragged in to decorate the festive rooms where a marriage is being celebrated, and who are told to sing in the midst of the gabble of conversations, the noise of food being served, and the shouts of drunken guests; who are elbowed by waiters doing their job, while they accompany themselves on their wretchedly dirty, battered harps; and to whom they throw a few sous, easing them out of the door immediately afterwards.

France does not possess a body for national music-making on a large scale. France does not possess great national works of music based on subjects that recall the important moments in its history and celebrate the emotions cherished by the nation. France does not even possess a national concert hall where a large audience can go to hear noble works majestically performed.

Every time there's been an attempt to set up a concert hall in one of the public buildings, music, and the architectural features it demands, are the last things to be considered; or rather, they are not considered at all. Word has gone out: Here's our concert hall, it'll do for *putting on balls*, for *drawing the lots for conscription*, for *a club*, for *elections*, or for *patriotic banquets*.

France doesn't possess any religious music. What is known by that name in our churches is no more than an indecent and ridiculous parody, when it's not a remnant of barbarity. There's not a church in France that possesses a choir with as many as forty voices. The French clergy are in general hostile to music; the Parisian clergy almost neutralise the isolated attempts of composers to perform their religious works by *forbidding women* to take part.

The musical sections of the French army are shabby, weak, incomplete, and unworthy of it, and unable to hold a candle to those of Austria, Prussia, and Russia.

The worthy attempts being made by choral societies in Paris, under the direction of M. Hubert, will never achieve totally effective results since women are not allowed to belong.[2] A choir without sopranos, loud, numerous, and experienced, is an orchestra without violins, a military band without clarinets.

---

2   Joseph Hubert (1810–78) was inspector of the teaching of singing and became director of the Orphéon (succeeding Wilhem) since 1842. Berlioz had applied unsuccessfully for this post.

Théâtre de l'Opéra-Comique: Premiere of *Le Caïd*, Comic Opera in Two Acts, Libretto by M. Sauvage, Music by M. Ambroise Thomas

JD, 7 January 1849

It's cheering to find how excited Berlioz is to be able, for once, to offer almost unstinted praise to a singer, in this case Delphine Ugalde.[1]

It's rather a good idea to set the opera in the capital of French Africa.[2] From this bizarre mixture of manners and costumes emerge comical contrasts and situations likely to lend unexpectedness and variety to the musical style. But these contrasts, piquant though they may be, cannot exempt the librettist from attaching an interesting plot to them and inventing a theme that is piquant and original. Unfortunately, it seems as though he said to himself: 'Here's a frame, the composer will add the picture'. So, here's this frame in two acts, a gilt frame, decorated with pearls, muslin, lovely Arab heads, and French moustaches, not to mention the heads of Negros, a eunuch, and a muezzin.

1　The premiere had taken place on 3 January at the Opéra-Comique. The librettist was Thomas-Marie-François Sauvage (1794–1877).

2　Algiers: The city, initially conquered in 1830, was included in 1848 as one of three departments: Oran, Algiers, and Constantine.

I'm afraid I may commit more than one mistake in this analysis. Despite all my concentration, I took a long time to understand what was happening; words reached me only indistinctly or didn't reach me at all. The dialogue, written in verse, unlike the general usage of the Opéra-Comique, added to my puzzlement.

Clearly, in its physiognomy and comic nature, the opera is close to two works that have brought popularity to M. Grisar: *L'Eau merveilleuse* and *Gilles le ravisseur*, not forgetting *Le Tableau parlant* which Grétry was not alone in painting, and whose libretto did not merely make a frame.[3] Here's what I thought was the plot of *Le Caïd*:[4]

The curtain goes up, it's a square in Algiers, it's still dark with no sun in the sky. A small troupe of Arabs, marching in step, utters this familiar cry: 'Be quiet! Let's hide! No movement! Let's be silent!' (in verse, naturally). We gather that they're stalking somebody and that they don't want to be spotted.

They slip silently away in the dark, while they may. Now others join in with the fray. The Caïd, rather fat, with a misshapen back and a definite lack of authority, fears that he might encounter a throng who do him wrong, then give him a whack, then 'Into the sack!' This terrible gang, thinks he, will just drop him into the sea.

Unless I'm mistaken, that last paragraph is in rhyme: it's real free verse, opéra-comique style. I beg the reader's pardon, it's a distraction. I'm far from abandoning prose and I'm sure readers will be glad when I get back to it. So, our hunchback would be glad to complete his morning walk without accruing any more humps. There's no question, he has very vicious enemies and very good reasons for mistrusting them. It's beyond a doubt.

He's not gone ten yards when a horrible blow on the back lays him low. 'Help! Murder!' he cries. A gallant fellow chases away the assassins and calls for help. He's delighted to see a young girl passing by. She's easy on the eye, her skirt's very short. With a groan and a snort, he begs her support. 'They have broken my bones!' and in pitiful tones he cries, 'My poor head! I'm dying! I'm dead!'

---

3   *The Magic Lake* and *Gilles the Abductor* are by the Belgian composer Albert Grisar (1808–69). Grétry's *Le Tableau parlant* (*The Talking Picture*) was premiered at the Opéra-Comique on 30 September 1769.

4   A Caïd is an administrator, judge and tax collector. It is remarkable that Berlioz, here and elsewhere, apparently chose to offer synopses on the basis of what he heard in the theatre, without using the printed librettos normally available in time for the premiere. This is why he is so appreciative of singers' good diction; the Conservatoire itself was in the business of teaching *music* and *declamation*.

Ah, there we are! It's too much for me, rhyming has come back with a vengeance. It would be very strange if it turned out that I couldn't write prose any more, doing the opposite of M. Jourdain.[5] But that's the result of innovation, or rather renovation, because at the end of the last century you frequently found verse being used in opéra-comique. It's M. Sauvage's example that's inserted verse into my body. So, let's see whether I can 'de-rhyme' myself. The young girl who ran to the shouts of the Caïd and his defender is a French milliner (in whom, I fancy, there's not a hint of poetry) with whom the defender, a Gascon hairdresser, is deeply in love. They're even engaged and, were it not for the rather scanty state of their finances, they would be bearing the same name and living under the same roof. The Gascon has an idea, a brilliant idea which should very soon bring him some money. It has not escaped his notice that the Caïd under obligation to him is one of those simple beings you could make believe that Abd-el-Kader is going to be president of the French Republic, or the Pope a member of the Institut.[6] The brilliant idea therefore consists in persuading the good fellow that he, the Gascon, possesses an infallible secret that protects Caïds from attacks with sticks and ambushes in the night. (No rhymes there … So, all's well, I'm now writing more or less like anybody else). The simple Caïd says, 'Fiddlesticks!' The Gascon replies confidently, 'No more than the truth! 'My dear Frenchman, sell me your secret!' ' I'm afraid it will be rather expensive for you'. 'How much then? 'A thousand boudjous' (or boudjoux, or bouts de joue, which would enable our Gascon to cut a certain dash in Algeria).[7]

How come people want us Frenchmen of France to spell these new words of African French correctly? Our dear compatriots the Bedouins use the following versions: a 'burnous' for a cloak; 'razzia' for looting; a 'sheik' for a chief (never mind this word, which a philologist has assured me is merely French with an Arab accent); 'silos' for grain cellars; a 'smala' for … I can't remember what; 'boujous' for a certain amount of money. The outcome is that we're obliged to send our young citizens to finish their university studies in Algeria, to Constantine, Oran, and Blida, and to become familiar with this lovely language by spending several years in desert high society.

---

5   In Molière's *Le Bourgeois gentilhomme*, M. Jourdain is astonished to learn that 'I've been speaking prose for forty years without realizing it, and I'm the most grateful person in the world to you for having explained that to me'.

6   Abd-El-Kader (1807–83), Algerian general and politician who fought French colonists in 1840 but was defeated in December 1847 (so a recent event), unlikely to become president, just as the Pope would be unlikely to become a member of the Académie des Beaux-Arts (often referred to as the Institute).

7   Berlioz's pun may mean that on returning to Gascony, the young man's health will be better, physically and financially; 'bouts de joue' (near-meaningless taken literally) may be intended to suggest healthy pink cheeks.

I return to my Gascon. 'A thousand boudjous', he says, 'take it or leave it'. The Caïd finds the cost exorbitant; something I can't express an opinion about, for the prophet can take me riding pillion on his mare Borack if I know what a boudjou is worth.[8] But the Caïd changes his mind. 'All right then', he says, 'I'll buy your secret at the price of a treasure far greater than the sum you're asking for. Get into this palanquin; my slaves will take you to my residence; I'll follow you and we can do the deal'. They cover the Gascon in a rich cloak; what am I saying? in a burnous; and the ingenuous Gascon allows himself to be carried. A Gascon always knows which way his bread is buttered. The Caïd, sly-boots that he is, may be trusting enough to believe in the hairdresser's talisman against violence, but not to the point of failing to find a way of buying it for nothing. He has a daughter, fine fellow that he is; he will give her to the hairdresser without a dowry and, in his opinion, Zaïde's lovely eyes (she's called Zaïde) are worth more than those of his money-box for a Frenchman ... of France.[9] He has good reason to be specific since Frenchmen abroad, young though they may be, are grasping, as tough as oak, and the whole world knows not to put a finger between them and its bark.[10]

Unfortunately, Zaïde has spotted a superb drum-major passing beneath her balcony whom she takes for a general, and to whom she has given her heart through the window (they're starting to have windows in Algiers). The non-general is beside himself with joy at having aroused the interest of such a pretty lass; he wants to settle the matter on the spot and take Zaïde away; determined, if the government kicks up a fuss, to send his drumstick to the minister and leave France to do whatever it can. Here's our lad entering the Caïd's harem as if he were returning to barracks, swaying on his feet, waving the plumes in his cap and singing 'rataplan' in a way to delight people who like that kind of thing. It appears Zaïde's one of them, as she's all smiles for her fine conqueror; she gets him to smoke a hookah, drink coffee, eat some jam, etc.

But sadly here comes our hairdresser to interrupt this delightful tête-à-tête. They set him down in Zaïde's bedroom, a bedroom apparently open to everyone. He wants to know why the Caïd has brought him to this charming spot; Zaïde too would be quite glad to know the destination of this hairdresser in a burnous sent by her father; as for the drum-major, his hand

---

8   Al-Borack (al-Burāk) is the prophet's winged horse, often described as a mare with a human face; Berlioz's 'pillion' ('en croupe') means mounting behind the rider. The boudjou was worth 1 franc 80 centimes: the figure in the libretto is 20,000 boudjous.
9   A reference to lines in Molière's *L'Avare* (*The Miser*).
10 A French proverb that says it's always dangerous 'to put your finger between the tree and its bark'.

is already on his sword to ask the Gascon to explain himself. What a curious group of people! Meanwhile a fourth curiosity arrives: a feminine and jealous curiosity. Our little French milliner enters to try out one of her bonnets on the lovely Zaïde. When she sees the hairdresser, the headdress falls from her hands. 'What's he doing here?' 'I don't know'. 'What are you doing here?' 'I don't know'. But wait, here's the noble Caïd and all will be explained. 'Daughter, I've chosen a husband for you …' Without waiting for him to finish, the drum-major, who couldn't imagine this meant anybody but him, comes forward twiddling his moustache: 'Present', says he. 'Who is this tall idiot?', says the Caïd. 'Here, my darling daughter, is the man my love has chosen for you'. 'Me?', cries the Gascon, stupefied and uncertain of the role he should be playing. 'Yes, you; I've got your secret and I'm giving you my daughter; as you can see, she's young and charming, you can live with me and your only job will be to look after her happiness and yours'. – 'If you say *yes*', muttered the milliner to her hesitant lover, 'I'll scratch your eyes out'. – 'If you accept', growled the drum-major, 'my sword'll have your skin for a scabbard'. The hairdresser makes his decision, saying, 'No, I'm already engaged. Here's the girl who has my heart and duty. Not wishing to criticize your excellent lady, you can appreciate the sparkle of these eyes and the elegance of this figure, details you Muslims don't make much of, I know, but which we on the other hand value greatly. So, I return to my previous offer: a thousand boudjous'. Baulk, shout, struggle as he may, the Caïd was overcome by his terror of violence. He gives a sign to one of his slaves, who immediately produces a little box that's open, containing a dozen gold pieces adding up to the whole amount; from which I gather that a thousand boudjous are not exactly a fortune. The hairdresser takes the box and in return gives the Caïd a little pot of *lion pomade* [hair gel], recommending it as an infallible protection against being beaten with sticks. The Caïd, duly reassured, gives the drum-major his daughter's hand; after all, she had to marry someone, and the Gascon embraces the milliner. They're all happy and go off to the altar, with nothing to do but enjoy days of gold and silk.[11]

I give my word that this is all I could understand of *Le Caïd*'s libretto. And I listened with all my ears, looked with all my eyes; I even extorted silence quite sharply from the others in my box, who were saying rude things about the Opéra's administration. So, you can blame me for whatever you like, it's not my fault, I can't do any more. Ah! Pardon me, I remember

---

11 'Jours d'or et de soie': in a letter of 22 December 1848, Berlioz had used the formula 'Nous allons filer des jours *d'or* et tout ira de *soie*', incorporating 'les jours d'or et de soie', which was a common phrase in French classical poetry. But the italicization of 'd'or' and 'soie' suggests he may have had in mind a pair of puns: 'jours dehors' (days outside) and 'tout ira de soi' (everything will go of its own accord).

now: also in the piece there's a very amusing white eunuch singing in the same way M. Béfort did in Félicien David's *Le Désert* and getting drunk on a bottle of 'parfait-amour'.[12]

Well now, on this *poem in verse* M. Ambroise Thomas has managed to write a charming and lively score, full of energy and well-tailored to the talent and voice of each of his singers. The introduction to the overture, orchestrated in a new and striking manner, is too pretty to be so short, and the composer would have done well to develop it more; the following Allegro is full of fire and very cleverly managed. The syllabic choruses which open the scene are colourful and dramatically well conceived but seem a little difficult for the chorus who are not very familiar with this syllabic, forceful and rapid style; the precision and tuning of their performance left something to be desired. The main sections of the duet between the milliner and the hairdresser are extremely elegant, and the drum-major's couplets, with their refrain accompanied by six drums beating out the reveille, are pleasing in their frankly military style. The aria sung by the same singer a bit later is well constructed and shows off the agile vocalization that Hermann-Léon certainly possesses, but it gives too much the impression of having been added to the score afterwards to make the singer's role seem more important; it doesn't belong to the piece. The eunuch's aria as he downs his fill of parfait-amour is extremely funny; the ruse of giving him a high tonic A-flat to end a perfect cadence heading towards a low A-flat had the whole house rocking with laughter, and Sainte-Foy had to encore the piece.[13] This actor plays his role with an intelligence and modesty that show he knows how to get the best out of the negative qualities of his voice, and that he fully realizes the value of what he lacks. There was also vigorous applause for a number of passages in the role of milliner, glittering with life and with a boldness only surpassed by that of its singer, Mme Ugalde-Beaucé.[14] Then came an ensemble organized with a masterly hand, and a finale whose staging follows the pattern of Italian ballets, in which all the singers and extras make the same gesture at the same time, raising or lowering their arms, inclining

---

12   'Parfait amour' (perfect love) is a violet-coloured liqueur. The 'ode-symphonie' *Le Désert* by Félicien David (1810–76) was a great success for some time after its first performance in 1844, largely owing to its 'exotic' contents; Béfort must have used a high, thin tone to imitate the muezzin's call. Berlioz reviewed *Le Désert* cordially and conducted it twice in 1845.
13   Sainte-Foy: see article 31, note 10. Hermann-Léon: see article 34, note 1.
14   Delphine Ugalde, born Beaucé (1829–1910), French soprano and composer, had just given her first stage performance in Auber's *Le Domino noir*. From 1863 she sang in the Théâtre des Bouffes-Parisiens, including in Offenbach's *Orphée aux enfers*, and from 1885 was that theatre's director.

their heads, rolling their eyes, smiling or weeping like a single character in a Punch and Judy show.

Apart from the observations I've already made about the inexperience of some singers in the syllabic style, the performance of *Le Caïd* is good and leaves little room for improvement. Hermann-Léon and Sainte-Foy are, as I've said, very good in the roles of the drum-major and the eunuch; Boulo, whom I had never heard since his arrival at the Opéra-Comique, has a pretty tenor voice which will be extremely useful, and which he uses excellently in passages requiring agility.[15] I will only advise him to be careful over the metallic quality his high notes take on when he forces them too much. Henri as the Caïd is the victim of the assaults with sticks to whom these additions to his role are somewhat less than welcome, and his control over the staging is a model of efficiency.[16] Mlle Decroix, unless I'm mistaken, sings just the few notes allotted by the composer to the character I've baptized Zaïde.[17]

I've left Mme Ugalde-Beaucé (the milliner) for my last and principal volley of compliments. She is charming and she vocalizes as no-one in France is currently capable of doing. Her voice, which has a pure and distinctive timbre, is loud enough for the Opéra-Comique; at the same time, it is always perfectly in tune and its agility surpasses anything I have ever heard in this genre. Her *fioriture* are in general those that the composer wrote, because she has the good taste to improvise only rarely. She amuses herself with arpeggios of diminished seventh chords, leaps of a tenth, double appoggiaturas and all the accoutrements of her art of musical lace-making, and declares herself a complete singer, fearing neither heights nor depths, nor threads of sound, nor trills, nor the most unbelievable decorations that the most agile flute could hardly manage. This young singer, who sings what's more with utter grace and spirit, is a very great prize for the director of the Opéra-Comique and for composers. M. Ambroise Thomas, in the role he has just written for her, has, with as much skill as joy, allowed the facets of her talent to shine through. Even so, I feel I should warn her of a fault which it will, I think, be easy for her to correct. In words containing '*e*' followed by two '*l*s', as in *voyelle* or *dentelle*, or else an accented *e*, as in *fidèle*, she almost sings *voyalle*, *dentalle*, *fidale*. This is certainly not as bad as copying certain provincial sopranos who sing *voyélle*, *dentélle*, *fidéle*; but it's not graceful and

---

15 Jean-Jacques Boulo (1820–87), French tenor, had recently arrived at the Opéra-Comique; he sang at the Opéra from 1853 to 1859 and later taught at the Toulouse Conservatoire.

16 Louis-François Henri (1786–1855), French bass and stage director; he sang the small role of Brander in *La Damnation de Faust* in 1846.

17 Marguerite-Jeanne-Camille Decroix (1828–?), French soprano who went on to have a brilliant career at the Opéra-Comique and then at the Théâtre des Fantaisies-Parisiennes.

even has a deleterious effect on the timbre of the notes with which these syllables are paired. Then Mme Ugalde-Beaucé's voice assumes the character of Mlle Déjazet's, reminding us of the music hall and licentious jokes.[18]

Le Caïd has been a brilliant success: the name of M. Thomas has been showered with applause; Mme Ugalde, the next to come onstage, had to appear yet again accompanied by all the other artists. At least I heard them being urged by shouts of 'Everybody! Everybody!' Care should be taken: these outbursts of enthusiasm could end up overplaying outright successes to the point of boredom. It could easily happen, in copying *gli applausi di Roma* and the shouts of *fuore*, aimed at the prima donna, the tenor, the high bass, the low bass, the second soprano, the conductor, the painter, the librettist; shouts to which I remember having added my voice one evening by shouting 'the wigmaker', but he refused to come onstage.[19]

---

18   Pauline-Virginie Déjazet (1798–1875), French actress whose voice had been described in 1833 as 'shrill and shouty' ('aiguë et criarde').

19   'Roman applause': the word 'fuore' doesn't exist in Italian: perhaps Berlioz misheard 'furore', as 'fare furore' means 'all the rage'. Berlioz is surely evoking the claque, whose methods of bringing about applause are described in *Les Soirées de l'orchestre* (seventh evening); the organized claqueurs were known as 'Romans', their leader as Augustus.

50

Second Séance of the Société des Concerts: Beethoven, Haydn, and Others

RGM, 4 February 1849

Anyone who knows Berlioz's music could probably guess the likely tone of his comparison between the two composers. But at least Berlioz has the honesty to doubt its value ...

I don't think the review of this concert will occupy my readers for long (one always imagines one has readers). The concert was *entrancing*, it must be said, and the orchestra performed miracles, especially in Beethoven's First Symphony. You have to hear our violins and see them flying away in [the Trio of] the Scherzo, to believe in the possibility of such nuances being observed by thirty bows simultaneously. It's astonishing. I'm not talking about that pattern which wends its way through the wind section, as light and swift as a puff of wind: we know what our violinists are capable of technically. In any case, that in itself does not present any problems; it's the delicacy of the legato that calls for praise, because there are a score of ways of playing such a passage correctly, and a score of ways passably; this is the right, excellent, and marvellous way. The audience was thrilled and demanded an encore of the Scherzo. For Beethoven this symphony was the point of departure. Its form is smaller and its style less grand than in the symphonies that followed; that it even lacks the sublime aspirations that marked the composer's later works is beyond doubt. But such as it is, how far superior I find it to Haydn's G major Symphony (Opus 51) that we heard in the same concert![1]

---

1   This is probably Symphony no. 92 in the accepted ordering, known as the 'Oxford'. It was composed in 1788 for the Concerts de la Loge Olympique

I'm very far from lacking respect for Haydn's genius, and further still from belittling the admirable music in this same work, the Andante of which is delightful. But overall it's impossible to ignore the enormous distance that separates Beethoven's First Symphony from Haydn's Fifty-First. In the former we find energy, warm blood, strength, the brilliance of youth and a certain virtuosity in handling the orchestra; in the latter we find tranquillity, wisdom, the calm of maturity, a little too mature, and a limited use of the orchestra, comparable to the earlier composers for the harpsichord. Beethoven's symphony is proud and elegant; it walks upright, head high; it commands attention. Haydn's is more humble; it advances modestly; its look is respectful; it barely dares to raise its voice; it insinuates; it is resigned from the start to pass unnoticed and full of gratitude to those members of the audience who are kind enough to listen to it. It's music to dine to, written to ease the digestion of Prince Esterhazy, Haydn's patron. The first movement goes with roast beef, the second with game, the minuet with the sweet, and the finale with the dessert. As soon as the last chord has died away, the prince sent a glass of tokay to his *maître de chapelle*, several bottles of Rhenish wine to the players, and got up while letting everyone see he was satisfied with his position as enabler. I feel that's how things would have gone; from which anyone may infer, without unduly upsetting me, that they went quite differently.

This is why we can easily understand that Beethoven produced nine symphonies and Haydn 117.[2] 117 symphonies! That makes us gasp like Leporello's 'a thousand and three' or Paisiello's 170 operas.[3] Such overwhelming fecundity initially has something dazzling about it. What riches! What abundance! What profusion! It's a continual flow of inspiration, a downpour of ideas! So beneath these indefatigable pens, melodies pile up thickly and full of sap, like blades of grass on a great prairie falling under the sickle! ... Yes; but like those blades of grass, they too fade, and fading means turning into hay. You don't chop down oaks with a sickle. And then (an

---

founded by the Chevalier de St Georges (Joseph Bologne) and the Comte d'Ogny; not for Prince Esterházy, as Berlioz supposed. It owes its nickname to a performance in Oxford (1791), when Haydn was made an Honorary Doctor of Music. Opus numbers attached to certain Haydn symphonies are no longer in use.

2   The usually accepted total is 104. Berlioz may have misremembered the article on Haydn by Charles-Louis de Sevelinges, in Michaud's *Biographie universelle, ancienne et moderne*, vol. 19. Paris: Michaud, 1817, which was in his father's library; there it says that Haydn wrote 118 symphonies.

3   Leporello's catalogue of Don Giovanni's conquests contains 2065 names; 1,003 was the figure for Spain. Paisiello wrote at least eighty operas; the figure 170 is either hearsay or deliberate exaggeration.

awkward comparison) we still have those wretched rabbits who produce so many offspring, while lions have so few.

Never mind! 117 symphonies, it's quite a haul; and if Prince Esterházy heard them all, he must have been blessed with an extraordinary digestion. It's true that he dined every day, and that he maybe got through more than one at each meal.

Ah well … joking aside, it would be extremely interesting for us musicians to explore the whole of this strange collection. Undoubtedly, we should find things to study and compare, and if not always agreeable, at least highly instructive. I'd give a lot to be able to judge in that way how much stylistic variety Haydn was able to find while reproducing the same form of instrumental composition 117 times, because I don't think he ever deviated from it. Sadly, we're very far from possessing scores of his complete symphonies. As a result, we can only read and hear a very small number, and the study I'm talking of, being made on a small scale, loses pretty much all its value.

The fourth part of Félicien David's *Christophe Colomb* was played after the Beethoven symphony. It's a fine piece in which we recognize the colouring of *Le Désert* and that profound feeling for nature that many composers, including the most famous, have completely failed to master.

The scene of the calm sea is necessarily rather like that of the desert, but it's beautifully handled. It's followed by the thousands of utterly delicious sounds, at first indistinct, soon clearer, which seem to be wafted to the sailor by the offshore breeze; the young woman's song has an original and naïve grace; but the arrival and the cries of joy from this desperate crew sighting the new world, the salvos from the guns, the racket of disembarkation, all that is conjured up with a master's hand, and worthily crowned by a splendid final chorus, full of excitement. Perhaps there's some abuse of simplicity in this work, and an over-frequent employment of the same rhythms played at the same speed in all parts of the orchestra, which makes the instrumental impact seem less varied in its make-up than it really is. But this drawback is a boon for the public, which needs a certain effort of will on the harmonic front to manage the complication of two times two, and to assure itself that the result really is four. F. David, in taking this line, is assured of always being understood and immediately appreciated.

We also had the fine prayer 'Dieu d'Israël' from Méhul's *Joseph* and a flute solo from M. Altès.[4] This young performer was well received, and he really does play the flute remarkably. But we already knew that. The demonstrations in the street outside were responsible for keeping the public away,

---

4   Joseph-Henri Altès (1810–95), French composer and flautist.

being hesitant to venture out.[5] As a result the concert couldn't start until twenty past two. In the end though, it was a full house, and twelve hundred people, for a little time, could hear beautiful music and forget 'Les sanglantes mêlées, / Les longs roulements des tambours, / Les lointaines voles / Des cloches et des canons sourds…'[6] ('The bloody conflicts / The long rolling of drums / The distant volleys / Of bells and muffled cannons…') Volleys which, very luckily, nobody heard, but which they could have heard and with which everyone appeared greatly preoccupied.

---

5   Two days earlier, on 26 January, the government had tabled a law in the National Assembly on the rights of association, with the idea of banning clubs. This action, clearly impelled by the riots of the previous year, was the reason for the demonstrations.

6   Lines adapted (or slightly misquoted) from the poem 'La Curée' in *Iambes* (published 1831) by Auguste Barbier (1805–82), French poet and dramatist, one of the librettists of *Benvenuto Cellini*. He was describing the July revolution of 1830.

51

Third Séance of the Société des Concerts

RGM, 25 February 1849

This report is in the form of imaginary conversations, centred on a report of the concert itself.

> The Scene is the rue Bergère at 1.45 p.m.
> Dramatis personae: An Old Man, a Young Violinist, Me

THE OLD MAN (*calling out to me*): Sir! Sir!
ME: Good day to you, sir!
THE OLD MAN: Well, we've got a top-notch programme today!
ME: No need to tell me! I fancy it's the most magnificent one the Société des concerts has ever given its subscribers.
THE OLD MAN: Very likely: The Fourth Symphony, the *Euryanthe* overture, extracts from *La Vestale*, the *O Filii*, it's all marvellous![1] Oh! What a treat for me to hear *La Vestale*! (*turning to the young violinist*). That'll leave you in a terrible state, my dear young sir, if you're as sensitive to music as I was at your age!
THE YOUNG VIOLINIST: Yes, I'm told there are pretty things in *La Vestale*.

---

[1] The 'O Filii' is an unaccompanied choral motet by Volckmar Leisring (1588–1637), German composer, theorist, and clergyman. It lasts only around two minutes and is entirely in D minor until the triumphant *tierce de Picardie* (major third) on the last chord.

THE OLD MAN: Pretty things! No, the whole work is beautiful; there's not a weak note, not a note that doesn't strike home; it's a sublime score, my young friend, a work that flashes and burns, and which you don't describe as having 'pretty things'. That sort of talk is blasphemy.
THE YOUNG VIOLINIST: Forgive me, I don't know it.
ME: You don't know *La Vestale*?
THE YOUNG VIOLINIST: No, sir.
ME: Are you a pupil at the Conservatoire?
THE YOUNG VIOLINIST: Yes, sir.
ME: And a violin teacher?
THE YOUNG VIOLINIST: Yes, sir.
ME: And you're what – twenty-eight, thirty?
THE YOUNG VIOLINIST: I'm twenty-nine.
ME: I congratulate your pupils.
I turn to the old man: What do you think of our system of musical education?
THE OLD MAN.: I say it's disgraceful, and that you really have to *look at the column* in order to be proud of being French.[2]
ME (*to the young violinist*): You can't have much free time; even so, you could have read this score.
THE YOUNG VIOLINIST: Heavens above, when I read, I prefer the novels of Paul de Kock to everything else.[3]
ME: Ah! You're fond of literature?
THE YOUNG VIOLINIST: A bit.
ME: And the works of M. Paul de Kock?
THE YOUNG VIOLINIST: A lot; but I do read others as well.
ME: Do you know Homer's *Odyssey*?
THE YOUNG VIOLINIST: Homer? No. Did this book come out some time ago?
ME: Yes, a long time before the February revolution [1848].
THE YOUNG VIOLINIST: Too bad; one can't read everything. I'm going to get through the whole of Paul de Kock.
ME: You're right, he's a good author. You must be very keen on drama?
THE YOUNG VIOLINIST: Mad about it
ME: Have you read Shakespeare's plays?
THE YOUNG VIOLINIST: As if I would! I'm told they're as boring as anything. I even heard one of my pals reading the scene in *Hamlet* where

---

2   A patriotic song of 1818 by Émile Debraux, containing the lines, addressed the Vendôme Column in Paris: 'With what glory you are surrounded / By the panels that tell of so many brave deeds!'

3   Charles-Paul de Kock (1794–1871), popular novelist, dramatist, librettist, and song writer. He was very popular in his time, but also much mocked, as here by Berlioz.

someone kills a rat behind an arras; I thought I'd die laughing. If all his plays are like that, you'll have to admit ... [4]

ME (*grasping the old man's arm*): Tell these young literate musicians about *La Vestale*! ...

THE OLD MAN: What a country! What manners! What ideas! But that's where we've come to.

THE YOUNG VIOLINIST: Goodbye, gentlemen, *enjoy* yourselves.

THE OLD MAN: Ninny! Young lout!

ME: Little scoundrel! Young cretin! ... Let's go in. (*to the old man*) We'll meet up after the concert.

THE OLD MAN: Certainly. This isn't goodbye.

Scene 2: In the hall, 2–4 p.m.

The orchestra plays Beethoven's Symphony in B-flat [no. 4]. Loud applause after each movement, particularly the Adagio and Finale.

Enter the chorus. They divide into two groups: the smaller one, consisting entirely of men, climbs up the orchestra steps and sits at the top of the amphitheatre behind the highest desks; the other group, which is much more numerous and includes both men and women, takes up its usual place at the back of the stage. The orchestra gives a chord and is then silent. Then the larger of the unaccompanied groups begins Leisring's 'O filii', each phrase being repeated either whole or in part *pianissimo* by the group above them, in what seems to be simply an echo of the group lower down.

This enchanting hymn was splendidly performed, and the audience demanded an encore; it was repeated as perfectly as before. It's a success for the chorus. Among the audience, people are enquiring about this Leisring, who has written such a fine piece of religious music. Nobody knows anything about him.

The orchestra plays the pretty Andante from Haydn's Symphony Opus 75. We find the theme gentle and graceful, admirably presented and varied but the accompaniment by bassoon and oboe playing a seventeenth apart seems a little grotesque. Almost throughout there are only three orchestral parts, which led one critic to call it a trio for two needles and a pin. To which another replied 'Oh!' and didn't argue the point.[5]

---

4   *Hamlet*, act 3, scene 4. Hamlet calls out 'How now? A rat? dead, for a ducat, dead'. The 'rat' is actually Polonius; Hamlet's deed starts a train of events that culminate in his own death.

5   This must be Symphony no. 101, known as the 'Clock'. A 'seventeenth' is two octaves plus a third. When the Andante returns to the original major key, the 'ticking' accompaniment is played by bassoon and flute a seventeenth apart.

The soloists return, namely Mlle Dobré, Mlle Poinsot, and MM. Dupont and Depassio.[6] They sing the Vestals' prayer, 'Fille du ciel'. This three-part female chorus engages the audience at once and moves them by its melody, both noble and graceful. Mlle Poinsot, in the role of chief vestal, begins her solo 'De ce lieu saint' ('From this holy place') well, and continues it badly. In the middle of a phrase, she inserts a horrible appoggiatura and ruins the word 'univers', the pronunciation of which eludes her, by singing it on an A-flat. Mlle Dobré begins 'Je sens couler mes larmes' ('I feel my tears welling up') with a slight tremble in her voice; but she soon regains control and sings the role of Julie, especially in the prayer 'Ô des infortunés' ('O unlucky ones') with an artificial accentuation, but one that's acceptable and often moving. M. Dupont brings an over-tender colouring to the role of Licinius, and M. Depassio, without ever reaching the terrifying impassivity of the elder Dérivis in the role of the Supreme Pontiff, nonetheless brings out its basic character. His voice is very beautiful and he sings in tune, even if he skated over two or three words that he should have articulated more slowly and emphatically. One feels this Olympian style is new to him. The finale arrives; the whole audience is gripped; you see listeners gasping and shaking, carried away by this inexorable rhythm; some clasp their hands, others desperately, and two young ladies hide at the back of their box to conceal their convulsive sobbing from the audience.

But the silence remains profound; you can judge it by the first pause, where the voices and orchestra go silent, while the solo tam-tam stretches out its funeral sighs. At the return of the soprano melody, on the $^6_4$ chord: 'De son front que la honte accable' ('With his forehead struck by shame'), the audience, shaken, exasperated and convulsed by emotion, makes an unconscious, involuntary movement as though to stand up, but without a sound. Such are their respect and admiration that not a single exclamation is heard. They are suffocated and suffering, but they're calm. Their fearful enthusiasm is held in by the pressure of a Titan's hand. They want to hear everything, everything, right up to the last note of the ritornello. Then, suddenly, a single cry escapes and rings round the hall, the cry of twelve hundred voices, joined by the shouts and noises of all kinds voiced by the two hundred electrified performers. Applause is not enough; there are gesticulations and thumps from fists and feet. The violins and basses join in with a hail of notes from their bows, while some raise their arms to the heavens and others are overcome with nervous laughter. It's a tumult to make you dizzy.

---

6   Mlle Dobré: see article 34, note 1. The French soprano Anne-Euphrasie Poinsot (1825–1906) later sang at the Opéra; Berlioz praised her in Halévy's *La Juive* for one of the best débuts for a long time (*CM* vol. 7, p. 433). Dupont: see article 6, note 3. The French bass Jean Depassio (1824–71) also joined the Opéra in 1853.

Then comes the overture to *Euryanthe*, performed by the orchestra with an astonishing fury, emerging purple in the face from the Spontinian blaze. This overture is a sublime work, as well as bold, young, lively, poetic, and displaying a masterly technique. But we're too exhausted by what we've just heard to appreciate it fully. The programme has been a superabundance of riches. Finally, we leave. The concert is over.

Scene 3: In the courtyard, 4.30 p.m.

A crowd of people with eyes aflame, tearful, red, pale, exhausted by overwhelming sensations. Everyone gives the impression of coming out of a dream. We shake ourselves, we breathe again.

THE OLD MAN. (*spotting me*): Goodness me! I can't take any more!
ME: Nor can I. Until tomorrow, my nerves are a wreck.
THE YOUNG CRETINOUS VIOLINIST: Well, gentlemen, I'm delighted to have heard that; the finale was especially effective.
ME (very coldly): Yes, that's the word, effective.
ANOTHER YOUNG LOUT (joining us): There really are some quite lovely things in that *Vestale*.
THE OLD MAN: (ironically): Aren't there just? I see you're a connoisseur.
THE YOUNG LOUT: All the same, they're right not to stage it; it wouldn't be a success, it's too old-fashioned.
AN OLD LOUT OF A CONTRAPUNIST (interrupting him): Also, it's very badly written. Spontini could never string two chords together; his accompaniments lie underneath the tune *like a handful of hairs on a soup*. He's no musician. But what's the matter, Monsieur Berlioz? are you feeling ill?
ME: Yes, in your company I'm feeling very ill; I feel very ill listening to you; I feel very ill knowing that there exist people of your sort and like these two whippersnappers [*myrmidons*]. And I shall only recover on the day when, knowing you're all in a sack with plenty of cannonballs at your feet and hanging by a string above the Seine or some other even less salubrious spot, and if, while you cry for help, I can cut the string.
THE OLD LOUT AND THE TWO YOUNG ONES (together): Thanks a million! What a charming fellow!
ME: May you get cholera! Go to the devil! Meanwhile, you can count on me; I shall make a point, if I can, of treating you as I do spiders and scorpions.
THE INTELLIGENT OLD MAN (digging his fingers into my arm): Bravo! The crowd disperses; the three cretins, laughing, go into a tobacconist's and light their cigars.

52

Sixth Séance of the Société des Concerts

RGM, 8 April 1849

Here, in the first two paragraphs of a much longer review, is Berlioz once more campaigning for composers' rights ... for which a useful German word is 'Werktreue'.

Let's climb the Capitol and give thanks to the gods![1] A great event took place in the first part of this concert. It was a veritable proclamation of principle; someone had the nerve to recognize that performers owe fidelity and respect to the great masters; that it is not their job, as interpreters, to alter and distort the original offered for their interpretation. Finally, to sum up, here was the brutal frankness of confessing this awkward but unarguable fact: there is no conductor, violinist, flautist, horn player, nor even a drummer, capable of giving Beethoven lessons in orchestration. Maybe one day it'll happen: but for the moment this precious teacher is nowhere to be found.

Indeed, let the future decide, for better or worse! Let's go for it! 'Fortune favours the brave!' [2] Whoever risks nothing has nothing! After all, the public won't eat us: LET'S PLAY THE FIFTH SYMPHONY WITHOUT CORRECTIONS; let's keep the contrabasses at the start of the Scherzo; be prepared![3] It's twenty-two years they've been kept on the leash, those

---

1   This quotes a prayer by Scipio Africanus, facing his Roman accusers, and recalling his victories over the Carthaginians.
2   'Let's go for it': strictly translated, this would be 'Let's throw our cap over the windmills!' ('Jetons notre bonnet par-dessus les moulins'). 'Fortune favours the brave' translates Virgil's 'Audaces fortuna juvat' (*Aeneid*, X, line 284).
3   Cellos and contrabasses open both the Scherzo and its Trio; Berlioz may be referring to the opening of the Trio which elsewhere he compared to 'les ébats d'un elephant en gaieté' ('the frolicking of a tipsy elephant'): *À travers chants*

wretched contrabasses; twenty-two years during which the Société des concerts of the Paris Conservatoire have been giving Europe the fine example of enlightened support to the glory of poor Beethoven, who had used basses there *to such poor effect* and *what's more, impossible to play*. But now, let's see what that'll produce, let's light the fuse of this bomb. One must try out the new; sometimes you have to stand out a bit in order to grip the public's attention. The pretty cello solo Beethoven had never thought of had been installed for twenty-two years; never mind! Let's burn our boats and may God protect France![4] The contrabasses shall play! And they did play in Beethoven's symphony. Yes, good heavens, it's as I say. And those unperformable contrabass parts were performed extremely well, and their poor effect struck everyone as a very fine effect! It makes one smile! When all's said and done, Beethoven had a certain instinct for the orchestra that sometimes, in his case, replaced technique and taste. Anyway, we got away with it!

Joking aside, M. Girard needed considerable courage to challenge a usage that had been implanted in the Conservatoire for so long.[5] M. Girard must have been afraid of being accused of disrespect towards … tradition. But no doubt believing it was preferable not to show disrespect to … the score, and that he was there to transmit Beethoven's thoughts faithfully, not to disfigure them, he remained true to his task; and Beethoven's C-minor Symphony, in Beethoven's orchestration, was, thanks to M. Girard, heard for the first time in the Paris Conservatoire on Sunday, 1 April 1849, at 2.15 p.m.

(1862 edition, p. 35; English translation, p. 21). At this period, it was evidently played just by cellos or even perhaps, as Berlioz implies, a single cello.
4   'Dieu protège la France' was inscribed on French coins of the period.
5   Girard: see article 12, note 32.

Industrial Exhibition, Musical Instruments: The 'Droit des Pauvres' Applied to Instrument-Makers; MM. Érard, Boisselot, Weulfel, Sax, and Vuillaume

JD, 21 August 1849

By 1849, Berlioz had turned his long-standing proclivity for sarcasm into a fine art, again at the expense of the 'Droit des pauvres' and its collector: the poor-tax levied on income, not only profits, payable by organizers of entertainments including concerts (see also article 34).

'Why do people go on making instruments?' you will ask. – Because we're still teaching musicians in Conservatoires and elsewhere. – But why, you will add, do we persist in teaching music to these poor wretches? – Good Lord, because the habit has been around a long time, because certain music venues still keep their doors open, because a small number of people are determined not to abandon the pleasure they get from music, and still indulge more or less in this excellent art. No doubt the time will come when these *eccentrics* will be quite rare in France, when all the opera houses will be shut, when Conservatoires no longer exist, and when those musicians who haven't died of hunger will have taken up a *useful* trade. But the time for this triumph of positive ideas over the empty dreams of poetry and art has not yet arrived; nothing is as tenacious as ancient habits. In any case Athens, Babylon, and Memphis were not demolished in a day. Everything takes time.

Besides, the Opéra is already closed and, if one is to believe the general rumour, its future doesn't look rosy even if it gets to open this winter. We don't know whether the Théâtre-Italien will manage to put on some operas. As for concerts (I'm not talking about those more or less numerous gatherings of idlers who are treated to chromatic scales on a keyboard and the simperings of tired romances); as for concerts, I say, their number will undoubtedly be much reduced, and that will be a real problem for the collector of the *droit des pauvres* who, quite apart from the satisfaction he has felt hitherto in collecting part of the products of musicians' labours, has always enjoyed honouring major concerts with his presence, and so encouraging the serfs who work for him. Perhaps, taking into account the interests of this estimable protector of our art, the government will nevertheless encourage musicians to put on concerts; but as this practical move cannot, after all, provide any kind of compulsion for a public more and more reluctant to pay money for listening to music, I fear that our noble protector will not collect much of it, and won't look so kindly on our efforts ... It's a serious business.

The enslavement of blacks has been abolished and this has ruined a crowd of excellent people who were very happy to get rich without doing anything.[1] There remained the slavery of French musicians which, by and large, brought in a mere hundreds of thousands of francs for our noble collector and, even if we haven't been emancipated, there's our dear gentleman reduced to the condition of a settler in Guadeloupe!! ... This is truly serious! Let us turn our eyes from this dismal spectacle![2]

The authorities should, in my view, pay a little compensation to the administrators of hospices and to our noble collector. As concerts are bringing in practically nothing for him and the opera houses are dead or dying, why not replace the *legitimate* part our collector takes on the gross receipts from concerts and theatrical performances with a corresponding *levy* on the product from the sale of musical instruments, since instrument makers are still at work? ... It's a very simple idea and I'm surprised no one has thought of it before. There's no doubt that such a legitimate tax will be paid as promptly as possible. MM. Érard, Pleyel, Boisselot, Sax, Vuillaume, Gand, and a score of others will even be proud to comply with it.[3] Inspectors will be sent to look over their products and receipts and, once the inspection is

---

1   Slavery was abolished in France by a decree of 27 April 1848. The man who accomplished the abolition, Victor Schoelcher, was a good friend of Berlioz until his rejection of Napoleon III led to a break in their friendship.
2   A remark often found in literature of the period.
3   Érard, article 10, note 2; Camille Pleyel (1788–1855), French pianist, composer and piano maker; Boisselot, see article 10, note 6; Vuillaume: see article 14, note 9; Charles-Adolphe Gand (1812–66), French violin maker, attached to the Conservatoire.

over, these gentlemen will say to M. Érard or M. Sax, for example, 'You've sold 160,000 francs worth of pianos, or 80,000 francs worth of saxhorns, we have the *right* to an eighth and even a quarter of your gross receipts; give us 20,000 francs, M. Érard and you, M. Sax, 10,000 francs. Excellent! The collector is satisfied'. And he will be. Those who might doubt his satisfaction don't know our good collector and his generosity. Nobody is more generous than him. The law authorizes him to take a *quarter* of our gross receipts, but he takes only an eighth. Suppose a musician puts on a concert whose costs amount to 1,000 francs; his receipts come to 800 francs; the law allows our collector to take 200 francs, and he takes only 100 exactly. Can one take unselfishness any further? …

So, I hope people will take steps as soon as possible to see that musical instrument makers are at last given the honour of satisfying the collector and indemnifying him for the considerable losses caused by ungrateful musicians, who are currently refusing to work for him. And this operation, I repeat, will be simple and easy. Instrument makers have, it's true, been making considerable losses over the last eighteen months; they sales have been halved, and their workmen have asked to be paid half as much again; but, when all's said and done, they still live; they even have the imagination to try and perfect their instruments, and some push audacity to the point of inventing new ones. These inventors are, I confess, not numerous; and this year they've abstained from showing the public their latest discoveries. I shall not, therefore, reveal their secrets.

As to the *new* improvements publicized at the 1849 Exhibition, they don't amount to a great deal. M. Érard has added to the piano a system of pedals like that on the organ, which allow the performer not only to modify and prolong the sonority of the strings, but also to give more resonance to the bass octaves using just the pedals. Sebastian Bach, the most radical organist known to us, was not content to attack the organ keyboards with his four extremities; he had the idea of adding to them a little stick held between his teeth, with which, by moving his head, he could strike the keys.[4] In this way he could, in certain passages, play thirteen notes at once. The famous singer Lablache, using a system he modestly chose not to advertise at the Exhibition and without using his feet, is the only person so far to play twenty-four and even thirty notes on the piano at the same time! It's true that nature has favoured him to an exceptional degree.

---

4   This is an almost direct quotation: 'He [Bach] was so fond of full harmony, that beside a constant and active use of the pedals, he is said to have put down such keys by a stick in the mouth, as neither hands nor feet could reach'.
    Charles Burney, *A General History of Music from the Earliest Ages to the Present Period*. London, 1789, p. 593.

M. Wolfel has added an adjustable screw to the piano which makes the tuner's task much quicker and easier.[5]

M. Boisselot, the clever piano maker from Marseille, has done even better. His invention will render really important services to piano playing, especially if you combine them with Érard's pedals. It works as follows: we know that until now piano pedals had two uses: one, to damp down the sound of the instrument by removing *two* of the three strings for each note out of the way of the hammer, which struck simply *one single string*; the other, to suspend the action of the dampers and so let the strings sound for the entire length of their vibrations. But this important effect, which bad pianists abuse so cruelly, cannot be limited to any particular range of the instrument: when the *soft pedal* is in use, the whole keyboard is subject to the action of the dampers. M. Boisselot has found a way of prolonging the vibration of *a single note*, leaving all the others subject to the dampers. This produces excellent effects of a staccato over a held accompaniment: effects which could be achieved in the past, but only by keeping a finger on the key whose sound was to be prolonged, and so immobilizing one of the player's hands. Thanks to M. Boisselot's invention, it's enough for the pianist to strike the note whose sound he wants to prolong more forcefully than the others, and he can abandon the key immediately without the string ceasing to vibrate. A low note can therefore continue to sound in the lower part of the piano while both hands are operating in the upper part, three or four octaves above the bass note.[6]

So much for what I can say about improvements to the piano. I'm not aware of anything being invented for the organ, the mélodium, the harmonium, the psalmodium, the antiphonium, the cacophonium, and other bastard offspring of the organ which mew, sigh, bark, and wail around their papa, making the Exhibition hall where this bunch of noisy brats is assembled a no-go area for musicians.[7] When these yells are joined by the racket of two or three pianos letting fly with their *fantaisies* in different keys at the same time, it's enough to give any musician blessed with some aural sensitivity an attack of *delirium tremens* or cholera at its worst. Tell me about the shops of Pleyel and Érard: there, nobody's playing preludes. These gentlemen don't need to advertise their products; everybody knows how splendid they are. They surround themselves with a wonderful silence, and those

---

5   Jean-Guillaume-Charles-François Wolfel or Weulfel (1804–?), Parisian piano maker.

6   The invention is probably by Louis Boisselot, son of the founder of the Marseilles piano makers (see article 10, note 6); it anticipates the third (middle or Steinway) pedal on modern pianos.

7   On the mélodium see article 42, note 7. Psalmodium and antiphonium appear in dictionaries of ancient music; 'cacophonium' is of course a joke.

hearing it appreciate its charm and majestic eloquence. If I needed to buy a piano, I'd go to Érard or Pleyel, merely because neither of them exhibits his instruments in the Exhibition.

Sax behaves likewise, I'm happy to say. Can you imagine a small army of instrumentalists all blowing away together at the elder and younger brothers of the baritone saxhorn, the sons of the bass saxophone, the mothers and grandmothers of the treble clarinet, not to mention the fearsome children of the tuba, the incompetently blown race of trombones, with or without valves, and the raucous family of natural and valve horns? This *Asiatic* concert would defeat all the precautions of the architecture to ensure the solidity of the Exhibition's building; we should see beams cracking, walls splintering, curtains torn to shreds, and ceilings collapsing with widespread mayhem. But no, these giants of brass and wood remain silent beneath their tent of glass, and pedestrians can circulate in absolute safety. The next-door neighbours of Sax's shop, the wise *friends* of this ingenious artist, '*Imitent* ... son silence autour de lui ranges' ('Surrounding him, imitate his silence').[8]

One of them, M. Barteh [*sic*], has fitted a slide to the natural horn like the slide found on English trumpets; this would have been useful before valves came along.[9] We may also notice, among one inventor's objects. brass instruments including all *their keys* or 'corps de rechange'.[10] The only result of this innovation is to make the instrument heavier and more fragile without improving the timbre and without making the embouchure any easier. There's also a signal trumpet which works on compressed air. Might this idea not have been suggested by the notion of a gigantic steam organ entertained some years ago by M. Sax?[11]

Among the makers of wind instruments, M. Godefroy has made flutes a speciality. He has just bought from the famous Boehm a new patent for a metal flute which is said to be excellent. M. Tulou has stayed with the old system of flute making and is not indulging in any modifications to an instrument from which he, fine player that he is, always draws such lovely sounds.[12]

M. Vuillaume, apart from his valuable imitations of the old violins of the masters (which he freely admits), exhibited this year a monster contrabass,

---

8   'Ses gardes affligés / Imitaient son silence autour de lui rangés'. Racine, *Phèdre*, act 5, scene 6.
9   Almost certainly Charles Bartsch, a Paris wind-instrument maker.
10 'Corps de rechange' are crooks; tubes of varying lengths fitted into natural brass instruments so that they can play in different keys.
11 Signal trumpet: Military bugle. Sax's steam organ: see article 44, note 3.
12 Vincent-Hypolite Godfroy (1806–68), French flute-maker; Theobald Boehm (1794–1881), German flautist and flute-maker; Jean-Louis Tulou (1786–1865), French flautist, flute-maker and composer.

beside which standard contrabasses are no more than pocket fiddles for a dancing master.[13] A special mechanism replaces fingers too small and weak to press these enormous strings onto the fingerboard. This gigantic wasp would buzz most usefully *beneath* an orchestra of two or three hundred musicians, as long as one gave it merely the long, fundamental notes of the harmony. A number of these mastodons have been included in German festivals. I'm sorry to say that, while making this instrument which is of limited use, M. Vuillaume has not been tempted to produce something about which I have often talked to him, and the nature and impact of which seemed to him worth considering. The instrument in question was a *percussive string* instrument, intended to produce the low tremolo, either *piano* or *mezzo forte*, *very dense* and in several parts, which the combination of a tremolo on the bows of the contrabasses, together with rolls on the timpani, renders only very imperfectly.

Because it's in this area that there remains the most to do. Orchestral percussion instruments are truly in their infancy, and the technique of resonance from sounding bodies being struck has hardly been studied, with the exception of the metal strings of the piano. Or at least, this study has so far been unproductive. The percussion instruments we have in our orchestras are, with the exception of the timpani (the sound of which is rarely good, its tuning being erratic and its resonance restricted); these instruments, I repeat, drums, bass drum, cymbals, and triangle, despite the use one can sometimes make of them, are leftovers from the barbarism of the Middle Ages; they declare a real link between our orchestras and the little discordant bands of Eastern peoples – a link that puts us to shame.

I've said nothing so far about the instruments exhibited by M. Sax. This famous inventor, despite the multifarious obstacles that people continue to put in his way, is still going forward and perfecting the numerous families of wind instruments on which he has worked, and those which owe their existence to him. These are mainly the families of the saxhorn, the saxotromba, and the saxophone. The first of these comes in six sizes: soprano, alto, tenor, baritone, bass, and contrabass. The saxhorn produces a sound that is both strong and gentle. The saxotromba's sound is less weighty; it derives from the saxhorn and various other known instruments, namely horn, trumpet, and trombone. M. Sax has regularized and standardized the mechanism of these different instruments, both the old ones and those invented by him, so that if you know how to play one of them, you also know how to play the

---

13   Pocket ('pochette') or 'kit' fiddles: see for instance Degas, *The Rehearsal*, c. 1873–78, Harvard Art Museums/Fogg Museum, for a fiddle-playing dancing master. The monster contrabass is the Octobass which Berlioz discusses under the heading 'New instruments' (including Sax's) in the second edition of his *Grand Traité*.

rest. If, for example, you know how to play the valve cornet, you can also play the valve horn, the valve trombone, the trumpet, the bugle, and all the saxhorns and saxotrombas. But given that the fingering and the embouchure of these fine instruments are straightforward, it doesn't follow that you can play them in a way to bring out all their finest points, or make nice sounds or powerful ones in solos and ensembles; in other words to ensure that they lose nothing of their quality, you must practise them over a long period and with good teachers. And here we come across one of the most serious weaknesses that one has to point out, given the state of French music-making.

A violinist, cellist, or pianist works ten hours a day for eight or nine years to acquire a standard technique, sometimes without success. Yet we expect a soldier, for instance, who can hardly read music, to play a saxhorn or a trombone really well a mere six months after one of these instruments has been put in his hands! From this follow the doubtful tuning, the faltering, ugly sound, the vulgar phrasing and, as a result, the instrument's negative impact. Give a marvellous Stradivarius to a scraper, and he'll burn your ears off, if you have any; the same goes for the most wonderful of Sax's brass instruments. You should ask MM. Forestier, Dieppo, and Caussinus how long they worked before they could play the cornet, trombone, and ophicleide as they do.[14] The same question could be put to the members of the Distin family who, armed with five of Sax's instruments, made a great name for themselves in France, Germany, and England, and who at this moment are touring North America with such success.[15]

We remember, even in Paris where everything is so quickly forgotten, the marvellous purity of sound these fine artists drew from their brass instruments, from the saxhorn especially – their fine tuning, their mellowness, and

---

14   Joseph Forestier (1815–82), French horn player and composer; Dieppo, see article 13, note 4; Joseph-Louis-Victor Caussinus (1806–99), French ophicleidist and composer.

15   John Distin (1798–1863) started his career as a slide-trumpet and keyed bugle player in the Grenadier Guards Band with whom in 1815, just after Waterloo, he had travelled to Paris. Sax patented the saxhorn family in 1845 and 'the resemblance of the saxhorn to existing instruments involved Sax in a long series of lawsuits. Yet by giving his instrument a new name and creating a uniform family of matched instruments he established the saxhorn as a principal section in French military bands [...] There were originally five sizes of saxhorn, extended in the 1850s to include the sopranino and the very large saxhorns ...'. Hugh Macdonald, *Berlioz's Orchestration Treatise*. Cambridge: Cambridge University Press, 2002, p. 303. Berlioz used saxhorns in *Les Troyens*. He seems to have contemplated using tenor and bass saxophones in the scene in heaven in *La Damnation de Faust*, but the two staves preceded by the instrument names are blank.

the strange charm they found in the sweetest, most tender melodies ... Who would have believed, eight years ago, that French instruments played by Englishmen would make a world tour like this to such applause? However, these instruments were still more or less closely allied to the trumpet. We may expect quite different results from the young family of saxophones, when true virtuosos, comparable in stature to those I've just named, will make this new and magnificent instrument heard as it should be heard. The effects composers will be able to draw from it within the orchestra, and above all for dramatic music, are incalculable. The voice of the saxophone, whose family consists of seven members of differing sizes, lies somewhere between that of brass instruments and that of the woodwind; it also shares, though with far greater power, the sonority of the strings. Its principal merit, for me, lies in the varying beauty of its *accent*: sometimes serious and calm, sometimes passionate, sometimes dreamy, or melancholic, or indefinite, like the faint echo of an *echo*, like the indistinct melancholy of the breeze in the woods or, better still, like the mysterious vibrations of a bell long after it has been struck. No other existing musical instrument, to my knowledge, possesses this curious sonority bordering *on the limit of silence*.

Only the *decrescendo* and *piano* of the singers in the Russian Imperial Chapel, those marvellous choristers for whom God must envy the Emperor Nicholas, can give an idea of the delightful half-tints, these crepuscular sounds of the saxophone which, applied with skill to the unfolding of some poetic inspiration, would plunge the listener into an ecstasy that I can imagine, but cannot begin to describe ... [16] But so far no one has written for this new voice, and the young M. Verroust, one of the excellent bassoonists in the Opéra's orchestra, is, I think, the only person currently making moves in this direction.[17] In this he has to start from scratch, both in teaching the instrument and in playing it. As for the development of the instrument itself, it's complete and, apart from some perfecting of detail, the task of its inventor, M. Sax, is finished.

---

16   Berlioz had visited Russia in 1847. Much impressed by the sacred music by Dimitry Stepanovich Bortnyansky, he arranged two pieces with Latin words in the hope that Catholic liturgies might also use them.
17   Charles-André-Joseph Verroust (1826-87), French bassoonist.

54

The Death of Johann Strauss

JD, 4 October 1849

Berlioz had devoted part of a JD *feuilleton (10 November 1837) to the concerts given by Johann Strauss senior in Paris: 'It's curious that the arrival of a German orchestra, whose pretentions barely extend beyond playing waltzes, should be a musical event of such great importance…The name Strauss was known to us thanks to the music publishers who have brought out his waltzes in their thousands, and to Musard who has played some of them, but that was all; and of the orchestra's precision, fire, intelligence, and rare feeling for rhythm, we had absolutely no idea'.* [1]

While the final rehearsals of *La Fée aux roses* were taking place at the Opéra-Comique in Paris, the city of Vienna was mourning one of its favourite artists.[2] Strauss has just died. This melancholy organizer of balls, during which his orchestra would deliver such ardent melodies, such abundant joy, and sometimes also such outbursts of passion and tenderness that they brought tears to the eyes, has just laid down his pen and his bow. I am not one of those who say: 'It's not important; it's just one waltz-monger less!' I say it *is* important, because Strauss was an artist in every respect. Some of his rivals turn lovely operatic music into appalling dance music; he on the other hand wrote such charming things for his dance orchestra that they could have made the fortune of many an opera. I can see him still on his podium in the Salle des Redoutes [Redoutensaal], with six or eight hundred Viennese

---

1 Johann Strauss the elder (1804–49), Viennese violinist, composer, and conductor, rather than his son of the same name. Berlioz's feuilleton continues with a discussion of 'The future of rhythm', among his most interesting theoretical statements. Translation: *Berlioz Society Bulletin* 212 (January 2021), pp. 43–53; excerpt in Barzun, *Berlioz and the Romantic Century*. New York, 1969, vol. 2, pp. 336–9. Strauss's funeral cortège (27 September 1849) was followed by a crowd of c. one hundred thousand.
2 Opéra-comique by Halévy, premiered 1 October 1849.

beauties swirling around at his feet, dancers lost to the world, drunk on movement and harmony, who obeyed him with such love, encored him with such energy in the intermissions, applauding him and covering him with flowers ...

What's more, Strauss rendered an eminent service to music by developing in some of the public a feeling for finesse and even for the elegant graces of rhythm. He's the creator of the syncopated dance, and it's to him we owe our deliverance from the insipid waltz, the insipid rhythm we thought was an inevitable component, as we still believe to be the case with marches and many other forms of music. Vienna then has lost one of its greatest charms; it's a Viennese gentleman who says so, writing to me, 'No more Volksgarten, no more masked balls! Vienna without Strauss is Austria without the Danube; Vienna is in tears over its lost joys!' Strauss, accompanied by a huge crowd, was carried by the members of his orchestra as far as Döbling, a village near Vienna, where he lies next to his rival Lanner, who was buried five or six years before him.[3]

---

3   Joseph Franz Karl Lanner (1801–43). Strauss had started out as the violin soloist in Lanner's orchestra.

55

The Death of Chopin

JD, 27 October 1849

Although Chopin seems to have had a low opinion of his music, Berlioz admired his piano-playing and compositions. There was some friendly correspondence in the 1830s including a dinner invitation partly in Italian that begins: 'Chopinetto mio, si fa una villegiatura da noi à Montmartre …'.[1]

After a long and terrible period of agony, Chopin has just died.[2] We shall not, in his case, use the regular formula and say that his death is a loss for art. Sadly, Chopin had been lost to music for some time. His exhaustion and sufferings were such that he could neither play the piano nor compose; even the shortest conversation tired him to an alarming extent. By and large he tried to make himself understood by using sign language. This was the reason for the kind of isolation in which he chose to live the last days of his life, an isolation that many people criticised, some attributing it to a disdainful pride, others to depression, both of which were utterly foreign to the character of this charming, supreme artist. Far from being gloomy, in the days when his sufferings were still tolerable Chopin was displaying a witty cheerfulness that lent an irresistible attraction to the meetings with his friends. He brought to every conversation that humour which was the principal charm and essential character of his rare talent.

His piano music has started a school. The most original grace, the unexpectedness of melodic shaping, the boldness of harmony and the independence of rhythmic accentuation are united to a whole system of

---

1   The note is dated from a few days before this rural party on 5 May, where the guests Berlioz mentions to his sister Adèle (letter of 12 May) were de Vigny, Antoni Deschamps, Liszt, Hiller, and Chopin: 'We chatted, discussed art, poetry, thinking, music, drama, what is life, in the presence of nature and under the Italian sky we've had these past few days'. *CG* vol. 2, pp. 180–1.

2   Chopin died on 17 October 1849.

ornamentation which he invented, and which remains inimitable. His piano études are masterpieces in which we find concentrated the outstanding qualities of his style and his most striking inspirations. We would even place them above his famous mazurkas which, as soon as they appeared, brought Chopin a wild success, especially with the ladies, and made him the favourite of all the aristocratic salons of Europe. This abundance of exquisite melodies, their allure both proud and serene, their disdain for anything vulgar, their restrained or urgent passion, their divine delicacy, their ceremonial grandeur, all these show a kind of affinity with the ways of the elegant world for which they seem to have been made.

Furthermore, Chopin, despite his magnificent pianistic talents, was not a man for the crowd, a virtuoso of large halls or grand concerts. He had given up such spectacles long ago. Only a small circle of chosen listeners, whose true desire to hear him play he could trust, could persuade him to go to the piano. What emotions he knew how to arouse! In what passionate and melancholy reveries he allowed his soul to wander! It was usually towards midnight that he let himself go with the greatest abandon; when the bigwigs had left the salon, when the current political topic had been dealt with at length, when all the scandalmongers had come to the end of their anecdotes, when all the traps were set, all the lies consumed, when everyone was tired of prose; then, in obedience to the silent prayer of some beautiful, intelligent eyes, Chopin would become a poet and sing of the romantic [*ossianiques*] loves of the heroes of his dreams, their chivalric delights, and the sorrows of the absent fatherland, his dearest Poland, always eager to conquer and always vanquished. But except under these conditions, which every artist should be grateful to him for demanding, it was pointless to appeal to him. He even seemed to be irritated by the curiosity his fame engendered, and he would slip away as soon as possible from an unsympathetic milieu if bad luck had left him stranded there. I remember a stinging retort he uttered one evening to the owner of a house where he had dined. Hardly had the coffee been served, when the host went up to Chopin to say that his guests, who had never heard him, were hoping he would be kind enough to go to the piano and play *a little something*. Chopin instantly refused in a manner that left not the slightest doubt of his feelings. But the host insisted in an almost insulting way, as of someone who knows the value and purpose of the dinner he has just provided. Chopin cut the discussion short, saying to him, in a voice that was faint and interrupted by a bout of coughing, 'Ah! Monsieur! … I have … eaten so little! …'

Despite the considerable proceeds from his published music and from the lessons he gave, Chopin did not leave a fortune; those unhappy Poles, whom exile so often brought to his door, know where that fortune went.[3] In his last days Chopin's lifelong admiration for Mozart led him to want the immortal *Requiem* performed at his funeral. His excellent pupil, M. Gutmann, heard this request with Chopin's last breath.[4] Immediately all the necessary preparations were made; thanks to the active intervention of the Abbé Deguerry, the archbishop has waived the prohibition which made the performance of the *Requiem* impossible.[5] As a result, female singers will be able to contribute to the ceremony, which will take place in the Madeleine church next Tuesday.[6]

---

[3] The implication is that Polish exiles benefitted from Chopin's generosity.

[4] Adolf Gutmann (1819–82), French pianist and composer of German extraction.

[5] Jean-Gaspard Deguerry (1796–1871) was curé of Saint-Eustache from 1845 to 1849, then of the Madeleine until his death in 1871; he was murdered during the Commune together with the archbishop.

[6] Among the soloists at the funeral on 30 October were Luigi Lablache, who had sung in the same work at Beethoven's funeral in Vienna in 1827, and Pauline Viardot.

56

A Method of Telephony by M. Sudre

JD, 17 November 1849

This is the last section of a feuilleton which includes a long review of an opera by Maillard and an account of music performed at a prize-giving in the Sainte-Chapelle. Jean-François Sudre (1787–1862), French violinist, composer and pedagogue, trained two friends to play and interpret his musical code. A given note would represent a word or a letter of the alphabet. The trio toured France, answering questions from the audience using Sudre's violin. A military application was soon suggested: a bugler could transmit orders to a regiment by playing an appropriate tune. In the end this promising idea came to nothing because the system was too vulnerable to wind and weather.

M. Sudre is currently offering us a new and melancholy example of the fate suffered by all inventors in our inattentive, forgetful, and jealous society. For twenty years now he's been fighting, swimming against the current, talking, writing, experimenting, and proving that a discovery of the greatest importance for armies and navies, and even for the rapid propagation of peace-making ideas is in his possession. He proved that this discovery is his, that he made it on his own, and that subsequently he has perfected and simplified it to the point of making it extremely easy to use; and for twenty years he has been ignored, made fun of, given promises that haven't been kept, had his confidences shockingly abused and, in the meantime, the poor man exists on his own resources and those of his friends. Acoustic telephony or telegraphy is the art of transmitting orders and information over long distances, using a tiny number of sounds in various combinations. M. Sudre first used the bugle's basic notes (c^1–g^1–c^2–e^2–g^2) as his auditory signals; now he works with just three (g–c^1–g^1). With these three notes he can send 3,159 orders. Naval capacity is only 1,815 (on a clear day), using thirty-four flags, pennants or ropes. Two minutes are enough to send three orders a distance of nearly 4,000 metres. As a result, these sonic signals can be sent at night as well as in the daytime, either in calm weather or in the midst of fog and rain. Using telephony costs nothing, since the smallest group of soldiers includes men whose job is to sound the bugle.

In a very short time, the telephonic method can be taught to those soldiers given the task of transmitting orders and of interpreting those they receive, as the inventor has proved many times. To the expressed objection that the bugle is not strong enough to send sonic signals over great distances, M. Sudre has responded as follows: 'Give me eight pieces of canonry and, using them, I will dictate whatever you like to a monitor possessing the secret of my method, and placed at the extreme limit of what a piece of heavy artillery can reach'. The experiment was made in the presence of M. le duc de Montpensier and several senior officers. M. Sudre, being assured that the eight artillerymen at his disposal could fire at the precise moments he ordered, transmitted very fast, with scrupulous accuracy and at a vast distance, the following five commands, chosen on the spot by M. le duc de Montpensier: 'Gunners, to your guns!'; 'The enemy are abandoning their position'; 'How long can you hold your present position?'; 'Send me a posse of light infantry!'; 'Report to headquarters!'

The prince and all his retinue were struck by such conclusive proof and warmly congratulated M. Sudre on the excellence and obvious usefulness of his ingenious invention. All the orders and details were delivered thirty times to make sure that proof was beyond question. When these produced the same results, the war minister, the navy minister, the Academy of Fine Arts, and a considerable number of officers and artists were obliged to agree that the problem had been entirely solved, that the usefulness of this method was clear and its employment both reliable and easy.

Having spent the little money he possessed and twenty years of his life on this project, M. Sudre, also prevented from secretly telling his secret to foreign powers who would have paid dearly for the information, M. Sudre, I suggest, had a right to receive some honourable recompense. Some time ago, in an *eighth* report on the telephonic method, in return for the rights the inventor donated to the government for his secret, the sum of 50,000 francs was allotted to him as a state recompense. This offer being accepted without demur by M. Soudre, thinking that was the end of the matter, gave detailed instructions as to the use of his method. Meanwhile, it has still not been officially accepted, the 50,000 francs have not been paid, and the poor inventor is in desperate straits and, if he doesn't go mad, will die of hunger: it's an out-and-out scandal, the causes of which are to be discussed very shortly by the Assembly.

But this is the standard fate regularly suffered everywhere by those unfortunates in the grip of a new idea. Less than two years ago, serious articles were being written to prove the impossibility of the electric telegraph and the absurdity of the trials undergone towards its application.[1] Today, the thoughts of humanity spread like wildfire from one end of Europe to another and in half of South America, by means of this simple iron thread greeted with such ridicule, claiming that *contact with a magpie would be enough to paralyse the conduction of electricity*. Napoleon didn't recognize the future of steam power, and Fulton was, in his eyes, nothing but a fool, obsessed with his claims and trial runs.[2] Before long we'll have the same spectacle around a still more important discovery, the driving of airships by means of a combination of helixes and inclined planes. Clearly, once this has been demonstrated and put into practice, the intercourse between the many peoples that make up the human family will be changed entirely; an immense revolution will take place whose positive consequences are incalculable. That's precisely why the brave mechanic who wants to provide mankind with wings capable of braving the winds and gliding over the storm will be faced with even stronger and more obstinate resistance. He'll be ruined and will die of overwork; he's expecting this and ready for it. But flying in the vastness of space will, nonetheless, be available to us sooner or later, and our descendants will be amazed that their forefathers, assuming for centuries that there was no solution to this problem, should, when a corner of the veil had already been lifted, have insisted on crawling about on the earth's crust like so many lowly animals.

Time is a great teacher, it's true, but man a very slow learner.[3]

---

[1] In 1846–7, the 1846 law financing construction of an electric telephone line between Paris and Lille was the subject of reports and controversy in the *Journal des débats*.

[2] Robert Fulton (1765–1815), American engineer, is credited with inventing the first steamboat (the North River Steamboat), which made its successful trial journey in 1807. Berlioz is quite wrong in saying that Napoleon thought that Fulton 'n'était qu'un fou', since in 1800 he commissioned Fulton to design a submarine – the *Nautilus*, the first practical submarine ever made.

[3] This refers to a line from Corneille, *Sertorius*, act 2, scene 4. 'Le temps est un grand maître, il règle bien des choses' ('Time is a great teacher, it governs many things').

57

M. Niedermayer's *Messe solennelle*

JD, 27 December 1849

Berlioz habitually misspelled the name of Louis Niedermeyer (1809–65), pianist (a pupil of Moscheles), composer, and teacher of Swiss origin. He studied operatic techniques with Rossini in Naples, then settled in Paris in 1823. He was an important pioneer in the development of French song but was unsuccessful as an opera composer. He founded a 'Society of Vocal and Religious Music' in 1840 which came to be known as the Niedermeyer School, where Gabriel Fauré studied and Camille Saint-Saëns was a teacher.

Towards the end of last month, this remarkable work was performed in the church of Saint-Eustache through the efforts of the committee of the Association of Musical Artists.[1] I am not to blame if I haven't had the occasion before now to speak about it and give the composer the justice he deserves. But the impression this religious work made on me was not one of those that fades after several days, and I think it is still sufficiently clear in my head for me to write about it without presumption.[2]

I shall abstain totally from touching here on a question that's much in the mind of a small musical sect: a question answered by those followers of the

---

1   The mass was performed on St Cecilia's day, 22 November 1849. The choir numbered 250 and the work was conducted by Dietsch (on whom see article 8, note 1).

2   In fact, Berlioz seems to have made notes during the performance, using, remarkably enough, a sketchbook in which the earliest entries date back to 1832. See D. Kern Holoman 'The Berlioz Sketchbook Recovered', *Nineteenth-Century Music* VII/3 (April 1984), pp. 282–315; 'Notes for a feuilleton' (full transcription), pp. 312–13. Given the date, it was understandable that Holoman did not identify the work; in Berlioz's notes, Dietsch, Dupont, and Girard are named, but not Niedermeyer. Some of the jottings are used *verbatim* in the review; a few are included here thus: [sk:] in the text, or are mentioned in notes.

unthinking schism which, on the pretext of making *Catholic* music, prefers to have religious services without any music at all. First of all, these musical Anabaptists didn't want violins in churches, because violins remind us of theatrical music (as if theatres don't also have voices and, in their orchestras, violas, cellos and contrabasses, etc.). After that, the stops of modern organs, in their opinion, are too varied, too expressive, too beautiful. Then they started to condemn melody, rhythm, and even modern tonality. The moderates among them still allow Palestrina; but the hardliners, the Balfour of Burleys of these new puritans, won't accept anything but unaccompanied plainsong.[3]

One of them, the Macbriar of the sect, goes further still: with a single bound, he reaches the goal towards which all the others have been slowly walking, namely, as I've said, the suppression of religious music altogether. Shortly after the death of the Duc d'Orléans, I was in Notre-Dame for the funeral of this noble prince, so profoundly and rightly lamented.[4] The puritans, triumphant that day, had arranged that the entire mass should be sung in plainsong, and that the accursed modern tonality – *dramatic, impassioned, expressive* – should be utterly prohibited. All the same, the choirmaster of Notre-Dame felt he should compromise to some extent with current corruption and accompanied the plainsong with four-part harmony. He didn't feel strong enough to break his pact with impiety completely; no doubt 'sufficient grace' had not sufficed.[5]

However that may be, I found myself sitting in the nave next to our fiery Macbriar. While condemning modern music which *excites the passions*, he was passionate in a very diverting manner in his support of plainsong which, we will agree, is far from having such a fault. But he restrained himself well enough until the middle of the ceremony. There was a long silence and the congregation was remaining in a solemn and profound state of meditation when the organist, by accident, touched a note on his keyboard; this accidental pressure produced an A on the flute stop, lasting a couple of seconds. This isolated note rang out in the midst of silence and echoed round the cathedral arches like a gentle, mysterious moaning. At which my neighbour stood up transported and, with no respect for real meditations of those around him, cried out, 'It's sublime! Sublime! There's true religious music! There's pure art, in its divine simplicity. All other music is foul and impious!'

---

3   Balfour of Burley and Macbriar are puritan characters in Scott's novel *Old Mortality*.
4   Ferdinand-Philippe, duc d'Orléans (1810–42), who died of a fractured skull when the horses of his open carriage ran out of control, was the eldest son and heir of the 'King of the French', Louis Philippe (reigned 1830–48). He had been a staunch supporter of Berlioz.
5   'Sufficient grace': God's mercy toward those who only deserve punishment.

Well, good for him, there's a logical fellow! In his book, religious music should contain no melody, no harmony, no rhythm, no instrumentation, no expression, no modern keys, no ancient ones (they remind us of the music of the Greeks, pagans all). All he needs in an A, a simple A, sounding momentarily in the middle of a crowd that's silent and, it's true, moved and prostrate. One could still impinge on his ecstasy by pointing out that theatres too regularly and frequently make use of that sublime A. But one has to confess that his system of musical monotony (not the right place to use this word) is easy to adopt and extremely cheap. From that point of view, it has a lot to be said for it.

There's a brain disease which Italian doctors call *pazzia* and the English ones *madness*, and we might well think that it's making progress among the followers of the new musical church. I have among them a friend who has just recognized that Mozart's *Ave verum* WAS NOT CATHOLIC; from which one must, I fancy, conclude that my poor friend is now completely mad.[6] To sum up, friends, enemies, don't-carers [*indifférents*], Gregorians, Ambrosians, Palestrinians, Presbyterians, Puritans, Quakers, Anabaptists, Unitarians, more or less seriously suffering from *madness*, from *pazzia*, I say to all of you: *Raca*! and I go back to music.[7]

The outstanding qualities of M. Niedermayer's mass, as I see them, are first its true expressivity, its very pure harmonic style, extreme melodic suavity, clever orchestration, and very clear handling of the various melodic lines. We can add to that a virtue rarer than you might think, in France anyway: namely his respect for Latin prosody [sk: 'la prosodie est toujours excellente']. Nothing is neglected in this large score; altogether it's beautiful, often imposing, and almost every detail survives minute scrutiny. The *Kyrie* in B minor, a key rarely used in church music, is splendidly prayerful and sad [sk: 'expressif et vrai'], made still more striking by the imploring cry [sk: 'un grand cri'] on the word *eleison*, now and then set to a dissonance. After the central section for the *Christe*, sung by the semi-chorus, the return

---

6 Joseph-Louis d'Ortigue (1802–66), French musicologist and critic, and a conservative Catholic, was a colleague and friend of Berlioz to whom the latter used the familiar 'tu' form; this allusion to 'madness' is not to be taken literally. In 1857 d'Ortigue joined Niedermeyer in founding a religious music journal *La Maîtrise*, and in 1863 he succeeded Berlioz as music critic of the *JD*. Mozart's *Ave verum corpus*, a motet of 1791, is of course Catholic, but the authorities in the mid-nineteenth century may have considered it too expressive for church use.

7 Jesus used 'Raca', in Aramaic 'idiot'; the word addressed to a brother will have the speaker brought before the council and 'whosoever shall say Thou fool, shall be in danger of hell fire'. (Matt 5-22).

of the massed voices together with full orchestral backing produces a fine effect [sk and feuilleton: 'un bel effet'].

In the *Gloria* (in D major), after a rather traditional opening, I was struck by a very interesting fugal passage and a lovely dialogue between massed voices and semi-chorus [sk and feuilleton: 'dialogue entre le grand et le petit chœur']. The solo for bass voices at *qui tollis* is perhaps more ceremonial than imploring, given that this is a prayer; but at the word *miserere* the style returns to utter truthfulness. The fugue that concludes this part of the mass is well constructed, and in no way belongs to the category of fugues which, vocalizing on the word *amen*, remind one mainly of drunkards letting fly and tavern noises; even so I still found its allure too classically tumultuous.[8]

The opening of the *Credo* is written in the style of a proclamation of faith, brilliant, proud, stately, and the paragraph is remarkable for its breadth, well-constructed and developed at length. The orchestration here is rich and ingenious; only the trumpet-calls drawing attention to *Deum de Deo* seem to me unmotivated and ineffective.[9] The section on the mystery of the Incarnation, one so difficult to bring off, is one of the finest in the work. It's an unaccompanied chorus of intense, profound, and consistent interest, leading to an extremely artistic conclusion on the words *et homo factus est*, where the major mode finally breaks out radiantly and powerfully. On the word *crucifixus* the wind instruments groaning in the bass produce progressions which seemed to me original without being too mannered. The sound of the *Sanctus* is unusually magnificent, although in the second part (in E minor) the style weakens somewhat. In the *Benedictus*, where religious unctuousness dominates, the harmonious, delightful group of wind instruments play a series of chords that one finds rather hackneyed these days, despite all their charm. In the same movement, the vocalized lines of the semi-chorus seemed to lack clarity rather, something a more rigorous performance would perhaps correct.[10]

As for the *Salutaris*, which Alexis Dupont sang with a stylistic purity and a tone calling for the highest praise, it's an exquisitely beautiful hymn of mystical love; the whole audience, right from the start, was moved and

---

8   A tactful version of Berlioz's repeated complaints, directed even against Beethoven, about routine 'Amen' fugues, which he parodied in *La Damnation de Faust* and elsewhere said were fit for a chorus of devils. In the sketchbook he simply wrote 'comme toutes les fugues sur amen'.

9   In the sketchbook, the Credo is noted down as 'pompous, too much in D major ('pompeux trop en ré majeur'); the trumpets in 'Deum de Deo' 'seem pointless' ('on ne voit pas le but').

10 The sketchbook comments that the 'petit chœur' was sometimes out of tune ('quelques intonations manquées'). Again, the review appears kinder than the jottings made at the performance.

charmed.[11] The holy melody [sk: 'beau thème'] rises initially on an accompaniment of strings playing legato in the middle and lower registers, then continues beneath a harmonious line of brittle sounds on flutes and violins. It's entrancing. Finally, the *Agnus Dei* which completes this fine score, a movement of masterly construction and equally well performed, shows the bass voices in their most powerful register, conveying a striking and novel character of robust humility; it's the prayer of strong men.

A work like this places its maker in a position not easily attained by serious composers. Not an honour that brings in great riches, it's true, but one the true artist would not exchange for the overflowing *author's rights* earned by banal compositions, at which all our musical organizations are aimed. M. Niedermayer will not disappoint us, that's for sure.

The performance of this mass displayed a grandeur and exactness rare in Paris: four hundred professionals and amateurs contributed to it, under the expert direction of MM. Girard and Dietsch.[12] It is to the latter, an excellent composer who fulfils the post of choirmaster of Saint-Eustache with such talent, that we owe the return to our churches of musical events such as this, truly worthy of music and religion. We should be grateful too to the parish priest of Saint-Eustache who supports him to the best of his abilities and exerts all his influence in favour of these occasions.[13] Also the archbishop of Paris has allowed women to take part in these religious musical festivals, so that the most magnificent examples of the art are now possible, which was certainly not the case a year ago. And these splendid banquets of harmony are not the privilege of just a few: on the contrary, a large and attentive crowd is always eager to take part in them in our sacred buildings, whose size is often not enough to hold them all.

It's thanks to the efforts of the great Association of Musical Artists that M. Niedermayer's mass could be performed in this way. Even so, the difficulties of the enterprise were such that it needed the devotion and tireless activity of Baron Taylor to overcome them. Through his friendly relations with painters, sculptors, actors, poets and musicians, through the warmth with which he embraces and defends their various interests, through the authority his knowledge and taste have gained for him, and through the confidence he inspires and the results he obtains, M. Taylor, president of three Paris artistic associations, is the real minister of fine arts today. All he needed was the money; he's on the way to finding it.[14]

---

11   Dupont: see article 6, note 3.
12   Dietsch: see article 8, note 1. Girard: see article 12, note 32.
13   Berlioz conducted the first performance of his *Te Deum* in Saint-Eustache in 1855. Louis Gaudreau (1792–1872) was curé there from 1849 to 1858.
14   Baron Taylor: see article 24, note 2.

58

Gluck's *Alceste*

RGM, 17 March 1850

The editor of the RGM wrote the following preface to Berlioz's text: 'Since the excellent Philharmonic Society are to perform extracts from Gluck's Alceste *next Tuesday, we think we shall be doing a real service to our readers to quote the fine pages written by Berlioz on these same extracts'. The 'extracts' are actually continuous from act 1, scene 3 to the end of the act in the French version of the opera (1776), and not much changed, bar the language, from the Italian original of 1767. The text translated below quotes two passages from reviews previously published in 1835 (they appear in quotation marks in the article). Since Gluck's operas constitute such an idée fixe in Berlioz's writings, it's only right that these final words should celebrate* Alceste.[1]

The third scene opens in Apollo's temple. Enter the high priest, the priest who will conduct the sacrifice together with the censors and other necessary instruments, and finally Alceste leading her children, the courtiers and members of the public. Here Gluck applies an extreme of local colour; it's ancient Greece he reveals to us in all its majestic, beautiful simplicity. Listen to the instrumental movement (*aria di pantomimo*) to which the cortege enters; listen to this gentle, veiled, calm, resigned melody, this pure harmony, this almost inaudible rhythm of the contrabasses, whose undulating patterns steal beneath the orchestra like the priestesses' feet beneath their white tunics; lend your ear to the strange timbre of low flutes, to the intertwining of the two violin lines sharing the melody, and say whether there's any music more beautiful, in the ancient sense of the word, than this religious march.

---

1   Berlioz revisited his writings on Gluck's *Orphée* and *Alceste*, also considering the source of the latter in Euripides and previous operas by Lully and Schweitzer, for his book *À travers chants*. Paris: Calmann-Lévy, 1862; translated by Elizabeth Csicsery-Rónay as *The Art of Music*. Bloomington: Indiana University Press, 1994.

The ceremony begins with a prayer, the first words of which, 'Dieu puissant, écarte du trône' ('Mighty God, dismiss from the throne'), pronounced by the high priest, are separated by three heavy chords of C on the brass, first fairly quiet ('à demi voix'), then rising to a fortissimo. Nothing is more imposing than this dialogue between the pontiff's voice and this stately harmony of the *sacred trumpets*. After a brief silence, the chorus take up the same words in a fairly brisk passage in §. The strangeness of the form and melody strike us with astonishment; surely you expect a prayer to be a slow movement, and in quite another metre from §. So how does this passage, without any loss of seriousness, combine a kind of tragic agitation with a strongly marked rhythm and brilliant orchestration? I'm strongly inclined to believe, since the religious ceremonies in antiquity were always accompanied by symbolic leaping and dancing, that Gluck was preoccupied with this idea and wanted the character of his music to chime with this practice. The harmonious ensemble that ensues, on stage, between the choral voices singing and the chorus's movements as they process around the altar, proves that, despite the probable ignorance of the most experienced choreographers as to the true ritual of ancient sacrifices, the composer's poetic instinct has not deceived him in guiding down this path.

The high priest's recitative with orchestra 'Apollon est sensible à nos gémissements' ('Apollo understands our wailing') seems to me the most telling application of the element in the composer's system that consists in employing the orchestra only in proportion to the *degree of interest or emotion*. Here the strings begin on their own, in a unison which unfolds to the end of the scene with a growing energy. At the moment when the priest's prophetic exaltation begins to manifest itself – 'Tout m'annonce du Dieu la presence supreme' ('Everything alerts me to the supreme presence of the god') – the second violins and violas begin an arpeggiated *tremolando*, interrupted from time to time by a violent blast on the basses and first violins.[2]

The flutes, oboes, and clarinets only enter successively in the intervals between the inspired pontiff's interjections. The horns and trumpets still remain silent, but on the words 'Le saint trépied s'agite, tout se remplit d'un juste effroi' ('The holy tripod is shaking, everything is filled with terror'), the massed brass let forth their long repressed blast of sound, the flutes and oboes add their feminine cries, the violins' tremors are doubled, and the terrible pounding of the basses shakes the whole orchestra: 'Il va parler' ('He's about to speak'). Then there's a sudden silence: 'Saisi de crainte … et de respect, / Peuple, observe un profond silence./ Reine, dépose à son aspect / Le vain orgeuil de la puissance. Tremble!' ('Seized with fear and with respect, / Ye people, observe a profound silence. / Queen, set aside

---

2   Berlioz uses 'basses' to mean cellos and contrabasses together.

when it appears / The vain pride of power'.) The word 'tremble' on a single pitch, while the priest, with a distracted glance at Alceste, points to the low-lying altar on which she must place her royal head, crowns this extraordinary scene in sublime fashion. It's prodigious, it's the music of a giant, music of which the possibility, before Gluck, had never been suspected!

We come now to the scene with the oracle which follows on from the high priest's recitative after a complete silence: 'Le roi doit mourir aujourd'hui, si quelque autre au trépas ne se livre pour lui' ('The king must die today unless someone else volunteers to forfeit their life for him'). This sentence, almost entirely on one note, and the sombre trombone chords that accompany it, were imitated, or rather copied, by Mozart in *Don Giovanni* for the few words spoken by the Commendatore in the cemetery. The following chorus is impressive; it tells of the stupor and consternation of a people whose love for their king does not extend to sacrificing themselves for him.

I shall indicate here an important tradition, ignoring which would enormously weaken the impact of this powerful scene. Here are the details: at the end of the Largo in triple time that precedes the agitated coda 'Fuyons, nul espoir ne nous reste' ('Let's flee, there's no hope for us'), the high priest's part in the score places the words 'Votre roi va mourir' on the six notes c-sharp–c-sharp–d–d–d–f in the medium range and starting on the chorus's penultimate chord. In performance, on the other hand, the high priest waits for the chorus to finish, and in the midst of this mortal silence delivers his 'Votre roi va mourir' in his upper octave like a cry of alarm giving the desperate crowd the signal to run away.[3] So everybody scatters wildly, abandoning Alceste who has fainted at the foot of the altar.

Rousseau complained about this Allegro agitato that it expressed a confusion of happiness and terror; to which one may reply that here Gluck found himself at the point where the two emotions meet, and that as a result it was almost impossible for him not to respond in kind.[4] The proof is that, from the shouting of a multitude rushing from one place to another, the distant listener could not, without previous information, be sure whether the emotion felt was of fear or wild gaiety. To make my point crystal clear: a composer can certainly write a chorus whose cheerful character cannot possibly be misinterpreted, but the inverse is not true, and the agitation of a large group of people expressed in music, when it is not dealing with hatred

---

3   The Priest's role has a number of alternatives including singing these words an octave higher; but he ends on another d rather than f. Possibly the singer sang f instead. That the cs are actually sharp is overlooked in the French editions of this article.

4   Jean-Jacques Rousseau. 'Fragmens d'Observations sur l'Alceste italien de M. le Chevalier Gluck', in *Collection complète des Œuvres de J.J. Rousseau*. Geneva, 1782, vol. 16, pp. 353–8.

or vengeance, will always come close, at least in matters of movement and rhythm, to the rhythmical forms of widespread joy. It's possible to find a less arguable fault with this chorus, namely that it doesn't develop. It's too short, and its brevity detracts not only from the musical effect, but from the stage action, since in the time taken by the eighteen bars it lasts, it's extremely difficult for the chorus to find time to leave the stage without entirely destroying the last half of the scene.[5]

The queen, left alone in the temple, tells of her anxiety in one of those recitatives that Gluck alone knew how to write; this monologue is sublime. I don't believe one can find anything comparable for truth and form of expression, to match the music (because a recitative like this is as much admirable music as the finest aria) of these words:

> Il n'est plus pour moi d'espérance!
> Tout fuit … tout m'abandonne à mon funeste sort;
> De l'amitié, de la reconnaissance
> J'espérerais en vain un si pénible effort.
> Ah! L'amour seul en est capable!
> Cher époux, tu vivras, tu me devras le jour:
> Ce jour dont te privait la Parque impitoyable
> Te sera rendu par l'amour.[6]

On the fourth line, the orchestra begins a crescendo, a musical image of the overpowering idea of devotion that begins to grow in Alceste's soul, exalts her, burns within her, leading to the outburst of pride and enthusiasm: 'Ah! l'amour seul en est capable', after which the delivery becomes headlong, the passage accelerating with such energy that the orchestra, abandoning the possibility of following it, stops aghast, and doesn't catch up until the end, when it dissolves into chords full of tenderness on the last line. In the famous aria 'Non, ce n'est point un sacrifice' ('No, this is no sacrifice') which is both aria and recitative, the most complete awareness of the composer's tradition and style are the only guide for conductor and singer; there are frequent tempo changes, some of them not marked in the score. For example, after the last held note, where Alceste sings 'Mes chers fils, je ne vous verrai plus' ('My dear sons, I shall never see you again'), she must halve the tempo, making the crotchets as long as the dotted minims of

---

5   Here Berlioz seems to be saying that the noise of singers rushing for the exits could distract from the music that follows the chorus.

6   'No hope for me remains! / Everyone flees … everything abandons me to my sad fate; / Of friendship, of gratitude / I would hope in vain for such a painful deed. / Ah! Love alone can do this! / Dear husband, you will live, you will owe me your life: / This life of which pitiless Fate was depriving you / Will be restored to you by love'.

the previous movement. Another passage, and undoubtedly the most striking, would become complete nonsense if the speed was not managed with extreme delicacy: it's the second appearance of the phrase 'Non, ce n'est point un sacrifice! Eh! Pourrai-je vivre sans toi, sans toi, cher Admète?' ('No, it is no sacrifice! / Ah! How can I live without you, dear Admetus?').

This time, as she completes her phrase, Alceste, struck by a desolate thought, stops suddenly on 'sans toi'. A memory wrings her maternal heart and stems the heroic passion that was taking her to her death ... Two oboes raise their lamenting voices in the short interval left by the sudden absence of voice and orchestra; immediately Alceste sings 'Ô mes enfants! Ô regrets superflus!' ('Oh my children! Oh useless regrets!'). She thinks of her children and believes she can hear them; distraught and trembling, she looks around for them, responding to the orchestra's disjointed pleadings with a pleading that's crazed and convulsed, and which tells as much of delirium as of distress, making the unhappy woman's efforts to resist the beloved voices incomparably more moving as she repeats, one last time, in a tone of unshakeable resolution: 'Non, ce n'est point un sacrifice'. Truly, when music reaches this degree of poetic elevation, one has to feel sorry for the musicians charged with delivering the composer's thoughts: talent is not enough for this overwhelming task; at all costs, it requires genius.

Many Italian, French, and German prima donnas have deservedly made reputations as excellent singers of the most famous modern compositions, yet could not, without covering themselves with ridicule, touch the works of Gluck, likewise some of those by Mozart. One can think of several acceptable Ninettes, Rosines, and Sémiramises; of how many Donna Annas and Alcestes could one say the same?[7]

The recitative 'Arbitres du sort des humains' ('Arbiters of mankind's fate') in which Alceste, kneeling at the foot of Apollo's statue, pronounces her terrible vow, displays an unusual example of orchestration, in that the voice is almost doubled throughout at the unison and octave by six wind instruments – two oboes, two clarinets, and two horns – over a tremolo on the whole string band. This sort of orchestration is very rare: I don't think anyone had tried it before Gluck. The effect here is of a solemnity that suits the situation to perfection. At the same time, we may notice the unusual sequence of modulations the composer uses to link the two great arias Alceste sings at the end of this act. The first 'Non, ce n'est point un sacrifice'] is in D major; the following recitative which I've just mentioned begins in D but ends in C-sharp minor; the high priest's solo as he returns to say that Alceste's vow

---

[7] Characters in Rossini's *La gazza ladra* (*The Thieving Magpie*), *Il Barbiere di Siviglia*, and *Semiramide*; Donna Anna in Mozart's *Don Giovanni*.

has been accepted, begins in C-sharp minor and finishes in E-flat; Alceste's final aria 'Divinités du Styx' ('Gods of the Underworld') is in B-flat.[8]

Alceste is alone once more; the high priest has left her, announcing that the ministers of the god of death will find her at sunset. Fate has struck; only a few hours remain for her. But the feeble woman, the trembling mother have disappeared, to be replaced by someone who, driven out of her true nature by the fanaticism of love, is now impervious to fear and, with no hesitation, goes to pound on the gates of hell.

In this paroxysm of heroic bravery, Alceste summons the gods of the Styx to challenge them; she is answered by a raucous, terrifying voice; the joyful shout of the infernal denizens and the fearful fanfare of Hell's trumpet strike for the first time on the ears of the beautiful young queen who is about to die.[9] Her courage is not at all shaken. On the contrary, with a surge of energy she harangues these hungry gods, discounting their menace and disdaining their pity. She does have one moment of tenderness, but her courage returns and she exclaims 'Je sens une force nouvelle' ('I feel new strength'). Her voice slowly rises, its inflections becoming more and more passionate: 'Mon coeur est animé du plus noble transport!' ('My heart is full of noblest feeling!'). Then after a brief silence, returning to her fearless harangue and deaf to the barking of Cerberus as to the menacing call of the shades, she repeats 'Je n'invoquerai pas votre pitié cruelle' ('I shall not ask for your cruel pity') in such a way that the strange sounds of the abyss disappear, overcome by the final cry of this passion mixed with anguish and horror.

I think this first act of *Alceste* is the most complete manifestation of Gluck's abilities, abilities which will perhaps never be reunited to the same degree within the same individual: powerful inspiration, unimpeachable reasoning, stylistic grandeur, abundance of ideas, profound knowledge of how to dramatize the orchestra, expression that is always true, natural, and picturesque, apparent disorder that is merely a wiser kind of order, simplicity of harmony and patterning, touching melodies and, above all, an immense power that terrifies any imagination capable of appreciating it.

---

8   The original Italian words of this aria begin 'Ombre, larve'. Despite his admiration for Gluck, Berlioz wasn't afraid to criticize him; in an article of 1861 he points out that the music has been altered to its detriment for the French version. The article is reproduced in *À travers chants* (see this article, note 1; 1862 edition, p. 172; English translation, pp. 113–14).

9   This 'shout' is orchestral; the chorus is not involved. In the Italian *Alceste* (1767) there is a scene with Alceste in the underworld, but it was removed from the French version.

Index of Names

Abbey, John, 65–6
Abd-El-Kader, 249
Adam, Adolphe, 13n40, 156–60, 175, 210, 217n7, 233
Albert, Prince Consort, 111, 195, 197
Albertazzi, Emma, 45–6
Alembert, Jean le Rond d', 204
Alexandre, Édouard, 217n7, 228
Alizard, Adolphe, 43, 79, 103, 121, 144, 188–9
Albrechtsberger, Johann, 173
Arnaud, Abbé, 96
Auber, Daniel, 79, 89, 141n21, 169n1

Bach, C. P. E., 99
Bach, J. S., 81n29, 104, 141n22, 268
Baermann, Heinrich, 43
Baillot, Pierre, 70
Balfe, Michael, 108n1, 231
Balzac, Honoré de, 3, 4n8, 6, 9, 15
Barbaja, Domenico, 59, 60n4
Barbier, Auguste, 258n6
Barroilhet, Paul, 116–17, 120–2, 128, 169, 218, 221, 223, 227
Bartsch, Charles, 270
Barzun, Jacques, 14, 20, 192
Batta, Alexandre, 75, 77, 108, 111, 229
Batta, Laurent, 229
Beaumarchais, Caron de, 2, 38, 102, 242
Beethoven, Ludwig van, 9n23, 16–17, 43–4, 54n12, 77, 78, 81n29, 84, 87–8, 98, 102–3, 123–5, 141–2, 145, 152, 160, 173n2, 192–4, 196–9, 224, 239, 255–7, 264–5,

278n6, 285; *Fidelio*, 23, 102; Symphonies: No. 1, 255–6; No. 2, 143–4; No. 3 (*Eroica*), 32; No. 4, 113, 261–2; No. 5, 183, 264–5; No. 6 (*Pastoral*), 22–4; No. 7, 107, 131; No. 9 ('Choral'), 34, 43
Béfort, Louis, 252
Bellini, Vincenzo, 47n3–5, 48n2, 56n15, 58, 145, 162
Benda, Georg, 99
Benedict, Julius, 76
Bériot, Charles de, 70, 164, 200, 202
Berlioz, Hector, musical works: *Benvenuto Cellini*, 11, 43, 59n3, 64n6, 67, 76n10, 77n15, 79n18, 81n30, 95n4, 104n10, 109nn3–4, 221n6, 222n8, 258n6; *La Damnation de Faust*, 82n32, 161n10, 169n1, 202n23, 253n16, 272n26, 285n8; *Grande Messe des morts* (Requiem), 13, 85, 191; *Harold en Italie*, 10, 18, 81n32, 162, 165; *Roméo et Juliette*, 1, 10, 18, 43n3, 80n23; *Symphonie fantastique*, 7n18, 9, 14, 18, 20, 104n10, 141n23, 159n6, 162–3, 167n2, 175n11, 176n15
Berlioz, Hector, literary works: *Grotesques de la musique, Les*, 216n5; *Memoirs*, 1, 2, 4, 12, 75n3, 113n1, 137n12, 141n21, 142n24, 155n8, 160n8, 183n13, 199n12, 209n2, 231n1; *Soirées de l'orchestre, Les*, 126n1, 192, 254n19; *À travers chants*, 264n9, 287n1, 292n8

INDEX OF NAMES

Bertin, Louis, Armand, Édouard, 3n7, 11, 12–13, 192
Bertin, Louise, 11, 35
Bertini, Henri, 114
Berton, Henri, 136, 139n17, 180, 245
Bertoni, Ferdinando, 182n11
Bettini, Alessandro, 225
Bézard, Jean-Louis, 75n3
Blaes, Arnold-Joseph, 43
Blanc, Charles, 244–5
Blanchard, Henri, 80
Blangini, Giuseppe, 183n12
Bocage, Pierre, 166
Bocquillon, Guillaume, see Wilhem
Boehm, Joseph, 174
Boehm, Theobald, 90, 270
Boetticher, Louis, 201
Boieldieu, Adrien, 139n17, 183
Boisselot, Louis, 64, 266–7, 269
Boisselot, Xavier, 64
Bortnyansky, Dimitry, 273n27
Boulo, Jean-Jacques, 253
Bologne, Joseph, 256n1
Bourbier, Virginie, 166
Brémond, Matthieu, 223
Branchu, Caroline, 39n2, 97n8, 179–80
Breidenstein, H. K., 195
Burney, Charles, 53n8, 268n15
Byron, Lord, 16, 95

Callinet, Louis, 65–6
Carafa, Michel, 80
Carpani, Giuseppe, 14, 20n2, 21–2, 26
Caraccioli, Domenico, 96
Castil-Blaze, 160n9, 182
Catel, Charles-Simon, 99, 19, 139
Caussinus, Joseph, 272
Cavaillé-Coll, Aristide and Dominique, 130

Chaix, François, 211
Charles X, 5, 6, 139, 190
Cherubini, Luigi, 80n25, 102n3, 134–42, 157n4, 180, 190–1, 245; *Ali Baba*, 140–1; *Lodoïska*, 135–6, 157; *Médée*, 100, 136; Requiems, 135, 140, 143–4, 190
Chevillard, Pierre, 164
Chopin, Fryderyk, 76n11, 81n29, 82, 91, 125, 162n1, 276–8
Chorley, Henry, 232n2, 236n5
Choron, Alexandre, 104, 141
Cimarosa, Domenico, 45, 99
Cinti-Damoreau, Laure, 169
Clari, Giovanni, 98–9
Carafa, Michel-Henri, 80
Coche, Jean-Baptiste, 90
Corneille, Pierre, 95, 281
Cossman, Bernhard, 164
Czerny, Carl, 76n7, 162n1

Dalayrac, Nicolas, 21n3, 70, 99, 102n3, 137n13, 245
Danjou, Jean-Louis, 66
Mlle Darcier, Célestine, 161
David, Félicien, 252, 257
David, Ferdinand, 75
Davison, James, 236
Debain, Alexandre, 217n7
Debraux, Émile, 260n2
Debussy, Claude, 20
Decroix, Marguerite, 253
Dehn, Siegfried, 175
de Kock, Paul, 193, 260
Degas, Edgar, 271n24
Déjazet, Pauline, 254
Delannoy, Marie-Antoine, 75n3
Depassio, Jean, 262
Dérivis, Henri, 39–40, 78, 180, 188, 262
Dérivis, Prosper, 112, 117, 121
Deschamps, Antoni, 125, 276

Deschamps, Émile, 80
Desmarets, Jean, 164
Despléchin, Éduard, 227
Devienne, François, 102n3
Dieppo, Antoine-Guillaume, 84, 107, 272
Diéterlé, Michel, 227
Dietsch, Louis, 49, 190–1, 213n14, 282nn1–2, 286
Distin, John, 272
Dobré, Marie, 169, 188, 262
Döhler, Theodor, 76, 91, 162–3
Donizetti, Gaetano, 56n15, 67–73, 108, 145–6, 231n; *La Favorite*, 79n18, 222; *Lucia di Lammermoor*, 47n3, 47n5, 68, 81, 145
D'Ortigue, Joseph, 284n6
Dorus, Louis, 107
Dorus-Gras, Julie, 76, 117, 169
Dragonetti, Domenico, 215n3
Dufaure, Jules, 244
Dufresne, Louis, 165
Dumas, Alexandre, 6, 15, 82, 95
Dumersan, Théophile, 193n3, 215
Dumilâtre, Adèle, 227
Duponchel, Charles, 67, 79, 82, 127n2, 141n21, 222n8, 233, 238
Dupont, Alexis, 43, 103, 128, 262, 285
Duprez, Gilbert, 49, 58, 59n3, 68, 72, 78, 127–8, 169, 180, 188, 220–2, 238, 241, 243
Durante, Francesco, 52, 99, 105
Duriez, Armand, 164

Érard, Pierre, Sébastien, 63, 64n1, 65n10, 66, 266–70

Falcon, Cornélie, 238
Ferrière Le Vayer, 80
Fétis, François-Joseph, 7–8, 11, 14, 219n2, 236
Flaubert, Gustave, 9n25, 234n2

Florian, Jean-Pierre Claris de, 41
Flotow, Friedrich, 223n1
Forestier, Joseph, 165, 272
Franck, César, 91n5, 141n22
Franco-Mendès, 200
Francoeur, François, 182n11
Friedland, Ferdinand, 231
Fulton, Robert, 281
Fuoco, Sofia, 243

Gade, Niels, 173
Gand, Jean, 267
Gallus, Jakob, 99
Ganz, Moritz, 200
Garcia, Eugénie, 81
Garcia, Pauline: see Viardot
Gardoni, Italo, 220, 223
Gasparin, comte de, 190
Garrick, David, 53n8, 159–60
Gaudreau, Louis, 286n13
Gazzaniga, Giuseppe, 135
Gibert, Jean-Baptiste, 75n3
Girard, Narcisse, 81, 265, 282n2, 286
Girardin, Delphine, 80
Girardin, Émile, 3
Glinka, Mikhail, 172–7, 202
Gluck, Christoph, 1, 4, 7, 15-16, 38–40, 49–53, 55–6, 61, 78, 87–8, 92, 96–7, 102n2, 135n6, 138, 140, 153, 157, 178, 179n3, 180–2; *Alceste*, 15, 52, 61, 87, 97, 100, 140, 179–80, 181n8, 212, 240, 287–92; *Armide*, 25, 61, 97n10, 100, 102, 107n15, 179, 181n8, 199, 212, 215, 240; *Echo et Narcisse*, 61, 97, 100; *Iphigénie en Aulide*, 61n6, 100, 180; *Iphigénie en Tauride*, 52, 59n2, 61, 87, 94, 97n8, 100, 112, 115, 135n8, 213; *Orphée (Orfeo)*, 49–53, 55, 61, 87, 96–7, 131, 154, 181n8, 182, 202, 240; *Paride ed Elena*, 52; *Telemaco*, 52, 209

Godfroy, Vincent, 270n23
Goethe, Johann Wolfgang, 239
Gordon, William, 90
Goubaux, Prosper, 77n16
Gouffé, Achille, 90
Gounet, Thomas, 16
Gounod, Charles, 10, 91n5, 141n22, 159n7, 205
Graun, Karl, 99
Grétry, André, 21n3, 59n2, 70, 99, 105n14, 107n16, 136n11, 157–8, 245, 248; *Richard Cœur de Lion*, 102n2, 209; *Zémire et Azor*, 208–11
Grisar, Albert, 248
Grisi, Giulia, 45, 47, 78
Gros, Antoine, 58
Guadagni, Gaetano, 53
Guelton, Sophie, 43
Gutmann, Adolf, 278
Gyrowetz, Adalbert, 216

Habeneck, François, 18, 81n32, 104, 131, 1698, 210n6
Halévy, Fromental, 126, 221, 242n6, 262n6, 274n2, 64n7, 76n10, 79n18
Hallé, Charles, 76–7
Hamel, Marie-Pierre, 66
Handel, Georg Friedrich, 23, 28n2, 29, 99, 104n11, 124, 141n22, 202, 239
Haydn, Franz Joseph, 2, 14, 21, 24, 27–8, 112–14, 200, 216n4, 224, 255–7, 261; *The Creation*, 21, 28n2, 29n5, 169
Heine, Heinrich, 6, 8, 80
Heinefetter, Kathinka, 121
Heller, Stephen, 76–7, 91
Henri, Louis-François, 253
Henselt, Adolphe, 176–7

Hermann, Léonard (Hermann-Léon), 169, 252–3
Herz, Henri, 9, 162, 177, 228–9
Hiller, Ferdinand, 59n3, 81, 276
Hoffmann, E.T.A., 122n8, 176
Hubert, Joseph, 246
Hugo, Victor, 2, 6, 11, 13, 15, 35. 67, 95, 119, 193
Hummel, Johann Nepomuk, 76n9, 84
Hurteaux, Auguste, 72

Ingres, Dominique, 11, 12
Isouard, Nicolas, see Nicolò
Ivanoff, Nikolay, 174–5

Jacob, Maria, 227n17
Janin, Jules, 11
Joly, Anténor, 67–71
Jourdan, Pierre, 211
Jouy, Victor-Joseph, 182
Jullien, Louis-Antoine, 231n1

Kalkbrenner, Friedrich, 76n2, 80
Kant, Immanuel, 75n3
Kastner, Georges, 82, 83–9
Kratki, see Schmezer
Kreutzer, Léon, 6
Kreutzer, Rodolphe, 21n3, 125n3, 135, 139n17

Lablache, Luigi, 45, 47–8, 76, 111, 268, 278
Lacépède, Comte de, 28
Lachner, Franz, 164
La Fontaine, Jean de, 1, 151n1, 179n1
Lagrange, Anna de, 238–43
La Harpe, Jean-François de, 97, 211–12
Lamennais, Abbé, 75n3
Lanner, Joseph, 275

INDEX OF NAMES 297

Leclerc, Pierre, 64n7, 65
Legouvé, Ernest, 77
Legros, Joseph, 52–3, 61n7
Leisring, Volckmar, 259, 261
Lemercier, Maria, 211
Leo, Leonardo, 99
Le Sueur, Jean-François, 13, 14, 37, 99, 136–7, 139, 165n11, 180–1, 183n13, 194, 245
Levasseur, Nicolas-Prosper, 78
Lind, Jenny, 201, 220n4, 239
L'Isle, Claude de, 81n31
Liszt, Franz, 7n18, 9, 48n7, 62n8, 64n6, 74, 76nn8, 11, 81n29, 91, 108, 111, 114n3, 118–19, 123–4, 130n2, 141n22, 145, 159n6, 176–7, 192–201, 276n1
Louis XVIII, 139
Louis-Philippe, 6, 11, 13, 15
Lully, Jean-Baptiste, 97n10, 287n1
Lvoff, Alexei Fyodorovitch, 176

Mainzer, Joseph, 81, 90
Marcello, Benedetto, 98–9, 105–6
Marcellus, Comte de, 194
Marié, Claude, 81n31, 108, 121
Mario, Giovanni, 47n4, 128n7
Marmontel, Jean-François, 135, 208–9, 211–12
Martini, Jean-Paul, 54, 139
Massart, Lambert, 123–5
Massart, Louise, 6, 124n3
Masset, Nicolas, 81n31
Massol, Eugène, 109, 187
Mayer, Charles, 174
Mayr, Simon, 99
Méhul, Étienne, 24, 32, 37, 42, 136, 139n17, 180, 216, 230n4, 245, 257
Melani, Jacopo, 27
Mendelssohn, Felix, 43n4, 76n6, 77, 131–3, 143, 166–8, 173–4, 199, 200n19, 209n2, 232

Mérimée, Henri, 175
Meyerbeer, Giacomo, 8, 9, 43n4, 67, 85, 87–8, 105, 141n21, 169n1, 174, 217n7; *L'Africaine*, 219; *L'Étoile du Nord*, 219; *Les Huguenots*, 24, 43n3, 76n10, 80n33, 81n30, 88, 201, 219–20, 239–40; *Le Prophète*, 50n2, 161n10, 219, 240; *Robert le diable*, 76n10, 88, 119, 124, 127, 128n7, 219–20
Michelangelo, 95
Michelet, Jules, 6
Mocker, Toussaint, 161
Moeser, Auguste, 200
Molière, 79, 122n8, 127n3, 157, 249n5, 250n9
Montpensier, Duc de, 280
Monsigny, Pierre-Alexandre, 70, 156–8, 209
Moore, Thomas, 16
Morel, Auguste, 79–80, 168
Mozart, Wolfgang, 28n2, 32, 49, 79, 88, 98, 108n1, 115, 117, 120–2, 135, 143, 224, 231n1, 232, 239, 278, 284; *Don Giovanni*, 116–22, 135, 145, 162, 289, 291; *Le nozze di Figaro*, 45–8, 122; *Die Zauberflöte*, 147, 224n13
Musard, Philippe, 80, 224, 274
Musset, Alfred de, 6

Napoléon I, 33, 37, 94, 136–9, 145, 181, 183, 281
Napoléon III, 10, 13, 95n2, 267n12
Nathan-Treillet, Claire, 91n7
Nau, Maria, 43, 79, 109, 121, 223, 227
Naumann, Johann, 99
Nerval, Gérard de, 15
Nicolò (Isouard, Nicolas), 139n17
Nodier, Charles, 6

Nourrit, Adolphe, 58–62, 75n18, 180n4
Novello, Clara, 199

Onslow, George, 174

Pacini, Giovanni, 48, 201, 240
Paër, Ferdinando, 80, 139n17
Paganini, Niccolò, 89, 187, 225
Paisiello, Giovanni, 38n1, 70, 99, 102, 137, 256
Palestrina, 99, 101, 104n11, 207, 283
Pape, Jean-Henri, 64
Pâris, Claude-Joseph, 65n8
Pastou, Étienne, 91
Paulin, Louis, 240–1
Pergolesi, Giovanni Battista, 99
Persiani, Giuseppe, 45–7
Philidor, François-André, 4, 70, 99, 102, 158n5
Piccinni, Niccolò, 38–9, 96n6, 97–8, 135n7, 181n8, 211n10
Pillet, Léon, 67n1, 126–7, 141n21, 223–4, 226
Pischek, Johann-Baptist, 201, 202n23
Pleyel (née Moke), Marie, 199
Pleyel, Camille, 64, 267, 269–70
Poinsot, Anne, 262
Ponchard, Louis, 127, 138
Porpora, Niccolò, 49, 99, 135n7
Portehaut (Porthéhaut), Jean-Baptiste, 241–2
Poulet, Alexandre, 95n1
Poultier, Placide, 126–9, 240
Poussard, Charles, 113, 146
Prévost, Ferdinand, 109, 121
Pubereaux, see Sainte-Foy
Pugnani, Gaetano, 24n7

Rachel (Élisa Félix), 95, 270n19
Racine, Jean, 95, 25n8

Rameau, Jean-Philippe, 99, 106–7, 151–5, 203
Ravel, Maurice, 20
Rémusat, Jean, 211
Ricciardi, Achille, 71–2, 81
Rignault, François-Émile, 164
Robert, Louis-Léopold, 58
Roller, Jean, 64
Romani, Felice, 56
Rossini, Gioachino, 10, 25, 45, 72, 59, 80n24, 81, 141n21, 146, 169n1, 172, 200, 206–7, 218–24, 240, 282, 291n7; *Barbiere di Siviglia, Il*, 38, 205; *Comte Ory, Le*, 226, 240; *Donna del lago, La*, 200, 225–6; *Guillaume Tell*, 25, 28, 30, 38, 44, 76, 114, 116, 126–9, 180, 205–6, 213, 221, 240; *Otello*, 28, 50n2, 73n16, 81n30, 92, 238, 240–3; *Robert Bruce*, 218–27; *Siège de Corinthe, Le*, 38–40, 205, 240
Rousseau, Jean-Jacques, 31, 54–5, 182, 289
Rousselot, Joseph, 69, 70n6
Royer, Alphonse, 5, 67, 73, 81, 218, 226, 227n16
Rubini, Giovanni, 48, 40, 70, 78, 89, 111, 121n6, 199, 225
Ruolz, Henri de, 82, 146

Sacchini, Antonio, 38–40, 70, 99, 102n2, 181n8
Sachs, Maria, 200
Sainte-Foy (Pubereaux), 161, 211–12, 252–3
Salieri, Antonio, 99, 181n8, 102n3, 179n3
Sand, George, ix, 130n2
Sarti, Giuseppe, 134–5
Sauvage, Thomas, 247, 249

INDEX OF NAMES 299

Sax, Adolphe, 228–30, 266–8, 270–3
Scarlatti, Alessandro, 99
Schiller, Friedrich, 239
Séchan, Charles, 227
Schlesinger, Maurice, ix, 5–10, 77n15
Schloss, Sophia, 199
Schmezer, Elise (Kratky), 199
Schoelcher, Victor, 267n12
Schubert, Franz, 49, 61–2, 80n28, 118
Schumann, Robert, ix, 7, 80n28, 173n4, 176n15, 236
Schweitzer, Anton, 287n1
Scott, Walter, 68, 223, 240n2, 283n3
Sedaine, Michel-Jean, 156, 158
Shakespeare, William, 1, 16, 18, 57, 94, 159–60, 166–7, 239; *Coriolanus*, 202; *Hamlet*, 57, 61, 160, 260, 261n4; *Othello*, 18, 19n55, 95, 240, 243, 260; *Richard III*, 111, 160; *Romeo and Juliet*, 80n23
Sigalon, Xavier, 95
Solovieva (née Verteuil), A. A., 177
Soulié, Frédéric, 95
Spontini, Gaspare, 4, 38, 40, 59n2, 79–80, 147n2, 178, 180–2, 207, 220, 240, 245, 263; *Fernand Cortez*, 108–10, 147, 181, 189n20, 240; *Olimpie*, 39n2, 180; *La Vestale*, ix, 30, 39n2, 79–80, 181–9, 213, 240, 259–61, 263
Staudigl, Joseph, 200–1
Stoltz, Rosine, 79, 281, 221–3, 225, 227n19
Strauss, Johann (the elder), 274–5
Strunz, Jacques, 69
Sudre, Jean-François, 279–81
Swieten, Gottfried van, 27–8

Taglioni, Marie, 119
Talma, François-Joseph, 25, 39n2, 136
Tamburini, Antonio, 45–7, 78
Taylor, Baron, 170n2, 286
Telemann, Georg Philipp, 99
Thillon, Anna (née Hunt), 71, 161
Thomas, Ambroise, 79, 91n5, 116, 156; *Le Caïd*, 247–54; *Mina*, 212–13
Tilmant, Alexandre, 164
Tilmant, Théophile, 487, 164
Tuczeck, Léopoldine, 201
Tulou, Jean-Louis, 270

Ugalde, Delphine, 247, 252–4
Urhan, Chrétien, 165

Vaez, Gustave, 67, 73, 81, 218, 226–7
Varin, Charles, 215n2
Vény, Louis, 165
Verdi, Giuseppe, 224
Vernet, Horace, 174
Véron, Louis-Désiré, 12, 141n21
Verroust, Charles, 273
Verroust, Louis, 143–4
Viardot (Viardot-Garcia), Pauline, 49–51, 54n10, 72n12, 81n31, 92–3, 112, 114–15, 131, 164, 202, 278n6
Victoria, Queen, 45, 111, 195, 197, 201
Vigny, Alfred de, 95, 276n1
Virgil, 1, 16, 25, 56, 154, 184n5, 202n25
Vogel, Johann Christoph, 135
Vogler, Georg Joseph, 99
Vogt, Auguste, 143–4
Vuillaume, Jean-Baptiste, 91, 266–7, 270–1

Wagner, Richard, xn1, 9, 49n1, 76n1, 236n5

Weber, Carl Maria, 43n4, 76n9, 84, 87–8, 92, 159, 173, 224, 230, 239; *Euryanthe*, 99, 144, 201, 259, 263; *Der Freischütz*, 24, 30, 92, 149, 160, 164, 182n10, 213, 221n6, 240; *Oberon*, 86, 99, 169, 213; *Preciosa*, 99; Piano concerto, 162–3, 199–200
Weber, Gottfried, 99
Weigl, Joseph, 99

Weulfel, Jean-Guillaume, 266, 269
Widman, Anna, 43
Wilhem, 82, 246n2
Winter, Peter von, 99
Wolff, Émile, 207
Wolff, Oscar, 198n9

Zerr, Anna, 163
Zimmerman, Pierre, 91
Zingarelli, Niccolò, 137

Printed in the United States
by Baker & Taylor Publisher Services